POST-TV

Piracy, Cord-Cutting, and the Future of Television

In the late 2000s, television no longer referred to an object to be watched; it had transformed into content to be streamed, downloaded, and shared. Tens of millions of viewers have "cut the cord," abandoned cable television, tuned into online services like Netflix, Hulu, and YouTube, and they watch pirated movies and programmes at an unprecedented rate. The idea that the Internet will devastate the television and film industry in the same way that it gutted the music industry no longer seems far-fetched. The television industry, however, remains driven by outmoded market-based business models that ignore audience behaviour and preferences.

In *Post-TV*, Michael Strangelove explores the viewing habits and values of the post-television generation, one that finds new ways to exploit technology to find its entertainment for free, rather than for a fee. Challenging the notion that the audience is constrained by regulatory and industrial regimes, Strangelove argues that cord-cutting, digital piracy, increased competition, and new modes of production and distribution are making audiences and content more difficult to control, opening up the possibility of a freer, more democratic, media environment.

A follow-up to the award-winning *Watching YouTube*, *Post-TV* is a lively examination of the social and economic implications of a world where people can watch what they want, when they want, wherever they want.

(Digital Futures)

MICHAEL STRANGELOVE has been called a "guru of Internet advertising" (*Wired*) and "the man who literally wrote the book on commercialization of the net" (*Canadian Business*). He is a lecturer in the Department of Communication Studies at the University of Ottawa.

Post-TV

Piracy, Cord-Cutting, and the Future of Television

MICHAEL STRANGELOVE

UNIVERSITY OF TORONTO PRESS
Toronto Buffalo London

ISBN 978-1-4426-4662-9 (cloth)
ISBN 978-1-4426-1452-9 (paper)

Printed on acid-free, 100% post-consumer recycled paper with vegetable-based inks.

Library and Archives Canada Cataloguing in Publication

Strangelove, Michael, 1962–, author
Post-TV : piracy, cord-cutting, and the future of television / Michael Strangelove.

Includes bibliographical references and index.
ISBN 978-1-4426-4662-9 (bound). – ISBN 978-1-4426-1452-9 (pbk.)

1. Television viewers – Effect of technological innovations on.   2. Television –
Social aspects.   3. Internet – Social aspects.   I. Title.

PN1992.6.S77 2015   302.23'45   C2014-908392-0

University of Toronto Press acknowledges the financial assistance to its
publishing program of the Canada Council for the Arts and the Ontario Arts
Council, an agency of the Government of Ontario.

 Canada Council   Conseil des Arts
for the Arts   du Canada

ONTARIO ARTS COUNCIL
CONSEIL DES ARTS DE L'ONTARIO

an Ontario government agency
un organisme du gouvernement de l'Ontario

University of Toronto Press acknowledges the financial support of the
Government of Canada through the Canada Book Fund for its publishing
activities.

Contents

Acknowledgments

Beyond my banging my head against a keyboard for four years, the writing of this book is also a result of my wife, Anne Strangelove, whose constant encouragement helped me persevere; my father-in-law, Professor Raymond St. Jacques, who provided a scholarly ear for bouncing ideas off and a keen eye for reading the final manuscript; Suzanne St. Jacques, for her input on the early manuscript; and a small group of friends whose living rooms, kitchens, and automobiles provided locations for some amateur ethnography as I explored their viewing activity. These members of the post-television generation include Chantal Trudel, who first drew my attention to the post-television habits of her tribe; Aneurin Bosely, who mastered the technical aspects of cord-cutting; John Curtin and Alida Cupillari, for insights into film editing and community television; Marc Fonda and Kim Easter, who along with their children shed light on the multi-screen viewing habits of the Netflix user, tablet owner, and television purchaser; Jamie Easter, who shared the insights of the Linux guru and smartphone wizard; Raymond Lacasse, who demonstrated to me that French Canada was also deeply involved in the disintermediation of the television industry; and my mountain-dwelling in-laws, Chantal St. Jacques, Pete Jansen, and their incredible girls, Emma and Sophie, who shed light on the uses of television, online and off, in the lotus land of interior British Columbia. This book, and my life, would have been greatly impoverished without these dear friends. I am also indebted to insights from numerous voracious pirates of digital entertainment whose names shall remain anonymous for obvious reasons. Finally, once again I am greatly indebted to the University of Toronto Press for their willingness to undertake this project and to Siobhan McMenemy for her skilful navigation of the publication process in her role as editor.

POST-TV

Piracy, Cord-Cutting, and the Future of Television

Introduction

A teenage girl called out to her friends who were playing along the shore of a duck pond, "Hey, let's go in the car and watch a movie!" The sun was shining, ducks were cruising along the shoreline in search of a handout, tulips were in full bloom. It was a perfect spring day in Ottawa. Yet, as far as the teenagers were concerned, all that sublime beauty was no match for the siren call of the family car's entertainment system. There were movies to be watched, after all.

When I was a teenager the phrase "Let's go in the car and watch a movie" had no meaning unless the intent was to go to a drive-in theatre. Had the teenager I overheard been just a bit older or perhaps a bit richer she might have reached into her pocket, backpack, or purse; pulled out a smartphone, a tablet computer, or some other mobile screen; sat down on the park bench; and watched a movie, television show, or YouTube clip. Or she might have filmed her friends and the ducks, uploaded it to the Internet, and then watched *that* movie. Clearly, when it comes to television, movies, and entertainment, much has changed.

Post-TV is an exploration of the audience's rapidly changing relationship to television, film, and the visual side of the entertainment system. Our connection with the cherished boob tube has been thrown into a state of flux because of the mass adoption of consumer electronics that connect Internet-delivered visual fare to global audiences. It would take over four million years to watch all the video that crosses the Internet each month. Six years after YouTube came out of nowhere, over half of all global consumer Internet traffic was taken up with delivering movies and television shows to online viewers.[1] The delivery of movies and television shows via the Internet will shortly consume the vast majority of Internet bandwidth.

The Internet is transitioning into an alternative vehicle for watching television and movies. This in itself would not amount to much except that at the same time content and audiences are spiralling out of control. There are rumours and dire forecasts of the end of network broadcast television. There is the possibility that the Internet will devastate the television and film industry in the same manner that it gutted the music industry. Changes are occurring in so many areas – technology, programming, advertising, business models, audience habits, and regulations – that it would be difficult to overstate the turmoil that the industry is facing. As Amanda D. Lotz observed in her book *The Television Will Be Revolutionized*, "Television as we knew it – understood as a mass medium capable of reaching a broad, heterogeneous audience and speaking to the culture as a whole – is no longer the norm."[2] Jennifer Holt and Kevin Sanson, editors of *Connected Viewing: Selling, Streaming, & Sharing Media in the Digital Era*, likewise suggest that in the near future audiences will witness nothing less than a "revolution in how screen media is created, circulated, and consumed."[3] Elvis is still on TV but the audience has left the building.

Television was once both the norm and the norm-setter. It established, or at the very least reinforced, normative social values, promoted consumer culture, created mass audiences that participated in widely shared stories (and, one might argue, widely shared illusions), brought families together in the domestic setting of the living room, and was a source of regional and national identities. Throughout the second half of the twentieth century, television scholars attributed considerable consequences to content produced by mainstream television: "Years of programming went by with scores of researchers documenting how television technology molded social habits, political strategies, marketing campaigns; fueled professional sports; corrupted society's values; and consumed elective time."[4] Television studies have served to reveal "many of the medium's festering sores," notes Jonathan Gray in *Television Entertainment*.[5] Gray also argues that "with perhaps the lone exception of our closest loved ones, very few other stimuli are as powerful."[6] If television of the twentieth century is no longer the norm, if the nature of this powerful stimulus is undergoing fundamental changes, then we are probably facing the erosion of related social patterns cultivated in the era of broadcast analogue television.

A recent spate of changes in society's relationship to television was driven by the transition from analogue to digital technology infrastructure. Digitalization of our entertainment, news, and information systems has led directly to a "major restructuring of social life."[7] Cellular phones have changed how we talk to each other, altered how we organize our time, and even normalized talking out loud in public to an invisible other during a telephone conversation. Social media has transformed the public sphere as over-sharing personal information ruins reputations while new techniques of public shaming further erode privacy in urban environments. Many parents would be shocked if they had full knowledge of what their children are doing and seeing online. Education is being massified and depersonalized through online courses, and retail stores are struggling to adapt to our online shopping habits. This restructuring of social life and audience behaviour continues with the growth of online television. Internet-induced changes in distribution and programming and new media technologies such as smartphones, mobile tablets, and wearable computers are responsible for widespread transformations of social life and are generating political and economic consequences. Mobile viewing, mass access to amateur and semi-professional video footage, ubiquitous television screens, new economies of television production, and many other features of contemporary life are coalescing into a post-television culture.

Until recently, there was little indication that the Internet would play a dramatic role in shaping the television industry. As recently as 2007 Lotz could write that it was too early to tell what impact the Internet would have on television.[8] Yet only four years later financial analysts described television services such as Netflix and Hulu as "providing a new market for older shows."[9] Streaming video services such as Netflix were responsible for encouraging US television networks to create more shows. Ironically, one of the earliest indications of a post-television culture is more programming. Not only has the online audience created a demand for *more* television programs, but television viewing in the United States is at record levels. Americans are spending 20 per cent more time watching television than they did in the late 1990s.[10]

What does it mean when we see the news headline "The Arrival of a Post-television, Techno-savvy Prime Minister"; a lecture named "Lost in Transition: From Post-network to Post-television"; articles entitled "Management Consulting for a Post Television Age," "Politics in the Post-TV Age," "Ordinary Witnessing in Post-television News," "Virtual Realities: Recreational Vehicles for a Post-television Culture?" or "Journalism in the Post-television Age"; and books with titles such as *Watching HBO in the Post-television Era* and *Transmission: Toward a Post-television Culture*? Clearly there is a sense that television is undergoing changes affecting many areas of life, such as consulting, politics, news, recreation, journalism, and culture. The "post" in "post-TV" does not indicate the end of television itself, but it does refer to the end of a particular way in which broadcast television structured viewing and the beginning of new ways of participating in television.

Consider Archie Bunker, a television character who represented so much of my generation's relationship with television as we grew up watching *All in the Family* in the early 1970s. Archie was often seen sitting in a chair that faced the family's television set in the living room. The chair, now housed in the Smithsonian Institute's National Museum of American History, was the epitome of the audience's relationship with television in the twentieth century. Archie was a "couch potato" and his chair was facing the "boob tube" (a relationship replicated decades later in television comedies such as *Married with Children*).

Fast forward to 40 years later and we find the audience involved in something called viewer-created television and consumer-generated advertising. Archie's character, played so well by Carroll O'Connor, was not seen making videos and uploading them to global audiences. He did not make clever advertisements of the products he loved (or cutting ones of the products he hated). He did not comment via Twitter or blog about the shows he watched. He certainly did not use Facebook to share clips of his favourite television scenes with hundreds of his online friends. He simply watched television and we in turn watched him. It was television viewing in its simplest situation.[11] This simplicity defined television's early character. Few things were easier to do than watching television.

Questions about television's essential character go back to its earliest years. One early interpreter of television, Marshall McLuhan, gained considerable attention because he challenged common assumptions about the character of television. McLuhan brought our collective attention to bear on the ubiquity of television's presence. Suddenly we were faced with something that seemed to be everywhere at once. A vast globe was reduced to a village wherein everybody became "profoundly involved with everybody else."[12] Forces such as the recent transition to a digital entertainment environment along with the rapid spread of social media have increased this profound involvement. Internet-facilitated social viewing, amateur and semi-professional videography, and related media practices bring with them new challenges to the identity and essential character of television. What is television in the age of the Internet?

In 1994 the mass adoption of the Internet was in its early years. The mediating and disintermediating effects of mobile consumer devices such as smartphones and tablet computers, the screens that pervade our visual environment, and the pop culture status of amateur videography were still a decade away when Peter d'Agostino and David Tafler wrote their introduction to a collection of essays titled *Transmission: Toward a Post-television Culture*. D'Agostino and Tafler argued that a new "post-television culture" has arisen and as a result "television no longer means television … Television has now become a bank machine, security monitor, information terminal, computer interface."[13] Two primary sources of this post-television culture are the mass adoption of the Internet and consumer video technologies. Along with media theorists such as Sean Cubitt, the authors saw in video "the possibilities for breaking television's hold" on consciousness and everyday life. Video promised to revolutionize television by allowing marginalized communities to maintain their values, define their own reality, and undermine the credibility of a "homogenized mainstream reality."[14] Video was seen as something quite apart from television, something that promised to democratize television and improve social life. The present convergence of video and television within the Internet makes any claims about their essential differences increasingly problematic. For a growing part of the global audience, video is television.

Television still has a stranglehold on popular culture and collective values, but its identity and future remain unresolved issues. There is confusion and uncertainty over what qualifies as television. As recently as 2008 Frazier Moore, a television columnist for the Associated Press, asked the question, "When did 'watching television' become an outdated term?"[15] Struck by how different his 13-year-old son's viewing patterns were from those of the analogue era of *All in the Family*, Moore noted that television viewing once meant turning our collective attention to a singular device – the television set. Now this thing once called television is available everywhere we go on an astounding variety of mobile consumer devices. Here we encounter another ironic condition of television in the post-television age. As television viewing becomes disassociated from a singular device, at the same time it becomes ubiquitous. In the post-television age television is everywhere. But this does not mean that it is simply more of the same old thing.

Media and change are almost synonymous terms in our minds. We tend to think of media in general and dominant media systems in particular as agents of change, and rightly so. As television diffuses throughout the social landscape it is morphing into something quite different from what it was and what it did in the twentieth century. Who creates it, how it is distributed, how we watch it, why we watch it, and how we pay for it – all this and more is undergoing change.

Television studies, suggests Georgina Born, "is increasingly entangled in the controversy over what television is to become."[16] Indicative of the controversy is a collection of articles published in 2013 under the title *After the Break: Television Theory Today*. Editors Marijke de Valck and Jan Teurlings note that "within television studies there seems to be a growing consensus that television as we knew it is irrevocably changing."[17] A general perception is that television is in a period of transition that has generated a "widespread idea that television is in crisis."[18] As a result of converging mediums that allow us to watch a film on a tablet computer, a television show on a desktop computer, and almost any visual content on any screen, the traditional barriers and distinctions between film studies, television studies, and new media studies serve little purpose in the face of transformations that "shake all media scholars out of their comfortable disciplinary ways."[19] As the chairman of the Academy of Television Arts and Sciences observes, "Television no longer refers to the box sitting in your living room – television refers to storytelling. The method by which our viewers experience those stories is truly irrelevant."[20] In this context of uncertainty *Post-TV* draws upon television and new media studies to explore how old media systems and new media innovations are changing the structure and identity of television. *Post-TV* makes connections between the way online property rights are asserted and contested; examines attitudes of the online audience, new industrial forms of television, and the political economy of television; and probes how all this affects social life. Identity, diversity, citizenship, news, and global conflict serve here as examples of life caught in the web of television's future.

Invariably, changes resulting from new media are subject to overstatement by both scholars and industry thought leaders. In an article tellingly entitled "Not the Apocalypse: Television Futures in the Digital Age," Jinna Tay and Graeme Turner raise a series of objections to what they call a "developing analytical orthodoxy" regarding the future of television.[21] This orthodoxy forecasts the imminent end of television. But such an orthodoxy (or straw man, perhaps) is not the inspiration for the chapters that follow herein. *Post-TV* is not an argument about the imminent demise of television. It is an exploration of the rapid transformation of television brought on by the great agent of change in contemporary society – the Internet.

There are dozens of different technologies and hundreds of different services in use for delivering television over the Internet. Two of the main categories of online television are Internet Protocol television (IPTV) and over-the-top (OTT) streaming video. IPTV generally refers to multichannel video service (also known as cable television) that is delivered over a private, dedicated Internet Protocol network. IPTV has been described as "basically a set of technologies and market strategies that allow telephone companies to compete with cable companies for current mass-audience TV viewers."[22] In contrast to this, services such as YouTube and Netflix are OTT streaming services that are transmitted over the public Internet. *Post-TV* focuses on what is known as over-the-top delivery systems that send video content over the public Internet. What follows is a non-technical discussion of how audiences redistribute, rebroadcast, view, pay for, pirate, and produce television shows and movies via the Internet. *Post-TV* explores the role that the Internet is playing in the transformation of television and its audiences. Video distributed over the Internet to a desktop, laptop, smartphone, tablet computer, flat-panel television set, or eyewear challenges common notions about the identity and future of television. Jonathan Bignell and Andreas Fickers suggest that "television operates to find an identity as a medium by establishing difference and similarity with other media."[23] Online video and related phenomena such as mass participation in amateur videography, the proliferation of mobile viewing devices, and new economies of production and distribution are producing differences and similarities that redefine television's identity.

The transformation of television is itself a matter of debate. Consider Tay and Graeme's argument that a "major industrial shift" in television has not yet occurred.[24] To make their case they point to the meagre adoption of IPTV. Nonetheless, surely it is an industrial shift when billions of individuals are exposed to videos that circulate on the Internet. A major industrial shift is seen in a collection of related forces such as mass online piracy, the creation of innovative commercial services such as Netflix, Hulu, iTunes, and Amazon, and new economies of production and distribution. We see the outlines of an industrial shift when Google, Apple, Intel, and Sony seek deals with the television industry to license content and launch OTT streaming television services. Technology companies entering into the business of producing and delivering television shows and movies are part of a shift to a digital, networked era of televisual entertainment.

Post-TV argues that a major industrial shift is occurring in the nature of viewing devices, modes of production, and distribution systems. The primary movers of this are not the television and film industries but the consumer electronics industry, the Internet, and the online audience. It is comparable to the shift that occurred in the music sector where we witnessed the failure of the music industry to adapt to consumer entertainment devices such as iPods and Internet-enabled home computers. By the time this shift was complete it was not the music industry that dominated the sales of online music – it was the computer industry.

The rise of the Internet as a new distribution medium and the proliferation of mobile viewing devices have generated a major transformation in how and why audiences use television. Audiences have reconfigured their use of television faster than the industry has been able to adapt. Baloo, an anonymous Internet commentator, expressed this change in the following terms: "I want to watch what I want, when I want, on whatever device I want – and there are plenty of others that feel the same."[25] *Post-TV* argues that there are many who feel the same way as Baloo.

One thing remains certain: the online audience is growing. Although the size of the North American audience is growing slowly, the amount of time spent watching online video is rapidly expanding. Growth across traditional television markets has stalled while increases in online viewing continue unabated.[26] Meanwhile, pay-TV penetration in the United States and Canada is experiencing unprecedented declines within an industry that many thought would never fade.

There is more at stake in the growth of online viewing than just changing audience habits, the diffusion of enabling devices, and Internet-delivered programming. The Internet acts upon the economy like a reverse form of alchemy – it turns what was previously gold into something that is considerably less costly. In fact, the Internet turns fee into free. A central force at work in the post-television age is the mass adoption of Internet-facilitated piracy practices. Michael Z. Newman suggests that piracy "confirms the value of television as ephemeral and disposable … a shared text which no one buys or sells."[27] Michael Geist, one of Canada's leading interpreters of Internet intellectual property law, notes that the television industry must now compete against so much freely available video content that "a growing percentage of broadcaster content has no market value."[28] Content loses value when the cost of access and distribution (particularly via digital piracy) is rendered negligible.

The long-term market value of television programming is under threat because of free online streaming services, online video subscription services, peer-to-peer downloading (which is mostly pirated content), and other emerging online options. Even YouTube has gotten into the act with online video rental services. The consequences of this are foremost on the minds of broadcast, cable, and satellite programming providers. As Geist notes, industry giants such as Bell Canada recognize that the value of their services are faced with steep erosion in the face of the proliferation of free.[29]

No market faces a frontal attack without a strong defence, and this is exactly what is happening. Entrenched broadcast players have benefited from favourable regulatory regimes and are striking back. Usage-based Internet billing rates are increasing, and incumbent players are calling for the imposition of broadcast-like regulations on Internet video services. Critical theory draws a sharp contrast between industrial imperatives (such as protected markets, regulatory capture, increased rates, and protection of the broadcast television ecosystem) and the social imperatives of culture, communities, and individuals. We see the primary industrial imperative revealed when executives insist that the current business models of the television and movie industry must be kept in place. For example, NBC Sports Group chairman Mark Lazarus called upon programmers and distributors to acknowledge the value of the pay-TV system and urged all parties to participate in "protecting the pay TV ecosystem."[30] Lazarus was reacting to the threat of uncontrolled online content and implored studios, networks, and broadcasters to preserve established arrangements between distributors and programmers.

Lotz's survey of the post-network era of television provides insight into how online television confronts the industrial imperatives of the twentieth-century television system. Lotz contrasts our increasing ability to control our own viewing experience with the industry's "drive for increased control over when, where, and how audiences viewed television programs."[31] As viewer choice and control increased it became imperative for the industry to alter production and distribution practices. Yet piracy continues to confound the industrial imperative of creating artificial scarcity, and emerging Internet-based modes of distribution threaten to undermine the television oligopoly itself. Nonetheless, the television industry will not go quietly into the night. As Susan Crawford has argued in *Captive Audience: The Telecom Industry and Monopoly Power in the New Gilded Age*, this is not an industry that welcomes competition or has the public's interests at heart. Crawford notes other industrial imperatives such as the consolidation of market power, deregulation, undermining community-owned networks, limiting upload speeds, and the shared interest in "maintaining the status quo."[32] It remains to be seen if the imperatives of a twentieth-century media system will continue to mould the viewing habits of the twenty-first-century audience.

Tay and Turner provide a cautionary tale as to why the so-called "end of television" orthodoxy may be overstated. Yet their argument insufficiently accounts for the major industrial shift of networked digital television, emerging online viewing trends, and the fundamental problem of maintaining a viable industry in the face of the transformation from fee to free. It may be true that visual culture remains "on the balance, anchored within the larger context of the home," but with each new generation of viewers this is less likely to be the case.[33] It certainly is not for the university students who populate my classes. Place is increasingly irrelevant for the audience. As I witnessed on the shore of the duck pond, it has been cut free and is adrift on the winds of change. For a generation that associates telephones with texting, friends with Facebook, and books with electronic tablets, television is everywhere they are, whenever they want it, and they want it for free.

An examination of emerging trends in online television audiences raises the question, "what is television?" The cellular phone changed the meaning of a telephone in the minds of many young people from something you talk with to something you use for texting. A comment made on Facebook by one of my students, Danielle Vicha, highlights how the social use of the telephone has changed in the past decade: "What ever happened to talking on the phone? Does this not exist anymore? I bbm, I text, I email, I twitter, I IM, I inbox. Can someone just call me instead of my phone beeping for something else?"[34] In a similar manner the meaning and uses of television have undergone considerable changes in the Internet age.

The online audience may come to think of television in a very different manner than the baby boomers of television's golden age. For over 50 years during the latter half of the twentieth century the dominant symbol of television has been a "box." Then the first decade of the twenty-first century saw digitization transform television's master symbol from a box to a flat panel. The popularity of flat-panel televisions occurred along with the simultaneous proliferation of flat-panel computer monitors. Flat-panel screens are now everywhere – in taxicabs, on the back of seats in airplanes, in family cars, malls, storefronts, concerts, and kitchens. The fat box became a thin screen, went forth, and multiplied. It grew to enormous dimensions and it shrank to ridiculous proportions. Now it is found everywhere that marketers think they might profitably capture our attention. There is little difference between a flat-panel television, a computer monitor, a laptop, a tablet computer, and the smartphones in our pockets. They are all portals to television. Television is no longer associated with authorized and regulated production systems, a universal and familiar device, or any device at all. As John Hartley argues, television is not something that has invariable features or "any *essential* mode of production, distribution, and consumption."[35] Television is not a discrete object or a privileged device. It is visual content that emanates from a wide variety of production systems, embodies all genres and narrative forms, and flows across multiple types of screens and into all manner of electronic gadgets.

Of course, television is more than just content and technology. It is also a symbol of fame, celebrity, and notoriety. To be on television is to be someone special. This special quality of television may also be changing. YouTube is providing the online audience with a lesson in how to get famous without being on television. Amateur videographers are achieving national and international fame through their viral videos, which feature their talents, crazy pets, or funny children. There is the possibility that as television content becomes divorced from any one "box" and gets intermingled with other forms of video content, such as amateur videos, the association of television with fame will become diluted across other media systems such as YouTube. In a highly fragmented media culture, television could lose its special status in the mind of the audience.

Canadian Online Exceptionalism and Ordinary Discontent

Canadians have been described as "the most voracious consumers of online video in the world."[36] We watch more videos and spend more time watching videos than any other country. My fellow Canadians watch almost twice as much online video as our American neighbours do. When Canada's national newspaper, *The Globe and Mail*, reported this story, readers wrote the following responses in the online edition

> We cancelled our satellite service because we have access to most ev
> thing we want to watch from a handful of TV network websites.
>   100 channels of crap for close to $100 a month through either R
> Bell. You can only watch what they will let you when they wa
> watch it. The same shows playing on 12 or more channels

time. Reruns out the wazoo. Twenty minutes of commercials for every hour of programming.

I've never owned a TV or paid for cable/satellite crapola. My Internet connection costs less and represents FAR greater value.

All across the globe these themes appear in readers' comments on on-line news stories about television. Even though television viewing is practically a universal habit, we encounter considerable discontent with television. Limited choices, repeated airings of the same shows, inane content, excessive commercials, and expensive bills are common complaints. This situation is not very different from the time of *All in the Family* except that now audiences have more choices. As far as the industry is concerned, the most fearful aspect of this choice is a phenomenon known as cord-cutting – cancelling a cable or satellite television service and using the Internet to access programming, and doing so mostly for free. Canadian online video consumption may set international records, but our discontent with television is shared across the globe.

Cord-cutting: Fringe Activity or Wave of the Future?

At present, only a minority of the television audience has participated in cord-cutting and abandoned their paid television services for cheaper online options. Nevertheless, there are indications that a growing number of consumers are dissatisfied with cable television and related practices of the incumbent industry. In 2013, two years after the *Globe and Mail* described Canadians' voracious taste for online video, the newspaper acknowledged that "cord cutting is definitely happening."[37] Millions of households disconnecting from cable television, historically unprecedented decreases in cable subscribers, tens of millions of paying subscribers of new delivery systems such as Netflix, and uncontrolled piracy of movies and television shows suggest that the industry is faced with a growing number of consumers who feel poorly served by the dominant model of television.

Cord-cutting is fuelled by the need to reduce household expenses in the midst of a harsh economy, facilitated by new products that offer an easy alternative, encouraged by the example of others, and socialized by an online culture defined by free information and entertainment. In 2010, a full 12 per cent of American cable users had cut premium cable services and 7 per cent cut out cable television altogether.[38] Five years after the invention of YouTube the US cable industry witnessed its largest dip in subscribers in the history of cable television. Was this a coincidence or the beginnings of a viable online alternative?

The experiences of those who have cut the cord and of cord cutters who have returned to the fold of pay-TV are captured herein. *Post-TV* provides readers with one of the first explorations of the values and opinions of cord cutters presented in their own words. We also encounter and analyse opinions about cord-cutting from television industry insiders. Scholarly analysis often leaves aside the vernacular discourse. Gerard H. Hauser suggests that the audience's ideas, values, and preferences should be treated as "a significant source of evidence deserving intense scrutiny."[39] When viewers' experiences are presented in the vernacular form we are confronted with the raw data of post-television cultural studies. Although industry opinion can be as biased as the audience's, the following also takes note of what industry thought leaders have to say about digital piracy, cord-cutting, and the online audience. When an established Wall Street analyst such as Harold Vogel suggests that cord-cutting is happening because "the psychology of the users is changing" and an entire field of new media studies suggests that the Internet is generating new ethics, values, and behaviour, we need to consider the possibility that the online television experience is diverging from the audience experience of the twentieth century.[40]

Post-TV provides the reader with a novel perspective on the online television audience. By placing piracy, cord-cutting, and related practices at the centre of the online viewing experience, *Post-TV* challenges the notion that television practice is "powerfully constrained" by regulatory and industrial regimes.[41] Questions of disintermediation, the relationship between distribution and market power, and the outlines of an emerging post-television culture are raised. The failure of the music industry to adapt to the desires of the online consumer and the woeful track record of the television industry's attempts at rolling out interactive television and related services suggest systemic failures to adapt to digital media and online consumer behaviour.

The television industry may be letting the audience slip through its hands as viewers migrate to more convenient and less expensive online options. A problem for one industry is usually an opportunity for another. Two of the largest high-tech companies in the world, Apple and Google, are competing against each other in the hopes of dominating the online television market.

The opportunity for the television industry to keep the audience in its corral may have already passed. The virtual migration to digital pastures is already well under way. Glenn Britt, former CEO of Time Warner Cable, noted in 2009 that "we're starting to see the beginnings of cord cutting where people, particularly young people, are saying all I need is broadband."[42] A year earlier almost one million US households relied solely on the Internet for television and didn't pay for traditional television services.

The newspaper industry is struggling to convert young people into regular readers and is having difficulty turning them into paying subscribers. They prefer to get their news online for free or from *The Daily Show*. It is the changing habits of the young that are transforming the music, news, and publishing sectors. The television industry must convert millennials to the habit of paying for something that they always acquired for free – a hard sell by any measure. The younger generation of Internet users is the canary in the coal mine and will indicate if death is in the air for the incumbent television industry.

The transformation of the Internet into a viable platform for watching video is only a few years old but the television industry is already being hit with daily doses of bad news. "Fewer young people watched TV on traditional sets over the past television season, the second consecutive year of decline as viewers face a proliferation of ways to watch TV show," reported the *Wall Street Journal* in May 2011.[43] In the spring of 2013 an article in *MSN Money* boldly proclaimed, "Television as We Know It Is Fading."[44] Other headlines sang the same song: "Network TV: An Industry in Decline," "Television News in Rapid Decline."[45] Along with these worrying headlines we witness the growth of "how to cut your cable" articles in blogs and magazines. In 2013 PBS published a book titled *Your Guide to Cutting the Cord to Cable TV*, GigaOM published *Cut the Cord: All You Need to Know to Drop Cable,* and Kalee Cole self-published *The Frugal Guide to Cutting the Cable Cord.* These phenomena point to Internet-driven changes in audience behaviour that demand the attention of television and new media studies.

Cord-cutting is definitely happening, but it is such a new form of audience behaviour that it remains surrounded by uncertainties. Is it driven purely by financial considerations? Will it remain a marginal audience experience or will it define the viewing habits of millennials for decades to come? Will bit caps and the high cost of bandwidth limit the spread of cord-cutting? To what extent are cord cutters willing to pay for online content? These uncertainties join a long list of other challenges facing the television industry: rising programming costs; a shrinking market for pay-TV; increasing competition for the online audience; and a new audience psychology influenced by the Internet's culture of free. These are some of the questions and issues addressed in *Post-TV*.

In 2012 around 3.4 billion movies were watched online through streaming services like Netflix. Not counting pirated movies, consumers watched 1 billion more movies online than the 2.4 billion movies watched on Blu-ray discs and DVDs. Indicative of the amazing speed at which the Internet is changing audience habits, the number of online movies viewed doubled between 2011 and 2012. Movie consumption is shifting from purchases of single physical discs to unlimited streaming services.[46] DVDs are not dead yet, but it is widely acknowledged that they are well on their way to being replaced because of Internet viewing habits. As one blogger noted,

> I have not purchased a DVD or Blu-ray movie in many years. Last one was *Pan's Labyrinth*, back in 2007. Since then, I have relied on services like Netflix to take care of my needs. This was before smartphones and tablets reached their full boom. Now, such services are available from most devices with a screen, making it even more convenient for the consumer ... Why would I purchase a more expensive DVD or Blu-ray disc? It costs about the same (most times more) as my monthly Netflix subscription and is far from offering the convenience that streaming services feature.[47]

These changes in television technology, industry structure, and audience habits are dragging us into a post-television culture. The following chapters will explore some of the more disruptive forms of online audience behaviour and speculate about their implications for the media industry and society. Control is a central theme in the history of television. As D'Agostino and Tafler noted about the new post-television culture, "there remains a question of control. Who controls the tools often determines the nature of the system put in place."[48] Chapter 1 looks at early attempts to escape control, such as community access television and video activism, the use of the remote control, and, more recently, online piracy. It is argued that the music industry provides important lessons for how the television and movies sectors could lose control over their content. Executives and research analysts within the television industry insist that the past of the music industry is not the future of television, but there are reasons to believe that industry thought leaders are engaging in wishful thinking.

Piracy is synonymous with the Internet, and online television certainly is no exception. Chapter 2 provides an extensive look into why the online television audience prefers free to fee, even if it means breaking the law. Chapter 3 looks at the specific case of sports television piracy and argues that the crown jewel of cable television, sports programming, is also at risk from new habits of the online audience. Online piracy has made it possible to get most television shows and movies along with a great deal of sports programs for free, so the question in the minds of many is, "why pay for cable?" Chapter 4 explores how the online audience has responded to the degradation in the value of a cable subscription by "cutting the cord" – cancelling their cable television and getting television over the Internet. Along with the rapid growth in cord cutters is a generation of online viewers who have never paid for a television subscription and may never do so. These "cord nevers" may be ahead of their time, but so were a few million Internet pioneers back in 1990. *Post-TV* provides a detailed exploration of cord cutters and cord nevers – pioneers of a new way of watching television that has struck fear in the hearts of television executives.

Chapter 5 looks into the viewing habits of the post-television generation. Viewing on demand, distracted viewing, mobile access, and social viewing are causing upheaval in the television industry. These habits are fostered by piracy as well as new types of online television services. Chapter 6 provides short case studies of online television services such as Netflix, Hulu, Amazon, Apple TV and iTunes, Google TV, and YouTube. These legitimate sources of competition for the online audience combine with illegitimate modes of pirate viewing and collectively threaten to disintermediate the incumbent television industry.

Chapter 7 argues that, contrary to the industry's dominant discourse, the risk of disintermediation grows as an oligopolistic old media system desperately tries to hang on to the status quo of twentieth-century broadcast business models. The television system attempts to maintain the value of content through the creation of artificial scarcity but the Internet creates conditions of digital plenitude. Finally, chapter 8 asks what happens to society when its super-peer undergoes radical transformation. Television is widely cited as being responsible for many aspects of social, political, and economic life in the twentieth century. If online content and audiences spiral out of control, how will this affect the social order in the twenty-first century? To answer this question *Post-TV* looks at diversity, citizenship, news, and global conflict in the era of the online audience.

The following analysis makes no attempt to provide an account of the global online television system or the vast varieties of national television systems. The focus here is on the United States and Canada, but many other national audiences are intertwined in the emerging post-television era. The United States may not be the future of the global television audience, but it remains the largest source of both legitimate television exports and illegally downloaded shows and movies. China may have one of the most controlled statist media systems in the world, but the Chinese are among the world's most uncontrollable and voracious digital pirates. No industrialized nation has escaped the effects of an online audience and digitized content but not all will be equally affected. One hundred million Americans and another one hundred million Europeans have not yet connected their homes to the Internet, so the post-television future that is unfolding is only one of many. Nevertheless, the issues and trends found within the contemporary American post-television landscape are consequential for global audiences. As Gray notes, "the American model of television itself is rapidly becoming the world's more common model."[49] It may be the case that online television itself will soon become the world's more common model of television.

It is not my intention to spell out the certain future of the online audience. The following chapters explore aspects of online audience behaviour that are far too novel to provide the foundation for forecasting the future. While I do argue that cord-cutting, digital piracy, increased competition, and new modes of production and distribution are rendering audiences and content more difficult to control, the future of the television system remains highly uncertain. Alternatives to a future of uncontrolled content and audiences could unfold if piracy were eliminated. If the television industry manages to cripple new forms of legitimate online competition, we could find ourselves in a future defined by the old television oligopoly. Alternatively, we may find the prospects of the audience defined by new types of oligopolies run by Apple, Intel, Google, and other current outsiders. All the major players within the television industry have launched their own online streaming services. If the television oligopoly manages to assert its current industrial imperatives, the future of online television might be defined by these limited services. As I said, my goal here is not to map out all possible alternatives or provide a detailed account of how the dominant players are adapting. The focus herein lies elsewhere: with the online audience, out-of-control content, and emerging business models that threaten to disintermediate the dominant players.

Post-TV acts as an unintended sequel to my previous book, *Watching YouTube*, which explored how the Internet has changed amateur videography and created a culture of mass participation in film-making. Reading *Watching YouTube* is not necessary for following the arguments made in *Post-TV*, but it should be understood that one of the forces affecting the online television audience is amateur videos. By now many readers will be familiar with YouTube. Many readers will have seen online videos from all manner of sources. Amateur online video represents how the audience has a choice for viewing more than just what is made available by the television industry. What follows is an exploration of the television audience's expanded powers of choice, new capabilities of rebroadcasting and production, and the democratization of global distribution. There are extraordinary implications for the audience and society when we can turn on our television sets and watch *All in the Family* as well as videos of our own family members.

1 From the Remote Control to Out of Control: Music Piracy and the Future of Television

One of the main reasons the Internet represents a threat to the television industry is written in the history of television itself, which is defined by recurring issues of choice and control. The television industry has a long history of trying to control audiences and limit choices. The appearance of a medium that is intrinsically difficult to control becomes all the more significant given the considerable efforts to control content and audiences since the early days of television.

Control takes many forms. The anti-competitive behaviour of media conglomerates and concentrated markets found across the globe are forms of control.[1] Media industries have long used regulatory policies to protect their markets while also benefiting from the effects of deregulation to expand into local and foreign markets. Even as the Internet has created new types of media corporations, such as Google and Facebook, the overall trend has been a degree of concentration of ownership in commercial media sectors that industry watchers have found alarming for over 30 years now. As Henry Jenkins notes, there are "a small handful of multinational media conglomerates dominating all sectors of the entertainment industry."[2] While others argue that this has no deleterious effect on consumers, culture, and democracy, such unprecedented power of cultural production, expression, marketing, and public relations concentrated in the hands of a few multinational corporations and private individuals is hardly something worth celebrating.

The scale of concentration in media markets is altogether remarkable. Robert W. McChesney describes media markets as "textbook examples of corporate-dominated oligopolistic markets ruled by a small number of firms." Media companies "are typically vast conglomerates that function as oligopolies in not just one market but in many."[3] In the United

States "four firms sell almost 90 percent of the music," six firms account for 90 per cent of revenues in the motion picture industry, and six firms control over 80 per cent of the cable television industry.[4] The level of media concentration in other national markets, such as Canada and Australia, is even higher.

Some voices argue that market concentration is good for consumers. Jeffery Church, economics professor at the University of Alberta, agrees that consolidation within the media industry, a small number of firms with large market shares, is beneficial.[5] One of Canada's four major media corporations, Shaw, went so far as to argue that consolidation within the media industry helps keep consumers "within the regulated system." Dwayne Winseck, communications professor at Carleton University, dismissed this claim as "repugnant," and rightly so.[6] Why should we celebrate less competition for consumers, which means less choice and more expensive products and services?

What consumers want is abundantly clear. They want television when they want it, where they want it. Time and again, as Winseck notes, both industry and regulators have the opposite goal in mind – keeping the audience in the current broadcast system.[7] Maintaining the status quo by keeping consumers watching television as it is offered to them by the existing broadcast system requires restricting competition, consumer choice, and freedom. This, in a nutshell, is the goal of incumbent players within the entertainment industry at the dawn of online television viewing.

One of the first technologies to give viewers control over the flow of television programming was the remote control. Audiences gained greater control over the array of viewing options through their remote control devices. Television viewers quickly discovered that the remote control can be used to mute the sound during commercials and switch channels to avoid advertising altogether. Articles celebrating the viewer's new power to avoid commercials appeared in newspapers as early as 1955.[8] Long before the remote control became widely used the broadcast industry attempted to frame viewer control as an illicit form of disruption.[9] In his analysis of the implications of the device William Uricchio notes that even the modest semblance of control afforded to the television audience by the remote control "terrified" the industry and caused "something just short of a panic among broadcasters and advertisers" because it undermined the ratings system.[10] Similarly, the authors of *Remote Control: Television, Audiences, and Cultural Power* suggest that television "controls us at a distance. It emanates from some place far away, yet it makes its presence constantly felt in our everyday lives. As the gadget we use to change channels, the remote control symbolizes the viewers' selection, control, and manipulation of television broadcasts. Our frustrated 'zapping' of commercials has become the American industry's worst nightmare."[11] If the humble remote control was the television industry's worst nightmare, one can only imagine what a terror the Internet must represent.

The remote control disrupted programming and revenues and foreshadowed how the rise of the online audience would affect the industry decades later. The general tendency of television audiences trying to gain more freedom is also inscribed in the early history of community (public) access television, pirate TV, guerrilla video, advocacy video, non-profit media associations, video activism, and related efforts. These alternative modes of television production arose in response to controls imposed by market and state forces which use dominant forms of media as "a tool for social control."[12] As early as the late 1960s public access television attempted to redress the imbalance of power within the commercial broadcasting system, which favoured private interests over public concerns.[13] In these pioneering days of public access television, activists and scholars looked forward to a time when grass-roots media would displace the communicative power of the state and the corporate sector.

My purpose here is not to retrace the history of alternative media organizations and forms but to note that their very existence attests to the nature of power within the political economy of television. Laura R. Linder's survey of the history of public access television in America places the issue of control at the centre of the television system: "How can people speak and hear noncommercial, localized voices and ideas when the majority of the media outlets are controlled by a few megacorporations?"[14] The structure of dominant media systems leads to the suppression of alternative voices and thus generates the impulse to find alternative outlets for expression. By their very nature dominant media systems invite the growth of oppositional media. John D.H. Downing describes these alternative media as constituting "the most active form of the active audience."[15] One might well add that the Internet enables this most active audience to become hyperactive. This aspect of television's political economy makes the arrival of a new televisual system such as the Internet all the more significant as a possible source of more viewpoints and voices. It also frames one way that the Internet will be used as a form of alternative expression – community-based online television beyond the control of government and market forces.

In her overview of the history of the video Portapaks and the independent television movement in the United States, Deirdre Boyle traces how video artists and activists (often one and the same) "challenged television's authority."[16] Representatives of the counterculture of the 1960s attempted to gain access to commercial television but "learned the hard way that television had no intention of relinquishing its power."[17] Writing about the contemporary situation in 1992 Boyle argued that free speech was being powerfully opposed and support for alternative media in America was at a new low. Within a few short years the mass adoption of the Internet would lead to a substantial increase in free speech capabilities and alternative media production and distribution.

The past of alternative media provides us with a few lessons to keep in mind at the dawn of the post-television era. Although the radical potential of alternative media has not yet been fulfilled, neither has the Orwellian conceit of corporate media overridden independent thought and action. Radical and community media have always existed on the margins but those margins are not fixed. Downing notes that "community-owned cable TV stations account for less than 3 percent of all cable stations in the U.S." but at the same time "new self-managed media have been mushrooming in country after country."[18] This suggests a thirst for viewpoints and programming that goes beyond what the state and the market are willing to provide. At the roots of television's history we find a struggle for control that continues to this day and defines post-television culture as a battleground over content and audiences.

Initially, viewing choices were made for us by television programmers. This was quickly interrupted by remote control devices that delivered a marginal increase in audience power. Alternative and community-based media extended the search for programming control and in many instances gave it a distinctly political character. The Internet has continued this shift towards the empowered audience to the point where it represents a problem for the entertainment industry. Yet there is no guarantee that audiences will continue to gain more control. The next stage could see our ability to choose displaced by computer programs known as adaptive agent technologies.

Used by companies such as Amazon, adaptive online shopping agents record your browsing and purchasing habits and then recommend further products that might be of interest to you. Television manufacturers are developing adaptive agents as a solution to the coming problem of having to choose from a menu of thousands of daily programs. Soon we will be faced with an overwhelming menu of choices. In the post-television future our choices might be made for us by software programmers and adaptive agent designers.[19] Our televisions, in whatever form they may take, will make viewing choices for us based upon our previous viewing decisions. In this near-future scenario there will be little need for viewers to make choices. The adaptive agent will displace viewer control because the software will "stay in touch with our changing rhythms and moods ... anticipate our every interest," and prove to be "nearly infinite in its capacities."[20] Now that is software you might want to marry.

The dream of such a perfect partner, one who can make all the right choices for us and guide us through the growing complexities of the digital consumer lifestyle, is an old one. It reaches back to the early days of science fiction novels and can be found in the writing of contemporary techno-utopians such as Nicholas Negroponte. In 1995, at the dawn of the Internet cultural revolution, Negroponte wrote *Being Digital*. This manifesto for a networked society asked us to imagine "a future in which your interface agent can read every newswire and newspaper and catch every TV and radio broadcast on the planet, and then construct a personalized summary."[21] Software agents will filter the digital world of news and entertainment for us and provide us with a highly personalized version of our tastes and interests. This was a vision that caught on among retailers because it promised precision-targeted delivery of advertising.

I have my doubts about the ability of choices to be so perfectly automated and seamlessly integrated into the habits of consumers and audiences. Every time I ask my students how they respond to Amazon's purchase suggestions they indicate that the automated suggestions have had little if any impact on their purchasing decisions. Yet it is probably unwise to underestimate the technological marvels that await us in the near future. Adaptive agent technologies are in their infancy. Negroponte's vision of the Internet delivering a perfectly customized version of all my information and entertainment needs in a "Daily Me" package could be part of the post-television future. The commercial sector is certainly intent on making it a reality.

Three-quarters of what Netflix customers choose to watch is the result of software-generated recommendations. The company's goal is "to learn individual viewing preferences so well that every recommendation is a hit with the subscriber."[22] Netflix knows what movies and television shows customers watch, when they are watching, whether a show is watched in part or all the way to the end, and even when viewers rewind to re-watch a particular scene or favourite star. Netflix wants to keep their subscribers from straying beyond their catalogue of selections. In short, it wants to own the eyeballs of the audience. If such a system defined the audience's experience, then the programmers of widely used adaptive agents would gain tremendous political and economic influence. These agents would have intimate knowledge of our habits and tastes and reveal our political values, sexual orientation, and religious beliefs.

It is a small step from having our needs served to seeing our actions controlled: "armed with an appreciation of the user that is developed through inhumanly attentive collection and analysis of user behavior, [the digital agent] is positioned not merely to serve, but also to shape (if not control) the actions of a user."[23] One of the ironies of a post-television future may be that commercial television gains more power over the audience, power hidden within a ubiquitous and seemingly harmless process of automated recommendations and guided choices. Will the agent adapt to our needs or will we be moulded to its purposes and designs? The possibility that preferences will be completely programmed is somewhat offset by the continuing influence of peers upon individual choices. People close to us are a significant influence on our viewing habits. Yet this may simply displace the issue – who or what is influencing our peers' tastes and choices?

A prominent characteristic of post-television culture is found in the various attempts by the industry to re-establish control over content. With the digitization and Internet-ization of the entertainment industry, television is transforming into something that is inherently difficult to control. As Julian Thomas notes, television is "no longer functionally dedicated to content of a particular sort of origin."[24] Television is no longer dedicated to delivering highly regulated content to paying audiences. The capabilities and freedoms this affords the audience are being undermined by incumbent industry giants every step of the way.

Dominant media companies attempt to restrict their customers from accessing content and products that are not part of the company's offerings. Michael Wolff described the battle between established distribution channels – Time Warner, News Corporation, Viacom, Disney, Comcast – and new technology innovators in the following terms: "The upstarts are geared to giving customers what they want (new products as well as the Establishment's products) when they want it; while the latter closely regulate who gets what, when and how, and on what complex and baroque payment methods and terms."[25] This is a struggle over the control of video: "Who controls video controls the media business, and, too, the culture. And, in a sense, everybody's lives."[26] Here Wolff may not be guilty of exaggeration. Much is at stake at the dawn of the post-television age.

The entertainment industry is trying to minimize the expanded choices that come with Internet technologies. Incumbent players do not want to compete against new services that expand viewing choices. The default strategy of the cable industry promotes devices and services that channel the user to preselected content choices available only from the cable company and its content partners. This mirrors an earlier strategy of containment that deployed remote controls dedicated to profitable aspects of pay-TV services and made accessing alternative sources of content difficult or impossible. Such control strategies have always faced audience resistance. Contemporary restrictive strategies are met with counter-strategies of jailbreaking and hacking.

Consider the example of Apple TV as a restrictive device that attempts to channel the viewer's experience to Apple's catalogue of products. Apple TV's programming and interface design make it difficult to access content outside of Apple's corporate ecosystem. Yet Apple TV and similar devices such as PlayStation, Xbox, TiVo, Boxee, and Roku have a global community of hackers that extends the usability of the devices far beyond the designers' intentions. This highlights the cat-and-mouse game played by media corporations and the audience. Media corporations try to contain the online audience within their products and content offerings. The old business model of viewing devices and services dedicated to content of a particular sort of origin is still with us. As Thomas notes, all around the world media businesses are trying to "restrict the capacity of consumers to share, store, and modify content."[27] Of course, consumers continue to hack media interfaces such as Apple TV so they can gain access to all of the content available on the Internet. Not all of the audience uses such hacks, but for those seeking to regain control over their media experience, help is always just a click or two away via Google.

In contrast to the extraordinary level of freedom afforded by the Internet, media industries seek a degree of control that exceeds what was possible and legally permissible in the analogue age of television. One example of this type of overreach is the FCC's attempt to re-engineer consumer electronics and make them conform to a regulation known as the broadcast flag. The broadcast flag proposal required devices that receive a television program to also read the instructions of certain types of embedded codes. These codes, or "flags," would "include information that activates controls in the reception device over whether or not a program may be recorded, stored for any period of time, or burned to a DVD."[28] In other words, consumers would not be able to do anything with their media that the industry did not allow. Under this set of regulations the consumer electronics industry would have had to re-engineer their devices to conform to the wishes of the US entertainment industry. The US Court of Appeals rejected the FCC mandate, but the entertainment industry continues to promote the legislation.

The broadcast flag was rejected as something that would trample the audience's fair rights to access content that is in the public domain. As Wendy Seltzer, attorney for the Electronic Frontier Foundation (EFF), notes, public rights would be "hard-coded out" of existence.[29] Limits on open-source development, interoperability, and technological innovation would have transpired and legitimate non-infringing activities would be disallowed. It is also doubtful that the broadcast flag would prevent piracy considering the army of dedicated hackers that would defeat such digital rights management technology. The entertainment industry was intent on implementing a system that ignored consumer rights and was willing to risk stifling innovation in the marketplace.

An earlier example of the television industry's attempt to stifle technological innovation and audience freedoms occurred in 1984 when Universal City Studios tried to stop Sony from selling video cassette recorder (VCR) machines. The US Supreme Court ruled that manufacturers are "not liable for creating a technology that some customers may use for copyright infringing purposes."[30] This ruling ensured that subsequent technologies, such as the personal computer, CD burners, digital video recorders, Apple's iPod, and Web browsers could make it to the market without fear of lawsuits from the entertainment industry. The EFF points out that peer-to-peer technologies are under similar legal assaults because the entertainment industry "has been trying to roll back the protections established more than twenty years earlier in the [Sony] Betamax case."[31] The trend here is clear – entertainment industries have continually sought to deny the public access to new technologies that expand the audience's control over content.

The ongoing attempts to limit audience freedoms and the FCC's willingness to ignore public interests are enabled by the "unique political influence of the broadcasters themselves."[32] We risk underestimating the nature of the threat if we lose sight of the collusion between elected officials and the entertainment industry. Legal scholar Anthony E. Varona notes, "With Members of Congress beholden to broadcasters for positive coverage immediately before and after elections, it is not surprising that the broadcast lobby has become one of the most obvious 'textbook' examples of an industry 'capturing' its regulators, and in this case, the Congress itself."[33] Examples of this collusion of interests abound. Congressman Howard Berman, an original co-sponsor of the infamous Stop Online Piracy Act (SOPA), received $337,000 in political contributions from the movie and television industry during the 2011–12 election period.[34] The 25 co-sponsors of SOPA received a total of $5,407,342, and the 40 co-sponsors of the PROTECT IP Act (PIPA) received more than $13.5 million from the television, movie, and music industries.[35] Comcast, News Corporation, and Disney spent a combined $30.6 million on Washington lobbyists in 2011. Collusion also manifests itself in the exchange of professionals between state and market systems. Thus we witness bureaucrats such as FCC commissioner Meredith Attwell Baker become senior vice president for government affairs for NBCUniversal.[36] This occurred four months after the FCC approved the merger of Comcast and NBCUniversal.

Collusion between the entertainment industry and the state reflects the logic of capitalism's media economy – a desire to control audiences and content while reducing the rights of the audience. After surveying a variety of attempts by the industry to encode anti-circumvention provisions into television technologies, Thomas concluded that "the new television, for all its promise, may end up less usable than the old."[37] There is the possibility that hardware and software could both contain "new rules for controlling the flow of content" and effectively unite all "household devices into one logical machine and thereby return us to the more manageable era of the stand-alone TV."[38] Likewise, in *The Future of the Internet and How to Stop It*, Jonathan Zittrain argues that the Internet is in danger of being subjected to a form of centralized control by corporations that would all but eliminate fair rights, piracy, end-user innovation, and the generative collaboration that has come to characterize the Net.[39] But thanks to the anarchic counter-forces of market competition and hackers, this dystopia has yet to arrive.

It is not only within the Internet that we find anarchy. There is no small amount of anarchy within capitalism itself. A coordinated effort by media, software, and hardware industries to engineer choice and freedom out of the consumer's world would create a market niche for consumer goods that allow the audience to do what they want with their devices and see what they want on their screens. The control logic of the entertainment industry is subject to the anarchy of the global marketplace. A widely felt need will not go unfulfilled.

DVDs (digital versatile discs or digital video discs) represent one of the latest chapters in the story of control versus freedom. Scholars variously see DVDs as initiating a shift of power and control from media corporations to consumers or conversely as "an extension of pre-existing marketing practices."[40] Building upon Gilles Deleuze's connection between emerging control societies and new forms of communication, Jo T. Smith proposes that the marketing of DVDs "invites the media consumer to contribute their time, attention and labor to emerging modes of social regulation and normalizing regimes."[41] Yet, as with all media systems, here again we encounter contradictory forces. At the same time that it promotes audience control the DVD also brings with it "new modes of action that can diagnose and act" against capitalism's control societies.[42] During the age of DVDs consumers were busy ripping them to make illegal copies and share them with their friends while corporations attempted and failed to control the duplication of DVDs through digital rights management systems. Internet-based entertainment systems embody similar contradictions of control and freedom. Post-television culture brings with it new modes of consumer management and surveillance and new opportunities for dissent.

The People Formerly Known as the Audience

In 2006 journalism professor Jay Rosen crafted the manifesto "The People Formerly Known as the Audience." Rosen was describing a shift in power between the audience and the media industry that was enabled by the Internet: "The people formerly known as the audience are those who were on the receiving end of a media system that ran one way, in a broadcasting pattern, with high entry fees and a few firms competing to speak very loudly while the rest of the population listened in isolation from one another – and who today are not in a situation like that at all."[43] The manifesto struck a chord with the Internet community and media professionals because it spoke to basic issues of control and freedom. Even media moguls are aware of the changes audiences are going through offline and online.

Rupert Murdoch, chairman of the News Corporation and one of the world's richest media tycoons, observed that consumers "want control over their media, instead of being controlled by it."[44] The television industry pays lip service to giving audiences television everywhere they want it. But as audiences and industry move online the intention is to reassert control over eyeballs. Consider the following from Ann Kirschner, vice president for programming and media development for the National Football League: "We already own the eyeballs on the television screen. We want to make sure we own the eyeballs on the computer screen."[45] Kirschner made this statement in 1995. Ten years later Murdoch acknowledged the actual desires of the online audience. Yet it remains to be seen if television moguls have really given up trying to control the online audience and own their eyeballs.

Rosen touches upon an important issue when he notes that owning the eyeballs of audiences is little more than a "fantastic delusion" that "gave its operators an exaggerated sense of their own power and mastery over others."[46] Could it be that executive decision-makers are so filled with an exaggerated sense of power that they overestimate their ability to control online audiences? If the media industry suffers from delusions about its ability to control the audience, then the Internet may have a detrimental impact on the effectiveness of business plans.

The economy of the television industry is based on a simple formula, a business model shared by the media and entertainment industry. The *Economist* succinctly described this traditional business model as "based on aggregating large passive audiences and holding them captive during advertising interruptions."[47] As aspects of online television business models, passivity and captivity are ill-suited to a highly productive, active, mobile online audience. Can an industry that has been built on the pretensions of owning eyeballs, controlling audiences, and force-feeding advertising to viewers sufficiently transform itself in the age of networked digital media consumption?

The Content Formerly Known as Costly

The fundamental problem for commercial television and film industries is that they must find a way to build a business in an online environment which treats all content, all private property, as public property. Either by design or by accident, online media content in all its varieties wants to be free. The first generation of Internet businesses tried to work around this by creating online destinations that attracted large audiences and then charging advertisers for the privilege of reaching those audiences. By 2009 publishers and broadcasters were "beginning to discover, however, that advertising alone is not providing the sustainable digital business model they expected for their expensively produced content."[48] Led by Murdoch's News Corporation, major media corporations are watching closely as newspaper publishers experiment with paywalls and online charges. The future of such business models is highly uncertain. Whether it is news, music, movies, or television, it is quite difficult to get the online consumer to pay for content and to do so profitably.

Even when online content is profitable it can cause considerable grief to an industry. Consider the much heralded success of iTunes, an online content service which presents "a source of endless frustration for the music industry."[49] Apple achieved success with iTunes by "manhandling the major record labels during a series of now-legendary negotiations" that resulted in a pricing agreement music executives quickly came to regret.[50] So while the standard line of thinking suggests that iTunes represents the potential for enormous profit from the online sale of entertainment content, it may also represent a looming threat for the film and television industry. Apple's success with iTunes provides the television and film industry with a warning: an industry's content can end up in the hands of another industry and be sold at a much lower price than it once cost consumers. Whatever one might conclude about the success of Apple's efforts to sell music online, piracy remains rampant and accounts for 95 per cent of all music downloaded from the Internet.[51]

Do Consumers Prefer to Pay?

Television executives insist that the Internet will enhance and not erode their audience count and revenue streams. Yet there are striking similarities between the swift rise and normalization of music piracy and the current trends in television piracy. By paying close attention to the recent past of digital music, we stand to gain insight into the future of television.

The music industry reacted to the rise of digital piracy by trying to stem the tide with the marketplace, technology, and legal actions. With the majority of all downloaded music falling into the category of piracy, we can declare the attempt to control content and consumer behaviour a failure. According to the International Federation of the Phonographic Industry (IFPI), in 2010 alone digital piracy cost the global music industry an estimated $1.5 billion.[52] Although such industry voices are known to inflate statistics as part of their public relations campaigns, no one can doubt that digital piracy has been very disruptive for the industry. The IFPI claims that during the first decade of the twenty-first century "the global recorded music industry based on selling and owning recorded music shrunk by more than 50 per cent."[53] When millions of young consumers choose to behave in a certain way there is little, if anything, that governments and industry can do.

During the first decade (1999–2009) of rampant online piracy the Recording Industry Association of America (RIAA) repeatedly insisted that pirates could be converted into paying customers of digital music services – "the best way to deter piracy is to offer fans compelling legal alternatives" – but piracy has not been deterred to any significant degree.[54] Of course, we can hardly expect the RIAA to provide a factual assessment of music piracy. Is there really any such thing as a compelling alternative to free? The notion that piracy can be stopped, or significantly diminished, through the offering of a compelling legal alternative (one that invariably costs money or involves annoying ads) is found in industry, press, and academic opinions. The notion operates as a statement of faith in the belief system of capitalism.

Consumers, it is fervently believed, would actually prefer to pay for goods. Even within institutions that are usually diametrically opposed to the actions of the RIAA we find this conviction. Fred von Lohmann, an attorney with the EFF, sounded very much like RIAA public relations when he suggested that "if you want to stop casual piracy you have to offer a compelling legal alternative."[55] Both industry representatives and consumer rights groups are saying the same thing – consumers want to pay for stuff that they can otherwise get for free. Yes, some consumers do prefer to pay, but the experience of the music industry suggests that, when given a choice between pay or free, many online consumers choose free. This bias towards free does not negate the obvious fact of a vibrant marketplace in cyberspace. Online music streaming brings in around $1 billion (US), streaming rights for online television and movies is adding billions of dollars to studio coffers, and worldwide spending on digital media and entertainment is forecast to hit $1 trillion by 2017.[56] The *Economist* magazine summarized the digital economy in the following terms: "The internet is at last contributing to media-industry bottom lines. But it will not restore the newspaper or music businesses to their previous size. The economics have changed for good."[57]

When they first appeared on the consumer's radar there were indications that free streaming music services such as Spotify might lead to a reduction in music piracy.[58] There is also the possibility that access will replace ownership as the primary value among consumers. In Sweden, home of Spotify, the world's largest streaming music service, physical sales of music decreased by 24 per cent during the first half of 2013. A similar trend is occurring in the United States, where the sale of single digital songs is declining as streaming music becomes more popular.[59] Music lovers are shifting from physical purchases and digital downloads to streaming services.[60] This trend confirms Patrik Wikström's suggestion that "concepts such as ownership and acquisition have slowly become increasingly irrelevant."[61] Yet, contrary to Gregory Steirer's similar claim that online viewing services "seem certain to increasingly rule out or disable traditional forms of media collecting," the cable cutters and cord nevers that I am familiar with have vast digital archives of music, television shows, and movies.[62] Ownership and collecting as a part of consumer culture are unlikely to disappear anytime soon. Thus we still see claims by media scholars such as "Americans are more comfortable with things than with access."[63] We have not yet arrived at the "Age of Access" forecast by Jeremy Rifkin, wherein ownership and markets "play an increasingly diminished role in human affairs."[64]

Reflecting on the collapsing sales of movie DVDs, one market analyst suggested that "consumers simply are not interested in owning content any more. Content is so easy to access on-demand, why buy it, especially given the dramatic price differential between buying and renting?"[65] Yet the rise of an access-oriented consumer culture, where people pay not to own something but to access a copy of something, would merely shift the nature of piracy without eliminating it. Access itself would be subject to widespread piracy. Netflix subscribers share their paid account login passwords with an additional ten million viewers.[66] A similar pattern exists among users of paid video services such as HBO Go and Hulu Plus. We are already witnessing the beginning of widespread access and authentication piracy. Netflix has plans to reduce the amount of account sharing, but such efforts may prove ineffective if hackers find a way around any new authentication systems.

Writing in the *New York Times* about his experience as a cord cutter, Nick Bilton related how sharing access passwords to HBO Go, the authorized online source for the television series *Game of Thrones*, was a widespread practice.[67] All of Bilton's cord-cutting friends admitted that they used various forms of piracy to watch *Game of Thrones*. Friends do not let friends miss good television. Even Bilton did not hesitate to resort to piracy to see the latest episodes. "HBO told me that 'Thrones' would be out on DVD in eight months, so I experimented with the piracy option, too. It took me all of 22 seconds to begin watching the latest episode through the illicit route of an online storage service and an illegal BitTorrent site."[68] This casts doubt on industry plans to limit piracy through online authentication schemes such as Time Warner Cable's TV Everywhere initiative. Curiously, even this news story repeated the "people will pay" thesis when it quoted the editor of *TorrentFreak*, Ernesto Van Der Sar (a pseudonym), as claiming that the only way to stop piracy "is by making legal content easier to access and offering it at a reasonable price."[69] Yet many consumers will measure the promise of easy access and reasonable pricing against "22 seconds" and "free."

Why did there arise such a consensus that consumers will pay for something that they can get for free? Because analysts asked consumers, and "overwhelming year-over-year survey data" suggested that "people will pay for a subscription service that has all the perks, and none of the hassles, of a free system."[70] Nonetheless, sometimes there is a vast gulf between what consumers say they will do and what they actually do. This is particularly true when there are moral implications to the consumer's behaviour. Individuals want to be seen as doing the right thing in public but are quite willing to break laws in private. For over a decade now the market has been asking consumers to pay for something they can get for free and so far many consumers have responded with a resounding no.

In 2002 Farhad Manjoo wrote in *Salon* magazine that "it's amazing how many people seem to agree that legitimate music subscription services can become a viable alternative to free trading."[71] A decade later the massive sales of digital music through iTunes had not made a dent in online music piracy. The belief that the market can provide a compelling legal alternative to music piracy has persisted for over a decade. Even as recently as 2011 analysts were insisting that Apple's new iCloud music service would provide "a compelling legal alternative that should act as a piracy deterrent," a sentiment echoed by Victoria Espinel, the coordinator of US intellectual property enforcement.[72] Likewise, a government-sponsored watchdog in the United Kingdom insists that "the growth of the legal online music market is the best way to tackle online copyright infringement."[73] But these are highly biased voices working from within the centre of capitalism's belief system. An industry analyst, an intellectual property enforcer, and a government-sponsored consumer group all repeat the same tenet of capitalist faith – consumers prefer to participate in the marketplace on terms set by corporations.

This tenet of capitalist faith resurfaces year after year. Writing in May 2013 the editor of an industry newsletter confidently told readers, "If you provide a reasonably priced, legal alternative, most people will use it and traffic to sites that typically host pirated content goes down."[74] Yet piracy persists. It does not seem reasonable to argue that the past 20 years of the commercial development of the Internet has utterly failed to provide a reasonably priced and legal way to access content. Plenty of such commercial services exist across a variety of content sectors. The problem is not the lack of legitimate digital services, fair pricing, or usability. By mid-2014 this was finally acknowledged in the pages of the *Australian Financial Review* when Andrew Harris said, "If music industry experience is anything to go by, making shows such as *Game of Thrones* available immediately on any device at the right price will not solve our piracy problems." Harris observed that despite the fact that the music industry already delivered on the consumer's demand for online availability, ease of access, and reasonable price, "the piracy issue still has not been solved … [because] it's impossible to compete with free."[75]

The music and television industries face an intractable problem: a large percentage of consumers prefer not to pay for certain types of content. In an era in which conventional wisdom suggests that the market offers the most efficient solution we are confronted by a problem that cannot be solved by the market. When it comes to certain types of transactions surrounding certain types of goods and services, many people prefer not to participate in the market.

Digital Music Piracy: The Future of Online TV?

The impact of digital piracy on the music industry's revenues remains a matter of debate. The industry typically cites piracy as the source of all its woes. Yet some academic studies conclude that the loss of revenue resulting from online piracy is negligible.[76] Other studies conclude that digital piracy actually increases sales.[77] Most academic studies suggest that piracy significantly erodes the sales of physical music, yet the impact on digital sales appears to be positive. A recent analysis of 16,000 Internet users by the European Commission found that both online piracy and legitimate music streaming services lead to marginal positive gains in the online legal sales of digital music, and "the vast majority of the music that is consumed illegally by the individuals in our sample would not have been legally purchased if illegal downloading websites were not available to them."[78] Whatever the case may be, it is highly unlikely that piracy is a problem soon to disappear. Apparently, even media empires do it.

Bell Canada was ordered to pay over $1 million in damages and fees when it was found guilty of facilitating the piracy of its competitor's satellite television signals. Senior Bell managers "knowingly communicated false data to the CRTC [Canadian Radio-television and Telecommunications Commission] related to the piracy rate of its TV distribution system."[79] Bell is not the only media company willing to lie to regulators and facilitate the piracy of its competitor's television signals. Operational Security, a secretive unit within Rupert Murdoch's News Corporation, has faced repeated accusations that it encouraged piracy of its competitor's pay-TV products.[80] Murdoch is even suspected of "playing God in British politics." Writing in *The Globe and Mail*, John Doyle suggests that there is a decades-long pattern of interference in government affairs: "MPs and former MPs explain how they were put under surveillance by News International and their every movement recorded. This happened because they questioned some policy that favored the Murdoch media companies. And, as it turns out, the police were often in the pay of the Murdoch papers too."[81] One can see how the attempt by media empires to seize the high moral ground in the piracy debate may ring hollow in the ears of the online audience.

In 2005 I wrote that "online piracy is nowhere close to being eliminated" and argued that it would be all but impossible to eliminate digital piracy.[82] There are some indications that I may have been wrong. Even as newspapers around the world were reporting on the rising rate of television piracy in 2011, the *New York Times* observed that the tide was changing in France: "Studies show that the appeal of piracy has waned in France since the so-called three-strikes, or graduated response law, hailed by the music and movie industries and hated by advocates of an open Internet, went into effect. Digital sales, which were slow to get started in France, are growing. Music industry revenues are starting to stabilize."[83] Yet I have my doubts.

Music piracy went down sharply after the collapse of Napster and then rose dramatically. It may well be the case that the French government just drove piracy further underground as consumers reacted to the new law by increasing their use of anonymity tools such as virtual private networks (VPN). In any event, the drop in piracy has not led to a dramatic increase in revenue for the French music industry and video market.[84] A 2013 report commissioned by the French Minister of Culture found the Hadopi "Three Strikes" program was ineffective.[85] The French anti-piracy program cost the government tens of millions of euros but only recouped 150 euros in fines. Here we see a considerable amount of public money being spent on a futile effort to preserve twentieth-century notions of private property.

More than three years after various countries implemented graduated responses such as France's three strikes program, a study by Rebecca Giblin concluded that there is a "startling lack of evidence" that graduated response programs are either successful or effective.[86] Curiously, powerful right-holders repeatedly claim the opposite about these programs. Once again we encounter the counterfactual quality of claims made by media and entertainment corporations. Giblin also noted that in certain countries such as New Zealand the introduction of a graduated response program led to a decrease in peer-to-peer (P2P) traffic, whereas the use of VPN (encrypted downloading) rose dramatically.

There are other exceptions to the general upward trend in music piracy. New laws in Sweden allowed companies to find out more information about illegal downloaders and resulted in an apparent reduction in piracy behaviour.[87] Yet between 2009 and 2012 there was a 40 per cent increase in the use of online piracy services that mask pirating behaviour.[88] Germany has seen over 100,000 prosecutions for illegal downloading with the result that the piracy rate apparently dropped to 6 per cent. An authoritarian response to piracy may be a factor in the Pirate Party becoming the third-largest political party in Germany. Yet as P2P piracy becomes a target of legal action, piracy shifts to hard drive swapping, phone ripping, darknets, cyberlockers, and other illegitimate modes of exchange. Mark Mulligan, former vice president and research director at Jupiter Research, suggests that Germany's piracy problem went offline. Germany became "Europe's largest non-network piracy market, actually exceeding P2P penetration."[89] In Norway a recent decline in digital piracy has been attributed to the growth of music and television streaming services.[90] Norway may yet prove that piracy can be reduced when adequate legitimate streaming services provide consumers with affordable content. Conversely, almost a third of UK Internet users who use streaming services also engage in piracy.[91]

In the first six months of 2013 streaming music increased by 24 per cent in the United States but "overall sales of albums and track equivalents were down by 4.6% over a year ago."[92] Piracy and streaming entertainment services are interconnected behaviours, but it is too early to

conclude that growth in streaming services will lead to a proportional reduction in piracy. By the end of 2013 worldwide sales of music were flat, iTunes revenue was in steep decline, and industry analysts were suggesting that digital sales may have peaked. The majority of online music listeners were consuming free streaming music, while only 25 per cent were paying for streaming services such as Spotify.[93] Once again we encounter a situation where the majority of media consumers do not pay for content. This could prove to be the future of online television and movies.

We do not have a clear picture of the total number of digital pirates or whether online piracy is declining. A 2010 study suggested that P2P piracy decreased from 16 to 9 per cent of all US Internet users since 2007, but this study just measured P2P piracy and did not account for the rise of newer methods of illegal downloading or illicit streaming.[94] Warner Music claims that 13 per cent of Americans are avowed pirates.[95] In the United Kingdom 18 per cent of Internet users are digital pirates.[96] Over 80 per cent of reported piracy takes place in international markets.[97] China has a piracy rate of around 90 per cent and the worldwide piracy rate (average) is 42 per cent. A study commissioned by NBCUniversal claims that in January 2013 some 432 million unique Internet users illegally downloaded copyrighted material, up 10 per cent from 2011.[98] The entertainment industry is not out of the woods just yet.

Each defeat of a major illegal downloading site and each new restrictive law tends to set off a wave of expectations that illegal downloading will soon be brought to an end. Thus Flora Rostami notes, "On June 27, 2005, many believed that the beginning of the end of all P2P technology and illegal downloading of copyrighted materials had finally arrived." In June 2005 the US Supreme Court ruled against Grokster, an online music service that was facilitating illegal downloading. Nonetheless, seven years later "online services reminiscent of those exploited by the defendants in the Grokster case continue to thrive. In the end, neither type of litigation strategy, either against the file-sharing program owner or the individual downloader, seems to be a viable option for the content industry's goal to eviscerate, or even merely reduce, illegal downloading."[99] When one type of technology is defeated in the courts another rises to take its place. When the industry forces Internet service providers (ISPs) to reveal individual names behind an Internet address, the hacker community responds by circulating programs that will hide an individual's Internet address and identity. Each move by the music industry and the state is matched with an effective counter-strategy by the online community. Litigation has not been a complete failure, but it has hardly stemmed the tide or changed the culture of the Internet.

Between 2003 and 2008 the RIAA sued approximately 35,000 American consumers for digital piracy. This nefarious legal effort saw the RIAA engaging in outrageous acts such as seeking more than $1 million in damages from a graduate student who allegedly illegally downloaded seven songs.[100] The music industry's attempts at litigation have been a wasted effort. After admitting that Sony had not stopped to "calculate the amount of damages we've suffered due to downloading," Jennifer Pariser, Sony BMG's head of litigation, revealed that Sony had spent millions on litigation against online pirates and that "we've lost money on this program."[101] One of the world's largest music companies had not bothered to figure out exactly what real damages had been wrought by illegal downloading and was losing money on its litigation efforts against tens of thousands of Americans.

Conventional wisdom assumes that there is a direct and indisputable relationship between illegal downloading and declining music sales. When powerful commercial interests are at stake it may be best to subject such wisdom to close scrutiny. The relationship between illegal downloading and music sales is neither direct nor clear-cut. More than one study has reached the conclusion that many who engage in music piracy are simply not part of the market: "most copyright infringement on P2P networks is of content that otherwise would not have been purchased."[102] It may be the case that many digital music pirates would never have bought the music they steal in the first place. Another study concluded that "digital music, not online music piracy, substitutes for physical album sales."[103] It is doubtful that any amount of similar conclusions by further studies will shift the attitude of the industry and the policymakers under the sway of well-funded propaganda campaigns.

Sales of physical albums in the age of digital music players declined because people prefer music acquired from online sources. Both physical CD and DVD sales are collapsing as consumers move away from hard-copy formats for entertainment products. The music and television industries are being disrupted for reasons that go far beyond illegal downloading. Rather than face the fact that the consumer's world has undergone an extreme transformation, the music industry has responded with propaganda tactics, bold lies, intimidating lawsuits that often trample our fair rights, and secret negotiations with governments. On top of it all, they would have us believe that they hold the higher moral ground against illegal downloaders.

You know the war on digital piracy has reached feverish heights of rhetoric and propaganda when illegal downloading is conflated with terrorism. The RIAA and the IFPI have been busy propagating the notion that there is a sinister connection between digital piracy and terrorism. Industry-supported websites boldly proclaim that terrorist organizations are "involved in the fabrication, distribution and sale of counterfeit music and other intellectual property infringing material to raise funds for their operations."[104] Hey kids, if you illegally download Rick Astley's "Never Gonna Give You Up," you are buying lunch for a terrorist sleeper cell. The piracy–terrorism connection is nothing more than an industry fabrication, "an implausible claim that has circulated in industry literature since at least 2004," according to a report published by the Social Science Research Council.[105] Industry-funded misinformation campaigns have not created an atmosphere conducive to rational civic debate.

In 2008 the *Guardian* reported that the UK government attempted to set "a secret target to reduce illegal file sharing of music and films by up to 80%" before 2011 (they failed to keep their plan a secret and to reach their goal).[106] Guided by the music industry's propaganda, the United States is attempting to universalize a much stricter set of intellectual property rights implemented through secret trade negotiations of a most extraordinary nature, such as was seen with the Anti-Counterfeiting Trade Agreement (ACTA). In both cases the United Kingdom and the United States were found to be secretly drafting legislation with the cooperation of the entertainment industry. Secret negotiations are continuing in the form of the Trans Pacific Partnership trade negotiations.[107] Vested interests in the back door, public policy and ever more punitive laws out the front door.

One of the most extraordinary attempts to eliminate piracy made global headlines in the winter of 2012 when the US Congress went to vote on the infamous bill known as the Stop Online Piracy Act (SOPA). The law and its Senate counterpart, PROTECT IP Act (PIPA), would have given the US government the power to censor any website anywhere in the world. Many of the top cybersecurity experts in the country said that the proposed censorship mechanisms could be easily bypassed. Nonetheless, Congress was intent on passing SOPA, but something happened that quickly eroded congressional support. The Internet community got wind of the bill and social networks sprang into action. On 18 January 2013, many of the most famous Internet websites went black in protest against the bill. Wikipedia, Google, Amazon,

Craigslist, Wired, Tumblr, Mozilla, Reddit, Techdirt, the Center for Democracy and Technology, and tens of thousands of other sites changed their home pages to black to protest SOPA and PIPA, bills sponsored by none other than the RIAA and the Motion Picture Association of America (MPAA). SOPA and PIPA suffered a humiliating defeat at the hands of Internet activists, ordinary citizens, and new media corporations. Many felt that the entertainment industry was willing to wreck the Internet if it meant saving their business models.

SOPA set new media companies such as Google against the most powerful entertainment corporations in the world. Laurie Cubbison, director of writing at Radford University, describes the implications of the bill's failure in the following terms: "At one time the major media conglomerates who run the movie, television and music industries dominated copyright policy, but in 2012 Internet companies and consumers challenged and defeated two bills championed by these media conglomerates, indicating that copyright policy will no longer be dominated by content owners."[108] Of course, it may take more than a few defeated bits of legislation to deflate the power of the corporate sector. Nevertheless, the Internet does hold forth the promise of a reinvigorated citizenry.

SOPA may go down in history as one of the worst public relations disasters. The Internet protest against SOPA globalized an issue that previously didn't have a large audience.[109] Nevertheless, it is doubtful that Hollywood is about to change tactics. A month after the failure of SOPA, Al Perry, a senior executive at Paramount Pictures, toured American law schools and made the counterfactual claims that copyright infringement was "theft plain and simple" and that bills like SOPA "simply didn't raise First Amendment concerns." At Yale Law School Perry's comments "were followed by a rebuttal from Brooklyn Law School Professor Jason Mazzone, who pointed out that Perry's remarks had completely ignored limitations on copyright such as fair use," and at the University of Virginia, "Perry's remarks were followed by a rebuttal by Art Brodsky of Public Knowledge, who argued that Hollywood's failing profits had less to do with Internet file-sharing than with the industry's failure to produce good movies and come up with innovative business models."[110] Perry's claims had even less credibility among the online audience.

What is it about digital piracy that causes industry lobbyists to engineer misinformation campaigns, governments to engage in gross acts of legislative overreach, secret trade negotiations, and misguided policy goals, and the entertainment industry to be willing to alienate pretty much the entire Internet community? Whatever the nature of the moral terror that has dug deep into the skin of our culture, the propaganda effort has had an effect on business. With their thinking carefully guided by the music industry itself, investors have come to the conclusion that this is a war that will be won.[111] Or so conventional wisdom would have us believe. Yet conventional wisdom appears to have turned a blind eye to China, where "only 10 or so online digital music service providers out of 7000 are legitimate."[112] Within the Internet, music acts as de facto public property. As we move into a post-television future there remains the possibility that television and movie content will also act as de facto public property within the Internet. It may come to pass that most online television and film content will be exchanged beyond the confines of the marketplace. Chuck Tryon and Max Dawson documented an example of this emerging anti-economy of digital entertainment, a 19-year-old female Northwestern University student who, like many of her peers, regards online content as free: "my budget [for entertainment] is probably $0. I use my cousin's Netflix, so I don't pay for it. And I watch streaming or HBO Go, things like that are free – a friend's HBO Go so ... I don't pay for it."[113]

Writing in the *Guardian* Ben Goldacre responded to one of the many overinflated claims that have come to characterize the music industry's rhetoric – illegal downloading in the United Kingdom cost the economy "billions of pounds and thousands of jobs." Goldacre suggested that the music industry had inflated the level of its losses by ten times any reasonable estimate. When the journalist confronted the government body, the Strategic Advisory Board for Intellectual Property (SABIP), with knowledge of the exaggerated findings, SABIP refused to address the issue. Goldacre concluded his investigation with this comment: "as far as I'm concerned, everything from this [music] industry is false, until proven otherwise."[114] I am inclined to agree. Indeed, other academic studies have also concluded that the music industry has been providing the public and policymakers with misleading data.[115] When one such report was published by the London School of Economics, the MPAA countered with a literature review of studies that affirmed that piracy leads to a loss in revenue. This literature review featured a footnote on the first page stating, "We thank the Motion Picture Association of America (MPAA) for providing generous funding to support this study."[116] Of course, there are plenty of words other than "generous" that could be used to describe such a relationship.

Inflated claims are a standard part of the music industry's public relations campaign and are an old propaganda tactic. Do not just tell a lie;

tell a *very big lie* and repeat it as often and as loudly as possible. Thus in 2009 we witnessed an industry website, TheTrueCosts.org, boldly announcing that intellectual property theft costs the United States no less than 750,000 jobs and steals $200 to $250 billion annually from US industry. That is some well-funded terrorism. The claim gets repeated by feckless journalists, quoted in Wikipedia articles and scholarly journals, and parroted by the US Department of Commerce, Customs and Border Patrol, the Federal Bureau of Investigations, and the US Chamber of Commerce as if it were some newly discovered proverb by Jesus himself. In 2010 the US Government Accountability Office released a report saying what many suspected all along: these figures "cannot be substantiated or traced back to an underlying data source or methodology."[117] In other words, and like so many of the music industry's claims, the figures were entirely made up.

One of the most definitive analyses of piracy is *Media Piracy in Emerging Economies*, a three-year-long joint effort by 35 researchers that was published by the Social Science Research Council. Their conclusions contradict most of the conventional wisdom around the subject and provide a sobering correction to the outrageous claims and demands of corporations that seek greater control over copyright and common culture. The researchers found "little evidence ... that enforcement efforts to date have had any impact whatsoever on the overall supply of pirated goods. Our work suggests, rather, that piracy has grown dramatically by most measures in the past decade." The report notes that most of what we think about digital piracy has been carefully guided by the industry itself: "What we know about media piracy usually begins, and often ends, with industry-sponsored research." Although industry press releases confidently proclaim that piracy inflicts enormous economic costs, "most of the industry researchers we spoke with showed considerable circumspection about their ability to accurately measure either rates or losses." The industry itself simply does not have a clear understanding of what harm is being done. The best that can be said is "piracy is clearly ubiquitous."[118]

Piracy has not reduced the level of creative economic activity by artists, nor can it be said to have degraded growth in content and creative sectors of the economy relative to the overall economic performance.

The number of new albums released more than doubled in the period, from 35,516 in 2000 to 79,695 in 2007. The number of Hollywood films released ranged between 370 and 460 in the 1990s and between 450 and 928 in the 2000s, with the peak year in 2006 and some 677 produced in 2009. Software industry growth has been dramatic, averaging 20%–30% annually until 2009. The video-game sector averaged nearly 17% growth between 2005 and 2008, with growth rates in 2007 and 2008 of 28% and 23% … the core copyright industries in the United States averaged 5.8% growth between 2003 and 2007 – well above the roughly 3% annual US growth rate in the period. According to the World Association of Newspapers and News Publishers, total media and entertainment spending posted an annual growth rate of 5.3% in the United States between 2002 and 2008 and 6.4% globally. Losses to piracy need to be placed in this context of overall industry growth – and in some cases remarkably rapid growth.[119]

Contrary to industry claims, the content industry is doing fine. As one study concluded, "the drastic decline in revenues warned of by the lobby associations of record labels is not in evidence."[120] Yet we must recognize that certain product categories are being disintermediated by the rapidly changing online environment. Legal low-cost competition is coming from streaming services such as Spotify in the United Kingdom and Hulu in the United States, Redbox rents videos for as little as $1 in the United States and Canada, and the sales of single songs in digital format is replacing the higher-cost album. Two forces driving all these changes are piracy and legitimate competition. Piracy "resets consumer expectations around cheaper, on-demand availability. But increasingly, the pressure on the high-end market comes from legal innovators at the low end."[121] Piracy has been a source of incredible innovation in the marketplace and leads to lower prices and more convenient services. No wonder incumbent industry players hate piracy. It has led to competition in price and service, which is great for consumers, but hurts the bottom line of large media corporations.

Piracy is less of a threat than are legitimate new products, services, and business models. Industry representatives tend to blame their losses on the popularization of Internet piracy that was kick-started with the launch of Napster in 1999. Yet online piracy is only one of many changes in consumer habits brought on by the proliferation of DVDs, video games, cell phones, the switch from albums to digital singles, and an aging population less interested in buying highly formulaic music genres that the studios crank out year after year. Given all these various forces, the contribution of piracy to the music industry's decline is "hard to specify and is a matter of considerable disagreement in the research literature."[122]

Macroeconomic analysis is notoriously complicated so it comes as no surprise that contradictory conclusions surround the assessment of the health of the entertainment sector. Nonetheless, a common theme does arise across the literature – any declines in the areas of music, television, and movies are due to a complex array of factors that go far beyond piracy. The best we can say about the precise economic impact of piracy on music sales is that we simply do not know.[123] But we do know one thing for certain – people are not listening to music or watching television the same way they did in the twentieth century. Online music piracy provides five important lessons for thinking about the future of the online television audience.

1 Piracy has become normalized among online audiences and particularly so among young consumers. Free is far more compelling than fee.
2 The perception of consumer behaviour within industry and government is warped by the belief system of capitalism. Conventional wisdom promotes an idealization of consumer behaviour ("they prefer to pay") and an overestimation of the power of laws and the influence of public relations campaigns.
3 An entire industry can lose control over its online content.
4 Attempts to place unreasonable limits on digital content and the online audience will be met with a consequential political backlash.
5 It is unlikely that all sectors of the marketplace, including content industries, new media corporations, and consumer electronics firms, will act in a unified manner to reduce online piracy. The vested interests of the entertainment industry are not the same interests that motivate sectors such as consumer electronics and innovative new media companies. This means that as long as hundreds of millions of consumers want to engage in digital piracy, there will be legitimate and illegitimate businesses willing and able to facilitate mass online piracy.

Summary

A direct parallel cannot be drawn between the habits and consequences of music and television piracy. Listening to music is not the same activity as watching television or a movie, and digital music files are much smaller than digital files of television shows and movies. Nonetheless, the recent history of online music is rife with lessons for the television and movie industry.

The accessibility of online content cannot be easily controlled. If people want digital content for free, the chances are they will find it for free somewhere on the Internet. These are not rhetorical statements. They represent the real world of online consumer behaviour. The entertainment industry has a long and ignoble record of trying to stifle technological innovation and audience freedoms. Their disregard for the rights of the audience combined with their use of propaganda tactics, falsified data, regulatory capture, political collusion, and naked self-interest has all but stripped the music, television, and movie sectors of the high moral ground. As a result, the online audience expresses considerable contempt for the industry, its lobby organizations, and politicians who speak on their behalf. No wonder many Internet users feel justified when engaging in digital piracy.

The music, film, and television industries have misidentified their main problem when they set sights on illegal downloading. Illegal downloading is not the industry's mortal enemy. Their problem lies elsewhere, with rapidly multiplying sources of entertainment found on large, small, and tiny screens and in multiple locations from cars to pockets and purses. The new ecosystem of fixed and mobile Internet-enabled screens are draining audiences away from traditional sources of music and television and fragmenting entertainment budgets.

Legitimate alternative technologies and innovative new media businesses are competing on price and convenience while incumbent players are preoccupied with a twentieth-century mentality of control.

2   Television and Movie Piracy: Simple, Fast, and Free

In 2012 the government-sponsored New Zealand Science Media Centre informed the press that "New Zealanders are ready and willing to pay for legitimate alternatives to illegally downloaded movies and television content, but they aren't being given the options fast enough."[1] When the *New Zealand Herald* reported the story online, readers wrote over 100 comments that provided insight into the dilemmas facing the post-television audience. Most of the comments reflected a willingness to pirate, disparaged the available legitimate online television services, and complained about the state of the national television industry.[2] Their comments reflected an audience that is aware of the structure of the global television industry, contemptuous of incumbent industry leaders and political managers, and self-justified in their online piracy behaviour. Readers also indicated that they would pay "for a service that delivered the latest movies and TV shows as easily as pirates can offer them" but it looks like New Zealanders will have to wait a long time for such a comparable service.[3]

Television piracy, according to the *Economist* magazine, "gets less attention than film or music piracy, but it is no less widespread."[4] In economic terms, which are by no means the primary terms for analysing piracy, illegal downloading functions "as a remedy to the shortages caused by market failures."[5] It makes it easier to find entertainment goods not immediately available in the local marketplace. Of course, piracy also operates as a substitute for legal purchases within the marketplace. Scholars disagree on whether or not major online piracy sites such as the defunct Megaupload hurt the movie industry. Brett Danaher and Michael D. Smith found that Megaupload displaced digital film sales.[6] In contrast, another study of the impact of Megaupload found that box office revenues increased for movies with smaller audiences. The researchers suggested that smaller movies benefit from social network effects. Pirates who do not want to pay for a movie download the product, watch it, and influence the opinions of non-pirates, which leads to more purchases of the movie.[7] This conclusion reflects an abundance of anecdotal stories about how young, mostly male consumers use piracy to check out a movie or television show prior to purchase.

Online piracy of television and movies takes two main forms: downloading complete files (similar to downloading a music file) or streaming a show or movie. Downloading a movie typically takes a few minutes or longer while streaming a movie has the movie begin within a few seconds. Both methods tend to use peer-to-peer (P2P) systems such as BitTorrent. These two modes of accessing legitimate and illegal sources of content generate the majority of Internet traffic. Files range in size from approximately 700 megabytes for a movie to 10 or more gigabytes for files that contain an entire television series.

Increasing bandwidth speeds are rendering large file sizes irrelevant to many users. Australia is launching a high-speed National Broadband Network, which will dramatically decrease the time it takes to download pirated television shows and movies. John Porter, CEO of the pay-TV network Austar, spoke about the industry's fears:

> driving a superhighway into everyone's living room is gonna just totally enable peer-to-peer piracy. So, if we in the television industry don't go to school on the failings of the music industry in relationship to piracy and creating really user-friendly ways of acquiring media through micro payments and very simple user interfaces, we're gonna end up with the same kind of statistics that someone quoted earlier, which is half our business is gonna be gone.[8]

The television industry's fears that the past of the music industry is their future are justified. The two most pirated shows of 2011, *Dexter* and *Game of Thrones*, saw higher levels of piracy than the actual number of legitimate television viewers. Sometimes piracy can create an illegitimate audience that is larger than the actual television audience.

Digital networked communication technology renders control over the flow of content extraordinarily difficult. Audiences have become accustomed to illegal online services that have the distinct advantage of being simple, fast, and free. Even before the rise of mass participation in digital piracy, audiences had been socialized into the habits of piracy. Consider the example of the European Union, where piracy rates for pay-TV subscriptions that rely on set-top boxes were estimated to be around 30 per cent in 2003.[9] These set-top boxes were physically circumvented by various illegal means. An industry study of UK audiences conducted five years later found a similar rate of 32 per cent of the population involved in various forms of media piracy.[10] Also following this pattern, a multi-country survey found that 31 per cent of Internet users are not willing to pay for online content at all.[11] This suggests that Internet-enabled piracy should be seen as an extension of a pre-existing mindset among consumers. A significant percentage of consumers will go out of their way to avoid paying for entertainment products. Piracy rates vary too greatly across nations to propose that there is any global constant rate (such as 30 per cent). Nevertheless, the percentages shown here are suggestive of resilient anti-market consumption patterns.

In a Massachusetts Institute of Technology (MIT) conference presentation boldly titled "Piracy Is the Future of Television," Abigail De Kosnik suggested that "illegal downloading is the most usable and feature-rich [option], and bears the greatest potential for pioneering new modes of audience engagement, as well as new global revenue streams, related to television products."[12] De Kosnik proposes that the broadcasting industry should emulate the advantages of pirating: convenience (it is easy to keep a television archive in a single place and a uniform format), ease of merging a television archive with a friend's collection of pirated shows, and ease of organizing an archive.[13] Similarly, Axel Bruns notes, "Streaming media was once described as a second-rate, slightly gimmicky form of television; today it can be argued that television has become a less convenient form of streaming media."[14] De Kosnik and Bruns are suggesting that a better way of watching television is evolving outside the control of the television industry itself. Internet piracy is a new type of mass media that contains the content of old media but discards the context of the market economy.

Online piracy has so many advantages that even those within the television industry are making use of it. Writing in *Maclean's* magazine, Jesse Brown relates how "in a field where people need to watch movies and television episodes regularly for professional reasons, piracy is simply the quickest way of doing so." He describes various ways in which "movie industry folks" use piracy for professional reasons because "piracy is simply the quickest way" of getting the job done. Brown speaks with authority on the matter: "I've known employees of entertainment companies who [illegally] download torrents of videos that they've produced themselves!"[15] I have spoken with workers in the television industry and heard similar stories. So has screenwriter Julie Bush, who relates that "many showrunners and executives I know not only pirate stuff all the time but also privately endorse the idea that piracy is good for the industry, a great way to advertise, and essential to building a healthy audience."[16] De Kosnik's argument that illegal downloading is the most user-friendly and feature-rich option gains traction when it is a tool used by professionals within the television industry. Brown invites us to imagine "if Hollywood was using file-sharing technology for the same practical reasons we all do: not because they love stealing, but because they hate waiting for tiered release dates, hate waiting for ads and previews to end, and hate wading through digital locks that make sharing content difficult."[17] It would seem that the entertainment industry has given us a lot to hate.

With the growth of the Internet, piracy has been transformed into a new form of mass behaviour – almost everybody is doing it for one reason or another. Manuel Castells and Gustavo Cardoso observe that in various ways we all engage in piracy, including media corporations and law firms that seek to criminalize piracy, and thus they propose the notion of "piracy cultures."[18] The online television audience provides insight into digital piracy culture. Abigail De Kosnik's microanalysis of one individual's social network of film piracy demonstrates continuities with older piracy cultures. She says, "Internet file sharers, for the most part, repeat the behaviors and psychological motivations of earlier collectors."[19] De Kosnik identifies an aspect of Internet piracy that departs from pre-digital piracy in one significant way: "Digital collector-pirates are at far greater risk for severe legal and financial punishment for their activities than their predecessors were."[20] Piracy cultures are a result of "a very significant proportion of the population" using alternative channels for obtaining content.[21] These piracy practices of everyday life "might either evolve toward new institutionalized market practices and a changed perception of the law, or remain counter-cultural movements, although ones shared by large portions of the population."[22] Piracy cultures of the post-television era represent an oppositional force to the on-demand culture of digital entertainment that governments and media corporations are attempting to propagate. Chuck Tryon describes "on-demand culture" as characterized "not by universal access but by the process of limiting and restricting when and where access is available."[23]

Of course, the television industry is not likely to embrace piracy cultures or radically change its business model. We see this reflected in *Variety* magazine: "the folks who produce the vast majority of programming in the country have a vested interest in maintaining the status quo."[24] Others similarly suggest that "content owners want to keep premium TV and movie content on the Web more scarce, and want to protect the lucrative business of syndicating hit shows to TV stations and cable networks."[25] Yet making content more scarce on the Internet does not seem like a readily attainable goal.

People pirate television shows not simply because doing so is free. Pirating has costs associated with it, such as the Internet connection, subscription services to value-added pirate sites, computer hardware replacement costs, and time. Nevertheless, the incumbent television industry has failed to offer free online access that matches the flexibility and ease of use experienced by the online pirate. Thus De Kosnik concludes that "piracy is the easiest, simplest, most feature-rich means available for acquiring TV by means of the Internet."[26] Free, easy, simple, and feature-rich – this is not something that can be yanked out of consumers' hands without a fight. Even high-tech billionaires like Google co-founder Sergey Brin acknowledge that legitimate commercial services fail to meet the standard of convenience and ease of use established by piracy. "When you go on a pirate website, you choose what you like; it downloads to the device of your choice and it will just work – and then when you have to jump through all these hoops [to buy legitimate content], the walls created are disincentives for people to buy."[27]

Television piracy is at significant levels and on the rise. A 2013 UK-government-sponsored study found a rising incidence of piracy, with one in six Internet users illegally accessing digital entertainment. The frequency of piracy rises to 33 per cent among those who regularly watch online television and films. A three-month period saw 52 million television program files and 29 million films illegally downloaded in the United Kingdom.[28] According to one industry study, Americans are the most prolific pirates of US-produced television content (11.6 per cent of global total), followed by the United Kingdom (8 per cent) and Canada (8 per cent).[29] The study also claimed that piracy increased 400 per cent from a year earlier. Television piracy rates exhibit enormous variation across region, age, income, and ethnicity. For example, the executive vice president of international business for News Corporation, Rajan Singh, observes that within the United States, "the fact is, piracy in the South Asian community is huge."[30] Members of this community use illegal set-top devices that enable piracy of live and on-demand television from South Asia.

Media theorists such as Tarleton Gillespie have argued that the Internet will be wired shut because of increasing copyright controls. Gillespie claims that the manufacturers of consumer electronics, such as those currently used to access pirated television, exercise "near-monopoly power" over content and "are being drawn into tighter and tighter collusion with culture owners such as the television industry."[31] Yet by the early 1990s in the United States, half of the widely used Videocipher II television receivers were illegally hacked to descramble channels.[32] Such signal hacking of more advanced technologies continues to this day. Clearly, the television and content industries hold little sway over the widespread use of illegally modified set-top boxes that facilitate piracy. The Internet in general, and television content in particular, are far from being wired shut.

Care must be taken when citing piracy statistics. As mentioned, piracy rates derived from industry-sponsored research have a "very loose relationship to evidence."[33] The questionable quality of research conducted in the service of industry lobbying efforts and the lack of a substantial body of academic research on television and movie piracy leave us with a void in concrete estimates of television and movie piracy rates. As recently as 2011 an international survey looked at peer-to-peer piracy, the use of file-locker sites such as RapidShare and Megaupload, and personal sharing of media files and concluded that "we have seen no studies that explore this high-end personal-media ecology in any detail."[34] Piracy rates fluctuate with the appearance of new technologies, changes in local laws, and new value-added commercial services (such as Hulu and Netflix). One study concluded that television piracy decreased in the United States as services like Hulu and Netflix made streaming a more viable option.[35] The rise of streaming services may be leading to a decline in P2P piracy of television. We do not know if this decline is reflected in other methods of pirate television viewing, such as the use of file-lockers and illegal streaming services.

Online discussion forums about television and movies are littered with references to piracy. The television industry is aware of the impact of piracy on its business and is testing various new strategies for the online release of shows. In March 2012 the American television network CW made shows such as *The Vampire Diaries* and *Gossip Girl* available on CWTV.com or Hulu Plus within eight hours of airing on television. Previously, online audiences had to wait three days. By April a fifth of

CW's audience was watching its shows online, twice as many as a year earlier. This may have had an effect on CW's regular prime-time audience, which fell 14 per cent.[36] CW made the change to a quicker Internet release of their shows in response to high piracy rates: "about 20% of all streams online of CW programming were of the illegal variety, with levels reaching 28%–29% for 'Vampire Diaries' and 'Gossip Girl.' Even worse: 50% of that piracy occurred within three days of the premiere broadcast."[37] Advertising revenue is closely tied to ratings in the first three days of a show's broadcast; thus CW was facing a potential loss in revenues. The changes that the CW network are undergoing represent the industry's shift towards multi-platform, multi-screen television. By 2014 CW's online audience grew by 60 per cent from the previous year.[38] The industry has little choice but to meet the audience's demand to watch television wherever they want.

Peer-to-peer Internet traffic is predominantly made up of American television series flowing out of the United States to foreign markets.[39] Why is this happening? The industry delays the distribution of popular American television shows by months and even years. "Television networks have been very slow to adopt the global simultaneous release practices of the major studios. Until recently, even major English-speaking markets like Australia waited a year or more for the broadcast of American hits."[40] The gap between the initial release of a movie or television show and its availability in other markets leads the audience to resort to online piracy to get the desired product. The larger the gap in time, the greater the audience's involvement with illegitimate solutions. The networks are aware of this and are beginning to adapt the introduction of new shows to the context of a global, technologically sophisticated, and very impatient audience.

In March 2012 the Fox Network staged a worldwide premiere of *Touch*, a new television drama, by releasing the show simultaneously in 100 countries. Executives in the television industry believe *Touch* is the beginning of a new business model that will reduce online piracy.[41] The show's creator realized that audiences will get the shows they want to see off the Internet if they cannot get them on television. This dawned upon him after he saw hundreds of fans of *Heroes* at an event in Paris before the show was available on television in France.[42] Piracy is forcing studios and networks to accelerate their worldwide rollouts of shows and movies. In what is known in the movie industry as "day-and-date worldwide strategy," an increasing number of television shows are being released simultaneously in multiple foreign markets alongside the domestic premiere. Recent shows such as *Missing, Body of Proof, The River*, and *The Walking Dead* (second season) all used such a strategy.

There is a limit to how fast television networks can release a show to foreign markets, though. "A network typically doesn't have the time to make all the adjustments necessary to take a production from completion to international distribution given that some episodes aren't locked until just a day or two before broadcast."[43] This suggests that there will always be some forms of market failure that cannot be corrected and thus create a need which piracy fulfils.

Piracy is not the only reason networks are changing their strategies. US shows are facing stiffer competition from local productions; as a result, foreign markets "don't need us as much as they used to, they have their own shows," notes Marion Edwards, president of international television at 20th Century Fox Television Distribution.[44] Because of the weakening demand for US television shows in foreign markets, the American networks are responding with more flexibility in how their shows are made available to foreign markets. As is often the case, online piracy is only one of many complex forces driving us into a post-television era.

What is behind the rise in digital television piracy? Faster Internet connections; a greater variety of online content; the increasing availability of online television shows, sports events, and movies in high-definition (HD) format; a proliferation of large and small mobile screens (tablet computers, laptops, smartphones, and so forth); the increasing cost of cable television; changing social norms regarding certain types of property and theft; a demand for instant access to entertainment products from foreign markets; and simple economics are all contributing factors. "Nobody's going to pay you for something they can get for free," notes economics professor Glenn MacDonald.[45] Of course, this is not quite the whole story. People do pay for bottled water. They also pay for online access to movies, television shows, sports, news, pornography, and many other video products.

A report by Digital TV Research estimated that 177 million homes in 40 countries watched shows online in 2010, a number that will grow to 415 million homes by 2016 with revenue growing to $21.5 billion.[46] These estimates only include legitimate paying subscribers. In any event, video is the future of the Internet and there is a lot of money on the table. Americans paid to watch an estimated 3.4 billion movies online in 2012.[47] Even in China, a veritable hotbed for all forms of digital piracy, the top company in the online video business is valued at $3.5 billion (US).[48]

The *Economist* magazine points out that China has the largest online video audiences with 450 million viewers.[49] Television content in China is heavily censored by the government. This has had the effect of driving the audience away from traditional television to online video. According to admittedly unreliable government news sources, traditional television viewing in Beijing captured only 30 per cent of households in 2012, down from 70 per cent three years earlier. This suggests a mass migration from state-controlled television to less heavily regulated online video. Pirating entertainment content has been described as "one of the most common forms of media consumption in China" and has significantly diminished political and industrial restrictions on available media content.[50] The control mentality of both the state and the traditional television marketplace appears to be driving audiences to the freer pastures of online viewing. Contrary to widespread expectations that China will eventually conform to Western trade demands and audience habits, it may prove to be the case that China represents the future of online audiences and media content – substantially beyond political, legal, and industrial control.

Another industry study claims the online video market will grow by an average rate of 35 per cent annually from 2010 to 2015.[51] The findings of industry studies can be overstated, but remarkable growth rates are not new to Internet-related phenomenon. Cisco forecasts that 90 per cent of all Internet traffic will be video by 2015.[52] Moving pictures have been the dominant entertainment medium for almost 70 years. It comes as no surprise that the Internet is evolving into a predominantly video-based medium.

Television piracy takes place even when network websites make shows and movies available online. One study noted, "Every one of the ten most pirated TV shows, in fact, can also be streamed for free on sites like Hulu.com, veoh.com, or major TV network Web sites."[53] Many feel that legitimate commercial streaming services do not deliver the same quality as can be found on pirate sites: one consumer commented, "I have Netflix and will still download the same movie they offer off of the Pirate Bay because the quality sucks."[54] In 2008 when Fox's *Prison Break* premiered, over a million people illegally downloaded the first two episodes even though it was freely available on Fox.com.[55] People used their favourite pirate sites perhaps out of habit or out of a desire to avoid advertisements. Anyone outside the United States could not watch the show on Fox.com or Hulu. So a show with 6.5 million viewers saw an additional 1 million viewers resort to piracy to get what they wanted. When it is in the industry's best interests to gain the largest possible audiences for their shows, it is simply mind-boggling that there is so much resistance to piracy's ability to increase viewership.

In a widely read lecture presented at the Australian Film, Television and Radio School entitled "Piracy Is Good?" Mark Pesce observed that "TV producers want their programming to be watched as widely as possible – by everyone ... This assertion seems so basic, so fundamentally essential to the economics of television, that it's very hard to understand why *anyone* (other than a broadcaster being cut out of the value chain) would get upset about piracy of television programming."[56] Pesce tells how he pirated the re-visioned *Battlestar Galactica* series that was debuted on SkyOne in the United Kingdom in 2004. Long before his local Australian broadcaster Network TEN ran the show Pesce downloaded and watched all 13 episodes of the first season.

The American SciFi Channel delayed broadcasting *Battlestar Galactica* for over two months, so of course practically every science fiction fan around the world downloaded the series illegally in the meantime. According to the logic and arguments of the television industry, this mass piracy of *Battlestar Galactica* should have wiped out any economic return from the series. Yet mass piracy "appears to have the reverse effect ... *Battlestar Galactica* has been the most popular programme ever to air on the SciFi Channel."[57] Online piracy acted like word-of-mouth advertising for the series and turned out to be a powerful source of promotion.

Piracy as promotion is not a rare phenomenon. It happened to the BBC series *Doctor Who*. It is a familiar, but unofficially acknowledged, marketing strategy within the software industry, and it defined the very roots of fan cultures across a variety of genres. Henry Jenkins argues that Japan's animation industry grew from $8 to $80 billion (US) in a decade, "in part because Japanese media companies paid little attention to the kinds of grassroots activities – call it piracy, unauthorized duplication and circulation, or simply file-sharing – that American media companies seem so determined to shut down."[58]

The role of piracy as promotion is debated among scholars. Part of the problem in determining if it is harmful or helpful is that "the boundaries between piracy, promotion, and sharing are far from clear."[59] Where one activity stops and the other begins is often difficult to determine. Nonetheless, it is doubtful that piracy would have the same promotional effect in all areas of the world, on all genres of television viewing, or with other entertainment products such as sports.

Piracy is not merely an issue of a few companies trying to profit illicitly from illegitimate services. Every desktop computer, smartphone, and tablet computer connected to the Internet is a potential source of pirated material. Masses of people all across the globe actively promote piracy outside of market contexts, without profit motives, and beyond the effective reach of laws. In the case of streaming television piracy, "most video feeds come from individual users who use television receivers attached to their computers to transform the television signal into a digital stream and then broadcast the stream to other users."[60] Axel Bruns calls this do-it-yourself (DIY) distribution "guerrilla re-broadcasting" and notes that "there are unlikely to be any effective technological solutions to prevent DIY re-broadcasting."[61] Aggressive legal action and extensive public relation campaigns have not yet led to a significant reduction in piracy rates.[62] A 2009 headline in the *New York Times* declared, "Digital Pirates Winning the Battle with Studios."[63] The same headline could be written today. There is little reason to hope that digital rights management solutions will stem the tide of piracy in the context of online media streaming. Automated digital rights management (DRM) removal from streaming media is feasible, can be done in real time, and has proven effective against Microsoft, Netflix, Amazon, and Hulu.[64]

Canadians consume more American television than any other nation and thus express a particular sense of entitlement and outrage when they are denied access to American online television. Andy Forssell, a senior vice president of Hulu, hears numerous complaints from Canadian audiences over geo-blocked content and receives "a lot of angry emails from Canadians who consider what we were making available online to be their birthright."[65] Hulu uses a technology called geo-blocking to prevent people from accessing content if they live outside of the area covered by its territorial distribution agreements. Therefore, most of the world cannot legally access Hulu's content. Software tools such as virtual proxy servers allow the online audience to circumvent geographical restrictions. Typing in the phrase "how to access Hulu" in the Google search engine returns links to thousands of blog pages and instructional videos on how to circumvent Hulu's access restrictions. The piracy community is technically adept, well informed, and helpful, particularly so for Canadians who cannot access content on Hulu because of the limitations of licensing restrictions.

Michael Z. Newman described this type of illegal file-sharing activity as a reflection of Canadians' "frustration and resentment over the inability to share a common culture with those beyond their borders. File-sharing ameliorates this sense of being wronged by cultural institutions." Piracy arises out of a "sense of a justified entitlement to popular culture, as well as a sense of the illegitimacy of this access's denial."[66] Curiously, online comments on a *Toronto Star* news article revealed American citizens working in Canada who felt affronted that, even though they are US citizens, they could not access Hulu while in Canada. Meanwhile, a Canadian working in the United States was "equally frustrated with Canadian broadcasters like Slice and Showcase geo-blocking content for non-Canadians ... I had to resort to tracking down shows like *Project Runway Canada* posted illegally on YouTube."[67] As it turns out, geo-blocking affects online audience members on both sides of the Canada–US border and leaves them feeling alienated from the broadcast system.

Hulu attempts to extend the dominant industry practice of creating artificial scarcity. Producers and broadcasters "use streaming clearances to make Hulu resemble the broadcast space [of television] by making episodes scarce pending syndication deals and DVD releases."[68] This leads to episodes, entire seasons, and movies being pulled without notice. When shows are pulled from Hulu, viewers resort to piracy. Piracy rates of some television shows were reported to have doubled when Hulu changed its policy and forced viewers of the free version of Hulu to wait eight days before they could watch its shows. Sheila Seles argues that this indicates "a fundamental misunderstanding of the online space on the part of content providers."[69]

While people pirate content to avoid paying, piracy also introduces people to material that they later buy, as seen in the comments of anonymous online viewers: "Piracy is expensive to me, because it creates a desire for the movies, music, and shows, and informs me of what's available in the market."[70] In another online discussion debating the ethics of television piracy one viewer wrote, "*Walking Dead* was on AMC's website last year for the first episode. I watched it myself and then had to pirate it to show my girlfriend when they stopped showing it there. Guess what happened? I bought all the comics! And the DVD!"[71] Although almost every television show and movie is available on the Internet for free via piracy, consumers are still willing to pay for entertainment.

Movie Piracy

Movie piracy is no less a problem than television piracy. Recent industry-sponsored studies claim film piracy represents a significant percentage of the overall market of all film revenue: Russia 81 per cent, Brazil 22 per cent, India 90 per cent, United States 7 per cent, United

Kingdom 19 per cent.[72] The MPAA claims that around 25 per cent of broadband users have pirated a movie from the Internet.[73] A study by Jie Bai and Joel Waldfogel found that among Chinese college students 50 per cent of all movie viewing is unpaid via piracy.[74]

As with music and television piracy, no one has a precise picture of the scale of the problem, which may be growing in some areas and shrinking in other regions. Movie piracy may have declined by as much as 10 per cent in Australia.[75] Streaming television services were cited as being responsible for a collapse in piracy in Norway. After the introduction of Netflix there, television piracy declined by more than 72 per cent.[76] Such declines may be offset by increased piracy via cyberlockers such as RapidShare or they may be a harbinger of more declines as commercial streaming services spread across the globe.

As recently as 2007 empirical studies of movie file sharing were rare and data on the issue was limited.[77] A 2009 study of 12 countries found that 38 per cent of the population was downloading films from illegal sources.[78] The numbers rose to a whopping 80 to 95 per cent in Russia and China. The MPAA claims that Russians download 31 million copies of American movies annually.[79] Some studies found that film piracy hurt paid consumption while others argue that digital piracy has little or no effect on the marketplace.[80] Curiously, one study from Carnegie Mellon University found that Internet and broadband growth led to a $1.4 billion (US) *increase* in DVD sales between 2000 and 2003.[81] Another 2007 study noted that the movie industry's claims about online piracy "have not been reflected (so far) in overall industry revenue." During this nascent period of online video, the movie industry was said to be experiencing "robust growth in revenue."[82] Three years later empirical studies on movie piracy were "scarce" and results remained "ambiguous."[83]

At the time I wrote *Post-TV* there had been little change in the state of the field. As Brett Danaher and Joel Waldfogel concluded in a 2012 study, "the effect of piracy on movie revenue remains unsettled."[84] This level of uncertainty within scholarly studies provides a stark contrast to the MPAA's claim that American movie studios were losing $6.1 billion annually in global revenue, with worldwide losses totalling $18.2 billion in 2006.[85] Whatever the impact of piracy may be, the movie industry is doing quite well: "Since 2002, the U.S. movie industry has seen a $9–10.5 billion business in domestic box office revenues, with successive record-setting years in 2007, 2008, and 2009. International distribution brought in some $16.6 billion in 2007, $18.1 billion in 2008, and $19.3 billion in 2009."[86] By 2013 international distribution brought in

$25 billion (US). Only in DVD sales do we see a consistent and dramatic decline in revenue. Regardless of the high levels of movie piracy over the past decade, and in direct contradiction to the claims of devastating loss made by the MPAA, "Hollywood achieved record-breaking global box office revenues of $35 billion US in 2012, a six per cent increase over 2011."[87] A new record was set again in 2013 with global box office revenues hitting $35.9 billion. It is difficult to reconcile the claims of loss made by the entertainment industry with their actual revenues.

Looking at the top ten most pirated movies via BitTorrent, as recorded by TorrentFreak, shows an indication of the volume of worldwide movie piracy: 86,670,000 downloads in 2009, 92,480,000 in 2010, 74,880,000 in 2011, 77,450,000 in 2012, and 74,700,000 in 2013.[88] This data does not necessarily indicate declining piracy rates given that we do not know how much illegal downloading has shifted to file-lockers and other new piracy methods between 2009 and 2013. Also, annual movie piracy rates are very sensitive to the relative popularity of blockbuster movies made in any given year. Movie piracy went up in 2009 and 2010 largely because of the enormous popularity of *Avatar*. Data will need to include a wider range of piracy methods before we can get a clear picture of the full extent of movie piracy behaviour. Nonetheless, we are probably looking at hundreds of millions of movies being pirated over the Internet every year.

The MPAA reports growth in overseas film markets that are experiencing rising standards of living among the middle class.[89] In many of these overseas markets, such as China and Russia, US copyright law has little influence. This growth highlights the difficulty in assessing the impact of movie piracy as the majority of piracy occurs in foreign markets, yet foreign markets are where Hollywood is seeing enviable increases in revenue.

On the surface, the increase in revenue in overseas markets suggests that rising economies may see falling levels of piracy, yet the issue is not so straightforward. As the authors of *Media Piracy in Emerging Economies* note, conventional wisdom draws a direct correlation between increasing economic development and decreasing rates of piracy. The authors are sceptical of this "narrative of progress" that informs the enforcement conversation. Movie piracy is "primarily determined by shifts in technology and associated cultural practices, from the rise of compact discs (CDs) and video compact discs (VCDs) in the 1990s, to the explosive growth of digital video discs (DVDs) in the early 2000s, to the more recent growth of broadband Internet connections." The claim that piracy will decline as income increases is questionable because "industry research methods simply do not permit reliable estimates of change at this level of detail."[90] Technology, not the economy, appears to be the determining factor in piracy rates.

As is the case with television, the movie industry practice of windowing – delaying releases in overseas markets – increases the demand for pirated content. One study found that "the longer the lag between the U.S. release and the local foreign release, the lower the local foreign box office receipts. Importantly, this relationship is larger after widespread adoption of BitTorrent than before."[91] The industry has adjusted its release strategies, with the average release window falling from 10.5 weeks in 2004 to 4 weeks in 2010.[92] The study concluded that the mass adoption of BitTorrent since 2004 by online pirates did not erode domestic US box office revenue.

MPAA data shows that the combined Canada/US market totalled $10.2 billion, "down 4 per cent compared to 2010, but up 6 per cent from five years ago."[93] Academic analysis argues that domestic American studio revenues have declined in growth since 2004 but that is "widely attributed to a spate of poor movies and a defection of movie consumers to video games and other electronic media."[94] Even Universal Studios president Ron Myers admitted, "We make a lot of shitty movies."[95] A surge of bad movies has accentuated the impact of post-television media habits. Old media is losing its audiences to the compelling and highly attractive forces of new media.

A champion of the Motion Picture Association of America, Senator Patrick Leahy once called movie piracy a threat to "all of the value" created by *The Dark Knight*, a film he appeared in briefly. What happened to the movie in the hands of online pirates and how it performed at the box office says much about the overblown claims of the MPAA and politicians who lobby on the industry's behalf. *The Dark Knight* made headlines around the world because it was circulating on pirate sites long before it was seen in the theatres, and it "became the most pirated film of 2008. It also broke all box office records and earned over $1 billion worldwide."[96] If piracy is indeed a threat to "all the value" created by such a movie, then it appears to be a very weak threat. In fact, pirates may represent some of the entertainment industry's most loyal customers. People who engage in online piracy are also more likely to pay for streaming and downloadable content or buy DVDs in store.[97]

Unlike the situation faced by the music industry, the age of widespread online movie and television piracy has just begun. Executives within the movie industry fear that they will follow in the footsteps of the music industry, and they are probably correct. "We think this is likely," conclude the authors of *Media Piracy*. Low-cost alternatives, the proliferation of rental kiosks such as Redbox, and online piracy will probably hasten the collapse of the DVD market: "Americans may one day face a $50–60 billion domestic movie industry rather than a $60–70 billion one."[98] This is not great news for the industry but it is hardly a digital apocalypse. There may also be an indirect benefit to the entertainment industry from piracy within underdeveloped global markets. Piracy acts as a form of promotion in economies that cannot afford high ticket prices: "if piracy has caused the loss of potential revenues for Hollywood companies, it has also, to a large extent, enhanced the circulation of their contents in these markets – preparing, in a sense, the ground for future legal exports."[99]

The United States of Piracy

In many ways, the industry's efforts to control online piracy of television, movies, and music has backfired. The industry's overreach, its questionable production of piracy statistics, and its attempts to criminalize mass behaviour via moves such as the Stop Online Piracy Act have created a new type of body politic – the United States of Piracy. The "United States of Piracy" was Tilman Baumgärtel's keynote speech at a conference on media piracy. He suggests it is possible to write the history of creativity and the arts as "an ongoing, collective process, where everybody steals from everybody else. Or at least, where no man is an island when it comes to good ideas." Baumgärtel also argues that piracy is the foundation of shared cultural experiences, innovation, and national identity and an essential component of a healthy economic system. Pitted against the United States of Piracy is an entertainment industry that, if left unchecked, threatens "restricting and locking away free culture ... I am not alone in my impression, that what we see right now in the realm of Intellectual Property has started to become an obstacle to creativity and development in many areas."[100] Our origins as a United States of Piracy and the risk that our culture may be locked up and placed under the control of powerful corporations provide the larger context for examining television and movie piracy.

Perhaps one of the most important features of movie and television piracy is not lost revenue but the social construction of a piracy epidemic and its implications for the wider social order. Behind the attempt to criminalize mass behaviour of the online audience are claims that are distinctly ideological. Ideas are being produced and disseminated that are in the interests of dominant economic and political groups. Madjid Yar argues, "The expansion of proprietary copyrights, and the criminal-ization of their violation, is part of a larger 'game.'"[101] The goal of this game is to reduce competition, stifle innovation, and consolidate control of culture itself.

Manufactured statistics that inflate piracy rates and industry losses are transformed into facts and these "facts" become the basis for new draconian policies. In this way new policies and laws actually produce the very behaviour they falsely claimed existed in the first place: "the tightening of copyright laws *produces* more 'copyright theft' as previ-ously legal or tolerated uses are prohibited, and the more intensive policing of 'piracy' results in more seizures; these in turn produce new estimates suggesting that the 'epidemic' continues to grow unabated; which then legitimates industry calls for even more vigorous action."[102] Yar has a point – the industry is not working in the public's best inter-ests and is playing a dangerous game.

The public has stood up and taken notice of the power grab that is under way in the guise of a war against online piracy. Consider the fol-lowing comment from an online news reader: "The new piracy is steal-ing our rights to enjoy what we have purchased and sell it when we are done. Virtually all digital content precludes the right to resell. It also precludes the right to back up (technically ripping DVD's is against the law), the right to modify the file, or change the file to a format you can better enjoy on more of your gadgets."[103] The industry's various at-tempts to criminalize mass piracy have created an impulse towards political action in the Internet age. We see this collective response mani-fested in numerous countries with the rise of new political parties such as the Pirate Party, a sign that piracy cannot be dismissed as deviant economic behaviour. It is vital resistance to the overreach of govern-ments and the corporate takeover of culture.

Online movie piracy was barely on the public's radar ten years ago, but signs of public discontent with the entertainment industry ap-peared as early as 2002 (though certainly earlier than that). That year, writing in the *Guardian*, film-maker Alex Cox spoke of the "war against the pirates" and described the MPAA as "a rich lobby group, with powerful allies in the World Trade Organization and an international copyright regime which favours corporate profits over individual free-doms." Cox questioned the credibility of the MPAA's claims about lost billions of dollars in revenue and highlighted their failure to gain the high moral ground: "Corporate multinationals, wielding unchecked power, terrify me far more than kids with video cameras."[104]

Ten years later, again in the *Guardian*, Antonia Senior reflected on how the extent of copyright infringement among the online audience has been overstated and how attempts to regulate their behaviour have led us "back where we started – with unenforceable rules and an anarchic web."[105] Trying to predict the future of the Internet is a mug's game, particularly when we seem to keep arriving at the place we once all were. Enforcement has largely failed and online audiences and content remain pretty much as they were 10 and even 20 years ago – out of control.

Back in 2003 a headline in the *New York Times* declared, "Studios Moving to Block Piracy of Films Online." Journalist Laura M. Holson told readers how Hollywood executives had learned from the music sector's failure to deal with piracy and were launching a "coordinated offensive to thwart the free downloading of films before it spins out of control." The industry's offensive included measures such as a nationwide piracy awareness campaign in theatres and embedding electronic watermarking on movie prints. Guards were posted in theatres that premiered movies and outfitted with night-vision goggles so they could catch anyone who dared to videotape the film. The film industry also convinced school boards to include lesson plans, thinly disguised industry propaganda, in 36,000 classrooms in the form of "stealing is bad" educational materials. It is odd how no one has ever managed to get "corporations influencing school curriculum is bad" messages embedded in education materials. The industry knew this would not be enough though: "Hollywood executives agree that to succeed in changing minds, they have to come up with easy and cheap online alternatives to free downloads."[106] Almost a decade later the headline "Scant Gains in War on Piracy" appeared in *Variety* magazine. A 2012 industry panel on piracy prevention and countermeasures "drew a picture of a movie industry settling into a grim cold war it can only win with a diminished definition of victory." The industry was still struggling to control camcorder piracy in theatres, which the MPAA claimed was "the source of over 95% of movie piracy." Digital watermarking and digital rights management technologies were having "mixed success achieving … relatively modest goals."[107] The control of movie piracy remains a distant dream for the industry. Education efforts have failed. DRM schemes have failed. The online audience is still waiting for an easy and inexpensive online alternative to the "simple, fast, and free" formula of online movie piracy.

On the surface it may seem that not much has changed. Television and movies continue to flow freely and illegally across the Internet. Yet there appears to be a politicization of piracy. Decades of overreach and gross exaggeration by corporations and governments have created a justification for online piracy in the minds of many. Thus an individual in the Philippines declares, "Most politicians and big-time business men are really crooks … we take from those who have too much to begin with."[108] Both outside and inside the United States the discourse of online piracy reflects the audience's feeling that corporations have struck an unfair bargain and piracy is a way to correct the overreach of the too-powerful. Examples of piracy and anti-corporate sentiments abound within the Internet. Piracy, says one Internet user, is "the consumer routing around a greedy and uncooperative corporation."[109] For another Internet user, pirating television and movies led to expanded intellectual horizons and learning a second language: "If it weren't for piracy and torrents sites I wouldn't have seen all the documentaries and other educational material that I have in these few years, which gave me more knowledge about the world than the poor education system we have in my country (and as I hear, in lots of others)."[110] Education and literacy are the foundation for a healthy citizenry. Perhaps online piracy may one day replace television as the great educator.

In the online discourse surrounding the topic of piracy the themes of corporate greed, corporate-state collusion, corruption, and overreach are commonly seen. Of course, online conversations also manifest points of view that are against piracy and supportive of laws and the actions of corporations. The Internet is not a homogeneous community.

Baumgärtel warns against "romanticizing media piracy." The pirates he knows well in the Philippines "are far from being the resistance movement against international information capitalism that some would like them to be. On the contrary, they might be the most aggressive and most developed – illegal – version of capitalism."[111] Yet I do not think we can easily strip the politics of consumption from piracy. Yes, there are those who are "into" piracy strictly because it is a way to make money or avoid paying any money. Can a complex, global, and diverse phenomenon such as piracy be reduced to mere economics? If so, it would be an extraordinary exception in the study of consumer behaviour. Doing so would require ignoring the testimony of an online audience expressing real concerns and motives. These motives include the expressed desire to subvert copyright law.[112] The discourse of digital piracy is littered with political references and indications that the online audience is aware of corporate wrongdoing, overreach, and the general threat to culture that initiatives such as ACTA and SOPA represent.

Not every 14-year-old teenager illegally downloading *Avatar* is a card-carrying member of the Pirate Party but his or her involvement in piracy may be part of a consciousness-raising journey. Not all piracy is politically motivated, though there is a distinct element of "subpolitical participation" which Simon Lindgren and Jessica Linde have identified within the cultures of online piracy that can "contribute to feelings of freedom, autonomy and participation."[113] Yiannis Mylonas's analysis of piracy culture in Greece arrives at a similar conclusion: "The vicious attacks on society by transnational and local neoliberal [intellectual property] policies expose the irrationality of capitalist rationality to the vast majority of the population" while also generating new possibilities for social change.[114]

Television and movie piracy does more than simply promote private individualized viewing. As Jinying Li notes, movie piracy creates an alternative public sphere wherein piracy consumption of suppressed films provides a space for marginalized identities. In contrast to the pseudo-public that is created through state censorship and media corporations, online film piracy's affordability, accessibility, and diversity offer "a much wider and inclusive cinematic spectatorship than the hegemonic form of theatrical screenings." Within heavily censored media environments such as China and Russia, illegal downloading of censored independent films highlights the political function of movie piracy as an "underground information-circulation channel."[115] In a similar fashion online film piracy has circumvented state censors across the globe and participated in creating a vibrant alternative public sphere. Indicative of participatory networked forms of representation, after the fall of Mu'ammer Gaddafi, Libyan cinema exploded and the Internet played a role in building awareness about the country's new film culture.[116] Li intriguingly proposes that the state and market's anti-piracy efforts are "the best indication of the political potential of the alternative public sphere." Thus we see that piracy is not merely a matter of property rights and theft. In the post-television era, piracy's "unruly organization of cultural distribution" provides the foundation for new social orders.[117]

In certain instances piracy proves to be a politicizing agent in the Internet age. The grievous actions of corporations and the state are educating the online audience in the economic system's "strategic colonization of fundamental social commons, such as culture, intellectual goods, as well as human creativity and communication."[118] Likewise, Jonas

Andersson finds that online piracy serves to "lay bare the arbitrary nature of copyright as well as the arbitrary nature of the privately ordered online regimes" of multinational media corporations.[119] Patrick Vonderau describes the role of the illegal service the Pirate Bay as "contributing to normalizing the idea of copyright infringement being fair use, or indeed, a social norm."[120] Martin Fredriksson sees in piracy a "spontaneous response to a malfunctioning market that embodies a potential critique of that market and the property regimes that it upholds."[121] Brett Robert Caraway also suggests that the tension between the gift economy of the Internet community and the commodity-exchange economy of capitalism is "symbolic of a potential rupture in the social relations of capital." The recent commodification of culture under late modern capitalism creates conflict with "a much older tradition of communing [sharing] that stretches back centuries."[122] Alexander S. Dent argues that piracy is a "necessary response" to unfair international laws.[123] In the 1960s we learned the personal is political. In the post-television era, online civic society is discovering that piracy is political.

Critical theory reminds us that there is "nothing natural with property because property is not a pre-political natural attribute to individuals. The naturalisation of property relates to liberal ideology and is a political construction."[124] In capitalist markets the property claims of corporations serve to maintain monopolies and control prices.[125] In this context piracy becomes an ideological target just as socialism became an ideological target in the mid-twentieth century because it represented the possibility of a viable alternative. According to Mylonas, piracy practices demonstrate "the possibility of a democratic economic model" and are criminalized because "capitalism requires the eradication of non-capitalist, non-market models of economic behaviour."[126]

In a post-communist world online piracy provides an ideological target for a capitalism intent on eliminating all possible rivals. The politicization effect can be seen in events such as the persecution of the Pirate Bay, leading to the formation of the Pirate Party in Sweden, and this political movement spreading to other countries. In Canada interest in copyright made its way to the front pages of the national newspapers. As a result of repeated attempts at legislative overreach by a Conservative governing party and interference from American lobbyists, Canadians "now have a politics of copyright to talk about."[127] Copyright is perceived as closely connected to cultural destiny and motivates grassroots political action when corporate property claims are overextended. To reduce piracy to a simple equation of theft, as is done in the dominant discourse, is to risk arriving at the point where we are forced to answer the question, "are you now or have you ever been a member of the Pirate Party?"

Digital piracy is as complex as the global village. It encompasses a set of issues as varied as globalism under capitalism, shifting cultural norms, gender, class, identity, and age. Corporations and governments would have us believe that it is merely a straightforward issue of theft. In their minds, theft is theft and that is the end of the matter. But an increasing number of media and legal scholars are questioning the entertainment industry's attempt to frame piracy as simple theft.

Stuart P. Green, a professor at Rutgers Law School, suggests that theft law was thrown into a state of confusion as a result of the American Law Institute issuing a Model Penal Code in 1962: "In a radical departure from prior law, the code defined 'property' to refer to 'anything of value.' Henceforth, it would no longer matter whether the property misappropriated was tangible or intangible, real or personal, a good or a service. All of these things were now to be treated uniformly." As the decades rolled by and the information age kicked into high gear, patents and copyright became a lucrative part of the economy in every industrial nation. Green argues that this in turn led to lawyers and lobbyists from the entertainment industry "and their allies in Congress and at the Justice Department" attempting to enact laws such as SOPA. Such laws reflect a rhetorical strategy to enshrine the notion that downloading is stealing. However, this rhetorical strategy to change how we think about theft has failed. "The problem is that most people simply don't buy the claim that illegally downloading a song or video from the Internet really is like stealing a car. According to a range of empirical studies, including one conducted by me and my social psychologist collaborator, Matthew Kugler, lay observers draw a sharp moral distinction between file sharing and genuine theft, even when the value of the property is the same."[128]

Green suggests what we should learn from the failed attempt to change how people think about digital piracy: "we should stop trying to shoehorn the 21st-century problem of illegal downloading into a moral and legal regime that was developed with a pre- or mid-20th-century economy in mind. Second, we should recognize that the criminal law is least effective – and least legitimate – when it is at odds with widely held moral intuitions."[129] Again we encounter the accusation that the entertainment industry is trying to apply twentieth-century notions of property to a twenty-first-century media system. The Internet has come packaged with a moral code that is specific to the digital lifestyle. Hundreds of millions of people simply do not buy the argument that downloading television shows and movies is theft. This is part of a wider cultural shift that is occurring as we move into the post-television age. Not only is the status of property changing, the status of television itself is changing.

Television's Changing Status

In an article that appeared in *Television and New Media* Newman makes an intriguing argument that piracy is engendering a shift in television's social status.[130] Television's cultural identity is shifting from feminine to masculine and from private to public good. When the audience acts as programmer, when it makes choices about what is of value and worth redistributing through piracy networks, television is no longer seen as a feminine, low-class, and passive experience bounded by the marketplace.

During the broadcast era of my youth, television was regarded as a public good available for free to anyone who owned a television set. In this formative period television had a cultural status described as feminized mass culture. In the early study of popular culture, masculine denoted good high culture and feminine denoted bad commercial culture. Television has long been framed as a debased medium, one widely thought to be a "threat to intellectual culture, childhood development, and social cohesion." Mass involvement in television piracy is seen by Newman as an indication of the rising social status of television viewing. Piracy is a practice "typically linked to youth, masculinity, class, and technological sophistication. One seldom finds the less legitimate and more ephemeral forms of television, feminized and devalued genres such as daytime talk shows and local news, circulating in the P2P networks." File sharing also legitimates television by moving it away from the old audience position of a passive couch potato to a much more active stance. The formerly passive viewer is transformed into an "advertising-avoiding television programmer" (one of the often seen motives for engaging in television piracy is the desire to avoid commercials).[131]

Under the influence of piracy, television viewing gets stripped of its devalued content; transforms the passive audience into active seekers, redistributors, and programmers; and frees it from the commercialized taint of advertising. Thus illegal distribution renders television "more culturally respectable by masculinizing it, articulating TV with activity and discernment rather than the more feminized and passive character-istics that earlier defined it."[132]

Television's initial cultural status was defined by its content, which was controlled by networks and broadcasters, and the audience's pos-ition was controlled by the largely one-way character of the technology. It stands to reason, then, that if mass involvement in piracy changes how content circulates, what content circulates, and how active the audience can be in the entire process, it is conceivable that the social status of television is open to change as well.

Newman also sees television piracy as a form of audience resistance to the transformation of television from public good to a private good. Television was once free. The past few decades have seen cable broad-casters successfully change television into something the audience pays for twice. We pay with the labour of having to watch advertising and we pay our monthly cable bills.

Television piracy is also transforming the national identity of tele-vision. All around the world people express a feeling of entitlement to television shows, regardless of those shows' point of origin. Conversa-tions about piracy within online television communities reveal "a sense of entitlement to television and a frustration with the structures that slow or forbid transmission of American shows to viewers in other countries." Newman suggests that television's value is being trans-formed from a locally owned property into a "cosmopolitan trans-national culture."[133]

Behind television piracy stands a set of forces that are potential change agents in areas far removed from economic arguments or sim-plistic moral equations. Piracy could initiate "new positive evaluations of television," rendering it "more culturally legitimate than it had been."[134] The forces of digital piracy that are drawing us into the post-television age could increase the cultural esteem surrounding a medium traditionally associated with corrupted values and crude mass tastes. Yet the argument over television's changing cultural status from femin-ine to masculine also reflects ideological issues regarding the legitim-ization of commercial television in the digital era. Michael Z. Newman and Elana Levine argue that the commercial and academic discourses that celebrate the shift from passive and feminine to improved viewer agency, intelligence, and masculinity "implies a progress narrative that naturalizes gendered hierarchies with their assumption that moving forward technologically means moving away from the feminized past and towards a masculine future."[135] Newman and Levine rightly note that in the end, "praising the television industry for finding new ways to monetize our attachment to TV" overlooks how it also serves to perpetuate "hierarchies of taste and cultural value and inequalities of class and gender."[136] After all, when the industry speaks of the new powers of the digital audience, they are only concerned with those powers that increase engagement, advertising recall, and purchase frequency. Not all agency is equal or desirable.

Summary

Television piracy is widespread, normative behaviour among the young. It is pervasive in many foreign markets, beyond legal or technological remedies, and likely to grow with the inevitable deployment of faster Internet connections and the ongoing adoption of broadband among households. Many people will opt for illegitimate services even when the same content is freely available on commercial websites. Piracy is seen as a superior method of accessing content – free, easy, simple, and feature-rich – while the television and movie industries are burdened with contractual obligations and a control mentality that prevents them from effectively delivering a compelling alternative. Nonetheless, television and movie piracy rates may see declines in certain markets as the online audience adopts commercial streaming services. Or not.

In the fast-evolving world of the Internet anyone who wants to see the future of television and movie piracy should download the latest disrupter, which takes the form of a program called Popcorn Time. This multi-platform, open-source media player provides an interface that looks almost exactly like Netflix and organizes movies and television shows by genre. Popcorn Time is essentially a free, easy, simple, and feature-rich interface to millions of torrents, pirated television and movie files that are streamed to your screen and come with a wide variety of language subtitles. As *Forbes* explained to its readers, "not only is the interface elegant and easy to use but it seems like it will be almost impossible to take down."[137] While Popcorn Time itself may succumb to lawsuits, it has set a new standard in piracy programs that is nothing short of revolutionary.

A common explanation of television piracy is that it is a response to failures within the market. Media corporations are accused of failing to deliver the right options and not meeting demand in a suitable fashion. Yet the motivations for piracy may extend far beyond issues pertaining to the market itself. Whatever the root causes of mass participation in media piracy may be, it is highly unlikely the television industry will acquiesce to the demands of the online audience and make its content freely available on terms that are fully satisfactory to the audience. The values and belief systems of media corporations are entrenched in the twentieth century and hamper the ability to adapt to the demands of an online audience enabled by twenty-first-century digital technology and accustomed to free, easy, and simple.

There is an inherent conflict between the piracy culture of the online audience and the culture-on-demand digital marketplace promoted by media corporations. Piracy claims reflect ideological interests of some of the most powerful multinational corporations. Online piracy can be a politicizing agent and the foundation to alternative public spheres. It may also be changing the social status of television.

3 Sports Television Piracy: They Stream. They Score!

With over 219 million viewers the 2012 Olympic Games in London was the most watched television event in US history. The London Games also set records for online television viewing, delivering 159 million video streams of events and 20.4 million hours of online video.[1] The London Games demonstrated that a mass audience can be reached through commercial online television. It also demonstrated that Internet audiences will use illicit means to view sports online when they are dissatisfied with a commercial service. Technical problems and NBC's inferior commentary on the Olympics had Tara Jenson

> scrambling for other ways to watch live. Jenson, a Linux system adminis-
> trator in Minneapolis, set up two virtual private networks (VPN) to by-
> pass NBC's broadcast, one on her home media server and the other on her
> iPad, tethered to a 4G hotspot, so she could watch at work. Her preferred
> coverage? The BBC, which is notably devoid of "NBC's dumb commen-
> tary," she said.[2]

NBC tried to shut out cord cutters from the walled garden of live online coverage, but many viewers circumvented the gateway to BBC's free online video feeds that were meant only for UK audiences. There was even a Silicon Valley startup, AnchorFree, backed by funding from Goldman Sachs, that provided software for circumventing the BBC's online gateway and thus avoiding paying for cable television access to the Games. NBC reported that all this online viewing activity "did not cannibalize the coveted prime-time audience."[3]

The fundamental problem facing the sports television industry is that it relies on exclusivity in an era of digital plenitude. Brett Hutchins and David Rowe describe the effects of online digital plenitude in the following terms: "Significantly lower barriers of access and cost have multiplied the number of media companies, leagues, clubs, and even individual athletes that can produce and distribute content for online consumption. Lower barriers have also allowed large numbers of users to access, appropriate, and share live sports footage."[4] All this adds up to a fight over the distribution of sport content.

Sports is an exceptional area of television viewing. Unlike movie and television show audiences, sports fans want to see their events live. Thus they are not likely to be satisfied with illegal services that upload entire games for future downloading. Sports fans do not want to download the game after it is over. They want to see it as it happens. Writing in the influential online publication paidContent.org, Daniel Frankel notes, "As perhaps its most popular and perishable video product, sports is rightly considered TV's most resilient asset when it comes to the forces of digital video recorders and cord-cutting. Fans generally prefer not to time-shift sports, and they don't 'catch up' with their favourite teams via Netflix viewing binges."[5] It is widely thought that the desire to see sports events in real time on television will keep the audience tethered to the cable, but this tether is getting thinner with each passing year. Sports fans may be a key indicator of the viability of cord-cutting – ditching paid television services for free access to legal and illegal online alternatives (see chapter 4 for more on cord-cutting).

One of the biggest attractions for sports fans is regional games. Fans who want to see their local teams have limited options: "cut out cable and they'd have to go to a sports bar or buy a ticket to see their favorite club's home games."[6] Some sports events like the Super Bowl can be viewed live and online for free. As Frankel observes, "You can see a lot of the action without paying a cable bill."[7] Sports associations such as Major League Soccer do have online services that stream live games. These services typically suffer from two drawbacks – they carry an additional charge beyond your regular cable bill and they do not allow fans to see their local team's home games. In the end, they require you to pay more and you still do not get access to the games you really want to see because of local blackout rules. Fans such as Colleen Peters relate how they subscribed to a service such as MLB.TV only to discover that they are still "denied access to watch our favorite teams play online."[8]

A fan's favourite local team typically has its home games licensed exclusively by regional sports broadcasters and is contractually committed to multi-year broadcast licensing deals. This arrangement is a significant source of revenue for teams. Time Warner Cable is committed to paying the Los Angeles Lakers $3 billion (US) for 20 years' worth of future games. That is a $3 billion bet that the broadcast system is going to remain unchanged over the next two decades. Thus Frankel concludes that neither the broadcast industry nor the sports associations "appear eager to disrupt the current model."[9]

Billions of dollars' worth of future revenue are tied up in contractual arrangements that assume that the broadcast system is going to maintain control over content and audiences for decades to come. For example, in 2010 Turner Sports and CBS signed an $11 billion 14-year contract for the broadcast rights to the NCAA tournament, including digital and new media platforms. The broadcast industry is adapting business models to the online audience, but they may be overestimating their ability to control audiences and content in digital environments. These lucrative deals are extensions of twentieth-century broadcast business models that depend upon controlled content and corralled audiences.

The sports industry may be in the midst of an economic bubble created by inflated television rights and player contracts. Consider the case of the Cincinnati Reds' first baseman Joey Votto. In 2012 Votto signed a ten-year contract worth $225 million. Players are getting contracts in the hundreds of millions of dollars and teams in the tens of billions of dollars – all based on cable rights fees. The sports industry is able to command such enormous fees because every cable subscriber in the United States pays close to $100 per year to sports television networks, regardless of whether they watch sports at all. This has created a large cash flow to teams and significant valuations of a team's equity. Within the sports industry this rights-fee boom "is premised on the assumption that cable and satellite providers will forever squeeze their customers at the whims of Regional Sports Networks, and that the customers will forever tolerate it, and that the FCC will forever endorse it."[10] The inflated valuations and paychecks have been cited as one of the sources for rising cable subscription costs. It seems unlikely that the sports industry will be able to continue to charge increasing rates to all cable subscribers and sustain an inflated sports economy when the television system is in the midst of disintermediation from various online alternatives. Of course, one of those alternatives is the most difficult one to control – online piracy.

Studies of illegal sports streaming note that fans do not insist upon a high-quality reproduction of their game.[11] They are more concerned with immediacy than visual quality. On the matter of low resolution and the online television experience, Joshua Green argues that this is "completely consistent with television's traditional low-fi aesthetic."[12] Of course, for every rule there is an exception. As one viewer says, "I'm still waiting for HD sports to come alive online ... until then I must keep my cable TV (as unfortunate as that is)."[13] Note how having to pay for cable television at the dawn of the post-television era is seen as "unfortunate." This viewer will not have to wait long. High-definition sports will be widely available on illegal streaming services sooner rather than later. While in the past live streams did suffer from low quality, "time and technological advances have seen exponential improvements" in the visual quality of pirated broadcast streams.[14]

The illegal streaming of sports is on the rise across the globe. During the 32 days of 2014 FIFA World Cup in Brazil there were no less than 20 million viewers on illegal streaming websites.[15] One popular streaming site, Firstrow Sports, has almost ten million unique users worldwide and millions of dollars in estimated revenues. The BBC reported that the Premier League shut down over 30,000 illegal online streams of its television matches in the 2011–12 season. Yet even such an effort made only a small dent in the illicit flow of programming: "It is a case of 'whack-a-mole.' One disappears and another one comes back online."[16] In one month alone (July 2008) 90,690 illegal streaming channels were created at the portal Justin.tv.[17] Illegal streaming of Major League Baseball increased by 25 per cent from the 2007 season to the 2008 season.[18] The audience size for pirated online streams of sporting events ranges in the "thousands for the majority of streams, or the low 100,000s for the most popular streams."[19] According to an online copyright protection agency, unauthorized live streams of sporting events can attract over one million viewers.[20] Some argue that illegal live streams "may be the last straw in tipping most clubs in the EPL into bankruptcy."[21] Certainly, all this is not good news given that half of the English Premier League (EPL) clubs are considered technically insolvent.

Popular sporting events regularly generate hundreds of unauthorized streams from illegal websites offering fans free live re-transmission over the Internet. Thus far there are few if any effective legal remedies to the illegal streaming of sports. Legal action, even when successful, is usually an "after-the-fact" solution that does not stop the initial violation from happening. Illegitimate streaming services that are taken down through successful legal action often propagate to other websites across the globe. Fans report that it is getting easier to access real-time illegal sports streams: "The pirate feeds don't cut out nearly as much as they used to, and, so far, the feds haven't been able to sue them out of existence."[22]

Illegal streaming of sports events is a global phenomenon that has been aided by free broadcast software, which makes it possible for almost anyone on the Internet to capture an event and stream it to others at little or no cost. The hardware costs for becoming a do-it-yourself online broadcaster is as low as $50 for a television tuner card. The combination of low entry costs, minimal technical knowledge, and freely available software has made illegal streaming of sports and other television content a very widespread phenomenon. Most of the students in my courses admit to using illegal streaming services to supplement their viewing, sometimes even while in class (other professors' classes, I hope).

Will loyalty to their teams discourage fans from undermining the home team's revenue via online piracy? This certainly did not happen with music fans. A study of the fans of elite English football suggests that a combination of corruption and hyper-commercialization has helped to justify the use of illegal content.[23] Why would fans not make use of free illegal transmissions when their leagues and favourite players are regularly seen engaging in corrupt activities and when fans feel they are being gouged for the price of a ticket and a packet of crisps? For many, piracy is seen as normative behaviour. It's not a crime, it's a lifestyle. Over half of those who engage in online piracy do so because they feel that "everyone does it."[24]

There are signs that sports television is in trouble. With few exceptions, such as the Super Bowl, both ratings and the total audience size for sports programs in the United States have declined steadily since 1970.[25] An aging population is also having a negative effect on the sports industry. It is unlikely that aging sports fans will be replaced "by a younger population with the same numbers, interests, and purchasing power" of their predecessors.[26] Nonetheless, the value of broadcasting deals among major American sports leagues doubled from 1990 to 2006.[27] Television revenue has shot upwards while audiences have declined. On top of declining audiences sports broadcasting is also faced with the disruptive chaos of the Internet.

As with the wider television industry, sports broadcasting's business model rests on creating artificial scarcity. The economy of sports broadcasting is characterized by high barriers that make it difficult for new companies to enter into the market. Government policies often create local monopolies or oligopolies, existing contractual arrangements discourage competition, and firms are faced with enormous start-up costs. These barriers have limited "the number of media companies and sports organizations able to create, control and distribute quality, popular sport content."[28] The economy of sport content rests on a mid-twentieth-century broadcast-rights model that gave exclusive rights to popular sports that, with very few exceptions, could only be seen on television. In the economy of sports broadcasting this exclusivity was enabled

> by the considerable expense of setting up and maintaining broadcast technology infrastructure, the limited supply of and access to broadcast spectrum, state regulation, and intense market competition. This is an economic order that consistently stimulated demand by guaranteeing a 'scarcity' of distribution channels for high-quality, popular content – only a limited number of television networks possessed the production and distribution capacity and capital to broadcast major sporting competitions and events.[29]

The sports economy and the contractual relationships within it are disrupted by the rise of a new medium that changes who can create, produce, and distribute content for online audiences.

In response to the growth of the online audience, sports organizations are supplementing their existing broadcast revenue streams with the sale of exclusive rights to new media such as the Internet and mobile phones. These new media platforms have created a situation that Brett Hutchins and David Rowe described as "outright chaos" for all involved in this economic sector. Chaos and disruption in the sports sector do not bode well for the rest of the entertainment industry. Rupert Murdoch, widely seen as one of the most influential people in the global sports business, claims that "sport absolutely overpowers film and everything else in the entertainment genre."[30] If sports broadcasting is disrupted and thrown into outright chaos by the online audience then the rest of the entertainment sector had best head down to the bomb shelter. New media is exploding across the television landscape.

The sports industry has been schizophrenic in its response to the online audience. Incumbent organizations blessed with substantial television revenues are "seeking to protect and maintain their accustomed high level of control" over the production and distribution of their content, while smaller players are "changing their business practices to embrace the creative and superabundant distribution opportunities afforded by the Internet."[31] Note how the incumbent players default to a position that attempts to preserve their "high level of control" when faced with new media threats. This control over the online audience is far from comprehensive. Quite literally, hundreds of millions of people all over the world use YouTube, digital piracy, and many other available means to evade the industry's practices of controlled distribution. Meanwhile, the dominant players within the industry respond with plans for increased control and new ways of charging for content. In industry and academic literature on the subject of online television this theme of preserving control occurs time and again. This raises a central question about a post-television future – can they do it? How much control can the market exert over online content and audience behaviour?

A control mentality was at work when both the 2007 Pan American Games Organizing Committee and the 2008 Australian Olympic Committee tried to stop athletes from blogging during the games. Here we witness a twentieth-century control mentality trying to stop a twenty-first-century media phenomenon – DIY online publishing. The twentieth century lost the battle. For better or worse, athletes are becoming content producers.

The sports industry has failed to stop the illegal transmission of sporting events over the Internet. Legal attempts to do so increase resistance and resentment among fans.[32] There have been successes, but digital piracy of sports media content is on the rise. Indeed, one could reasonably say that we are in the age of mass piracy. It is a behaviour shared by hundreds of millions of people. Hutchins and Rowe suggest that the sports and television industries have been "caught off guard" by individuals and organizations that use the Web to undermine the exclusivity of television and "are yet to fully comprehend" the essential character of the Internet.[33] More than information wants to be free. Much more. Digital plenitude disrupts the business models of traditional television. What is the future value of a business sector that sells exclusivity rights to content when many fans simply do not care about copyright and know how to access illegitimate sources of sports entertainment for free?

Hutchins and Rowe describe the various struggles over online sport content during the past decade as "the first wave of major conflict and ongoing change in the media sport economy." They also suggest that television will maintain its "preeminent role" in the live broadcast of events.[34] Yet I wonder how long that pre-eminence can be maintained in the Internet era. The problem facing the industry is as big as its entire fan base: "The problem facing professional sports leagues is that anyone with a camera phone or computer now has the ability to widely disperse what they are viewing, hearing, or thinking; thus, fans put themselves in direct competition with the licensed materials owned by the professional sports leagues."[35] What is the meaning of scarcity and exclusivity when athletes turn the camera on themselves, when so many fans have video cameras and every aspiring sports commentator has a blog?

As recently as 2011 Brett Hutchins could rightly state that academic research on digital piracy had largely overlooked the sports sector. Hutchins found a number of similarities between online sports piracy and entertainment piracy in general. Media corporations and sports organizations are guilty of "relentless media industry propaganda and suspect claims of damage."[36] As is the case with other sectors of the economy, no one is certain just how much damage online piracy causes in the domain of sports. Also following in the footsteps of television and movies, the inevitable transition to high-speed broadband among millions of households means that piracy of sport content is destined to get worse before it gets better (if it gets better at all).

Technological solutions such as digital rights management tools have proven as ineffective as legal actions. Prevailing counter-piracy strategies have failed to deliver results and "media sport industry leaders yearn for the replication of a closed analogue-broadcast system on the Internet."[37] As with the rest of the entertainment sector, the impulse appears to be towards the preservation of existing business models and the use of legal action to stifle innovation and competition. The news is not all bad. Hutchins concludes by noting that "the overall value of sports television coverage deals signed internationally shows no signs of collapse and audience numbers remain healthy."[38]

The sports canary in the Internet coal mine remains alive and well but there can be no doubt that the audience is shifting to online sources. Behind the phenomenon of online sports streaming is more than just a few commercial enterprises offering illicit services. The piracy mode of viewing is supported by an army of volunteers working in the Internet gift economy.[39] Sports fans are particularly active in the DIY approach to re-transmitting television over the Internet. Through streaming services such as Justin.tv, fans "follow a 'gift-economy' logic[;] they re-broadcast what sporting events are readily available to them on their local TV channels, and in turn profit by being able to watch the sporting events rebroadcast by fellow users from elsewhere in the world."[40] In essence, the Internet has created a globalized gift economy that directly competes with capitalism's market economy. Here are the outlines of a new economy that emerges with the post-television audience, one that is part of "a larger trend towards user involvement in television broadcasting."[41] The irony of Apple's newly branded product, iTV, is that it comes preloaded with iDistributor, iVideographer, iBroadcaster, iSportsCommentator, and, of course, iPirate. The challenge before the incumbent television industry is to control how the people formerly known as the audience participate in television broadcasting.

We see the outlines of a post-television sports culture when journalists of major dailies admit to engaging in illicit forms of audience behaviour. Writing in the *Toronto Star*, staff reporter Raju Mudhar related how he joined in on March Madness, the NCAA Men's Division Basketball Championship finals, by going online at work in search of a game to watch. Mudhar surfed to CBS's online stream of the games but found that it was blocked in Canada. The message in his browser read, "Location Blackout. You are geo-restricted from this content." The league was attempting to black out the Canadian online audience in accordance with contractual arrangements. This did not present a problem for Mudhar: "I just zipped my browser over to adthenet.tv, the once busted but still going strong central hub of illicit sports streams, and immediately got the St. Louis–Michigan State game. It was simple, fast and free, all lessons that online sports providers could learn from."[42] It is indeed noteworthy how the phrase "simple, fast, and free" reoccurs within both industry and academic descriptions of online piracy.

Mudhar reflected on the meaning of his experience for the future of television and concluded that the Internet "will eventually kill TV – or at least morph to become the main source of how we get all our entertainment," but the sports audience still has a long way to go, "particularly if you want to go the legal route." In the meantime, both Bell TV and Rogers were offering streaming services for March Madness, but they cost the subscriber an additional fee and yet more money when they exceeded their bandwidth allowance watching all those games. So the online audience is left with one legitimate choice – pay more, then pay again. Mudhar accuses sport and communication companies of "half-heartedly serving up options online." Again it is clear how the audience is underserved by legitimate online options, opts for illegitimate viewing options that are simple, fast, and free, and looks forward to a post-television future where the Internet is the main source of all our visual entertainment. Mudhar's experience of March Madness confirms Hutchins's observation that, with rare exceptions, "affordable and comprehensive official pay-per-view Internet sports services are few and far between."[43] Piracy of television content is a highly compelling option. One of the first victims of the post-television sports audience may prove to be the World Wrestling Entertainment (WWE) corporation. Stock analysts blame online piracy for undermining WWE's pay-TV business model.[44]

All this is not to say that industry efforts to adapt to online audiences have completely failed. NBC's online streaming of Monday Night Football garnered an average of 300,000 online viewers per game.[45] NBC also streamed Super Bowl XLVI to 2.1 million viewers while simultaneously broadcasting it on television. NBC claimed that its live stream of the Super Bowl was a success but viewers complained of repetitious advertisements, poor connections, poor resolution, and failed (dropped) streams, leading Rebecca Greenfield to write in the *Atlantic*, "Streaming just can't compete for sports viewers, so they're still willing to pay to see their games. For now."[46] Among television experiences that are measured by 101 million viewers (Super Bowl) and tens of millions of viewers (major league sports), online audiences make up only a fraction of the audience. Nonetheless, that fraction is a large and growing number.

The NCAA March Madness Live online streaming service garnered 26.7 million visitors and served 10.3 million hours of streaming video during just the first three rounds of the 2011 tournament.[47] MLB Advanced Media (BAM) streamed 18,000 live sporting events in 2011 and delivered over half a billion streaming video feeds to online viewers. BAM claims to be the largest source of live-streamed sports events with 2.2 million subscribers to paid products, 25 per cent annual growth, and $600 million in revenue in 2011.[48] Nonetheless, the MLB streaming service still blocks home team games. One customer wrote, "The local blackouts are described in small print and in a way that doesn't make sense to the average buyer. I've had 3 friends all tell me about how awesome this was and didn't realize they wouldn't be able to watch the local team live. When I called last year to complain and cancel the service, the MLB.TV rep said that this was their biggest problem and drove everyone nuts!"[49] And this is after paying $14.99 for the MLB.com At Bat app as well as the $100 or $125 MLB.TV package.

Reflecting on his consumption of illegally streamed sports, Mudhar noted the "moneymaking double dip" that can come with online viewing.[50] Whether you are paying for the online content or not, you might end up paying for the extra bandwidth you use viewing the content, particularly if you are on a mobile device. Consider the experience of Brandon Wells. After he bought a new 4G iPad he sat in his car and watched streaming March Madness games. The consequences of his actions caught him off guard. Watching a mere two hours of college basketball "burned through his monthly wireless data allotment of two gigabytes."[51] High-bandwidth network devices such as the latest iPad encourage users to watch more online video and rack up higher charges when they exceed the gigabyte limit on their mobile or home Internet subscription. Writing about Brandon's experience in the *Wall Street Journal*, Anton Troianovski concluded, "Something has to give: Either consumers will have to get used to paying more or wireless carriers will come under pressure to change their pricing models."[52] What impact bandwidth caps will have on the growth of the online audience remains uncertain.

The industry appears to be moving away from free streaming of sports entertainment towards for-fee services. These fees tend to be modest, ranging from $125 to $169 (US) annually, so the question arises as to why charge at all when so many simple, fast, and free illegitimate options are available. As one sports commentator complained, "It is amazing to me that as soon as you get comfortable and used to something that 'SHOULD' be free, BAM! you get gouged for yet another fee."[53] Writing in *Forbes*, Fred Dreier offered this intriguing explanation of the commercial motives behind moving towards subscription-based streaming. Dreier speculates that cable companies are using the registration and payment routines behind paid streaming services to acclimatize the online audience to the authentication process of TV Everywhere, Time Warner Cable's answer to online piracy. TV Everywhere allows Time Warner Cable subscribers to access content online if they use their cable bill to register for the streaming services: "they want the customer to know they can get the content on any device, so long as they keep paying their cable bill."[54] In the end it really comes down to this – will consumers be willing to pay for getting television on "second" and "third" screens, such as tablets and smartphones, when they can get the same content for free through illegitimate streaming services?

You have to wonder about the long-term viability of charging for online sports when the former head of the National Cable and Television Association, Steve Effros, remains sceptical: "Everybody is playing around with this [for-fee streaming services] and testing it, but to suggest it portends a major trend is way ahead of reality ... some people will find it worth paying to use, but I think most people won't."[55] Nonetheless, there is money to be made in streaming sports. One gets the sense that this mode of online viewing is well on its way when even President Obama has the NBA League Pass streaming service installed on his own iPad.[56]

The television industry's attempt to get the audience accustomed to paying for online content has similarities with the dilemma faced by the newspaper industry. Consumers generally regard online news as something that should be free. The news industry has been experimenting with online paywalls since 1998, asking consumers to pay for access to content. But there is so much freely available news content that consumers tend to go elsewhere when they encounter a paywall. Some paywalls have delivered results, but unless the majority of news goes behind paywalls consumers will find and use free alternatives. Clay Shirky had this to say about paywalls and news:

> The day they launched their paywall, the *Times* of London shrank its digital audience from a large multiple of its print circulation to a small fraction of it. This isn't a problem with general-interest paywalls – it is *the* problem, widely understood before the turn of the century, and one to which there has never been a convincing answer. The easy part of treating digital news as a product is getting money from 2% of your audience. The hard part is losing 98% of your advertising base.[57]

The attempt to erect paywalls in the newspaper and television sectors invites comparison to dying empires and raging emperors. Consider the remarks made in a lecture delivered at the University of Melbourne by Mark Scott, managing director of the Australian Broadcasting Corporation. Scott refers back to 2005 when little Caesar himself, Rupert Murdoch,

> said he wanted to "make the necessary cultural changes to meet the new demands of the digital native" [but now] says he's not going to respond to the demands of these digital natives. Instead, they – who have never in their lives paid for news online – will be asked to respond instead to his demands and start paying. The argument seems to be that people once didn't pay to watch television but now many do. We fought against timed local calls but now make them every day on our mobiles. Some of us might pay for recorded music we might once have illegally downloaded. And because we want to read and see this great content so badly, now we will pay for that.
> It strikes me as a classic play of old empire, of empire in decline. Believing that because you once controlled the world you can continue to do so, because you once set the rules, you can do so again. Acting on the assumption that you still have the power that befits the Emperor … when you want to charge customers for something that in this era is effectively generic, that

has many different free substitutes and is, by its nature ephemeral – mainly used and discarded – then the challenges you face are formidable.[58]

Murdoch's empire is threatened by digital plenitude. His response has been to erect paywalls against the hordes of virtual Visigoths, young netizens unwilling to pay for any digital content. Yet it remains to be seen if media empires can erect sturdy walls and control leaky content and unruly audiences. Rome did not fall in a day, but fall it did.

Scholar Victoria E. Johnson suggests that sports programming is blessed with a "unique predisposition to anticipate, ameliorate, and capitalize upon the transition from the network era to the post-network era and beyond."[59] As true as this is, it might also be said that sports programming is uniquely vulnerable to disruption by online audiences. Largely male, technologically sophisticated audiences have mastered accessing alternative sources of pirated content. The industry hopes to socialize this demographic segment into paying for online content, but the opposite could well come to pass. Sports audiences may lead the way in socializing others in the habits of pirate viewing. What will define the habits of this future television audience: commercial paywall initiatives such as TV Everywhere or illegitimate options best described as "Piracy Everywhere"?

In the winter of 2012 I asked my University of Ottawa students to raise their hands if they were regularly accessing pirated streams for viewing live sporting events. The vast majority of hands, both male and female, went up. The problem for business plans such as Time Warner Cable's TV Everywhere is that television is already everywhere, free, and easily accessible without registration processes. University students are living the post-television lifestyle in which we see online video change the way television content is consumed. Whereas the sports audience was once tethered to television's broadcast schedule, fans can now access what they want, what they missed, or what they want to see again on multiple fixed and mobile networked devices, including laptops in lecture halls.

An Industry Picture of Online Sports Consumption

In the fall of 2013 Chris Harper, a market researcher with Kantar Media Sports, released the "Global Sports Media Consumption Report."[60] Although industry research suffers from flaws such as vested interests and a lack of transparency and uniform definitions, this report nonetheless provides us with insight into the current state of the online sports audience at a time when data of any kind in this area is lacking. Harper notes that fans are "reluctant to pay for sports online" – an observation that mirrors a similar resistance to paying for digital music, news, television, and movies.[61] Sports consumption via mobile phones in the United States has grown from 21 per cent in 2011 to 35 per cent in 2013. A similar trend is found in fans' use of social media to follow sports, which rose from 15 per cent in 2011 to 25 per cent in 2013, with Facebook being the preferred platform.[62] Desktop computers are used by 29 per cent of fans, 23 per cent use mobile devices such as smartphones and tablets, and Internet-connected (smart) televisions are used by only 7 per cent of fans for consuming sport content.[63] US fans spend 3.8 hours a week consuming sports on traditional television and 2.5 hours a week consuming sport content via desktop computers and mobile devices.[64] Overall, 63 per cent of US fans follow sports online.[65] Only 9 per cent of fans pay to watch sports online and only 11 per cent express a willingness to pay.[66] This strongly suggests that, as with the music industry, online audiences will view sport content outside of direct market exchange. Unsurprisingly, sports audiences do not prefer to pay.

The Sociology of Live Pirate Streaming

The English Premier League's struggle against alternative football broadcasts provided an opportunity for Matthew David and Peter Millward to explore the sociology of piracy and live-streaming among fans. David and Millward studied how fans use local pubs to watch pirated broadcast streams of EPL matches.[67] They found that sports piracy facilitates social viewing practices that call into question aspects of Manuel Castells's theory of production and spatial division of labour. In Castells's model of informational capitalism, areas of innovation are populated by key players within networked cities while low-skilled support workers remain separated from the centre of the network.[68] In contrast to this highly segregated model the authors found that local pubs function as a milieu of innovation, a place where "the action" is to be found in the company of friends.[69] The pirated broadcast streams provide an occasion for local communities to assert a degree of autonomy and consume games "outside the control of the English football authorities and their member clubs."[70] Curiously, the authors found no evidence that illegal broadcasts in pubs threaten home match attendance.

Although fans themselves do not necessarily see their actions as political, David and Millward suggest that by using pirated broadcast streams and not attending football matches, fans are resisting the EPL's version of global capitalism while consuming EPL entertainment "by alternative means." Piracy provides fans with "alternative ways of maintaining their supporter-identities" that reshape the networked economy of football. The combination of a local community with networked sources of sport entertainment allows fans to "create new hubs or milieu of economic and cultural innovation."[71]

Whereas Castells's model of capitalism places support labour such as fans in passive, powerless positions on the margins of the social order, David and Millward argue that in pirated viewing the "scope for action, change and innovation spills out beyond elite control." Piracy viewing in the context of local gatherings enables fans to "choose how and where to watch matches and to create their fan cultures accordingly[;] they become significant players, able to challenge dominant practices, offer alternatives, and thereby themselves participate in the milieu of innovation." Football fans actively challenge the EPL's attempt to structure their viewing experience and define fan identity. Resistance to global capitalism, new possibilities of change and innovation, community and identity formation, and a "resurgence of locality" – all these dynamics suggest that digital piracy has implications that go far beyond the narrow interests of multinational corporations.[72]

The role of piracy in fan media consumption has been an overlooked aspect in the academic study of sports media. Raymond Boyle and Richard Haynes's *Power Play: Sport, the Media and Popular Culture* acknowledged that sport "is about to be dramatically affected by the Internet" and foresaw more control being placed in the hands of the consumer.[73] It is understandable that *Power Play*, published in 2000, made no mention of Internet-driven sports media piracy. This oversight was addressed in Boyle and Haynes's 2004 publication, *Football in the New Media Age*, where the authors note that an early form of sports pay-TV, ITV Digital, "faced a massive problem of piracy."[74] Before the rise of Internet-facilitated piracy of television, millions of fans had already gained illegal access to satellite and pay-TV sports channels. Piracy rates of early subscription sports television may have been as high as 60 per cent.[75] Boyle and Haynes also note that the online distribution of live football threatens to undermine the value of television broadcasting rights.[76] They are far from alone in this observation.

When we jump ahead in time to *Sports Media: Transformation, Integration, Consumption*, a 2011 collection of essays edited by Andrew C. Billings, the subject of the Internet enters into the analysis yet piracy of sports media remains almost entirely overlooked. This oversight is soundly redressed a year later with the publication of Hutchins and Rowe's *Sport beyond Television: The Internet, Digital Media and the Rise of Networked Media Sport*. Hutchins and Rowe argue that the rise of the Internet and digital television represents "a new media sport order" that is as significant as the rise of television itself in the 1950s and 1960s.[77] The authors lament "the difficulty of meaningful open debate about online piracy when industry propaganda and suspect claims of damage in the marketplace dominate the public messages in circulation."[78] As of 2012 the state of online sports piracy remained largely out of control. Unauthorized live Internet streaming feeds were available for almost any sporting event while DRM technologies and legal measures remained ineffective. There were even scattered reports of companies withdrawing from television broadcast-rights negotiations because Internet piracy was seen as devaluing exclusive rights.[79] As with other theorists of new media the authors also note that the development of online sport content produces greater consumer choice and "a countervailing urge for control on behalf of content providers."[80] At stake is the hegemonic control of popular sport content by media corporations and the possibility that sport content and audiences are spinning out of control.

Change does not come easy in this media sector. Andrew Kirton and Matthew David argue that sports broadcasters suffer from the same resistance to change that crippled the music industry in the early twenty-first century:

> The digital "revolution" has so far revealed a high level of resistance to change on the part of established corporate content providers and distributors. This pattern has been true of the recorded music industry, and it looks to be the case with the sports broadcasting industry. There will be continued attempts by those who principally benefit from existing economic arrangements to sustain them for as long as possible, but they look doomed to failure.[81]

Again and again we encounter the claim that regardless of all the various commercial online initiatives by media corporations, there remains considerable resistance to change.

After exploring various changes across the sports television landscape, Hutchins and Rowe conclude, "Media sport no longer revolves mainly around capturing and maintaining a singularly conceived mass audience and rigorously policing access to it."[82] If television broadcasters fail to maintain bundled content packages which force every American cable TV subscriber to contribute to the sports media industry, we will witness massive disruption across the entertainment system. As much as sports organizations bemoan piracy, they are the beneficiaries of a "sports tax" forced upon almost every paying television subscriber in the United States. Clearly, theft takes many forms in the entertainment industry.

ESPN

At this early stage of the online television audience "there is limited evidence of cultural and political democratization or flattened hierarchies."[83] Not only is there an ongoing struggle over rights between corporations and audiences, but the "upsurge in control" of online rights by telecommunications operators "has provoked open conflict with and among news media, television broadcasters, and sports organizations" over online content rights.[84] Curiously, while piracy practices among sports fans have a substantial impact on fan communities (as is manifested in areas such as resistance to global capitalism, new possibilities of change and innovation, community and identity formation, and a resurgence of the significance of local spaces), media practices based on official online sites such as ESPN.com have been found to promote "little substantive change" in dominant practices, gendered discourses, and promotion of consumer lifestyles.[85] Likewise, an analysis of fans' reaction on Twitter to the problems associated with the broadcast of the London 2012 Olympic Games reveals considerable unease within the broadcast industry over audiences taking an active role in television programming. Online environments such as Twitter provide a space in which the contract between viewers and television programmers is negotiated.[86] One analysis of the sports broadcast audience suggests that by the year 2023 the majority of the sports audience will have migrated to Web-based television, with the possibility of the switch occurring much faster.[87] Media corporations are aggressively promoting the online viewing experience. NBC plans to offer live digital streams of all its marquee sports events, increasing its volume of coverage from 300 online hours in 2012 to 4,000 hours in 2013. Meanwhile, ESPN.com offered up 17,600 hours of live event programming.[88] These trends suggest that we are bound to see substantial changes in online sports audiences and in the business practices of the media companies that seek greater control over content and audiences.

Depending on how you look at it, ESPN provides an example of either the unassailable nature of media conglomerates or their fragility. Sport journalists with the *New York Times* noted, "The more than $6 billion in cable fees flowing annually to ESPN from almost 100 million homes is threatened as growing numbers of consumers cut ties with cable providers to avoid rising bills for pay TV, turning instead to video streaming services." ESPN and its parent company Disney stand to lose billions of dollars if lawmakers in Washington legislate the de-bundling of channels within cable packages. Under current regulations an estimated 75 million American homes that never watch ESPN are forced to pay a monthly fee for the sports channel. John Skipper, president of ESPN, referred to this situation as a "beautiful business model."[89] Disney and ESPN executives have donated hundreds of thousands of dollars to elected officials in an effort to protect what others see as anti-competitive business practices and price gouging. Meanwhile, ESPN is faced with declining ratings and has lost more than one million subscribers.

While some argue that cord-cutting will never become mainstream because of sports television, it may be the case that the unfair economics of businesses such as ESPN actually generate incentives to cut the cord. Only a small percentage of American households are regular ESPN viewers yet every cable household pays for it. ESPN attempts to protect its online content through the TV Everywhere system that requires viewers to be authenticated with a TV subscription. I was curious to see how well ESPN's content has been walled off from non-paying viewers such as myself. A Google search for the phrase "ESPN free streaming" immediately led me to a site that provided pirated streams of all of ESPN's valuable content. Cord-cutting is far from toppling the ESPN empire at the moment, but as more sports content moves online, cracks are beginning to appear in its beautiful business model.

eSports

The online digital environment has given rise to a new category of virtual (or electronic) sports, also known as eSports. Three organizations are at the centre of eSports – Major League Gaming, the Electronic Sports League, and European Xtreme Gamers – which bring together amateur and professional gamers. Over 600,000 gamers visit the live-streaming site, Twitch, daily and the site garners 45 million unique visitors a month, up from a mere 3.2 million in 2011. One million gamers broadcast their game sessions each month. Online gaming franchises have logged over a billion hours of gameplay.[90] The most popular eSports events can attract half a million viewers.[91] Matthew DiPietro, vice president of marketing at Twitch, claims that "collectively, these events match and often beat broadcast/cable TV audience sizes."[92] Amazon acquired Twitch for $970 million (US), a deal driven by the reality that "for many people, watching elite gamers in action has as much appeal as watching professional football."[93]

eSports is seen as a genre of entertainment that combines hedonistic, competitive, and cooperative elements.[94] Admittedly, this is a much smaller media phenomenon than traditional television but it is indicative of how digital entertainment is creating new forms of online television. Twitch allows gamers to stream their gaming live to online audiences and suggests a future where the audience is the content of online television. This mode of participatory, interactive online video challenges the attempt to restrict the definition of television to the more familiar push-and-flow dynamics of broadcast systems. eSports events create the liveness, co-presence, and flow normally associated with traditional broadcast television. It may prove to be the case that new online forms of televisual entertainment such as eSports are so interactive that they do not translate into the realm of traditional television. As Tobias M. Scholz suggests, eSports has a distinct audience that is "solely reachable over the Internet and classical television has no place in it."[95] Finally, with the acquisition of the gaming website IGN.com by the News Corporation and CBS Interactive partnering with Twitch.tv we see the commercialization of the gaming community that may be laying the foundation for a form of virtual sports uniquely suited to post-television culture.

Summary

Piracy of sports television is growing and neither technology nor regulation holds much promise of significantly reducing sports TV piracy rates. The industry sees sports television as the one thing that will stem the tide of cord-cutting. This is perhaps a faint hope, given that sporting events only compose between 2 and 3 per cent of television's monthly programming.[96] Ten years into the early history of online television the traditional broadcast system still holds the centre, but the Internet is chipping away at the edges of the audience. Nonetheless, one gets a sense of things spinning out of control as content and audiences move into cyberspace. Do-it-yourself sports re-broadcasters provide an example of how the locus of distribution power is shifting in favour of the audience.

Following the rise of user-generated content, epitomized by amateur videographers on YouTube, a new era of guerrilla rebroadcasting is beginning to take shape. All over the world individuals are re-transmitting pirated television shows and live sporting events. This represents a new type of virtual television network operated by amateurs – a global pirate broadcasting system that duplicates and redistributes the content of media corporations within a gift economy. Meanwhile, the television industry's moral claims are substantially negated in the minds of many because of the industry's own illegal acts and hyper-commercialism.

The sociology of piracy among sports fans reveals complex and contradictory effects. There is a re-territorialization of local community-based viewing experiences that connect to global flows of pirated commercial broadcasts. Previously secure monopolies held by domestic broadcasters are undermined by the new milieu of economic and cultural innovation which is created when local pubs provide fans with pirated sport content. Television piracy changes patterns of consumption among sports fans and offers "the potential for a reform in the way social geographies are drawn."[97] Contrary to the general perception of Internet television and piracy, the online audience is not necessarily isolated nor is place rendered irrelevant. Locality gains significance as media corporations and the multinational sports industry lose control over the place of viewing. Television piracy leads to fan action moving beyond elite control.

It remains to be seen how tightly the sports audience will remain tethered to the television cable. The expectation is that the demand for live sporting events will keep this audience paying their cable bill. Yet this is a technologically skilled audience segment that is growing resentful of rising cable bills. The economy of sports television appears to be inflated at the very time when audiences are declining, the cable system is on the verge of disintermediation, and content is spinning out of control in cyberspace.

4 Television's Scariest Generation: Cord Cutters and Cord Nevers

Among the television industry's biggest fears is the phenomenon known as cord-cutting (also called cable-cutting).[1] Cord-cutting refers to individuals cancelling cable television subscriptions and turning to "over-the-top" services such as Netflix, Hulu, Boxee, iTunes, and YouTube, free over-the-air television, or simply pirating all their entertainment needs off the Internet. Small but worrisome declines are being registered across the television system. At the time of writing *Post-TV* it was still much too early to know how widespread cord-cutting would become. As yet we do not know how many will use the Internet as their primary source for television shows and movies. Nonetheless, cord-cutting represents a new form of audience behaviour that is growing and consequential for the television industry.

Driving the cord-cutting phenomenon is a host of factors, from rising cable subscription costs to innovative consumer electronic devices that deliver the Internet to television and television to the Internet. The overall effect of all these changes is that the audience is no longer tethered to the television set nor bound by the restrictions put in place on content by the incumbent television industry. Elliot Turner captured the character of this shift when he reviewed his new iPad: "The iPad alone brings cord cutting much closer to reality. One of the real consequences is that quite a bit of my personal cable-watching time has shifted to the Web."[2] Television viewing is taking place on desktop computers and mobile devices such as smartphones and tablet computers. Internet users are finding that the majority of their shows are available online, and people like Turner anticipate the day soon arriving when they will completely cut the cord and cancel their cable television subscription. Turner's iPad is part of the multi-screen phenomenon that is leading people to consider a cable-TV-free lifestyle. Owners of tablet computers are three times more likely to consider cutting the cord than the average adult broadband user.[3]

Also of great significance, Turner relates how a new viewing device such as a tablet computer led to a change in his television habits: "the amount of mindless time I spend watching actual TV has shrunk substantially … and has been replaced predominantly with much smarter content. I feel better for it at the end of the day too."[4] It may be that Turner is an exceptional example. The use of multiple screens can also increase overall television consumption. New media technologies are changing what we watch and how we feel about watching. A major shift in viewing habits is well under way. New consumer electronics and the digital plenitude of the Internet allow the audience to make choices about how and where they get television to a degree that simply was not possible in the twentieth century.

Cord-cutting behaviour takes two main forms. Some households cancel their pay-TV subscription and rely solely on OTT options. Others move to lower-cost pay-TV packages which they supplement with OTT options such as Netflix, Hulu, iTunes, Amazon Prime, and piracy, a choice know in the industry as cord-shaving. Television viewing behaviour is evolving into complex patterns that draw upon traditional distribution channels, various types of mobile and fixed viewing devices, and a growing suite of legitimate and illegitimate online options. One of the earliest demographic analyses of cord-cutting behaviour suggested that cord-cutting will have contradictory effects on television consumption. Among some households television viewing hours will decline, while among other households "viewership hours may actually grow."[5] Over-the-top services such as Netflix, multiple and mobile screens, and online piracy are a consequential "determinant of viewership patterns."[6] Viewing patterns change according to the various combinations of viewing devices, such as a family television set and a smartphone. The authors found that all forms of video streaming "make statistically significant marginal contributions to viewership hours" for both television shows and movies.[7]

In 2010 Nielsen announced that cord-cutting was a myth that was "busted" by their latest data: "for now the idea of a cord-cutting revolution appears to be purely fiction."[8] As recently as 2011 market analyst Craig Moffett boldly declared that "the fear of cord cutting is fading."[9] Crédit Suisse analyst Stefan Anninger also suggested that "cord cutting fears may have been overblown," and Miller Tabak analyst David Joyce described the cord-cutting phenomenon as a "fringe" behaviour among mostly young viewers.[10] After all, by the end of 2011 there were still almost 101 million US pay-television subscribers.

Industry executives also added their voices to the debate. In 2012 Disney CEO Bob Iger insisted, "We're not seeing some great interest in cord-cutting because I think, generally, consumers are happy with the quality and the variety [of channels] that they're getting, and the price-to-value relationship is generally good."[11] Iger reassured investors 19 months later that when it comes to cord-cutting, "we don't see evidence of this occurring."[12] Time Warner CEO Jeff Bewkes assured investors that "our best years are ahead of us."[13] Ariel Emanuel, CEO of the famous Hollywood talent agency William Morris Endeavor, declared that "cord cutting isn't happening."[14] As recently as summer 2013 Chase Carey, chief operating officer of 21st Century Fox, confidently informed shareholders that "consumers want a bundle, they just want a different bundle … We see no meaningful evidence of cord-cutting today."[15] Of course, the main audience for corporate executives is their investors. They are not about to admit to shareholders that the Internet represents any real threat to their business.

At an investors' conference the CFO of Time Warner Cable, Irene Esteves, also made a point of denying any threat from cord-cutting in the wake of the Nielsen report: "we're not really seeing it." Esteves dismissed charges that cable television is overpriced. "With an average pay TV bill of $75 a month for about 250 hours of TV viewing on average, the cost of pay TV amounts to only 30 cents an hour."[16] This is a highly deceptive way to frame the issue. Pay-television may only cost 30¢ an hour but it also costs $900 or more a year. That is a large pile of cash to a family struggling to meet mortgage payments. Esteves was quickly contradicted by her boss, Time Warner CEO Glen Britt, who explained to investors, "A lot of the people who are living paycheck to paycheck want our product, but simply can't afford it. Many entertainment executives are in denial about this, but it's happening."[17] Something is amiss when one of the top entertainment executives accuses his colleagues of being in denial about the high costs of the industry's products.

A growing body of evidence suggests that cord-cutting is real and growing. In 2011 some 1.5 million American households had cut the cord that year alone, the overall television audience declined slightly for the second year in a row, and Nielsen data demonstrated that "the number of U.S. homes subscribing to a cable, satellite or telephone company for a multichannel TV bundle isn't growing as fast as it used to."[18]

In 2012 an additional 1.08 million US pay-TV customers cancelled their subscriptions.[19] This is a small but significant phenomenon because it grew by almost 23 per cent over the last year. By May 2013 Nielsen reported that it had identified 5 million "TV Zero" American households that had opted out of traditional television.[20] Initially a sceptic, Moffett changed his tune from 2009, when he called cord-cutting an "urban myth," and in 2013 advised investors that "pay TV is unmistakably declining and the rate of penetration decline is accelerating. The very fact that there have recently been more new households being minted each year than there have been new pay-TV households is proof positive that cord cutting is real."[21]

The trend in Canada is smaller but growing rapidly. One study reported that a mere 1 to 2 per cent of the 11.7 million television subscribers cut the cord in 2012.[22] Another study reported that 4 per cent of Canadians cut the cord in 2007, 7 per cent in 2011, and 8 per cent in 2012.[23] In mid-2013 the audience measurement firm comScore suggested that approximately 16 per cent of Canadian adults had abandoned traditional television services and were relying entirely on the Internet for television content.[24] In the same year cable and satellite TV carriers shrank in size for the first time in the history of Canadian television.[25] Mario Mota, the primary author of *Canadian Digital TV Market Monitor*, explained, "While the recent decline in subscribers in Canada is small relative to the size of the total TV market, we now have two consecutive quarters of data for the Canadian market that confirm that cord-cutting is a reality here too."[26] This downward trend was not over. By summer 2013 the Canadian television market declined yet again, which meant three consecutive quarters of subscriber losses.[27] Nonetheless, in the fall of 2013 the consulting firm PwC insisted that "Canadians are not cutting the cords yet" and saw cord-cutting as posing no real threat for the next five years.[28] In May 2014 the Canadian Radio-television and Telecommunications Commission (CRTC) reported that the total number of television subscribers had fallen for the first time after years of slowing growth.[29] The drop was small, a mere 7,000 subscribers in 2013, but the decline occurred during a period wherein the Canadian housing market added around 170,000 households. Pay-TV growth is falling behind growth in the housing market.

Traditional television is losing its audience to online alternatives.[30] According to the *Wall Street Journal*, this new trend is unprecedented: "Prior to 2010, the pay-TV industry never saw a quarterly subscriber decline."[31] Another analyst noted that "the exodus is picking up steam."[32]

Between 2010 and 2012 the pay-TV (cable) industry experienced five quarters of declining subscribers. Meanwhile, 2012 was the second year in a row that witnessed a reduction in the number of homes with televisions. The pay-TV industry experienced its first full-year decline in subscribers in 2013 even with an expansion in US housing, "normally a surefire source of growth."[33] While such losses are often seasonally related, the year-on-year growth rate was below the level at which new households are being formed.[34] Declining numbers of subscribers within the pay-TV industry were all the more significant as over the same period the market saw an increase in new households, the labour market increased, and the economy improved.[35] The cable industry was reporting unprecedented declines during "the period of the year that tends to produce the largest subscriber gains."[36] Cable television was losing subscribers at the very time when it had every reason to gain new ones. As a result, the media analysis company SNL Kagan projected that cord cutters would rise to 10 per cent of US households by 2015.[37] What was only a single-digit phenomenon is becoming a double-digit threat.

Second-quarter results from 2013 provided yet more confirmation of declining pay-TV subscribers in the United States, as DirectTV, Cablevision, and Time Warner Cable all lost subscribers.[38] For the first time in television history we saw growth in the housing market but the decline of subscription television. Between 2010 and 2013 there were 3.2 million new US households, yet during the same period the pay-TV industry only added 250,000 subscriptions.[39] Analysts had previously suggested that a "housing recovery would pave the way for a boost in pay TV subscriber improvements" but clearly people are motivated to drop cable television by reasons more complex than just economic hardship.[40]

By mid-2014 television industry insiders were still debating the causes and extent of cord-cutting but data regarding online audience trends strongly suggested that disruption due to network effects was bound to grow. Over half of the US population streams television shows or movies at least once a week. Among US adults under the age of 35 no less than 67 per cent watched online video weekly. Over 7.6 million US households were cord cutters and one-third of adults had at least one television in the home connected to the Internet. Audiences that watched online video on a television are three times more likely to cut the cable TV cord, up from two times more likely just a year previous. Among those who watch video on their smartphones, the cord-cutting habit becomes even more prominent.[41] All data pointed in the same direction: the more one watched online television, used multiple screens, or watched mobile video, the more likely one would become a cord cutter. These trends gain significance as an increasing percentage of the global audience adopts mobile video, makes use of multiple screens, and grows accustomed to Internet-connected televisions. In other words, the general environment of the global television audience is increasingly tilting in favour of the cord-cutting lifestyle. This trend is confirmed when we consider that in 2013 fully 13 per cent of US millennials, people ages 18–34, made do without any pay-TV service.[42] It is easy to see why when it is increasingly easy to do so.

Many industry analysts and executives have been unwilling to see cord-cutting as anything other than an economic issue that merely affects young people and lower-income families. Bewkes told a conference audience, "Once they [cord cutters] take the mattress and get it off the floor, that's when they subscribe to TV."[43] Yet the majority of cord cutters are under 40, educated, and employed. Working professionals and university graduates who have cut the cord point to deeper motives arising out of a networked social environment unfamiliar to the twentieth-century television system. Evan Shapiro, an executive producer and professor of television management at New York University, explained the driving force behind cord-cutting in the following terms:

> As the two largest generations in history continue to graduate from college and into the workplace, they will demand a low-cost, efficient alternative for pay-TV service. If need be, they will make due [sic] with the various legal and illegal "over the top" avenues for getting the TV they want. What they will likely not do is pay for 500 channels when they only use 10. And, if the industry does nothing to change, a significant number of young viewers – the future lifeblood of the business – will abandon the platform completely. For those that don't believe this, please – *please* – see the music business.[44]

Piracy and cord-cutting need to be understood, at least in part, as audience responses to pricing issues in the marketplace. There is the simple motive of getting a better deal for your dollar. Consider the example of Mary Sherwood, an American who cancelled her cable bill initially out of financial distress because of unexpected medical bills. After becoming accustomed to free over-the-air network TV and streaming subscription services such as Netflix, Amazon Prime, and Hulu Plus, Sherwood told the *Miami Herald*, "Once you make the switch, I don't know why you would want to go back." Economic hardship was the initial motive, but Sherwood "can afford to renew the [cable] subscription now" yet she has not done so.[45] Sherwood behaved like the much maligned rational consumer of classical economic theory. This suggests that the explanation of cord-cutting needs to acknowledge that motives of the cord-cutting segment of the online audience go far beyond mere economic hardship. Rational choice and economic self-interest in a newly competitive television marketplace are also motivating online audiences to cut the cord and ditch the more expensive option of traditional pay-TV. Could it be that cutting the cord is the rational choice in today's television market yet the incumbent industry is intent on defending a poor choice that is not in many consumers' best interests?

On the one hand we see industry executives insisting that their products are fairly priced, if not a real bargain. On the other hand we witness some executives acknowledging that many consumers find $26 DVDs and $100 cable bills to be out of their reach. Britt's conversation with investors at a Morgan Stanley Technology, Media & Telecom Conference included the frank admission that the pay-television business "is fundamentally not growing."[46] The television industry has been increasing revenues in a mature market by raising prices. "What they're trying to do is grow by raising prices [but] it clearly is not sustainable," says Britt.[47] Cable bills in the United States have increased 38 per cent since 2000 and 77 per cent since 1996.[48] With wages remaining stagnant, cable prices in the United States have increased 6 per cent annually and were forecast to reach $200 a month by 2020.[49] Britt dismissed the threat of Internet video services by suggesting that "it is inefficient to transmit popular videos via the Web … The Internet is neither magical nor free."[50] Yet to a new generation of young netizens, the Internet *is* a magical place where you can get all the news, movies, and television shows you want for free.

Curiously, in the online comments to this news story one reader replied, "I'm in Canada and until recently I've been earning 44K a year, so spending $60–$80 a month on cable is not viable. I'd rather spend $8 a month on Netflix. I actually work for a cable channel and virtually none of the lower level staff (who don't still live with their parents) have cable."[51] Apparently, even many of the young staff at cable companies have cut the cord. Anthony Crupi described the situation to *Ad Age* readers:

It's counterintuitive to believe that Americans (especially the younger variety) will continue to lap up vanilla TV content. Time-shifting, mobile/ tablet streaming and online video now account for nearly one-quarter of total monthly video consumption. And last year, for the first time in two decades, the number of homes in the U.S. with TV sets dropped. Cord-cutting? This heralds the rise of a demographic that may never pay for a cable subscription – or so much as own a TV set – in the first place.[52]

The *Wall Street Journal* provided further insight into the growing cord-cutting trend when it noted rapid growth in the sales of television antennas. The company Antennas Direct was on track to double its 2011 sale of about 600,000 units. Using these antennas, consumers can access free television channels over the air. According to the company's customer survey, "the typical customer saves $96 a month by 'cutting the cord' on cable or satellite TV."[53] By May 2012 the demand for antennas was so great that Walmart began carrying two models in their US stores. Indicative of the impact that cord-cutting is having, a media market sector report published in *Barron's* lowered the outlook for Viacom "on an uptick in basic cord cutting" and lowered Time Warner's "because of continuing negative cord-cutting trends for premium-pay TV networks, where HBO is the dominant player."[54]

The industry is aware of the growing legions of cord cutters. Alisa Perren notes that anxiety over cord-cutting has led the cable industry to "heighten its call for authentication – in other words, to demand that consumers prove they subscribe to cable before they can gain access to programming online."[55] The problem with this plan, spearheaded by Time Warner under the moniker "TV Everywhere," is twofold. Any content that is digital can easily be pirated and any attempt to use technology to protect content online is inevitably circumvented by a global army of hackers. So there is reason to remain sceptical. Why would the television industry's authentication schemes be any more successful than the music industry's attempt to stop digital piracy through digital locks and other digital rights management technologies?[56] Speaking at the Variety Entertainment and Technology Summit in 2013, television executive Mark Greenberg called upon the industry to be "honest" and recognize that the main industry initiative for defeating cord-cutting, known as TV Everywhere, "has been a complete failure."[57]

HBO Go, which requires a cable subscription, provides an example of the limits to subscriber authentication schemes such as TV Everywhere as a method of controlling content and audiences. Perhaps as a result of HBO Go's restrictive cable subscription model, the popular HBO series *Game of Thrones* is also the most pirated television show thus far in the Internet's history, with over 25 million illegal downloads.[58] In just one day in 2013 over 1 million Internet users illegally downloaded the season finale. It is noteworthy that even with its record-setting level of piracy *Game of Thrones* also set a record for the highest DVD sales of an HBO series. The show's director, David Petraca, argued that the illegal downloads do not matter because television shows depend upon "cultural buzz" that piracy helps to generate.[59]

The Life of a Cord Cutter

In 2006 Dan Reimold, journalism professor at the University of Tampa, "cut" his cable cord and he has never looked back. Reimold is not living some fringe lifestyle devoid of television viewing. "I have a 42 inch flat screen. I watch TV all the time. I just don't watch regularly scheduled, commercially interrupted, monthly bill-required network and cable programming," he says.[60] What he does not do is this – he does not pay for television, at least not directly. He watches the New York Knicks games, presidential debates, movies, television shows, and other programming through free online streaming services and illegal downloading sites.

Reimold does not use any of the legal online substitutes for cable television such as Netflix, iTunes, Blockbuster, Hulu, and PlayOn. "Instead, some of us revel in the freedom and free price tag of less-than-legal downloading services and streaming sites," he admits.[61] Note that Reimold describes the experience of the cord-cutting online pirate in terms of not only "free" but also "freedom." From the remote control to cord-cutting and digital piracy, the audience has sought to escape the control of the television industry.

Reimold relates a number of lessons he has learned as a television-addicted cord cutter. Almost anyone can do it, but it takes time: "It took a day to figure out, a few months and lots of experimenting to master, and a year to feel like an expert." Downloading content (usually synonymous with pirating) delivers better quality than streaming content. Cord-cutting changes one's viewing habits. Fall premieres and the arrival of new episodes are no longer the highlight of the online viewer's life. "I am most excited when the shows' seasons end. Almost immediately, I download the entire season and watch the episodes straight through in a relatively short time."[62] Reimold's viewing is no longer directed by the prime-time schedule. Instead, he watches all the available episodes of a show and then moves on to the next show.

Cord-cutting requires effort to initiate and ongoing effort to maintain as a viewing lifestyle. Reimold describes his viewing experience as shifting from passive (turning on the television and being guided by the scheduled shows) to active (hunting online for shows, planning ahead and downloading overnight, noting the time of upcoming events like college basketball on his iPhone calendar so that he will not miss the real-time online stream). "The closest I come to channel surfing is Web searching. For example, a few months ago, I typed 'PBS' into a streaming site's search engine. Within seconds, I had a week's worth of documentaries and specials to watch."[63]

The life of a cord cutter is not perfect. Online streams fail. Illegal copies of movies have corrupted files, free streaming services are filled with advertisements, and the Web is filled with viruses. But in the end Reimold has not left mainstream popular culture behind. He has never felt "out of the loop" when it comes to discussing must-watch television. Oddly enough, the one category of viewing where he does feel left behind is commercials: "My students or friends will occasionally reference a new, hot commercial making the rounds on prime-time and I will have no clue what they are talking about. I used to jump onto YouTube to play catch-up, but over time I've made peace with my mostly commercial-free existence."[64] Reimold represents a new norm, a remarkable new pattern of audience behaviour rife with consequences for the television and cable industry. It is a pattern of audience behaviour that will be shared, in varying degrees, by an increasing number of North American households.

When PBS published Reimold's account of his experience as a cord cutter and a digital pirate, online readers engaged in a debate over the morality of illegal downloading. PBS redacted the article and removed links to torrent sites that facilitate illegal downloading. Jamie Allyant replied to the article with the comment, "PBS is not only right to publish this perspective, it is *needed*. For a comprehensive glimpse at cord cutting, the 'non-Netflix way' has to be addressed – ignoring it is irresponsible. It's how many of us watch TV nowadays."[65] One gets the feeling that the television industry is either ignoring the phenomenon or actively trying to wish it away.

Cord Nevers

A senior executive in the cable industry suggests that cord cutters may be the least of the television industry's concerns: "My biggest fear would be not so much people cutting the cord, but the younger generation coming up and never buying into [paid television services]."[66] In late 2011 media analyst Stefan Anninger coined the phrase "cord nevers" to describe the way teenagers presented a future even more frightening to the cable and television industry than hordes of cord cutters. Anninger saw the teenagers as "cord nevers" in the following terms: "They are growing up in an Internet-based video culture in which the mantras of 'why would I pay for TV?,' 'pay TV is a rip-off' and, 'I can find that for free on the web' are getting louder. We fear that some of these consumers will find pay TV far less relevant to their lives than do today's adults."[67]

Cord nevers are young Internet users who are growing up accustomed to pirating much of their entertainment needs from the Internet and who may never be converted to paying for television in any form. This new audience behaviour was captured in a comment on a news article about Canadian cord cutters:

> People under the age of 30 are, in large and increasing numbers, staying away from cable and satellite TV completely. Just as the bulk of people in this group shun telephone land lines, they are opting to stay away from the restrictive options cable/satellite offer. They prefer the freedom of movement afforded by laptops, iPads and the like. Being tied to a cord is losing favour at a much higher rate than this story is suggesting.[68]

Industry statistics may not be capturing the full extent of online audience behaviour.

Although cord cutters and cord nevers may never be more than a minority of the population they still represent a very real concern to a market for multichannel video service (cable television) that is mature. A mature market such as the television industry has very little room for growth. Thus we find the television industry's flagship magazine, *Variety*, warning its readers, "Households that want television already have it, and some TV execs worry that an increasing portion of the U.S. population may never want it."[69] People are changing their television viewing behaviour for a variety of reasons. Economic hardship, a willingness to pirate, and Internet streaming services such as Netflix are all said to be drawing subscribers away from traditional subscription models offered by incumbent players. These are forces that are creating a new norm among the younger audience. "Younger generations, who have approached television and technology in general with very different expectations than their predecessors, have introduced new norms of use," suggests Lotz.[70] After moving out of the dorm at Syracuse

University, 25-year-old Jordan Geddis decided not to get her own cable TV subscription. She gets all she needs online: "I can't imagine ever again being interested in cable TV."[71] Geddis is representative of one new norm.

Cord nevers live without cable TV, buy entertainment from online sources such as Apple's iTunes, frequently engage in piracy to get what they want from the Internet, and can't imagine ever needing a cable TV subscription. The Internet is overflowing with anecdotal evidence of this new generation of viewers. "I got rid of my cable service more than three years ago because all the shows I like are free, without commercials, and streaming on the Internet. I know that it is wrong but I don't care! 50, 60, 70 dollars a month for 60 channels of garbage," says one anonymous Net citizen.[72]

Rob Frieden, professor of telecommunications and law at Penn State University, describes the situation in the following terms: "The urge to 'cut the cord' and lower one's cable or satellite bill will become more compelling as new access opportunities develop and proliferate, even if they require payment."[73] The proliferation of viewing options, many of which do not involve a traditional television subscription, is changing people's behaviour and their expectations. The most influential shift may be the expectation to get television for free.

Ad Age magazine declared that the "cord nevers" demographic segment was "TV's Scariest Generation."[74] The appearance of TV's scariest generation was heralded by reports that the cable and satellite TV industry experienced its single largest decline in subscribers (580,000 in mid-2011).[75] Movie rental chains such as Blockbuster are facing bankruptcy. DVD sales are on a multi-year-long decline. Movie attendance in American theatres hit a 16-year low in 2011.[76] The signs of dramatic changes in media consumption are everywhere.

When Rebecca Greenfield conducted an informal survey at the offices of the *Atlantic* magazine she discovered that almost 43 per cent of her co-workers were cord nevers – they had never paid for a cable television subscription.[77] How big this segment of the Internet population will become is impossible to say at the moment. One industry report from November 2012 found that 13 per cent of US households who have broadband services did not have pay-TV.[78] Within this group of households that have broadband Internet, 2.6 million have never paid for any form of traditional television. These cord nevers are "disproportionately millennial" – 29 per cent are between 18 and 24. This trend led *Time* magazine to declare that "a new generation is coming of age, and so is their collective distaste for cable."[79] It is widely reported in the press that within the television industry the "prevailing ideology" is that when millennials "settle down and find jobs with more normal hours, they'll purchase cable subscriptions."[80] It remains to be seen if the Internet is not working in the opposite direction and socializing a new generation accustomed to digital plenitude (a greater number of affordable online alternatives such as Netflix) and highly allergic to cable bills that are edging towards $200 per month.

Industry analysts recognize the existence of a new pattern of audience behaviour that could create the scariest generation of television viewers. The changing patterns of viewing among TV's scariest generation are influenced by the ethic of online piracy. Digital piracy, digital plenitude, cord cutters, cord nevers, overpriced cable services, low-quality content sold in bundled subscription packages, and an industry that appears to be blissfully unaware of the real world of the online audience have combined to make a perfect storm, a disruptive gale blowing us into a post-television future.

From New Technology to New Values

Writing in the *Philadelphia* magazine Michael Callahan related to his readers what he thought was a new attitude towards television. While at the type of party executive editors and regular contributors to *Vanity Fair* tend to attend, Callahan overheard guests talking about television. During the conversation he observed how "watching television – or, more accurately, *admitting* that you are watching television – has become so very passé." As he nibbled on "gâteau de savoie and sipped the hosts' excellent wine," he overheard comments such as "Television bores me to tears," "David and I just had the cable disconnected, because we realized we weren't ever turning it on," and "I am just *soooo* busy – I only *wish* I could be one of those people who can hit the couch and watch TV!"[81] It is hardly new to hear certain types of people disavow television or regard it as something less than worthy of one's time, but perhaps something different from the familiar highbrow disdain of popular pleasures is afoot.

Callahan was not merely witnessing a drawing room drama centred on the display of high-culture tastes. He felt that he was listening to a "bragging contest over who can unplug the fastest," which has its roots in a "moral superiority complex." For Callahan this shift in values has something to do with deep cultural change: "While there is indeed evidence that TV viewing is on the decline – viewership of network programming among 18-to-49-year-olds, the coveted advertising demographic, plunged nine percent last year – I think the shift is more cultural than that. Not watching television has taken on the same currency as buying a hybrid or going gluten-free: *See? I'm better than you.*"[82] It takes more than one cocktail party to prove a deep cultural change in values, but the new media tsunami that has flooded all aspects of our lives has brought with it various shifts in values. The mass participation in digital piracy is suggestive of just such a shift. From sexting to conversations interrupted by cell phones to a general willingness to discuss our latest medical procedure on Facebook, indications of shifting values are all around us.

New Audiences, New Values

Watching online television reflects new values and attitudes. There is over half a century's worth of studies that explore the values and attitudes of the television audience but very little has been written about those of the cord cutters, cord nevers, television pirates, and other members of television's scariest generation. The following explores what the online audience thinks about television and the cable industry, investigates their motives for cutting the cord or never connecting the cable cord, and surveys the values that stand behind their peculiar actions.

A Difficult Beginning

Cord cutters readily admit that it takes effort to learn new television viewing habits. Eric Zimmett, a 2008 Penn State University journalism graduate, relates how "two years ago this month, I cut cable and moved into the streaming TV world, which at first was a bit rocky, but is now a more intuitive TV experience than ever."[83] This appears to be a common experience of the cord cutter – initially a difficult adjustment to new habits but eventually easy and intuitive.

Contested Narratives

The online audience is quick to contest the claims of television executives regarding the cord-cutting experience. In a *Globe and Mail* article David Purdy, vice president of video products for Rogers Communications, dismissed cord-cutting as a threat: "There's always going to be a small percentage of the market that is willing to go to great lengths not to pay for their TV signals."[84] One online reader replied, "Great lengths? Picking up a telephone and cancelling TV cable a few years ago took me less than three minutes. No problem whatsoever for me to click on bookmark links on my 24 inch iMac and watch TV and movies from all over the world now, Mr. Purdy."[85]

Freedom

Freedom is a key theme in the discourse of cord-cutting – freedom from paying and freedom from restrictive choices. Mark William Kennedy speaks of his experience in Norway: "I watch what I want when I want and for free. I also have my free over the air digital and free satellite stations (more than 50). So again, why would I want to pay for anything other than the basic Internet? It's very economical and not at all restrictive."[86]

Desire to De-bundle

The vast majority of the television audience pays for more channels than they actually watch. The standard industry practice known as bundling has consumers paying for a group of channels. Scholars have noted that "bundling requires consumers to purchase products in which they have little interest" and this reality has not been lost on consumers.[87] Bundling is very lucrative to the industry and the television lobby has resisted all efforts to de-bundle billing practices. Bundling usually occurs in oligopolistic markets such as the cable industry and serves to maximize profits at the expense of consumers.[88] A recent survey found that 92 per cent of consumers "want some type of à la carte programming offering from their multichannel service providers, but they're not willing to pay much for it."[89] There is no mystery as to why such a high level of consumer demand has gone unmet. RBC Capital Markets estimates that the American television industry stands to lose half of their subscription revenue if all 100 million multichannel television homes made the switch to à la carte services.[90] No wonder cable cutters frequently cite bundling as one of the reasons they cut the cord.

Payback

There is no love lost between cord cutters and the television industry. One gets the sense that after years of poor service and high fees the online audience looks forward to the industry getting its comeuppance. An anonymous Canadian writes, "I would LOVE in my lifetime to see Rogers and Bell out of business or in serious trouble. I really do not like the way media monopolies are allowed by our 'small government' Harper government these days."[91]

Evangelists

In almost every online discussion about cord-cutting there exists a theme of helpfulness. People share technical knowledge, describe various ways of getting free over-the-air television signals, and share links to legal and illegal online television and movie sources. For example, JimmyK wrote, "I am also thinking of cutting that cord. Sports held me back before, but now that all my teams totally suck, it's no longer a concern. I will miss the cable news networks however, such as CNBC," and received seven replies that told him where to get CNBC free online. JimmyK replied, "Just what I needed. I'm going to have a very enjoyable conversation with Rogers first thing tomorrow morning."[92] Cord cutters are effective promoters of cord-cutting.

Moral Justification

Cable cutters often rely on illegal downloading, illegal video streams, and satellite piracy to see all their shows. Their discourse reveals a sense of moral justification as cable companies are seen as greedy and stealing from customers. One cable cutter and satellite pirate writes,

> I would not mind paying if I have ability to pick and choose. But in order to get what I want to see I have to take a full package and then filter 70% out because I don't want [all the] channels included. Why do I have to pay $130 or more for maybe 30 channels? Is that stealing too or this is OK because big companies are involved? I canceled my cable a few months ago because my bill went from $98 to $135 plus tax and a few channels that I had before disappeared because "they don't make a profit" and still my price went up. That's not stealing?[93]

Of course, it is hardly surprising that the online audience is able to express moral justification for their piracy habits when there is a global debate about the greed of corporations and the 1 per cent who control the majority of the world's wealth.

The Sports Problem

Cable cutters both bemoan the lack of online sports and celebrate the amount of free sports programming. Cable cutters often supplement their Internet content with free over-the-air (OTA) television signals that they pick up with the help of an inexpensive antenna. For example, peekaboo from Toronto writes,

> As a sports fan hooked on cable for decades, I too thought I would regret cutting the cord in favor of OTA. Well I have been cable free for three years now and although I initially had some regrets on losing the premium sports channels, I have found that I actually watch TV more intently rather than channel surfing endlessly through countless useless channels that typically rehash the same content from one channel to the next, or replay the same mind-numbing reality show over and over.
>
> [using free OTA television] I get NHL Hockey on CBC and NBC, College Basketball on CBS, NBA on ABC, US football on NBC, CBS, and FOX, the latter without the CRTC's mandated simultaneous substitution rule. True I do not get Raptors or Blue Jay games anymore as they are no longer available OTA, but I gave up on these teams anyway. Saving $50 per month and getting as clear or clearer high definition picture quality legally without monthly bills, compared to the cable guy, seals the deal. Adios cable guy![94]

As discussed in chapter 3, many cable subscribers will not cut the cord until they can get all the sports they want via the Internet: "The only reason I still pay for my TV subscription is for live sporting events."[95] For those sport fans who do cut the cord, sometimes the need to see particular games diminishes and they adapt by watching a different selection of games. One Canadian explains how he adapted after cutting the cable.

> At first I missed CFL, MLS, and NHL games but then it occurred to me, these leagues and teams have turned their back on me. Screw 'em. I no longer pay to attend the live games; I never signed up for their specialty channels when I had cable. I don't buy their merchandise and I'm better for it ... I have started watching [American] games. The picture quality is insane, and the bands help me doze off.[96]

Avoiding Advertising

Cable cutters are a technologically adept segment of the online audience. This audience segment often takes steps to avoid online advertising while streaming television and movies. Thus one cable cutter recommends using "Firefox with Adblock software. Then you don't see any ads even in feeds direct from places like ComedyCentral."[97] After reading about Adblock I installed it on my Firefox browser, which took less than a minute to do, and it immediately transformed my Internet experience.

Some cable cutters are motivated to drop their pay-TV subscriptions because they feel that there are too many advertisements: "After 12 years of paying for TV, I finally cut the cord. The final straw for me was the distracting popups shown at the bottom of the screen in the middle of the shows. I mean really, think about. You are paying for the 'privilege' of being subjected to insistent advertising. How ridiculous is that? My average bill was around $100 month. That's over $12,000 a decade!"[98] Another cable cutter who watches television in the middle of the night writes, "I dumped cable not only because the price kept going up, I dumped it the minute I realized they were asking me to pay to watch commercials (infomercials) rather than entertainment shows during the hours I was most likely to watch ... when most of the channels of expensive extended cable are nothing but ads on the late night, why the heck should I keep paying more for less?"[99] A viewer from the United Kingdom also found the advertising to be too much to put up with:

> I stopped watching broadcast TV except on the BBC in the UK because there were too many ads (I then stopped watching the BBC channels, because iPlayer is a more convenient way of getting at the same content). When I tried watching TV in the USA, I was amazed anyone put up with it. You had at least twice as many ads as we did when it passed my tolerance threshold. I don't have a TV anymore, and I watch a lot more TV shows than I did back when I had one. Between iPlayer and DVD rentals, there's a lot of enjoyable content, and I know that if I sit down to watch a TV show for an hour then I will get an hour of entertainment, not 45 minutes of entertainment and 15 minutes of being annoyed.[100]

Advertising follows content and some members of the online audience find that certain types of content have too much advertising.

Another cable cutter relates how he grew tired of seeing advertising on television and cut the cable in 2009. He then used Hulu on the Internet to watch television.

> The first week of watching Hulu, I had to watch 15 seconds of commercial per half-hour show. I could tolerate that, so I was fairly happy. In week two, I had to watch one 30-second commercial per half-hour show; which was starting to annoy me, but which was just barely tolerable. In week three, Hulu started showing two or three 30-second commercials per half hour show.
>
> Seeing where this was ultimately headed, I stopped watching Hulu and subscribed to Netflix instead. That hit the perfect sweet spot, so that's where I stayed. Even Netflix's recent price increases (due to greedy studios raising what they charge Netflix) are way, way better than watching even one commercial on Hulu (which is run by the same TV people who flooded us with commercials to begin with). If the time ever comes where Netflix streaming has even one commercial, I'll cancel my Netflix subscription too.[101]

This viewer's experience of too many advertisements on subscription-based television is shared by others: "Hulu pisses me off because even if you pay for Hulu Plus you still get increasingly more commercials (seriously, they started with just a couple of commercials per show, now they rival over the air amounts)."[102] Paying for Hulu Plus and then being forced to watch numerous commercials is a common complaint among Hulu subscribers.

Consider the comment made by Craig Ott in response to an article about cable television and advertising in the *Wall Street Journal*:

> You would think that television networks would have figured it out by now. More and more of us simply will not waste an hour of our lives in order to watch 40 minutes of programming and 20 minutes of commercials. Aside from news and weather, I no longer watch any television with commercials; I haven't for several years. I would rather wait for the series I do like to be released on DVD or Netflix than have to put up with commercials. And I am not alone. Increasingly my friends and co-workers are telling me they are doing likewise. The networks have only themselves to blame, they forgot who the customer is and why we watch television. (Hint: It's not to watch commercials.)[103]

Most online news readers such as Craig Ott are also online television viewers, so they cannot be said to be universally representative of the television audience. Nevertheless, surely they are representative of something that should terrify the television industry. People are not simply moving online to watch the same television content in the same fashion. They are tailoring their viewing experience and jettisoning the elements that they despise. Few things are more despised than commercials and bad programming. If the advertising industry is hoping that the online audience will be more inclined to watch advertisements, they are in for a disappointment.[104]

Jeff Gaspin, former head of entertainment at NBC, is an example of the advertising-avoiding post-television audience. When he and his 13-year-old son watched *The Walking Dead* television series Gaspin used a variety of options including Netflix, iTunes, and the family DVR. "We learned a new behavior," Gaspin told the *New York Times*. Journalist Bill Carter relates how Gaspin and his son encountered the season's finale: "'We watched that live,' he said. 'It was not nearly as good. The commercials broke the tension. We had watched the other episodes with blankets over our heads. I hate to say this to the AMC executives and everybody else in the business, but I will never watch "Walking Dead" live again.'"[105] Gaspin found the OTT experience of online television viewing to be more convenient (he could watch it on his schedule, not the broadcaster's) and more emotionally compelling because of the absence of advertising. When he and his son returned to the fold of broadcast television to watch the season's finale, they found that the constant interruption from advertising ruined the viewing experience.

After Gaspin's story appeared in the *New York Times* Matthew Moskovciak wrote, "That's exactly the same experience I've had as a cord-cutter. The 100% commercial-free experience particularly lends itself to high quality cable shows like 'Mad Men', which I can't imagine watching with commercial breaks. Sure, I'll end up spending around $37 to watch the series via Amazon Instant in HD over its two-and-a-half month run, but it's well worth it, considering I'm still saving on cable and getting a better experience. Not to mention the fact that I own the shows and can rewatch them whenever I'd like."[106]

Online viewers may become so accustomed to not being interrupted by advertising that this ad-free experience eventually defines mainstream experience. The opposite may occur as online viewers are put in a position of being forced to watch more commercials. One cord cutter described her experience of advertising-free viewing in terms that should cause terror in the advertising industry: "I have kids and am lucky to watch an hour of TV a week. However, I did cancel my cable about a year ago and stream Netflix. My favorite aspect of this is that my four year old can watch what she wants and I don't have to hear her holler, 'I WANT THAT!' during every commercial."[107] Given that the primary economic function of television is the management of consumption, any interruption of television's ability to socialize wants represents a threat to the dominant economic system.

Rising Costs

Cord cutters frequently cite rising cable costs as a motive for cancelling their subscription. Keith Townsend, a blogger and self-described geek living in Lanham, Maryland, saw his cable bill increase one time too many.

> A little over 3 weeks ago I received my latest Comcast bill. I was shocked that the price had gone up yet again. This was the last straw for my wife who is a diehard cable user. She gave me the OK to cut the cord. I wasted no time in calling Comcast and scaling back to Internet only. I brought a Roku box, an Apple TV for my wife and subscribed to Netflix and Hulu Plus. My daughter is already a rabid streamer.[108]

Cable cutters often give a complex set of economic reasons for cancelling their television subscriptions and resorting to piracy. One cable cutter speaks of cable as costing too much, the greed of cable companies, paying "to be advertised to," and paying for unwanted channels.[109] Another complains of being forced to pay for multiple cable boxes in a household.[110]

Bandwidth Usage and Data Caps

Most Internet service providers (ISPs) impose data caps on subscribers. If an individual goes over a fixed amount of bandwidth usage they are billed extra. This is consequential for cord cutters as video streaming and downloading television shows and movies leads to more bandwidth usage. As recently as 2012 scholars noted that "relatively little work" among academics had considered the implications of usage-based pricing on the online television audience.[111]

One Canadian cord cutter found that his household rarely exceeded its ISP's bandwidth cap: "Canadian Internet services are good enough for casual mainstream TV watching, and even relatively heavy Internet usage, and as such should not prevent Canadians from shifting to on-line based TV and dropping their (expensive) cable TV subscriptions."[112] Barb Gonzalez, an American cord cutter, tells a different story: "Since I cancelled cable, I've had two months where my overages alone cost more than $200."[113] Another American cord cutter and Comcast Internet subscriber relates how he "finally logged in to the [Comcast] website and was a little shocked. I had been using an average of 100GB prior to cutting the cord and had a whopping 350 GB of usage last month. I'm already 100GB into my cap 10 days in."[114] Data caps may keep many viewers tethered to cable television.

Collusion

Cable cutters complain about what scholars have called regulatory capture. Regulatory agencies such as the CRTC and the FCC are mandated to act in the public interest but often behave as agents of corporate interests and guardians of media oligopolies. Canadian paulinwaterloo writes, "The CRTC has been for years in the pockets of the Bell, Rogers and Shaw empires and has clearly attempted to force all Canadians to sign up for these companies' offerings ... send a message to this industry-controlled puppet, the CRTC, and to our government who, in this case, are clearly not acting in Canadians' interests."[115] The online audience evinces a high level of awareness about the political economy of television.

What about the Children?

In some cases cord-cutting weans children off the television habit. Bobo Macoute writes, "I cut the cord 5 years ago. I have a great Panasonic Viera hooked up to Apple TV and a Blue Ray [*sic*]. My kid has an Xbox. If I watch TV it will be through an antenna, but I don't miss TV one bit, and I made my living in TV production since the early 80's. I'd be very worried if I was a broadcaster as my kids couldn't care less about TV."[116] This prompted a reply from canuck lefty: "I agree. My daughter is 22 years old, and she has no interest in cable. She and all of her friends watch all of the shows that they are interested in online. It's a new generation, and if the cable and satellite companies don't come up with a new model, they are going to miss the boat."[117] Cinemaven also replied, saying,

> My sons are 19 and 24 and neither chose to have cable when they left home and neither have their friends. My youngest lives in student housing with 4 other people and the university has a great lower cost deal if you want cable but none of them have been interested in the two years they've been there even though they'd be sharing the cost 5 ways. They have a giant TV for gaming but that's all the use it gets. My oldest watches anything he wants to online on his schedule and so do all of his friends … my iPad has got me using Netflix and much more online content so it's hard to believe the cable providers aren't worried because if an old lady like me is considering giving up that ridiculous bill every month, that means it's hit deeper than they're saying.[118]

Obviously, the older generation is aware of substantial changes in the viewing patterns of the young.

Alternative Content

Cord-cutting brings the online television audience closer to content that does not derive from the traditional television industry. Trevor Pott described how his cord-cutting led to him supporting "technology democratised content creation." Pott here refers to new modes of content creation such as crowdsourced productions. Pott donated money "to help crowdsource the creation of content I love such as *Sex after Kids*." Television content must now compete against a vast army of independent (indie) film-makers who use the Internet to distribute their films, often for free. Pott cites this online indie phenomenon as bearing "more blame for my cord-cutting than piracy ever will. The Internet gives indie artists the ability to distribute their works without having to fight the media giants for shelf space at the local box store."[119]

A Media Storm with a Centre?

While cord-cutting is usually seen to be confined to the young, this new audience trend extends well beyond cash-strapped university students and young people just entering the workforce. Cable cutters come from all walks of life, but there is a curious pattern of workers in the media industry who cut the cord. Consider how professional film-maker Morgan Spurlock notes that "a lot of friends of mine have already started to give up their cable subscriptions."[120] Dianne Nice, community editor for the *Globe and Mail*'s "Report on Business," also cut the television cord, subscribed to Netflix, and "told our TV company to shove off." Nice's family saves $1,020 in annual cable costs and no longer rents movies or watches commercials: "I no longer have to worry about my kids being influenced by TV ads. That's a savings I can't put a price on." In a trend also common among cord cutters, Nice found that her family's media consumption habits changed: "We've discovered we don't miss traditional TV fare and spend more time reading books in the evening rather than mindlessly flipping through channels."[121] It remains to be seen just how much disruption cord cutters create but the ingredients for trouble are all here: money saving, advertising avoiding, book reading – these are not the habits the television industry seeks to inspire.

The American writer Michael Wolff described his cord-cutting experience in *GQ Magazine*:

> I no longer have a television. I am box, satellite and cable free (I get my Internet access through a cable provider, but it provides me bandwidth, not content). A lot of content is available through a Google search. I filter what I want to see through friends, word of mouth and, increasingly, Twitter, and then watch it when I want to through a still-somewhat-cumbersome but effective process. I first check for free streaming on Netflix, then, if not available, go to a pay-per-view option on Amazon or iTunes. If not available there (that is, if content providers have not yet licensed them for à la carte sales), I go to a pirate site. The second season of *Downton Abbey* was a big event in America. But I was well into the series through an easily available pirate site.[122]

It would not be surprising if media professionals and content industry workers were at the centre of a change in media consumption habits that is rippling outwards through society. Among my own small circle of friends, two families have cut the cord – and both belong to the media industry, a journalist and a video editor. Journalists, professors, young adults working for cable companies, editors, film-makers – all have two things in common: the media industry and the cord-cutting habit.

No Regrets

It is quite common to see cord cutters say that they have not looked back since they cancelled their cable subscription. Responding to an article about cord-cutting in the *Wall Street Journal*, John Weber wrote,

"We cut the cord a while back and haven't missed it for a second. I can even watch WSJ live on my Roku if I haven't had my fill from reading the paper in the morning."[123] Likewise, John Damron replied, "We disconnected cable twenty years ago and never regretted the move."[124] Curiously, the *Wall Street Journal* article was about how cord-cutting is a "clumsy" experience that suffers from "weak content" but 11 out of 13 readers who wrote a reply contradicted the article's claims. Readers described their cord-cutting experience as "about as dead simple as you can get," "simple," involving "idiot proof devices," and, at worst, "adequate."[125]

Complicated Choices

Lotz describes the "complicated, deliberate, and individualized" nature of television viewing, a perspective captured in the experience of *Omaha World-Herald* columnist Rainbow Rowell.[126] After dropping cable television "because nobody in the house was watching it" and struggling with Netflix, Hulu, iTunes, a Wii, a DVR, passwords, surround sound, and remote control batteries, Rowell asks, "When did watching TV get this complicated?" She notes how her children think of television differently than do their parents:

> My kids treat our television like the replicator on "Star Trek" – *"We want to watch old 'Transformers' reruns. Make it so."* They think of the TV as something that gives them exactly what they want, whenever they ask for it. I think of the TV as more of a to-do list – a to-do list I can access only with a technical degree from DeVry. There's nothing spontaneous about my TV watching anymore.

Rowell finds that she has so much available to watch that she never turns on the television just to see what is on. Television has changed from a source of entertainment to a source of work and frustration: "In my house, adding a new show means going through all the services we subscribe to – Apple TV, Tivo, Netflix, Hulu Plus, Amazon, VUDU – then remembering their passwords, and then remembering which service lives in which device in our family entertainment center … Our entertainment center, in the last two years, has mutated out of our control. Too many options. Too many devices. Too much evolution, too fast. There are plenty of times when I think about watching TV and then decide that it's too much work."[127]

The television viewing experience of Rowell's family is complicated, deliberate, and individualized. It shows how the natives of the post-television generation, Rowell's children, treat television as a source of instant gratification that cannot be captured by network schedules. Cord-cutting has increased the family's choices while also increasing complexity. Multiple platforms, incompatible services, and complex interfaces render technology out of control. Yet the cable cord remained cut and the family keeps watching, even over breakfast.

It Does Not Always Work Out

When Raymond Griggs of Tampa, Florida, cut the cord, things did not work out as planned. Griggs heard from his friends how they had cut the cable and did some research. He found that he could save $80 a month so he cancelled his Verizon cable subscription, bought a Roku box, signed up for a 30-day trial of Hulu Plus, and bought an NBA League Pass for online sports viewing. The first time he tried to use his NBA League Pass to watch his team, the Miami Heat, on his laptop he found that the game was blacked out. He tried again the next night to watch another game but that too was blacked out. To solve this Griggs bought an ESPN live-stream service called PlayOn for $4.99 a month. That also did not go well: "after setting up a trial of PlayOn and getting it installed on the Roku, I navigated to ESPN and pressed play. I got to watch a screen buffer for at least 30 minutes. It was the worst experience just trying to get the game on. When it did finally work, it was almost half time. During the game it would freeze at times and buffer, I would have to back out and restart it. Really frustrating!" Griggs's experience of Hulu Plus did not fare much better. "I decided to also watch *Celebrity Apprentice* on Hulu Plus. But, when I got to the show, I see a box that says the show can only be watched on the computer. So even though I was on the Hulu Plus membership, I still had to watch it on my computer like the free membership. I again turned to PlayOn, which allows you to watch the free Hulu content on the Roku, found the show and hit play. The 1 hour show took almost 2 hours to watch. It kept buffering and freezing."[128]

Griggs described the next seven days of online television watching using a variety of legitimate paid-subscriber services as "misery." Five of the six sports games he tried to watch were blacked out, and playoffs were not included in his NBA League Pass. Griggs found online sports viewing via legitimate services to be "a mess" and Hulu Plus a "waste."[129]

In the end, Griggs called Verizon back and had his cable television re-connected. On one hand it appears that the masses are not yet ready for cutting the cable. On the other hand we find financial advisers such as the *Globe and Mail*'s Chris Umiastowski admitting that he avoids stocks such as Comcast, Time Warner Cable, and Cablevision because "it's easier than ever for people to cut the cord."[130]

The discourse of cord cutters reflects a wide range of other issues that define the common experience of the online television audience. Cord cutters often speak of benefits beyond saving money, such as discovering new shows, watching less television, and not seeing as much advertising. Cable TV viewers complain about the low quality of television content, decry the deceptive marketing practices and poor customer service of cable companies, and express a dislike of being tied to the broadcast schedule. Online discussion forums about television are also filled with debates over the ethics of piracy. The television broadcast and cable industry are often framed as acting deceptively and greedily and are seen as pirates of culture and policy. My impression after reading many such discussions is that many cable cutters do not see television piracy as unethical. This appears to be in keeping with the media culture that defines young people in particular. When over 80 per cent of young people see music piracy as acceptable, one should expect to see similar attitudes among the online television audience.[131] These attitudes may be coalescing into a lifestyle trend. Marketers of new apps that enable cord-cutting have begun to use phrases such as "the 'cord-cutting' revolution" and "a cable-free lifestyle."[132] Cord-cutting is being advertised as a value-added feature of some products. This is reminiscent of how Apple promoted the ability of some of its products to help consumers "rip, mix, and burn" media they download from the Internet.[133]

Finally, cord-cutting challenges the industry narrative of choice and freedom. Jinna Tay and Graeme Turner describe the US model of television as something that promotes a mythological perception of consumer sovereignty.[134] It is generally thought that the market, when freed from the confines of government oversight and intervention, leads to the consumer experiencing the widest possible array of choices and the greatest amount of freedom. Yet millions of consumers opting out of the cable system testify to a perceived lack of freedom and choice within the broadcast and cable system. Millions of cord cutters and cord nevers confirm Axel Bruns's suggestion that the technologies and processes of television "have now been outclassed by the Internet."[135] Even if cord cutters and cord nevers remain a fringe element of the television audience, they may nonetheless represent the beginning of "a disinter-mediation process which would see the gradual demise of broadcast transmitters and cable operators as their networks are replaced by the internet as a common communications carrier."[136] Only time will tell for certain. In May 2012 the US trade group the National Cable and Tele-communications Association launched a public relations advertising campaign that came to the defence of the cable industry.[137] The threat of cord-cutting compelled the cable industry to justify its existence. Per-haps it is best to leave the last word to Glenn Britt: "People will choose not to buy subscription video if they can get the same stuff for free."[138]

Summary

Young people are spending a whole lot of time on the Internet and with entertainment devices other than just television. The Internet is more than a new medium for television distribution. It is an alternative to the relatively passive activity of watching television. We still like to watch, but on the Internet there is much more to do and watch other than just television. This change in the media environment cuts right to the heart of the matter. The post-television world is not a world where television disappears or completely migrates online. In the post-television world, content produced by the television industry no longer dominates our visual culture. There are just far too many other types of screens out there with far too many different forms of entertainment for television to maintain the central place in our lives that it once had in the twenti-eth century.

Cancelling traditional television subscriptions, cutting the cable cord, and using the Internet for accessing television content is a trend that is growing and will continue to grow for some time to come. The post-television age begins with television literally leaving the confines of the "box" and its audience leaving the confines of the traditional market-place. The way a younger generation of viewers accesses content and watches television is radically changing. Although most of these chan-ges are still in their infancy, cord-cutting gives us reason to think that something unprecedented in the history of television is happening. The Internet has created television's scariest generation – a generation of viewers beyond the control of the incumbent industry giants, disdain-ful of copyright, enabled by digital plenitude, unwilling to pay for bun-dled content packages, and highly adept at finding alternative sources of visual entertainment.

Cord-cutting needs to be seen not as defining the inevitable future state of the audience but as something that is symptomatic of a deeper condition. The television audience now has the option of partially or completely opting out of the legitimate entertainment market. Cord-cutting demonstrates the way choice shifts in favour of the audience in the emerging post-television age. The audience now has the power to engage in do-it-yourself de-bundling. Fed up with paying too much money for too many channels they do not want to view, a growing segment of the television audience has responded by cancelling cable subscriptions and using alternative legitimate services like Hulu and Netflix to engage in à la carte viewing while supplementing these low-cost commercial services with digital piracy. A lack of choice and over-priced offerings are partial causes of cord-cutting but at its root is a much deeper change. The culture of media consumption itself changes when a generation arises that has always been able to choose what and where to view entertainment and to do so without paying for it. As is the case with digital piracy, cord-cutting is beyond the control of the industry. It may be less a price issue than an issue of never having been socialized to pay for entertainment.

The effects of cord-cutting ripple far beyond the loss of paying subscribers. Cord cutters frequently speak of their tastes changing. Viewers discover a world of alternative content, from indie films to amateur videos and crowdsourced productions. The online television audience does not care where the content comes from, as long as it is relevant and entertaining. Some cord cutters even speak of finding smarter content. Meanwhile, the television and movie industries labour under the false assumption that only they can create compelling content.

The television industry insists that it is offering consumers quality content at bargain rates, but cord cutters refer to the industry in terms of garbage, terrible customer service, greed, political collusion, and legal overreach. Cord cutters often see themselves as occupying the higher moral ground even when they are pirating content. The industry appears to be basing its business strategy on containment of audiences and content, but containment is unlikely in the leaky realm of the Internet.

Behind cord-cutting looms an even more frightful prospect for the television industry – cord nevers. Cord nevers stand as testimony to an online cultural environment that socializes mass participation in anti-market behaviour. The viewing habits of a growing segment of the online audience television have been dis-embedded from the context of market exchange and appear unlikely to be re-embedded through changes in legal regimes and technologies. This anti-market audience behaviour is one of the defining features of the post-television era.

Although many cord cutters describe their way of watching television as simple, there are numerous technical hurdles that must be crossed. Their experiences remind me of the early days of the Internet when modems and computers were a source of constant frustration to me. Who would have thought back in 1990 that such a slow, awkward, and geeky experience of amber screens and low ASCII email would grow to encompass billions of Internet users? We need to be cautious before we dismiss cord-cutting as fringe behaviour of the geeky few. That millions of people are willing to go out of their way, and sometimes go to great lengths, to cut the television cable attests to the strong desire among the audience for more control over their viewing experience. New media systems that offer more control, access to more content and more types of entertainment, lower prices, and the ability to act as a creator, producer, and distributor of content can transform entire industries. It would be remarkable if these forces failed to promote consequential change across the television and film industries.

5 Disruption: Viewing Habits of the Post-television Generation

Television viewing may have undergone more changes in the past ten years than it did over the entire twentieth century. In the twentieth century, changes to the structure of the television industry led to an expansion in content choices and more risqué sexual and violent content (think HBO). Remote controls along with VHS and DVD players failed to instigate revolutionary changes in viewing and content. Even DVRs did not lead to hugely disruptive changes in viewing patterns.[1] These technologies delivered more content from commercial and state production systems while giving the audience greater freedom as to when they could watch a show or a movie. The transformations wrought by the Internet are occurring on a much greater scale and across a wider variety of audience habits, technologies, and industry innovations. When Nielsen teamed up with Google to measure audiences, they discovered that 31 per cent of people aged 18 to 49 spend an average of 39 minutes per day watching television – far less than what is normally reported for the general population.[2] Members of this group are more likely not to subscribe to cable television. They also watch more videos on smartphones, are more likely to be heavy users of personal computers, and tend to be young, college educated, and affluent. This group is the leading edge of the post-television generation.

During almost 40 years of television watching from the 1960s to 2000, the biggest changes in my viewing habits were defined by black-and-white to colour, remote controls, and cable. I seldom used my VHS and DVD machines. None of these changes were particularly disruptive to my viewing or the industry. The viewing patterns of my generation varied little from Archie Bunker's – we sat in chairs in the living room and watched. In stark contrast, television recently spread across the landscape of everyday life and is even on our phones. Approximately 400 to 500 million video screens are scattered across the United States.[3] Television is available on many Internet-enabled devices and the variety of those screens continues to grow. Internet-enabled televisions, Blu-ray players, game consoles, eyewear, watches, and other streaming media devices are being used to access online content.[4] Video is dispersing from the television system to the Internet at a rapid pace. By 2016 the amount of video on demand moving across the Internet will be equivalent to 4 billion DVDs per month.[5] As a result of the productive activity of millions of amateur and semi-professional videographers, we are also seeing content arriving on our screens that did not originate from within the television system. The online audience is becoming accustomed to the pleasure of amateur content. Over 25 per cent of Canadians report that they find watching online videos on YouTube "more entertaining than flipping through channels and watching live TV."[6] The popularity of user-generated videos and the strong position of the US Public Broadcasting Service among the online audience is further indication that "the dominance of the big four broadcaster networks may be diminished in the online environment."[7] Television once offered the superior viewing experience but can no longer claim to do so.

The trends examined in this chapter are both very large and quite small. Streaming television shows is on its way to becoming mainstream in a media environment that sees audiences now spending more time on the Internet than in front of the television. Other viewing behaviour on platforms such as tablet computers and smartphones remains marginal but is growing at phenomenal rates. In the United States on a daily basis in 2013, a mere 7 per cent of consumers used a tablet to watch video entertainment and 12 per cent did so on smartphones (yet these numbers almost doubled from the previous year).[8] In the United Kingdom, Germany, Spain, France, and the United States 10 to 20 per cent of fans are using Internet-enabled mobile devices to consume sport content, but the penetration rates rise in China (46 per cent), Brazil (42 per cent), and Italy (26 per cent).[9] While the penetration rates of video game consoles and Internet-connected televisions are high and continuing to grow, only one-fifth of smart TV and game console owners use these devices for regular video streaming.[10] Nevertheless, very few commentators see these new forms of audience behaviour as inconsequential.

A study of online television consumption among Hungarian university students summarized the situation in terms of control: "Content is becoming increasingly independent from the platform [of the tradition-al television set] and the medium is increasingly in the hands of techno-logically empowered viewers."[11] Online television viewing behaviour includes "uncontrolled sharing" and uncontrolled online conversa-tions, leading the authors of the study to conclude that "in terms of control they [the incumbent television industry] are definitely losing weight" or influence over a "more active, even proactive" online audi-ence.[12] This loss of control is implied in the growing resistance to pay-ing for online video even as video subscription services grow. The percentage of Americans who say they are not willing to pay for a monthly online video subscription grew from 31 per cent in 2012 to 38 per cent in 2013. Likewise, the percentage of Americans who report that they watch mainly free video content grew from 60 to 64 per cent over the same period.[13] This unwillingness to pay for video content mirrors an unwillingness to pay for music and news. Billions of dollars will flow through the online video sector, just as iTunes brings in bil-lions of dollars in revenue for the music industry, but there is the pos-sibility that in the near future most viewing activity will remain outside the control of the marketplace.

Three common sources of complaints with the online viewing experi-ence are advertising, buffering or downloading wait times, and poor video quality.[14] The online audience often cites three reasons for watch-ing: to catch up on a missed television episode, to repeat a viewing, and convenience.[15] Another frequently cited reason is the desire to avoid commercials.[16] Of course, getting stuff for free is also a common motiv-ator. Studies that seek to identify motives for online video use typically find a wide variety of factors, including "timely learning, relaxing en-tertainment, boredom relief, companionship, escape and social inter-action."[17] Along with this grab bag of motives is the rather significant finding that watching online video has a "functional uniqueness" – on-line video gratifies audiences in a way that television does not.[18] As can be expected, motivations for using online video vary across culture, age, gender, and ethnicity.[19] Internet users find online television to be better than television in numerous ways, namely, "efficiency of search, interactivity, personalization, timeliness, usefulness of reviews and rat-ings, less cumbersome advertisements during viewing, instant replay, storage, and reliability."[20]

When motivations behind viewing and sharing of user-generated video content are taken into account, researchers reached the conclu-sion that television and online video "are quite different mediums."[21]

Likewise, Chuck Tryon argues that digital online delivery and mobility are creating changes that "point to a transformation of the experience and perceptions of movie and television viewers."[22] Post-television culture brings closer, more detailed monitoring of audiences as well as more personalized television viewing experiences. Time and place become less restrictive and platform mobility "offers a powerful expression of the cultural desire for a greater autonomy over when, where, how, and what we watch."[23]

It is becoming increasingly clear that the audience's experience of online video is platform-dependent.[24] Just as cinema, radio, and television delivered different audience experiences, smart televisions, smartphones, tablet computers, and desktop computers are delivering distinct audience experiences. The viewing habits of the post-television generation vary from platform to platform as different screens are used for "different styles of viewing."[25] Planned viewing occurs more frequently on large television sets while smaller, more mobile screens promote unplanned viewing. Internet-enabled televisions are the platform of choice for viewing long-form content such as movies while desktop computers and mobile devices are more likely to be used for viewing short clips and user-generated content. The availability of online content also leads to many changes in the way we view. Binge viewing, which was observed in the days of VHS and DVDs, may be on the rise as a result of the audience's access to larger catalogues of content. Nielsen reports that 88 per cent of Netflix users and 70 per cent of Hulu Plus users watch three or more episodes of the same television show in a day.[26] Seven out of ten American television viewers describe themselves as binge viewers.[27]

Viewing tends to shift between various platforms throughout the day. Online videos are frequently viewed on desktop computers during the day while audiences are at work, on regular and smart television sets during the evening, and via mobile devices while commuting.[28] Viewing videos while commuting varies according to available public transportation systems. Advanced industrial nations such as South Korea that have deployed extensive public transportation systems see greater use of mobile video than countries such as the United States, where approximately 75 per cent of commuting is done in single-occupancy cars.[29] Online video consumption is enabled and constrained by technological, structural, and cultural conditions.

Given the novelty of online and mobile viewing, these and many other observations regarding audience behaviour are bound to prove transitional and subject to qualification. Nevertheless, early studies are suggestive of current trends and avenues of further research. For example, consider a cross-cultural study that explored how Chinese and German audiences consume mobile video content. In contrast to German online audiences, Chinese users spent more time viewing videos uploaded by individual users. The study concluded that the consumption of online video is culturally inflected. Some cultures regard online video as entertainment while others see it as a serious information source.[30] Given that local culture has had a significant impact on television audiences, it stands to reason that local culture will also shape the perception and use of online video.

It remains uncertain whether online audiences consume more or less television. Some industry studies suggest that streaming services such as Netflix do not cannibalize traditional television viewing.[31] Within homes that have cut the cord, the use of a wide variety of viewing devices can lead to "markedly higher viewership hours."[32] Between 1999 and 2009 children's consumption of live broadcast television sharply declined but overall television viewing among this cohort increased significantly.[33] One of the more striking findings in an IBM study was the impact a mobile device has on television viewing: "Respondents in China, Japan and the U.S. watch substantially less regular TV as their use of mobile video increases. This trend is expected to accelerate in the other three surveyed countries as well."[34] Some viewers will watch more television as a result of the ubiquitous availability that mobile devices create and others will watch less as a result of alternative online experiences such as games. A recent study suggests that these two populations "tend to balance out" but it remains to be seen if this will hold true.[35] Industry voices such as Karen McCall, marketing manager for NBCUniversal, claim that as a result of mobile television platforms, "existing viewers will watch more TV."[36] Indeed, industry executives are united on the opinion that online viewing will enhance their hold on audiences, yet there is obvious self-interest in such a claim. In contrast to the claims of television industry executives, Nielsen reports that young US audiences aged 12 to 24 watch two-thirds the amount of traditional television of the US average.[37] Nevertheless, it is unknown if this audience segment is merely substituting one form of television access for another or actually watching less television. At this time it is far from clear what effect the Internet will have on how much television and movies audiences consume and what type of visual entertainment they will favour.

An IBM study, *Beyond Digital*, referred to the audience as "empowered ... demanding instant access to personalized content on their own terms" and at any time.[38] Consumption of digital content has moved out of the realm of early adopters and is now a mainstream behaviour.[39] This aligns with other surveys that indicate widespread consumption of online video in numerous regions. Over 71 per cent of adult Americans and 81 per cent of American parents are using the Internet to view videos.[40] One in four Canadians reports watching more online video than television programming while 16 per cent claim they watch the same amount of television as online video.[41] According to the CRTC one-third of Canadians watch online television "with the typical user watching three hours a week."[42]

A study of US college students' online video consumption highlights the continuing attraction of user-generated video and provides insight into viewing patterns that may shortly enter the mainstream. Among this audience segment, amateur videos are more commonly viewed than professionally produced content and almost 20 per cent of viewers also act as amateur content producers.[43] User-generated videos produce higher levels of satisfaction and "offer a wider selection of program genres to consumers and a more user-friendly navigation system than TV network sites."[44] Online content preferences also differ between genders, with females preferring pets, animals, dramas, and sitcoms and males preferring sports, vehicles, and late-night talk shows.[45] This suggests that online television will participate in reinforcing commercial media's representation of masculinity and femininity.

The challenge for the incumbent television industry is to channel these new behaviours into their commercial services. Not surprisingly, the industry sees the issue in terms of control. When five US industry vice presidents from HBO, Viacom, Dish, Discovery, and Comcast gathered together to discuss their online video strategies there was a conspicuous "underlying tension" between the panellists "about who, ultimately, controls the consumer experience."[46] Consumer electronics such as smartphones and tablet computers and novel modes of digital distribution have brought the issue of control to the forefront of industry conferences and strategic planning. In addition to cord-cutting and piracy, the television industry is adapting to audience trends that are driven by new media technology such as viewing on demand, distracted viewing, mobile access, and social viewing. Particular attention herein is paid to the issue of mobile televisual consumption.

Viewing on Demand

Online piracy, streaming services such as Hulu and Netflix, and sites that are home to amateur and semi-professional videos like YouTube and Vimeo have conditioned the post-television audience to expect to watch video when they demand to watch it, not when some company's schedule says they can watch. This television culture of viewing on demand and time-shifting is now normal audience behaviour.[47] The audience's expanded control over time runs up against what Mira Moshe calls "state time management," wherein the mass audience is "subject to traditional, linear, nontechnological principles" of regulatory frameworks.[48] This regulatory framework enabled the broadcast business model that still persists to this day. National regulatory frameworks developed in the twentieth-century broadcast era may not hold much sway over the behaviour of online audiences basking in the glow of international television flows.

Distracted (Multi-screen) Viewing

Smartphones, laptops, and tablet computers clutter the domestic landscape and have changed the nature of television viewing. Television still dominates our time but we are increasingly involved with other screens and other digital activities while watching.[49] The majority of online audiences divide their attention between multiple screens such as tablet computers, laptops, and smartphones while watching television.[50] This form of distracted viewing interrupts the flow of television viewing that was characteristic of the twentieth-century audience. When there are so many other, smarter screens in our lives we no longer give the "idiot box" our undivided attention. Yet there appears to be a limit to how much the audience wishes to engage in second-screen activity while watching television. As one analyst notes, "dedicated second screen apps that have built platforms around second screen activity seem to be trying different models in order to see what sticks. Overall, they've seen decent growth in audience size, but not dramatic growth. And lately it has looked flat."[51] Only 26 per cent of television programming viewed on mobile devices was from a broadcast or cable network's website or online app. As recently as 2013 almost 74 per cent of Americans who subscribed to traditional pay-TV services never purchased anything from their provider's video-on-demand catalogue.[52] This phenomenon, known in the industry as "cord cheating," speaks of the inability of the incumbent industry to meet the needs of the online audience. In other words, the incumbent television industry is having trouble corralling multi-screen viewers in their on-line corporate destinations. When it comes to who is providing the front end of online television delivery, cable and broadcast companies are being disintermediated by video subscription services that provide superior user interfaces and more content choices.[53] Not surprisingly, the television industry does not hold all the cards when trying to engin-eer the audience's online experience.

Post-television culture promotes a distracted audience that has enter-tainment options other than television immediately at hand. Data from Nielsen suggests that only 24 per cent of this distracted audience time is spent with content related to what is on television at that time. The rest of the distracted period of viewing is taken up with texting family and friends (56 per cent), visiting social networks (40 per cent), and brows-ing unrelated content (37 per cent).[54] Among sports audiences the use of a second screen during live broadcasts "often has very little to do with sports."[55] What remains certain is that the post-television audience is busy accessing the Web and each other while watching television. Hye Jin Lee and Mark Andrejevic argue that viewers who use second screens "are more likely to engage with commercial content."[56] Nonetheless, the relationship between multi-screen viewing and consumer activity can-not be reduced to a simple conquest of the audience by market forces and consumerist ideologies. There is considerable space for evasion, re-sistance, and non-market-based experiences within the evolving ecol-ogy of connected viewing.

The mobile- and second-screen experiences (which are often one and the same) highlight a contradiction between increased involvement with and distraction from commercial media. Max Dawson describes this contradiction in the following terms: "new handheld video tech-nologies can accommodate a variety of ways of engaging with the tele-vision text, including both distraction *and* attentive scrutiny."[57] Dawson also argues that all the multiple screens in the new television ecology should not be seen as "discrete, clearly defined entities, each with their own proprietary textual formats, narrative modes, visual styles, and viewing protocols" but as a totality that creates a collective aesthetic with properties which have long been central to television's formats, narratives, and styles.[58] In other words, the viewing experiences pro-moted within post-television culture are not utterly alien to Archie Bunker's children.

Across numerous industrial nations 75 per cent of adults surf the Web while watching TV.[59] According to Nielsen's data, "using a tablet or smartphone while watching TV is more common than not."[60] The Interactive Advertising Bureau (IAB) reports that 81 per cent of American viewers surf the Web and check email while watching television.[61] Among 18- to 24-year-olds a whopping 85 per cent are engaged with two screens at a time.[62] This multiple-screen viewing experience is combined with a multiple-use experience of television: "Younger consumers, those under age 25, rely on their TVs more for music, social media, going on the Web and communicating. Consumers with Internet-enabled TVs use their displays in a number of ways as well: 47 percent listen to music, 28 percent use social media, 26 percent surf the Web and 23 percent view photos."[63] In common with other studies, the IAB study also found that watching television on traditional sets declines as the number of digital devices rises in the home.[64] This does not necessarily mean that viewing hours decline with increased screens in a household. No parent will be surprised to learn that younger viewers are the most frequent users of cell phones while watching television.[65] Counter-intuitively, as the number of screens in use rises, so does advertising recall.[66] Online voting and shopping also increases among multiple-screen viewers. Multiple-screen users spend most of their mobile television viewing time watching broadcast and cable television.[67] This aligns with a study that found that users of video on demand within Flemish households "often choose to consume the same video content" as traditional television viewers.[68] Greater engagement with online shopping, commercial advertising, and normative content suggests that online audiences may suffer from the effects of deeper engagement with capitalism's ideological system. While Gerard Goggin notes that many scholars decry online television as a threat to common culture, it may be the case that it aggressively reinforces the most common of cultures – global consumer culture.[69]

The availability of multiple screens changes how any one screen captures our attention. Second screens can lure viewers away from the television (the "first" screen) for 30 per cent of the total viewing session.[70] The presence of a second screen, such as a tablet computer, decreased the average gaze length on the television. This may be why some television producers question the wisdom of facilitating second-screen experiences. Disney's digital entertainment vice president, Albert Cheng, explained that his network is rethinking the trend to complement television shows with second-screen experiences: "It's not a game that we want to be in."[71] Cheng sees the second screen as little more than a distraction for some of Disney's audiences. Likewise, the Fox News channel introduced more "breaking news" into prime-time programming in an effort to thwart digital distraction.[72] This is yet one more example of how the traditional television system is being forced to adapt to the disruptive habits of the online audience. Nonetheless, it is doubtful that we will see a general move away from industry-facilitated second-screen experiences. After all, that is where the online audience is going. We still like to watch, but television does not have the same powerful hold on our gaze that it once commanded. The audience has not left the building, but it is busy surfing the Web on laptops and tablet computers, checking Facebook, using Twitter, and texting friends about its favourite *Friends* episode.

To varying degrees multi-screen viewing is also distracted viewing and both can be mobile viewing. More than anything else, the audience of commercial television is supposed to pay attention to commercials. When it comes to the online audience's Twitter activity, as much as 30 per cent takes place during commercial breaks.[73] The use of Twitter rises in direct correlation to the number of commercial breaks. This type of audience behaviour may be indicative of an audience segment that has the attention span of a three-year-old on a sugar high. Here again we encounter contradictory effects; 38 per cent of mobile phone users use their phone to keep themselves busy during commercials, yet 35 per cent of mobile phone users will visit a website that was mentioned on television.[74] Thus distracted viewing both pulls us away and drives us to the marketplace – the intended destination of the commercial television system.

Mobile Access

By the end of 2018 there will be over 4.5 billion smartphone subscriptions in the world.[75] The number of mobile-connected devices now exceeds the number of people on earth.[76] Devices that facilitate mobile television viewing are some of the fastest-growing consumer electronics. In 2013 the amount of video watched on mobile devices such as tablets and smartphones doubled over the previous year.[77] By 2014 the mobile phone became the second most popular venue for watching television in America.[78] Mobile television occurs on far more than just smartphones and tablets and can be found on many different types of Internet-enabled mobile devices and *in* mobile devices such as cars and airplanes. Cisco Systems predicts that mobile video traffic will account for over 66 per cent of total mobile data traffic by 2017.[79] Smartphones alone have created a mobile video audience of approximately 240 million people worldwide, including 90 million Americans, using these new portable screens.[80] In Canada 33 per cent of smartphone owners and over 50 per cent of tablet owners are using their mobile devices to view online video.[81] North American audiences are now spending as much time using Internet-connected mobile devices as they are on more traditional online devices such as desktop and laptop computers.[82] These developments have led scholars such as Jason Farman to suggest that soon the "main medium people will use to access the Internet will be mobile."[83] The rapid deployment of auxiliary mobile screens combined with a noted impulse among some tablet owners to watch television online and cut the cable cord could equal one more force that spins audiences and content out of control.[84]

The rapid adoption of smartphones and the increasing bandwidth of high-speed wireless services are promoting mobile television consumption. The use of mobile devices for viewing television is not entirely new, as can be seen by advertisements promoting portable television sets in the 1960s. Nevertheless, it was not until the arrival of high-bandwidth Internet connectivity that we saw the mass adoption of phones and computers as mobile television platforms. The significance of mobile television has been described in terms of the facilitation of personal experiences and is not necessarily driven by a perceived need for mobility itself.[85]

With over 5 billion people now using mobile communication technology, we have entered an age wherein the individual experiences dramatically increased powers of global communication, production, and dissemination. James E. Katz sees these new powers of mobile audiences, consumers, and citizens as having the potential to "re-make the world."[86] Certainly, they are shaking the foundations of the television and entertainment industries. Mobile devices account for 40 per cent of views on YouTube. The growth in mobile video is so strong that Robert Kyncl, head of content for YouTube, believes that smartphones and tablet devices are becoming "the first screen, so when you talk about second screen, you are talking about the television."[87] Of course, this claim may prove to be more hype than insight.

Viewing television on mobile devices is still a novel activity, but using a mobile device is almost universal in a world of smartphones, portable video games, laptops, eReaders, and iPads.[88] These wireless consumer electronics are so popular that we are beginning to hear speculation about a post-PC era.[89] In 2013 the sales of tablet computers grew by 83 per cent while personal computer sales fell by 13 per cent.[90] The technology of television sets is also rapidly changing. The majority of new televisions are Internet-enabled and include Wi-Fi. Soon many new television screens also will include motion, gesture, or voice controls.[91]

All in all, "over one billion internet-enabled devices will be sold globally with less than one third of those devices being laptop or desktop computers."[92] The key point here is that a significant percentage of those 1 billion purchases – devices such as smartphones, tablets, game consoles, and Internet-enabled television – are the very things that enable disruptive patterns of television viewing. Hundreds of millions of consumers are buying devices that change the way they watch television.

Surprisingly, 52 per cent of smartphone video is viewed while at home. This viewing habit peaks between 8 and 11 p.m. Also counterintuitively, watching complete movies and television shows "now accounts for nearly 40% of smartphone video viewing every week ... videos lasting longer than 10 minutes accounted for half the total time folks spent watching online video."[93] Andy Forssell, senior vice president of content at Hulu, suggests, "I think you are seeing the U.S. start to edge toward something like the Japanese situation where you have kids watching a movie on a smartphone 10 feet from a 60-inch TV."[94] For the post-television generation bigger is not always better. Also surprising, mobile video consumers are less concerned about video quality than speed of delivery.[95]

The mobile television sector has a long history of commercial failures. The Italian mobile television marketplace faced failure in 2010. In this instance consumers were obliged to buy a new mobile device to access a small number of television channels and the telecom company used a technology that also has proven to be problematic in other regions.[96] Commercial success is not a foregone conclusion. An analysis of the market for the delivery of mobile sport content in Western Europe further highlights the difficulties that certain markets and regions face: "competing standards, high data costs, absence of insight into consumer demands and bargaining stakeholder power are carried as explanations for the slow market development of mobile television."[97] The shift to mobile Internet use will prove to be very disruptive to current business models in the media sector. Publishers and advertisers are reporting that advertising on mobile platforms generates "as little as one-tenth the revenue compared with desktop publishing."[98] This does not bode well for the television sector.

Yet to be seen is the type of economic model that will dominate the emerging mobile video ecology and if any one model will suit all regions and content types. Nonetheless, regardless of initial market failures in the early twenty-first century, there is little doubt that we are witnessing the "second coming of mobile television" as Gerard Goggin suggests.[99] What form this second coming will take remains uncertain. Even as Goggin draws our attention to the revival of mobile television, he also cautions against getting caught up in the hype generated by major industry players because of the "paradox of mobile TV: namely, it looks exciting, but the results so far are uninspiring."[100] Likewise, Goggin also describes the use of mobile television for broadcasting the 2008 Beijing Olympic events as "uninspiring" and "unimaginative."[101] Mobile devices are changing the sport media ecology, and "the divide between watching the game live at a venue, and its mediated representation elsewhere, has been seriously breached."[102] As an example of this breach Goggin points to fans of the 2012 Super Bowl, who uploaded 40 per cent more data than they downloaded – a phenomenon that threatens to undermine the corporate control over the representation of sports.[103]

While much attention is focused on the use of mobile technologies to access corporate media content, Lev Manovich draws our attention to "something else which so far has not been theoretically acknowledged: the movement of media objects between people, devices, and the web."[104] It is not merely people who are mobile in the new media context, but cultural objects, digital texts, have attained a new degree of mobility between people, technologies, and virtual spaces. Goggin argues that mobile movies do not recreate earlier uses of cell phones or cinema; rather they foster a new type of networked culture.[105] What the precise form of this networked culture will take remains to be fully revealed. Yet it is very clear at this early point in the evolution of a post-television culture that "those controlling the key nodes of distribution" – the motion picture and entertainment industries and the telecommunications industry – do not have the same degree of enthusiasm towards a more open culture as that found within the producer community.[106] In other words, the rise of mobile television is at the centre of a struggle between those who would control what the audience can see and on what terms and those who produce televisual content outside of the dominant industrial system. Once again we come face to face with the issue of control. Earlier commercial implementations of mobile television followed the often seen business strategy of walled gardens and proprietary technologies. It may well prove to be the case that the biggest influence upon mobile television culture is the more uncontrolled domain of the public Internet.

The implications of online television go far beyond the industrial imperatives of the entertainment sector and point to the existence of a ubiquitous network of mobile communication and culture production and exchange. Not explored in this book, but of great significance, are audience practices of mobile culture such as life casting, video blogging, video teleconferencing, gaming, and other forms of real- and near-real-time online multicasting by those who stand outside the dominant institutions of cultural production. Manuel Castells and others see in these and related aspects of mobile communication technologies a "profound social transformation."[107] Likewise Rich Ling and Jonathan Donner suggest that the mobile phone is part of a "crisis in control" and a "control revolution."[108] Mobile phone technologies deliver more autonomy to individuals but they also integrate social communication into the marketplace. Everyday conversations and representational practices are commoditized within corporate cell phone culture. Mobile video is one more piece of the complicated puzzle of digital networked capitalism. We would be mistaken to reduce its significance merely to a matter of the commercial interests of media and entertainment conglomerates. Much more is at stake here.

Mobile phones operate as a common tool for accessing and producing culture. Mobile media technologies are seductive devices that commoditize even as they are a source of amateur representational capabilities that have proven to be consequential. At the centre of mobile media culture stands the mass adoption of smartphones – communication devices that also record, upload to the Internet, store, and replay video. Goggin draws our attention to the consequential nature of this new media technology: "The use of mobiles for recording video has underpinned many facets of the postbroadcasting world."[109] Mobile video has created significant disruptions in areas as diverse as domestic life, work, education, politics, warfare, and policing. It is even responsible for an "informal reconfiguration of television" which Goggin sees as related to a "resurgence of informal economies."[110] The production and distribution of video is far from being fully contained by dominant institutions or completely constrained by the market economy.

Social Viewing

Social viewing is part of a contradictory set of forces which sees the audience increasingly watching television while alone, but doing so while connected to distant others. Television has always been a social experience but it is only at the dawn of the post-television era that the phrase "social viewing" became ubiquitous. People use Facebook, Twitter, smartphones, and other social networking devices to communicate with friends and strangers while watching television. Almost half of Americans visit social networks while watching television, and one in six will use sites like Twitter and Facebook to comment about television shows during broadcasts.[111] Social networking while watching television is even more common in countries such as China and India. The most socially active audience is sports fans. Sports constitutes between 2 and 3 per cent of television programming but generates almost 50 per cent of Twitter activity.[112] Online social interaction increases as the number of screens available to a viewer rises.[113] Mobility also has significant political impact upon sociality. Mobile audiences can route around limitations imposed by local networks and governments.[114]

We can see many of these forces at work in the life of Caroline Marques, an American high school senior who is studying abroad and who is highly representative of the post-television generation. Caroline describes watching television as "much more of an individual task done online." Her generation can "watch any show on our own schedule ... Thanks to (and because of) the Internet, we have an all access pass to everything on TV." Even though she is an international student living overseas, Caroline watches American TV shows shortly after they air. Her online viewing experience is mostly ad-free. Caroline also feels that the isolation of online television "steals a sense of community."[115] This aligns with research indicating that 84 per cent of people watch online television as mostly a solitary activity.[116] Yet aspects of online viewing are genuinely social, such as when I sit in front of my computer with my wife to watch Netflix, and some are distant shadows of the family gathered around a television set. Some scholars such as Sherry Turkle argue that Caroline's generation is drifting away from each other as they mediate their friendships through virtual connections.[117] Farman suggests otherwise and claims that mobile devices "produce social space," but the debate rages on over the quality of our virtual social connections.[118]

D. Yvette Wohn and Eun-Kyung Na explored the use of Twitter by television viewers and found that social media recreates a "pseudo 'group viewing' experience of television ... although users aren't directly interacting with specific individuals, they want to be part of a larger group."[119] Viewers use social media such as Twitter to recreate the experience of communal viewing. Even as television takes a virtual turn and enters the disembodied realm of cyberspace, we find that, as Jonathan Gray argues, "television is, has always been, and shows every sign of continuing to be, intensely social and communal."[120] Chuck Tryon suggests that in the light of Twitter and other social networking tools, Raymond William's description of analogue television as a form of "privatized mobility" needs to be updated in the digital age to "something closer to a more communal form of mobility."[121] Yet the communal mobility created by online television may mask an ideological process that privileges individualized content and suppresses the development of truly participatory and egalitarian modes of social networking.[122]

Mobility, Internet connectivity, and multiple devices bring expanded viewing options that produce complex audience choices. Consider the situation of Mike Duchock, an event coordinator and resident of Dallas, Texas. Multiple screens help Duchock maintain social viewing with his girlfriend while also freeing him from her particular viewing choices: "When she wants to watch *Grey's Anatomy* on his 50-inch plasma HDTV, he uses his mobile devices. 'Just the other night I watched my South Carolina Gamecock baseball game on the Watch ESPN app while I half-watched *Glee* with (her),' he says. 'There have even been occasions where I had one game on my iPad, another on my iPhone, and something else on TV.'"[123] Multiple screens accommodate the differing tastes and help keep this couple in the same room while watching television. "Watching shows on my iPad," Duchock says, "means we still get to be together, vs. me going to another room to another TV."[124] Is this couple alone together or just more together in the multiple-screen television environment?

Social viewing is promoted by the prevalence of social networks such as Facebook and Twitter. Audience use of Twitter can promote shows and can also lead to considerable negative publicity. Nielsen claims that the relationship between the volume of tweets (brief text messages) and ratings is a statistically significant causal influence that runs both ways. Broadcast television shows with large audiences experience an increased volume of tweets and "a spike in tweets can increase tune-in."[125] There is a strong correlation between online social conversations and television ratings: "Depending upon the timing, a 9% to 14% increase in online discussion appears to be capable of producing a 1% increase in a program's rating."[126] Naturally, the industry is looking closely at social media as a way of improving the audience metrics provided by Nielsen ratings. Tweets, also known as micro-blogging, drive audiences to a particular show and popular shows enjoy higher levels of social media activity. Yet this Nielsen study was produced with Twitter as a business partner, so once again we encounter the self-interested nature of data derived from the television and new media industries. Twitter wants to be an influential advertising and promotional medium. Curiously, the shows that generate the largest exchange of tweets are seldom the shows with the highest viewership. This suggests that those who use Twitter are not entirely synonymous with the mass audiences of traditional television. Twitter users tend to be young, technologically sophisticated urban dwellers.[127] Nevertheless, we get more insight into this audience segment from their use of social media and so do advertisers.

Academic research suggests that for some of the audience, Twitter enhances broadcast television and delivers a sense of liveness.[128] Twitter is also used by distributors to further engage the audience. For example, Howard Stern provided live commentary on Twitter throughout an HBO rebroadcast of the movie *Private Parts*. Social media is also creating a more engaged audience. Meredith Parker, a 23-year-old New Yorker, is driven to participate in the online conversations that surround her favourite show, ABC's *The Bachelor*: "Whether it's Twitter or Facebook, it's kind of forced me to watch it live that day. You have to keep up with your shows because of spoilers and just the general chatter."[129] Meredith uses social media while watching television because she does not want to miss out on the conversation and she does not want the online conversation to ruin a post-live viewing experience. Thus social media acts as a distraction and a seduction.

What is certain is that millions of viewers use Twitter during television shows to exchange opinions and that many television studios actively encourage this behaviour with the use of on-screen hashtags. This is leading to increased interaction between audiences, programs, and producers and engendering a hyperactive audience characterized by mobility and a desire to be part of production decisions. Mobile audiences reveal the audience's desire for more control over production and this has implications for scriptwriters and producers: "As more viewers reach for their mobile internet devices as they watch a programme to broadcast their thoughts via Twitter, we may witness an even deeper struggle for power between audience and media than is evident at present."[130] Yet this power struggle takes place within privatized corporate spaces that are designed to channel audiences towards the commercial interests of the television and advertising industries.

While the audience may gain some measure of power from the use of social media such as Twitter, they also become deeply engaged in television viewing and provide a form of free labour for the television and advertising sectors. The social side of online television increases the ability of media industries to engage in surveillance and exploit free audience labour.[131] Conversational flows generated by social television generate data that enable advertisers to more efficiently engage audiences and manage their consumer behaviour.[132]

Although there has been much industry ink spilt over the potential of Twitter, it is easy to overstate the social nature of this form of audience activity. For example, during television dramas almost two-thirds of viewers only tweet once per episode.[133] If this is free labour it certainly does not involve much work. By the end of summer 2013 only 18 per cent of American Internet users were on Twitter.[134] Nevertheless, José van Dijck reminds us that social networking tools attempt to shape and contain conversations for the benefit of the commercial sector: "the ultimate goal for a tool and service [such as Twitter] is to become the core of a mediated *social* practice in a *commoditized* environment – an environment where user needs are not the same as owner's gains."[135] Van Dijck notes that the intention behind these systems is to channel users "from social networking to commercial activity."[136] As television takes a new social turn we must continually interrogate the intentions and interests behind these commoditized spaces of network sociability.

The Future of Viewing?

Industry executives such as Jim Lanzone, president of CBS Interactive, present a fairly consistent narrative about the near future of television: "It's television everywhere. Before TV was just on your TV, and now you're essentially being able to access it on every device you can imagine – so your phone, your tablet, but even places like your refrigerator."[137] When we take into account technology that is under development but not yet fully deployed, the future of television begins to look more like science fiction. A report by Cisco Systems holds forth a scenario in 2031 where viewers can change the camera angles. During commercials "the irresistible aroma of pizza" wafts from your television set, the selection of content will be unlimited, the traditional concept of a channel will be meaningless, there will be a single interface and no more multiple boxes connected to the television, people will interact with their television sets via natural language and gestures, television sets will recognize the viewer's mood and respond accordingly by playing appropriate content.[138] Televisions will transform into all manner of screens, some expandable, flexible, wearable, and some covering entire walls. Yet no one screen will be dedicated solely to television.

Imagine a screen on your bedroom wall that displays a replica of your favorite painting. With a wave of your hand, you transform it into your personalized TV. When your program is over, a few more gestures transform the screen into a video-conferencing suite so you can say goodnight to your children at their grandmother's house. At bedtime, you set your alarm clock on the same screen, which darkens for the night. When it's time to wake, the screen slowly brightens to mimic the sunrise. In the future, these screens will not be purchased as "TVs" – the TV experience will be detached from a specific device. From the outset, the enabling devices or screens will be valued as multifunctional, multipurpose devices.[139]

The advertising experience of the future will shift from the current form directed at a large group of people to advertisements that are "laser-targeted to each viewer."[140] Television will encompass more of our senses: "Olfactory reproduction will enable viewers to perceive smells and taste in real time. Tactile reproduction will let them feel the impact on a driver as he crashes his car, or the waft of a sea breeze at the beach on a warm summer day. Above all, the experience will be natural and nonintrusive. Viewers will not need clumsy helmets or glasses, and will be able to 'disengage' from sensory stimuli as simply as turning down the TV's volume."[141]

Personally, I would tear my television set off the wall and throw it in the garbage if I started to smell junk food every time it showed up in an advertisement. Some of Cisco's predictions are likely to come true, others will end up as failed innovations, and still others will only be available to a small minority who can afford the technology and services. But here I am not concerned with what technological wonders will come to pass 20 years down the road. We have enough of such speculation coming at us from the marketplace's hype machines and have seen too many failures in the prediction business to be easily won over by seductive promises of the future. As it is, we are still coming to grips with what our crazy kids are doing with the Internet and television today. Can anyone claim to fully comprehend what is occurring right now in the television system?

Summary

I have shown in the first four chapters how digital piracy and cord-cutting have undermined the industry's command of property, price, time, and place. When combined with the forces of viewing on demand, distracted viewing, and mobile access, the overall effect is the disruption of television's core business model – the control of content, time, and place. This control of when and where a television show aired enabled the entertainment industry to aggregate individuals into mass audiences and was instrumental in creating the artificial scarcity that characterized entertainment content in the twentieth century. A show was only available on a television set when the broadcast schedule made it so. Consider the example of 1972, when every week 67 million viewers gathered together in living rooms everywhere and watched Archie Bunker misbehaving on *All in the Family*. Audiences gathered en masse around television sets to watch a particular show which, with rare exception, could only be seen then and there. Content scarcity was maintained because the distribution networks were also controlled by the industry. There was no Internet and no mass participation in online piracy.

The post-television generation is streaming and downloading television out of its twentieth-century box but is also being sucked into a twenty-first-century world where television is ever present. Audiences can watch a show or a movie anywhere, anytime, and often do so for free. A young generation of viewers has given up on traditional TV and may never return to the industrial mode of watching (and paying). These extraordinary changes in television viewing are not just found among high school and university students but increasingly are part of mainstream audiences across the globe. The habits of the post-television generation are highly disruptive to an industry that is based on forcing audiences to watch advertisements, controlling when shows are available, and profiting from the creation of artificial scarcity in an age of digital plenitude.

Over the coming years the consumer electronics industry is deploying hundreds of millions of Internet-enabled televisions and Internet-connected devices for viewing and interacting with viewers. Audiences are increasingly distracted and lured away by second and third screens while watching television. New mobile-screen devices such as tablet computers are fostering the cord-cutting urge. Even as the online audience experiments with cutting cable bills from their lives they are getting drawn further into a seductive world of social television.

Most of the trends that define post-television audiences are in a nascent stage and carry implications that are intensely contradictory. Online television is often characterized as highly social but is also a solitary experience. Audiences are gaining more powers of personalized viewing but are thereby subjected to intense monitoring by the industrial system.

An online world of uncontrolled sharing, viewing, and conversation is countered by the commoditizing logic of commercial social networking services. We may even reach the point where most viewing activity takes place outside the marketplace, yet the primary behaviour of simply watching combined with secondary behaviours such as social networking serves to reinforce the ideological grip of capitalism on global online audiences.

Post-television audiences still want to watch television, and the networked, digital, mobile environment makes television utterly ubiquitous for the wired and wireless masses. The twentieth century provided us with a lesson in television's potency. The twenty-first century may render audiences completely transparent and easily moulded to capitalism's regime of visual entertainment and consumption.

6 Innovation: New Sources of Competition for Online Audiences

It is a new world when retail stores such as Toys"R"Us and Target get into the video streaming business. Even public libraries are offering streaming services for book, music, television, and film audiences. It is indicative of the volatile nature of the Internet economy that Amazon, the world's largest online bookstore, is also positioning itself to compete for the online television audience. Time Warner, AMC Networks, CBS, and HBO all have their own video streaming services, but none come close to the market share of online audiences gained by Netflix and Hulu. Over half of American homes with broadband Internet connections had a Netflix subscription in 2014.[1] If there is a major theme in the following story it is that of disintermediation.

Netflix is the top provider of streamed films, while Hulu is the main provider of online television shows.[2] Both academic and industry analyses have described the incumbent television industry's response to these new models of online television in terms of "foreclosing strategies" that involve limiting new competition and maintaining scarcity.[3] Yet just as the music industry failed to capture the sales of online music, so has the visual entertainment industry also failed to be leaders in the sales of online shows and movies. It remains to be seen if the incumbent players within the television industry will achieve foreclosure on competition, audiences, and content in a networked digital environment.

This chapter explores how legitimate online television and movie services such as Netflix, Amazon, Hulu, iTunes, and YouTube structure the Internet television audience. These digital delivery systems are shaping the consumption practices of television and movie audiences. While some early market leaders may disappear in the coming years, they provide insight into patterns of online television viewing that may persist long after pioneering companies fade under the pressure of market competition and related forces. Years ago it was widely assumed that Microsoft would dominate online television but its flagship product, WebTV, rebranded as MSN TV, was shut down in mid-2013. What all of the following innovators have in common is that they represent a threat and at the same time are vulnerable to countermoves by the incumbent television industry.

Digital delivery systems are the latest in a long series of "next generation TV networks."[4] These new media companies represent a combination of experimentation and continuity with legacy business practices characteristic of the television industry. They also represent forces that are fragmenting the identity of television. Max Dawson suggests that television's identity fragmented as "new technologies of distribution and reception dispersed its content and functions across various sites and screens." This in turn has led to an "existential crisis" for television: "in addition to contemplating the perennial question of 'what is the future of television?' some commentators asked whether or not television had a future at all in a world in which computers, game consoles, iPods, and cellular phones all could receive and display television programming."[5] The growth of Netflix, Hulu, and iTunes does not signal the end of television but these new online services do suggest that television is undergoing a rather extraordinary transformation.

The rapid growth of a digital networked audience that exceeds one billion daily viewers is part of a series of changes that raises questions about television's stability and identity. Judith Keilbach and Markus Stauff argue that scholars have overstated television's past as a stable and clearly defined medium. Keilbach and Stauff depart from the common presumption of television as stable and homogeneous and reconceptualize television's past "as one of constant transformation."[6] They argue that constant transformations were "an essential feature of television during the reign of broadcast/network television" and as a result television gained cultural and economic power because it produced differences that fueled its own reproduction.[7] We can see differences being produced in online television – lower prices and new content, business models, and audience habits. These differences are adding high-margin revenue to the incumbent industry, expanding advertising possibilities, and perhaps most important of all, delivering television to a new generation of digital natives on their own terms. Thus, one way of conceptualizing a post-television era instigated by a digital environment is not as an end or radical break in the history and nature of television but as one more transformation in a long series of changes to technology, industry, audiences, content, and culture.

Perhaps nothing has challenged the identity of television more than its recent transformation into a digital technology. Ten years before the rise of networked digital television, Sean Cubitt argued that "video cannot be narrowed down to a subset of television, either in practice or theoretically."[8] As television takes on the digital form it moves closer to video, and now that the two are inseparable within the industrial and amateur systems of production and distribution, they both share a lack of a fixed identity and any essential or definitive form. Whereas theorists once drew sharp lines of distinction between video, television, and film, such distinctions are increasingly difficult to justify. Consider Cubitt's contention that video is the "worm in the bud" that will hasten the fragmentation of television's dominance and "will supersede TV itself."[9] The forces at work are far too uncertain, uncharted, and contradictory to project a linear progression from something called "television" to the new kid on the block, video. Cubitt was arguing for "a new hierarchy of visual communication."[10] Whereas television once defined "the pinnacle of an institutional and discursive hierarchy of video practices," video now emerges as the thing that brings an end to television's domination.[11] Yet the movement of the television industry and global audiences to online video challenges the notion that video has "a uniquely democratic mission" or that television and video have a fundamentally different ontological status.[12] Television, it turns out, is a snake that eats its own digital tail.

Keilbach and Stauff argue that when conceptualized as an experimental system, the difference between the past and the present of television becomes less clear and key features of contemporary television become "more ambivalent."[13] With amateurs and semi-professionals producing video content for global audiences, online bookstores such as Amazon investing in television programming, new media technology companies such as Google creating high-speed fibre-optic networks, and the world's largest semiconductor maker, Intel, claiming to soon deliver a "better form of television," the key features of the medium certainly do become ambivalent.[14] Nevertheless, when it comes to the difference between its past and present, a few developments inscribe the digital environment as distinct from TV as it used to be. Prior to the emergence of the digital environment, audiences did not function as distributors of television to the same degree that is occurring now. They certainly did not participate in the production of video content at the same level. Thus while ambivalences in television's identity remain, it may yet prove to be the case that we are indeed witnessing the emergence of significant differences between television's past and present.[15] Netflix provides an opportunity to explore one feature of contemporary television that simply did not exist in the twentieth century – tens of millions of paying subscribers to a streaming video service.

Netflix

When the post-television generation goes online seeking legitimate video services the results can be exasperating. *Globe and Mail* columnist Ivor Tossell reviewed iTunes and Netflix and found the viewing experience to be disappointing. Apple's iTunes embedded DRM software in their video products and as a result "you have 30 days in which to watch a file, but once you start watching, you have only 48 hours before it self-destructs ... Small wonder that many users still opt for pirated video."[16] The Netflix experience did not rate any better: "At the moment, Netflix Canada offers you the best of Hollywood's discount bin."[17] The US Netflix catalogue offers American customers a much better selection of movies. Tossell notes that Canadian Netflix subscribers "use several grey-market tricks, such as Virtual Private Networks and applications that fudge their Internet address, to gain access to the U.S. Netflix catalogue."[18] This shows how piracy is used by the post-television generation to enhance legitimate services that are stunted because of geographical licensing restrictions.

Canada was a test market for subscription-based video, which "performed above expectations" and did so regardless of Netflix Canada's woefully inadequate catalogue of television shows and movies.[19] Television is pretty mediocre as a source of entertainment and even worse when it is reduced to a small collection of old shows. Tossell's summation of the state of legitimate online television and movie watching in the spring of 2012 should by now sound familiar: "Canadians looking for a way to play digital video are faced with lousy options: convenient, legal services with poor selection; inconvenient legal services with middling selection and onerous rights management; and pirated downloads that offer exactly what consumers want to watch, when they want to watch it."[20] Regardless of Netflix's limitations, by April 2014 Netflix's Canadian subscriber base totaled an estimated 5.8 million, up from 2.5 million in 2013.[21]

In response to Tossell's experience of Netflix one *Globe and Mail* reader wrote, "Netflix takes a lot of flack, mainly from those who want the latest Hollywood blockbuster but for more obscure and 'artsy' movies it is excellent."[22] While customer opinion concerning Netflix varies greatly, the company nonetheless provides an extraordinary example of a commercial venture serving the post-television generation. Netflix began promoting a DVD mail-order subscription service in 1999. Over time it transitioned to offering streaming movie services that account for an incredible 32 per cent of North America's downstream traffic on the Internet.[23] By 2013 Netflix had over 40 million subscribers streaming 1 billion hours of video each month and anticipated annual revenues approaching $4.3 billion (US). This climbed to 50 million subscribers worldwide in 2014. Subscribers watch an average of 87 minutes of Netflix content every day.[24] Netflix is the largest online provider of streaming television and movies, with a 63 per cent US market share, followed by TV network online sites (49 per cent), Hulu (35 per cent), Amazon Prime (28 per cent), iTunes (25 per cent), and Hulu Plus (11 per cent).[25] Here the total market share exceeds 100 per cent because over 80 per cent of Internet users who stream shows and movies from the Internet typically make use of two or more online video providers.[26]

Netflix provides a movie service that is distinct from Apple's iTunes service. iTunes is a transactional video on demand (VOD) service that charges for each download of a movie while Netflix is a subscription video on demand (SVOD) service that provides an all-you-can-eat-buffet style of access to a menu of movies. Netflix controlled 89 per cent of the SVOD market in 2013.[27] Netflix's closest competitor, Hulu, has only a marginal market share while iTunes accounts for the majority of the revenue in the VOD market segment.[28] Apple and Netflix serve slightly different parts of the online video market. The majority of movie purchases through iTunes are new releases while Netflix serves up older titles. Consumers prefer renting movies on a subscription basis – a model Netflix uses which is very similar to subscribing to television but one that offers a permanent menu as opposed to a time-based schedule of offerings. In the words of business analysts, "the core value proposition" of Netflix and iTunes is actually very different.[29] Many consumers use multiple online video services so any advantage absent in one service is made up through accessing competing services. For example, Netflix subscribers enjoy unlimited consumption of older movies and often testify to using iTunes to access newer movies and Hulu to watch television shows.

The majority of Netflix's customers use a variety of devices such as Wii, PlayStation 3, Xbox, Blu-ray, TiVo, Google TV, and Apple TV to view video content on television screens. In 2011 Nielsen reported that 42 per cent of Netflix subscribers view their video content directly on their computers and 6 per cent on their mobile phones and iPads.[30] This aligns with the low reported rates of mobile television viewing. With the rapid growth of high-bandwidth mobile phones we may witness an increase in the amount of television viewing that takes place outside the home. Along with the desktop computer, another platform that is playing a significant role in new viewing patterns is game consoles. More than half of Netflix subscribers use their game consoles to stream shows and movies to their television set. By 2014 over 78 per cent of Netflix subscribers watched Netflix on an Internet-connected television.[31]

There are early indications that Netflix's success is hurting the ratings of children's shows on cable television.[32] Within households that regularly use Netflix, viewing of children's shows on regular, linear television declined. These Netflix households were watching just as much children's programming but their viewing was shifting from traditional television to online streaming. The difference between platforms was significant and caused alarm within the industry.[33] Streaming television shows via Netflix led to significant decreases in the ratings for some channels targeting children and teenagers, with steep declines seen among young boys. Streaming also led to repeat viewing shifting to online sources instead of through traditional television.[34] Also significant is the anecdotal evidence from discussion forums that children love viewing their Netflix shows on tablet computers. Young children use second screens and streaming services to watch their preferred shows while older siblings use the family television set to watch their shows. How we watch online television varies according to factors such as age and screen size.

The influence of Netflix on ratings is complex and contradictory. Netflix appears to encourage more television consumption.[35] Nielsen claims that the ratings for some television shows would be as much as 25 per cent higher if online views were counted.[36] Similarly, the presence of older episodes of serialized dramas such as *Mad Men* on Netflix has increased audiences for new episodes as they appear on traditional television.[37]

There is an open debate among television networks over the impact of Netflix. The chairman of Dish Network, Charlie Ergen, accuses programmers of shows such as *Mad Men*, *Breaking Bad*, and *The Walking*

Dead of having "devalued their programming content by making it available in multiple outlets," such as Amazon, iTunes, and Netflix.[38] In an age of digital plenitude Ergen was arguing for maintaining exclusivity: "it's been devalued because you can get it multiple ways and customers have more flexibility to get the programming. It's not quite the same as if something were exclusive."[39] Nevertheless, in this case online viewing appears to have expanded the audience. "*The Walking Dead* is the No. 1 scripted drama with Dish subscribers" and the highest-rated show for AMC Networks.[40] Netflix claims that it has been crucial to the financial health of the CW and AMC networks.[41]

Netflix's impact on the television industry goes far beyond ratings. After receiving 14 Emmy nominations for its original programming, the online service is gaining critical acclaim and cultural authority. David Bianculli notes, "It took HBO 25 years to get its first Emmy nomination; it took Netflix six months."[42] It is also "upending industry conventions – ordering an entire season of a series without asking for a pilot, withholding ratings and even throwing all of a new show's episodes online at once, in one big bundle, so viewers don't have to wait a week for the next installment of a series they love."[43] This is proving to be disruptive within the television industry and is altering audience expectations.

Netflix is said to have revived serialized TV dramas and is getting pitches from A-list scriptwriters before Hollywood gets a chance to see them. Netflix knows that it will remain in a fragile position as long as it is beholden to the incumbent television industry for its content, thus the drive to develop a track record in its own production capabilities. The industry also faces pressure from increased competition for content. With new entrants like Netflix bidding for exclusive rights to content come rising programming costs.

At the cost of $8 a month I subscribed to Netflix in May 2012. The process took three minutes and required a credit card or PayPal. My first impression was a bunch of shows I had seen before and a lot of recent bad Hollywood movies that I would not want to watch (or admit to watching). I searched for some British dramas I was interested in, such as *Ashes to Ashes*, and could not find them in the small selection. It was the same with the anime, science fiction, documentary, and foreign film selections – all very limited. The category "Classic Musicals" had a mere 11 movies in it. I finally found an episode of *Futurama* that I had not seen yet. It began streaming instantly but was far from HD quality, although nonetheless adequate. Later that night, instead of walking down to my local independent video store as planned, my wife and I pulled over some comfortable chairs from the living room, sat together in front of a 24-inch computer screen, and watched *The Illusionist*, a 2010 Scottish-French animated film directed by Sylvain Chomet. In spite of Netflix limitations I felt that I was experiencing something that could become a substantial threat to cable television and whatever was left of the video rental business.

Reflecting on my experience of Netflix over the following days I realized that there was a new "voice" inside my desktop computer. This was the voice of Netflix, which was now just a click away on my Web browser, silently enticing me to stop my research and writing of this book and explore its catalogue of shows and films. By subscribing to Netflix I had effectively moved the television from my living room to my office and now had to manage yet one more powerful force of distraction streaming towards me from the Internet – Hollywood. Slowly but surely my wife and I were being pulled into the post-television lifestyle. Netflix brought television to a new screen in my home and made it more present in my daily routines. Television crossed the boundary between my leisure world and my work world. This transition was facilitated by a feature of Netflix that allows you to automatically return to a show or a movie at exactly the same point you left it. As a result, I found myself taking short breaks from my day to spend a few minutes watching a movie, such as the 1981 animated classic *Heavy Metal*. The short-form viewing habit introduced to us through YouTube now inscribed a new form of television viewing. I found myself taking very short breaks from a long workday to watch a few minutes at a time of a movie or a television show.

Before Netflix my wife and I watched television shows together. We continued to watch television together after the arrival of Netflix but I also began to watch more shows on my own. Chuck Tryon argues that digital delivery systems such as Netflix participate in a pattern of promotional discourse within the television industry that has promised family harmony and togetherness since the post–World War II era. The promotional discourses of streaming services "emphasize that digital delivery can resolve domestic conflicts and create family harmony, ironically by encouraging individual, rather than collective forms of movie watching."[44] Tryon suggests that a notion of family harmony is part of an effort by Netflix to deepen subscribers' engagement with social media.[45] Through social media features of Netflix the system encourages individualized consumption while promoting the service as a builder of family harmony. It is too early to be certain but online television may privilege individualized, instead of shared, consumption.

It could be argued that Netflix is helping the film and television industry. Netflix derives most of its content from Paramount Pictures, MGM, 20th Century Fox, Sony Pictures, and Time Warner. Netflix spends over $3 billion annually to acquire streaming licences for its content. Les Moonves, CEO of CBS, described the relationship with Netflix in the following terms: "These deals are having a big impact on our financial results, adding meaningful, very high margin dollars to our bottom line."[46] Disney CEO Bob Iger says that new digital streams such as Netflix are adding to the company's growth and Disney is not seeing signs of cannibalization.[47] Jonathan Knee, director of the media program at Columbia Business School, described Netflix's position thus: "the robust success of a mere distributor is something incomprehensible and frankly, a little unnerving."[48] When the studios make their content available to Netflix they risk cannibalizing their own revenue streams, but the final outcome here remains uncertain. The CEO of Cox Communications, Patrick Esser, calls Netflix a "frenemy" of the cable industry and notes that 40 per cent of his cable television customers also streamed Netflix content.[49] Part of the reason why cord-cutting is on the rise can be found in the 35 per cent of Netflix's 25- to 34-year-old subscribers who choose Netflix instead of a pay-television subscription.[50] Another study claims that a fifth of US Netflix users have cut the cord.[51] These industry studies may be inflating the actual rate of cord-cutting among Netflix users but the fact remains that online competition and digital plenitude are motivating consumers to look for less expensive options. Netflix is the best friend and worst enemy of the television industry.

Netflix is trying to distinguish its brand by producing its own premium content, such as *House of Cards* with Kevin Spacey and a Norwegian gangster series called *Lillyhammer*. The company also built a 100,000-square-foot soundstage in Baltimore that can be used for feature film-making. Spencer Jakab provided the following assessment for readers of the *Wall Street Journal*: "However good Netflix's original programs, behind it lie thousands of mostly dated television shows and movies, and too few recent blockbusters."[52] How damning such criticism is depends on your perspective on television in general. Some of the most common complaints about broadcast and cable television are the poor quality of programming, the stale movies endlessly on repeat, and the small selection of shows. Television evolved into a mass medium in spite of its failure to deliver a quality experience, so the current low quality of online television services is not necessarily a major impediment to growth. Whatever happens to Netflix in the long run is less important than what it has demonstrated – tens of millions of consumers want to be able to legitimately stream television shows and movies directly to their computers and television sets if the price is right.

In the short term there is a limit to how transformative video streaming services such as Netflix can be in the United States, where broadband Internet is poorly deployed in rural areas. The United States ranks 19th in the list of nations with the fastest broadband.[53] Sixty-eight per cent of Americans use broadband at home but that still leaves 100 million Americans who do not have broadband even though it is available to 95 per cent of homes.[54] The lower quality of America's broadband network has not stopped tens of millions of American Internet users from signing up for Netflix and other streaming services.

Whereas television viewing united the population into a mass audience in the twentieth century, this century marks the beginning of a highly fragmented Internet-based television audience. This twenty-first-century audience engages in a variety of multi-platform viewing experiences. When YouTube and all other online video sources are taken into account the online audience is exposed to a much wider variety of content. Nevertheless, we must be modest in our predictions based upon Netflix and its audiences, as Trevor Barr notes; "making predictions is fraught with difficulty because the management of established commercial network television in the USA faces complex dilemmas as to what extent they might embrace the opportunity to offer more of their programming to new outlets, but also ensure no risk to their programming rights and to their lucrative advertising base."[55] One thing remains certain: Netflix is one more nail in the coffin of the physical DVD rental business.

Amazon

The online bookseller Amazon offers a video streaming service called Prime Instant Video. Between 2013 and 2014 Prime Instant Video almost tripled the number of streams it delivered and now surpasses both Hulu and Apple in streaming video usage. Prime's success demonstrates the rapidly changing nature of the online video sector. By March 2014 Netflix's share of the video streaming market reached 57.5 per cent, YouTube held 16.9 per cent, Amazon 3 per cent, and Hulu 2.8 per cent. Amazon is producing original content, but *Variety* magazine suggests that it is "trailing on all fronts – lagging on devices, subscription VOD, content acquisition, original productions – but is aggressively investing in each area."[56] In 2014 Amazon entered into an exclusive multi-year arrangement with HBO that gives Prime members access to premium content such as *The Sopranos*. This premium content only becomes available after three years of appearing on HBO, once again handing piracy a clear advantage.

Although Amazon is a distant second in the video streaming marketplace, it does represent the extraordinary nature of online business environments wherein a bookseller can transform into a producer and distributor of original and repackaged video entertainment. Amazon provides an example of how the incumbent television industry is facing new sources of competition in both production and distribution. It demonstrates that the cable industry's reluctance to provide à la carte alternatives to bundling has led to innovative online competitors stepping up and offering what consumers desire – less expensive options. Amazon also disrupts the power of gatekeepers within the movie distribution system by offering "the simplest avenue to distribution" and one that is the least restrictive, according to Joel Waldfogel.[57] Waldfogel argues that online video distributors such as Amazon enable audiences to gain access to a large and rapidly expanding catalogue of movies originating outside the major Hollywood studios: "These movies make up a growing and now substantial share of movie consumption in the box office, home video, and television."[58] Contrary to the claims of the incumbent entertainment giants, once again we find that networked technologies and the new environment of digital plenitude increases the rate of production within the media sector and expands audience choice. The barriers to both production and distribution are eroding and a renaissance of digital culture has dawned.

Hulu

Hulu is a free streaming service that was founded in 2007 and is mutually owned by Disney, NBCUniversal, and 21st Century Fox. It also launched a subscription-based service, Hulu Plus, in 2010 which, unlike Netflix, has advertising embedded in the video streams and provides paying subscribers with next-day content from five of the six major networks. By 2013 Hulu Plus had over 5 million subscribers paying $7.99 per month and revenue approaching $1 billion (US). Unlike Netflix, Hulu and Hulu Plus are only available to the United States and

Japan. However, through software tools such as VPNs Internet users can circumvent Hulu's geo-blocking.

By 2010 the US online audience was watching five times as much video (19.4 billion minutes) on Hulu than on the websites of ABC, CBS, NBC, Fox, and the CW.[59] In the first quarter of 2013 Hulu streamed over 1 billion videos to online viewers.[60] When it comes to gendered trends, women show a preference for online video services. Women make up 57 per cent of Netflix and 59 per cent of Hulu users. They also account for the majority of total time spent watching – 64 per cent.[61] Also noteworthy from Nielsen, "at the end of 2011, roughly one-third of consumers streamed long-form content such as a movie or TV show from the Internet through a paid subscription service like Netflix or Hulu-Plus."[62] Once again we find that the post-television generation is not the fringe – it is front and centre in the mainstream.

Hulu has the highest frequency of video advertisements, exposing viewers to an average of 48 each month. Also noteworthy, Hulu is responsible for over one-quarter of the total video advertisements viewed on the Internet.[63] This may become an issue down the road as much of the online television audience grows accustomed to the superior experience of advertising-free viewing through Netflix and piracy. Consider the comments of one former Hulu subscriber: "I got a trial for Hulu Plus, watched it exactly once, saw that there were commercials for a pay service and ditched it."[64] As a brand Hulu is in danger of becoming synonymous with too many commercials. Hulu's advertising-based business strategy may run into significant resistance from a new generation of college students who are described as having "unprecedented control over their reception or avoidance of advertising messages."[65] Industry executive Evan Shapiro describes Hulu as "great" and believes that "people like TV ads ... audiences won't mind watching the ads" because "the viewer actually gets to choose their own ad. Personalized, relevant and cool."[66] Freedom of choice gets reduced to choosing among advertisements. This is cool?

Meanwhile, directly contradicting Shapiro's questionable claim that people like advertising, Dish Network introduced an ad-skipping feature in their DVRs called Auto Hop. This new feature, which resulted in lawsuits from television networks, represents an "aggressive move to please the end customer rather than advertisers."[67] Brian Stelter, television reporter for the *New York Times*, suggests that Dish's move to keep audiences at the risk of alienating their content providers "stems from the persistent fear that subscribers will forego paying for television service and turn to Internet alternatives instead."[68] A cable network making it easier for audiences to avoid commercials suggests that the advertising-free viewing experience that can be found on the Internet via Netflix, piracy, and other means is putting pressure on the traditional television system.

Nothing degrades the television experience more than advertising. Some advertisements are indeed fun to watch, but most are not, and all represent an interruption of the viewing experience. Traditional television is being pushed into a corner where it must compete against the digital plenitude of the Internet and the superior experience of advertising-free viewing. The networks are desperately trying to compete against online television and some are willing to risk breaking the advertising model to do it.

Subscribers can access Hulu Plus on a variety of platforms, such as Blu-ray players, TiVo, Internet-enabled televisions, smartphones, Wii, PlayStation, and Xbox. Hulu delivers a wide range of movies and television shows from Disney, PBS, MTV, MGM, Viacom, NBC, Fox, ABC, CBS, Nickelodeon, and hundreds of other content owners. As with Netflix, Amazon, and Yahoo!, Hulu also produces its own in-house content. The corporate parents of Hulu question "whether giving their shows away online could put at risk the hundreds of millions they earn from traditional cable and satellite deals."[69] This conflict with other revenue streams and the risk of cannibalization may be why the corporate owners of Hulu tried to sell the business in 2011 and again in 2013. Among the interested buyers were Time Warner Cable and DirecTV.[70] No deal was closed and Hulu faced an exodus of senior executives "due to the uncertainty of Hulu's future."[71]

iTunes and Apple TV

Another legitimate video streaming service on everyone's mind at the moment is Apple's iTunes. Television and movie studios do not want to follow in the footsteps of the music industry and wake up one day to discover that Apple owns 80 per cent of the online video market. iTunes dominates the electronic sell-through marketplace for movies. Electronic sell-through refers to video content purchased for permanent ownership. Unlike paid-subscription models of streaming services like Netflix and Hulu, the electronic sell-through process requires consumers to pay a one-time fee to download and own a digital product. In 2011 the sales of downloaded movies exceeded the sales of physical DVDs for the first time. By 2013 iTunes customers were downloading 800,000 television episodes and 350,000 movies a day.[72]

Apple also offers a set-top box for online television viewing called Apple TV. In keeping with Apple's proprietary "walled garden" marketing strategy, this device is tied into other Apple products; as a result, "if you're not an Apple person – no iPad, no iPhone, no iPod, no Mac – you won't get much value out of this device."[73] Apple's strategy appears to be based on locking consumers into their proprietary products and then tightly controlling what content is available. This has made jailbreaking the Apple TV a popular counter-strategy for expanding the content and functionality available to users. As the *Globe and Mail*'s technology reporter notes, "Apple's ability to unilaterally dictate the rules of the game is slowly eroding."[74]

A revised version of Apple TV allowed users to connect to content from Netflix, Vimeo, and YouTube, suggesting that Apple is backing off its walled garden approach, although recent online comments and reviews also imply that little has changed: "the limitations of the Apple TV are infuriating: no apps, no Pandora, no Amazon, no Hulu, no browser, nearly impossible to find and stream your favorite radio station."[75] Unlike its iTunes online music venture, Apple's online TV option has failed to become a primary disrupter of a television industry that has been willing to walk away from Apple during content licensing negotiations. Apple is rumoured to be working on an Internet-enabled television set but so is everyone else. Nonetheless, one industry analyst speculated that within five years "Apple will push back against the current cable and satellite TV subscription models" and offer unbundled channels.[76] Apple may be influential and innovative, but is it big enough to unbundle the television industry?

The CEO of Apple, Tim Cook, sees the future of television in terms of controlling the key technology and dominating the market. He asks, "Can we control the key technology? Can we make a product that we all want?" – implying that the answer is "yes."[77] Yet it is hard to see how any one technology or consumer device will control the global flow of online content to a multiplicity of screens, operating systems, and consumer electronics. Twentieth-century methods of audience control cannot be easily imported into twenty-first-century networked flows of television content when piracy, jailbreaking, account sharing, and circumvention are widespread forms of audience behaviour.

Google TV

Google is an 800-pound gorilla in the online television market. No one is quite certain what the company is going to do next or if they could stop Google from doing it anyway. Major broadcasters and network studios have the advantage of their oligopolistic position in the market-place, but Google "has one tremendous asset over its rivals in broad-casting: Google can integrate platforms for user-generated content, television, search, advertising, social networking, and trade and marketing sites into all-encompassing business models, thus expanding the reach of advertisers across all platforms."[78] Nonetheless, as with Apple, Google is not immune to failure. Google's entrance into the set-top market with Google TV, launched in 2010, was a disaster. NBC, ABC, CBS, and Hulu all denied Google TV access to their content.

Consumers can access Netflix, YouTube, and the Web and connect Google TV to their desktop computers. Google TV shipped with a wireless remote control and a full QWERTY keyboard. In stark contrast to Apple, Google's design philosophy appears to be guided by a greater willingness to embrace interoperability.[79] Yet questions remain as to just how interoperable Google intends to make the online television experience. Consider the example of Google's Chromecast TV streamer, a $35 two-inch dongle that plugs into most new televisions and streams content from services such as Netflix and YouTube. Chromecast works by wirelessly transmitting content from smartphones, tablets, or desktop computers directly to your television. David Pogue informed readers of the *New York Times* that Chromecast was the "smallest, cheapest, simplest way yet to add Internet to your television."[80] High praise indeed. But as is often the case with "do no evil" Google, all is not as it may first appear. As Joshua Brustein explained to *Businessweek* readers, "This fits nicely into Google's stated philosophy of openness. But the company seems to be taking a step to make the device less open."[81] Brustein was referring to subsequent developments which suggested that Google was attempting to limit Chromecast to streaming approved content. Technology critics speculated that Google was attempting to shut out pirated content so as to entice media companies to cooperate with their business plans behind Chromecast, "and that means giving control to the people who make shows, rather than to those who watch them."[82] This fits with previous reports that Google is courting media companies for licensing television programming.[83] Television executives do not want to see the disappearance of the line that divides full Internet access and Web content from traditional television content. Nonetheless, for those who want full control of their television experience, and full access to the Web and pirated content, it is a fairly simple matter to connect a flat-screen television directly to the Internet so that the television screen acts like a computer monitor *and* a television set. This is what all of my cord-cutting friends have done and it is really quite amazing to see.

If Google TV does become a common feature in households (admittedly a long shot), it would erode the "distinction between a home page and a TV screen" and further complicate the definition of television.[84] It might also further complicate the experience of television. One of the uncertainties facing Google is the television audience's willingness to adapt to more complexity in their interface with television. While complexity is usually seen as a hard sell, complex interfaces did not stop the personal computer and the Internet from evolving into a mass market. Complex interfaces such as a keyboard bring with them expanded input possibilities and productive capabilities. It is possible that an increasingly complex television system that is tied into the Web will necessitate an interface that is somewhat more complex than a twentieth-century remote control, which, for the most part, was used to turn the television on or off, change channels, and adjust the volume.

The set-top box industry that specializes in connecting televisions to the Internet is in its infancy and will have to compete against a whole new generation of Internet-enabled televisions that are on the way. Even the interface is still under development. Apple is rumoured to be working on a television that will incorporate voice and face recognition. Both set-top box and smart (Internet-enabled) televisions face the unknown promise of convergence. It is generally assumed that people will want to be able to do everything on one screen – watch television, surf the Web, teleconference, and so on – but early experiments in interactive television in the twentieth century floundered on similar assumptions. Nonetheless, the Internet and television are converging and competing for attention on the same screens. Consider the example of Brittany and Dave.

Brittany Bohnet and fiancé Dave Morin used to plop in front of the television in their San Francisco living room with a smart phone in one hand and the remote control in the other, computers resting in their laps as they switched their attention from screen to screen. But with Google TV, the young couple can watch the latest episode of AMC's "Mad Men," check updates from friends on Facebook and on Flickr show off photos of Morin's marriage proposal ... all on one screen. "We have gone from hundreds of channels to millions of channels," Bohnet said.[85]

This couple's multiple-screen viewing experience collapsed into one screen with multiple functions and a complex interface (the keyboard). They exchanged one form of complexity – navigating between multiple screens and interface devices – with another. But here our sample is biased. Brittany runs the marketing campaign for Google TV and Dave is an Internet entrepreneur.

It may prove difficult to tear smartphones, laptops, and tablet computers from the hands of the television audience (it certainly is difficult to get my students to put them away while I lecture). Activities that once required multiple devices – reading a book, listening to a record, watching television, talking with distant friends – are now converging on a single screen. Google would like to own all those experiences but is unlikely to push competitors such as Facebook and Apple to the fringe.

This convergence of multiple media experiences in the domain of online television fulfils Sean Cubitt's 1993 prediction that "the video monitor will play an even more central role in social life."[86] For many digital natives, the thought of being separated from their various screens, especially their mobile screens, is all but intolerable. The rise of online television raises questions about how a ubiquitous screen culture will be colonized by new or old media oligopolies. How much freedom will we have to choose when so many corporate-owned databases and algorithms seek to influence our viewing and purchasing preferences? Google's desire to collapse multiple media uses into a single-screen experience typifies the corporate sector's desire to own and control audience experiences, data, and perhaps even desires.

YouTube

Google is also staking a claim in the television market through its video site YouTube. YouTube launched 100 channels of niche-oriented programming by Madonna, Disney, the *Wall Street Journal*, and others. Google committed to spending $100 million to market the new YouTube channels. Twenty of the channels gained 1 million views per week by 2012. YouTube has altered its business plan to emulate how television networks market their own programming. Google's strategy is to shift YouTube from relying on user-generated content to cultivating more premium, professionally produced content that will draw audiences and advertisers. This is part of a larger trend that sees Internet companies trying to reposition themselves as television networks.

YouTube delivers 4 billion videos every day to 1 billion users who watch a total of 6 billion hours of video each month, bringing in $3.6 billion in net revenue.[87] Over 100 hours of video are uploaded to YouTube every minute. When I wrote *Watching YouTube* (2010) it was highly debated as to whether YouTube would ever make a profit. Three years later the investment firm Morgan Stanley issued a research note suggesting that YouTube's annual revenue could reach $20 billion by 2020.[88] Rather surprisingly, "more than half of YouTube viewing in the U.S. takes place during traditional prime-time evening hours."[89] The world's largest collection of online video recently reorganized to function more like television. It now offers thousands of movies on a pay-per-download basis and has entered into a joint venture with 20th Century Fox studios to sell and rent movies. The irony of this is particularly rich as Fox's owner, Murdoch, once accused Google of being a "pirate leader."[90]

José van Dijck aptly notes that the technical conditions for YouTube and broadcast television are "progressively overlapping," and as a result "it is hard to tell any distinction between YouTube content and broadcast content because of mutual imitation."[91] The end point of online video, whether in the hands of amateurs or professionals, increasingly merges into the same goal, managed consumption: "technological toll keepers like Google guard access to the twenty-first-century entertainment universe, steering the creativity of users, the eyeballs of consumers, and the wallets of advertisers in the same direction."[92] This nefarious political economy of the post-television age brings with it increasingly sophisticated and often invisible means of consumer management. It also sees amateur video production and distribution captured by global media conglomerates such as Google and turned into unequal means of generating profit. Janet Wasko and Mary Erickson, along with a host of other critical media theorists, remind us that "one of the most worrisome aspects of YouTube's monetization strategies is the commodification of free labor."[93] Here they refer to the tendency of amateur videographers to add value to commercial services such as YouTube by freely contributing content. Without the massive catalogue of amateur videos YouTube's commercial value would be greatly reduced. In the twentieth-century television system the audience provided the free labour of watching advertising. In the post-television environment the audience is transformed into a source of free content which is repackaged, wrapped in advertising, and "sold" back to online audiences.

Thirty years ago television networks dismissed cable channels as too narrowly focused but ended up incorporating cable into their business operations. Robert Kyncl, the architect of YouTube's transformation into a competitor for television audiences, believes "it will happen again."[94] Kyncl wants to ensure that YouTube becomes part of online television viewing habits by serving professionally produced video content to niche audiences and transforming television as cable once did. YouTube's niche content, channels devoted to subjects such as pet grooming, could become a central part of the post-television generation's visual diet. It is already following a multi-decade-long trend in the fragmentation of the television audience. In 1985 *The Cosby Show* garnered 35 per cent of all US households. By 2011 the most popular television show, *American Idol*, won a mere 9 per cent of American television viewers.

YouTube's strategy is to deliver professionally produced content to narrowly defined audience niches and sell those audiences to advertisers who are targeting highly engaged and carefully measured audiences. The potential for YouTube to combine professionally produced content with significant audience reach is very real: "six of the top ten most-viewed YouTube videos in 2010 were scripted and produced."[95] YouTube fame is often far from accidental. YouTube can be said to further cloud the ontological status of television. As television moves online it begins to look more and more like a disjointed collection of video files. Meanwhile, YouTube is bringing order to the world's largest collection of video clips and trying to look more like television.[96] The forces of fragmentation and centralization are both hard at work in the post-television culture.

YouTube provides insight into the growing complexity of television. The new generation of screens, from Internet-enabled television sets to tablet computers, are agnostic. They are all able to receive YouTube and other Internet-derived video content. If they cannot do so consumers engage in criminalized actions such as jailbreaking to make their viewing devices agnostic. The television industry no longer has privileged access to a dedicated viewing device and the very notion of a "television" industry is also changing. As far as the viewer is concerned, there is only content from an ever-increasing diversity of sources. We are faced with what William Uricchio calls "definitional ambivalence."[97] This definitional ambivalence increased when YouTube won the

Primetime Engineering Emmy Award from the Academy of Television Arts & Sciences in 2013. Post-television category-bending phenomena such as YouTube transform the referent of "television" into a complex mix of professional, semi-professional, and amateur content that competes for attention across all screens. We are all Archie Bunker's children but we will never regard television in the same way as the baby boomer generation once did. Everything about television is rendered uncertain; "the medium's definition is in a state of confusion."[98] Our "definitional conceits" about the essential and distinguishing characteristics of television are being pushed "to the breaking point."[99]

Uricchio notes that one of the "oldest elements in television's definition was its potential for liveness."[100] Of course, aside from sports, breaking news, and rare events the majority of television viewing is not live. Any defence of television as a special category of liveness falls apart on the interrogation of the actual content of television. Indeed, it may be the case that the Internet will one day become the preferred medium for viewing and commenting in real time on live events.

Television theorists have also privileged Raymond Williams's notion of flow as the essential character of television. Flow describes how television programming and advertising breaks create a particular temporal experience. It is generally thought that the Internet does the opposite – breaks up the experience of time into small segments of distracted attention. Yet ever since the dawn of the Web people have described getting lost in the surfing experience and losing any sense of time. More recently, online television viewers such as Caroline Marques describe how "it's much easier to be sucked into an Internet frenzy and watch an unhealthy amount of shows or movies in one afternoon."[101] Marques experienced how flow manifests itself to the post-generation audience. The argument that online television is not really television because it lacks some essential character of twentieth-century television is misguided. Television is not a fixed experience defined by a particular industry structure, ontological status, or technological context. Consider Uricchio's argument that YouTube does not manifest flow because it offers "a set of equivalently accessible alternatives at any given moment."[102] This fails to account for how television, when seen as part of a larger entertainment ecosystem of the family room, is always competing against a plurality of accessible alternatives at any given moment. In many households television is experienced less as a flow and more as part of a riot, a carnival of competing sources of attention, conversation, and entertainment and often just a source of white noise that momentarily and only weakly holds viewers' attention.

The twentieth-century television system had a particular way of manifesting flow within the audience but flow is not unique to that century's television viewing experience. Uricchio is correct to argue that Williams's notion of flow remains vital to our evaluation and understanding of television.[103] Yet to argue as Uricchio does that there is a fundamental difference in the experience of time between television and YouTube overlooks significant aspects of the current moment in television's history. Television is becoming more like YouTube as it moves online and YouTube is becoming more like television as it deploys channels, professionally created content, subscription-based access, and ubiquitous availability. The argument that YouTube is categorically different from television falls apart when I can turn on my television and watch a complete episode of *I Dream of Jeannie* streaming in from YouTube or, conversely, turn on my computer and watch television shows on YouTube. Van Dijck proposes a variation on the concept of flow that recognizes that the audience watches television and YouTube as part of the same fluid routine. As a result, "YouTube at best creates a staccato flow of snippets that is easily abandoned by users, in contrast to the programmed flow of television stations."[104] It remains unclear how this is so different from the staccato flow of traditional television in a contemporary context of multiple screens, mobile audiences, and distracted viewers. Google is trying to re-engineer the staccato flow, the online viewing experience, into more of a "lean back" television style by pursuing content deals with major broadcasters and professional Web-content providers, serving as a television content "referral service" and "licensing the streaming of television shows and movies."[105] In other words, Google is working hard to make the experience of program flow and time on YouTube as similar as possible to traditional television.

The ambiguous distinction between YouTube and television grows as Google moves to position YouTube as a form of competition in the television and film marketplace. YouTube may not be trying to replace television but it is competing for the online video audience with on-demand subscriptions, film rentals, content partners, and original channels. Van Dijck's analysis of YouTube as a cultural form captures the ambivalence of television's definition when she concludes that YouTube competes with television on terms set by the television industry and, as a result, "YouTube appears to be distinctly different from television and yet ... cannot be seen separately from the latter."[106] Scholars who insist on rigid distinctions between television and online hybrid forms such as YouTube risk reinforcing the ideological strategy of the television industry. Van Dijck describes this discursive strategy as the industry's tendency to "point out that all alternatives are mere derivations of the only legitimate cultural form" – commercial television.[107] Uricchio also advises against trying to stuff YouTube into "an old media category" at the very time when the television industry "has stuffed itself into an unnecessarily small conceptual space" – wise words indeed.[108]

Van Dijck proposes that the analysis of YouTube as a technology, social practice, and cultural form substitutes the common terms of reference – broadcasting (technology), watching television (social practice), and programs (cultural form) – with the terms "homecasting," "videosharing," and "snippets" (video clips).[109] Doing so would provide television theorists with "a level playing field where socio-cultural values stand on equal footing with economic ones."[110] Van Dijck argues that introducing this new vocabulary "to name and define YouTube's generic technology, social practice and cultural form, is a step towards the creation of a more transparent media logic in which new platforms are not analyzed exclusively in terms of economics, but where a legal-economic perspective is functionally paired off with an integrated techno-socio-cultural viewpoint."[111] The definition of television should not be biased towards legal and economic considerations.

Van Dijck's proposal for a new vocabulary privileges aspects of YouTube that represent its formative years while ironically overlooking recent changes that mimic the role of television – long-form content, commercially produced content, video rentals, channels, sponsors, paid subscriptions, and the warm embrace of the advertising industry. The terms "homecasting," "videosharing," and "snippets" fail to capture these commercial aspects of YouTube. "Homecasting" also suffers from the danger of not accounting for any potential large-scale shifts to mobile uploading and viewing. Consider a similar weakness in Williams's description of television as a form of mobile privatization – a quality of television that gave the audience a window on the world in the privacy of their homes.[112] This quality of the twentieth-century television system gets turned on its head in the digital environment. The combination of widespread digital cameras and mobile viewing devices is turning television into something that deprives the domestic sphere of privacy as it transmits formerly private activity into the global videoscape.[113] Online television could be described as mobile de-privatization – we are all potential subjects of the video camera. We are the content of television.

The technology, social practice, and cultural form of online videos in general and on YouTube in particular remain complex, heterogeneous, and rapidly changing. Van Dijck's voice must be taken into account when she suggests that "media theorists and cultural critics need to pay more attention to the growing significance of user-generated content ... but they cannot simply accept the conventional models of the broadcast era."[114] Whatever vocabulary eventually dominates the analysis of You-Tube, we must reject the notion that YouTube is not some form of television because it fails to mirror the economic and technological structures of twentieth-century broadcast television. As Uricchio suggests, You-Tube's unique strength is that it provides us with "a transitional model to next generation television."[115] In 1993, over a decade before the rise of online video, Cubitt considered the growth of video culture and asked what would "a truly popular television look like? Amateurish, of course."[116] Perhaps YouTube and the dramatic increase in the production and distribution of amateur video are part of a transition to a truly popular form of television.

The new sources of online television are not merely providing an alternative distribution channel for the post-television audience; they are attempting to lure audiences with new content. Amazon, Google, Yahoo!, AOL, and other Internet companies are trying to undermine television's strategy of artificial scarcity – scarcity of good programming. Amazon recently created Amazon Studios to develop original content for its distribution services, Amazon Prime, Amazon Instant Video, and LOVEFiLM. Yahoo! has commissioned two original TV-length comedy series. Even Microsoft has entered the fray. It has hired CBS senior executive Nancy Tellem to run Microsoft's Xbox Entertainment Studios and develop original content. While it is generally assumed that the "Internet favours media content owners rather than media content distributors," this does not address what happens when distributors who are indigenous to the Internet, such as Netflix and Google, become content owners.[117]

There has always been plenty to watch, but there has seldom been much worth watching. Even as it operates as a blight on common culture the television industry also has created some of the best content. Internet companies have specialized in creating new online experiences and are moving into Hollywood's turf – quality original programming. But there is no formula that guarantees success. Microsoft has failed to become a market leader in any of its Internet-related ventures since the beginning of the Web. Google has demonstrated that it does not know how to create a successful social network platform and is unable to lure people away from Facebook, at least thus far. Apple has failed to be a disruptive force of innovation in the television sector as it once was in the cell phone sector. Individually, each of the new high-technology competitors for the television audience has tremendous obstacles to overcome, yet collectively they represent extraordinary forces of transformation that have revolutionized television in a very short span of time.

Empowering the Beast

Among television, film, and media scholars video has traditionally been associated with democratization, participatory culture, counter-discourses, resistance, activism, grass roots, and progressive social critique. When cable television arrived on the scene in the 1980s, video activists saw the potential for a cultural revolution, but the forces of marketization and privatization "meant the hoped-for cable-TV video revolution stalled."[118] As a source of non-commercial cultural production the Internet has inspired similar hopes. The irony of participatory online video, epitomized by YouTube, is that this locus of an unparalleled rise in self-representation and counter-culture video production is realigning itself with the broadcast industry, leaving critical theorists such as William Merrin to argue that "YouTube has little in common with either the countercultural spirit of the video movement or the decentralized and diverse information structures it hoped would emerge and resembles more of the very 'beast'" – commercial television – with each passing year.[119] There is reason to believe that the transformation of the Web into the future home of television and its increasingly fragmented audience may bring with it a beast even more fearsome than the commercial culture of the twentieth century. When we shift our viewing habits to online television we give up any pretence to a private home viewing experience. Essentially, we invite both old and new media corporations to spy on our every byte of digital consumption as we feast on digital plenitude.

Columbia University law professor Eben Moglen has made a compelling case for how we have given away our privacy in exchange for free services on the Internet. To summarize his argument, on the Internet "you get spying all the time."[120] This spying takes the form of companies monitoring all our actions and communications on the Internet and trading or selling that information to other companies and handing it over upon request to state agencies such as the US National Security Agency. Consider the scope of information Bell Canada collects from its customers: Web pages visited, location, app and device feature usage, television viewing, and calling patterns. As with all major media corporations, Bell is intent on eroding its customers' privacy in the pursuit of profit. Customers who purchase the so-called triple-play from media corporations – cell phone, Internet, and television service – give companies like Bell and AT&T enormous amounts of personal data. · Moglen rightly notes that on the Internet, "spying comes free with everything now."[121] Spying comes with everything we pay for online, including our television and movie consumption. For example, Hulu faced a class-action lawsuit for allegedly disclosing what viewers watch to other companies without their consent.[122]

The shift to online television is part of a larger trend in the development of high-technology smart homes that are networked to the Internet and a wide variety of commercial services. Whereas the "beast" of commercial television was once largely limited to a one-way flow of information coming into households on isolated, dedicated devices – television sets – the increasing integration of smart screens and Internet services into households is leading to the constant monitoring of household activity by corporations. Online television is just one piece of this puzzle. Lynn Spigel provides a critique of the smart home that allows us to see smart televisions and other post-television technologies such as smartphones, tablet computers, and networked home appliances as part of a powerful market system intent on eroding privacy and enhancing the management of consumer behaviour.

The smart home has been envisioned by architects since the 1920s and is available in various forms to the wealthy and the middle class. The smart home is smart because many of its appliances are embedded with software and sensors that are networked to the marketplace. Refrigerators that automatically order more milk before it is all gone, lights that dim or brighten automatically depending upon what you are doing, monitors that capture your heart rate, toilets that analyse your urine, and countless gadgets that help increase productivity while at home add intelligence and surveillance to the home. The smart home takes on the persona of a "companion" and defines new "post-human family relations where humans and artifacts are networked together in the performance of family roles associated with caretaking, relationship-building and affection."[123] On the one hand smart homes embody the middle-class value of luxury and on the other hand they subject the household to intense monitoring and data gathering. The smart home is part of the ongoing commodification of everyday life and is "predicated on corporate synergies, branding and especially lifestyle marketing."[124] Spigel's analysis brought to my mind a Microsoft television advertisement that portrayed a housewife getting a cup of coffee in her pyjamas and then *riding the escalator* to her bedroom office, where she explored online retail stores through the Microsoft Network. The home became completely integrated into the shopping experience. The smart home is also an extension of the office. Spigel notes that smart-home owners see their homes "as spaces for production."[125] The post-television generation will use their multiple screens to bring the workplace and the shopping mall further into the home. This, of course, is already well under way.

Our collective involvement with online television brings with it increased interactivity, which is promoted by the business community because the more we interact within commercial environments such as Netflix, YouTube, Google, and Facebook, the more we do the job of market research for corporations. The post-television generation is effectively "submitting themselves to new forms of observational feedback."[126] Every time I watch a movie on Netflix, buy a book on Amazon, say anything about myself on Facebook, or conduct a search on Google the economic system gains more information about my tastes and is better able to market to me. Smart televisions and smart homes are part of a trend that sees market research and observational science "being hardwired into the architecture of the home."[127] Our smart televisions are also broadcast centres, equipped with cameras pointing at us. We are encouraged to broadcast ourselves on YouTube while we narrowcast our preferences to marketing companies. The smart home is smart enough to measure our attitudes and values, sell that information to advertisers, and then sell us to ourselves. This process stretches back to the Taylorism of the early twentieth century, which saw the population socialized to "respond to and be observed by autonomous and anonymous measurement techniques."[128] The logic of the systems being deployed to create the post-television audience is an extension of the logic of capitalism. Domestic privacy is reduced to a romantic memory, a person's castle becomes a workstation, a bedroom transforms into a shopping mall, and every screen provides another opportunity to interface with the marketplace.

We have arrived at the point where a gleeful announcement by a company about a new product that enables a cable operator to "target ads to subscribers watching live TV on an Apple iPad based on activity from the device's Web browser" is seen as business as usual.[129] Our activity on the Web is used to enhance the effectiveness of advertising directed at us from online television. The mass deployment of the smart home comes with a new form of convergence as all of our formerly private domestic activity is combined with all our Internet interactivity and information gleaned from other data-gathering systems such as digital cash and digital wallets. The risk here is that the post-television audience will become perfectly transparent to marketers and highly susceptible to the manipulations of sophisticated shapers of private consumption and public opinion. The combination of smart homes and smart televisions promises to improve the manufacturing of consumption and consent. This is not merely the broadcast "beast" of the twentieth century. This is a far more powerful source of commercialized culture. Perhaps by collectively embracing smart homes, smart televisions, smartphones, clever fridges, knowing toilets, and related technologies we are making a terribly dumb mistake – granting the economic system more power over our individual lives and collective values.

What it means to watch television changes when it occurs across multiple screens and environments and within the multitasking contexts of a highly distracted post-television generation. Context is usually thought of as integral to meaning. The context of the television audience no longer resembles the twentieth-century audience's situation, and this suggests subtle shifts in the meaning of television. Joshua Green suggests, "Dis-embedding content from the technological and industrial strategies of broadcast television fundamentally disrupts presumptions about the context of viewing that have been central to the imagining of the television audience."[130] It is dangerous to presume anything about the context in which online television viewing occurs. The online audience seeks distraction from television while watching television and accepts complexity, low-resolution quality, inconvenience, and even solitude. The audience also begins to play the role of programmer and even distributor. Online viewing occurs in the form of binge-watching (consuming multiple episodes in one sitting), abbreviated snacking, and dozens of highly personalized variations. A common concept running across the tangled web of online television audiences is that of freedom. The new communities of users found in the Internet era of television bring with them a sense of meaning that may be deeply connected to the often heard refrain, "I want to watch what I want, where I want, when I want, for free." Freedom emerges as a key notion that defines the meaning of television for digital natives, pirates, and cord cutters in the digital networked era. Television studies have drawn a long, if not troubled, connection between the meaning of television and democratizing processes. Perhaps online television has a similar relationship to anarchy.

The digital plenitude that comes with legitimate and illegitimate forms of online viewing delivers more freedom of choice along with increased surveillance and means of avoiding surveillance (through virtual private networks and similar tools). At the centre of all these changes to distribution and audience viewing habits is that perennial issue of control – who will determine the ultimate character of the viewing experience? The Internet community is abuzz with a debate over the future of online television. As Josh Levy put it, if the incumbent television industry has its way, "you'll need a cable subscription to watch any TV show on the Internet."[131] In the doublespeak of the television industry, paywalls and forcing people to pay for bundled cable subscriptions if they wish to view television online is "about liberating content."[132] Yet, as the following chapter explores, it is far from certain that even the US cable and broadcast oligopoly has sufficient market power to control online television as Levy fears.

Summary

Netflix, Amazon, Hulu, iTunes, and YouTube demonstrate the potential of a viable online marketplace for video content and the threat that such a market represents to the incumbent industry. It is noteworthy that the least restrictive model of an online audience in terms of productive participation – YouTube – is also the largest source of users, amateur videos, and online video views. The least restrictive paid-subscription model – Netflix – has the largest amount of paying subscribers, with over ten times that of Hulu. The service that has the most restrictive geographical licensing, Hulu, has the least number of paying subscribers. From the point of view of the cord cutter it does not matter which online video provider has the largest or best catalogue, given that many cord cutters subscribe to more than one streaming service. As video streaming services expand their content libraries, they create a more robust online television experience that threatens to disintermediate the incumbent television and movie oligopolies.

It is too early to say for certain, but it appears that the online audience is acquiring a distinct preference for advertising-free video experiences. The online viewing experience may also be socializing the post-television audience in new ways of watching television that are poorly served by the incumbent industry. While online television ventures such as Netflix represent high-margin streams of revenue for the incumbent industry, they also threaten to devalue programming content by eroding exclusivity and scarcity. The motivation for the audience to cut the cable cord and look for less expensive ways of being entertained grows as audiences become more mobile, online content proliferates, and competitively priced television and movie services appear online.

Contradictory effects on the television system abound with increased revenue streams versus threatened business models, more effective ways to deliver targeted advertising versus more ways to become socialized in ad-free experiences, and more ways to become engaged in television versus more distractions from second and third screens. Online audiences increase the ratings of television shows but aggressively pirate desirable shows that are locked behind high paywalls. As television migrates across platforms and further infiltrates our lives it becomes more seductive and perhaps more addictive but for some also more advertising-free. Online television has reinvigorated the beast of commercial television but has also created a giant-slayer – the post-television generation.

7 Disintermediation: The Political Economy of Television

I began *Post-TV* with a look at music piracy as the predecessor to the habits of the online television audience. Online piracy represents the most extreme state of content and audiences out of control. Cord cutters and cord nevers represent the worst possible audience trends for the cable television industry – viewers opting out of paying for cable television. Representatives of the entertainment industry and financial advisers insist that piracy will be reined in and cord-cutting will remain marginal, but the possibility of significant disruption due to uncontrolled digital plenitude remains.

The television industry is aware of the changes taking place with the online audience and, regardless of their insistence that the status quo must be maintained, networks and cable operators have responded in a variety of ways. Release windows between territories such as the United States and Australia are collapsing in an effort to forestall piracy; every major channel, network, and broadcaster is providing various levels of access to content via websites; and most cable TV operators have some form of online video-on-demand service. The US television industry has implemented the TV Everywhere strategy of requiring authentication from cable subscribers before consumers can access online programming. Investment analysts believe that TV Everywhere will increase customer loyalty and add as much as $4 billion per year in subscription revenues.[1] Of course, there are certain risks to trusting what investment analysts have to say about the Internet. By 2014 only 21 per cent of pay-TV subscribers used TV Everywhere services at least once a month.[2] The use of the incumbent industry's authentication service is growing but it will have trouble competing against piracy's vastly larger catalogue, simplicity, and freedom. Writing in the *New York Times*, Molly Wood described the service in the following terms: "TV

Everywhere is still significantly less than everywhere, as even the industry itself admits, and the authentication process for watching shows is legendarily annoying."[3] Marvin Ammori, professor of law at the University of Nebraska–Lincoln, conducted a legal analysis of TV Everywhere and concluded that this business plan "rests on an illegal collusion and other potential violations of antitrust laws."[4] It is indeed curious how often one encounters the notion of collusion in the academic literature surrounding the television industry.

The industry has also implemented geo-blocking in the effort to maintain artificial scarcity across territories. Incumbent firms have invested in online delivery systems and acquired digital content studios. The effects of disintermediation will face counter-forces of remediation. Some cable distributors in the United States, the United Kingdom, and Sweden are already integrating Netflix into their own content packages. Meanwhile, one of Netflix's competitors, Amazon Prime, was developing a business relationship with CBS and HBO. Incumbent firms are busy integrating new streaming services into their syndication strategies and manoeuvring to prevent any one streaming media company from becoming the equivalent of iTunes in the music sector. This may prove difficult given that the efforts of the cable industry have been described as "predominantly fragmented and proprietary."[5] These are just some of the many steps that the industry has taken in light of the online challenges it faces.

It is unknown if the television and movie industries will avoid the same fate that other content industries have faced. The entertainment industry suffers from "pervasive uncertainty" about how to include the online audience in its operations and has been "unsuccessful in imposing traditional business models on the Internet."[6] It is far from certain that the incumbent players will eliminate competition from innovators, maintain profit margins, or continue to grow. The industry faces growing competition in production and distribution of content. This threatens to erode the artificial scarcity which lies at the foundation of media economics. Increased competition is raising content costs and content producers are innovating with new business models such as crowdsourcing. Each of these trends could change the economics of the television and movie industry and disrupt traditional business models.

Each sector of the entertainment industry is responding in various ways to the online audience. They may integrate new competitors into their operations. Cable operators may offer various degrees of unbundling to consumers. Media corporations may respond with mergers, acquisitions, and consolidation among incumbent firms. Comcast is making a $45 billion (US) bid to acquire Time Warner Cable. AT&T is seeking to acquire the satellite television provider DirecTV for $49 billion. Meanwhile, in Canada the largest telecommunication, media, and Internet (TMI) conglomerate, Bell Canada Enterprises, bought Astral Media for $3.4 billion. The reason for this merger is clear: Astral owns the premium television content (such as HBO Canada, the Movie Network, and 22 other channels) which represents "Bell's largest single content cost."[7] Owning content will make Bell's Internet services more profitable. Bell knows which way the wind is blowing. Content and communication providers around the world see their broadband services as a source of revenue-generating services. Providing access to content and services via broadband Internet is becoming a key source for generating new revenue in mature and competitive markets. Meanwhile, Bell's CEO, George Cope, has the audacity to claim that regulation of this market is bad for consumers and "the concept of monopoly is ... antiquated."[8] Apparently the concept of self-interest is alive and well.

We can see omens of disruption in the Canadian television sector with the challenges faced by Rogers Communication, which operates Canada's largest cable television network, wireless cell phone network, and publishing company. One in three Canadians has a Rogers cell phone. The *Globe and Mail* relates how "all of the company's main businesses are now either facing significant headwinds or are in decline."[9] Its cable television business is losing customers to competition from fibre-optic television services, Netflix, and cord-cutting. Rogers is serving mature markets that are not growing and as a result, "shareholders have earned almost nothing over the past five years, even when dividends are included."[10] The article was accompanied by 112 replies from online readers, most of which expressed disdain for Rogers's customer service, marketing practices, and price gouging. The highest-rated comment among online readers was this: "When Rogers finally goes under, I'll dance on their grave."

The following explores the possibility that the television industry's adaptive measures may not be enough to forestall the disintermediating effects of the Internet, which took a toll on other content sectors such as news, publishing, pornography, and music. What if the past of the music industry is the correct foundation for forecasting the future of the television and movie sector? What would happen if television's content and audiences not only remained out of control but the degree of anarchy, innovation, competition, and disruption grew to encompass a significant percentage of the mainstream audience? Mark Cooper, director of research at the Consumer Federation of America, describes the music industry as providing "the first major example of digital disintermediation."[11] Music companies share a number of common characteristics with television and movie companies. Their business model was based on bundled products, CDs that had a very high profit margin, and the industry itself was oligopolistic, dominated by four major conglomerates. Market dominance was achieved by the music, film, and television sectors through their control over distribution. This control is generally described in terms of monopolies and oligopolies. Of course today there are two more significant parallels. For the most part the products of the entire entertainment industry are circulated in digital format and are subject to very high rates of online piracy. Cooper argues that the recording industry functions as a "tight oligopoly able to engage in the exercise of market power."[12] Successful lawsuits by the FCC and state attorneys general in 2000 and 2002 for price setting stand as testimony to collusive market power, though "today the industry still remains a tight oligopoly with suspect business practices."[13]

Throughout the 1990s consumers were forced to pay for CDs that contained many songs they did not want. By 2000 there was significant consumer dissatisfaction with CD prices.[14] Digital consumer electronics such as iPods, the mass adoption of the Internet, and new consumer habits led to massive de-bundling in the music sector. The music industry suffered huge financial losses because they eliminated singles as a purchase option, forced consumers to purchase bundled products, artificially increased the price of CDs through collusion, and failed to adapt to the new habits of online consumers. Ultimately, the music sector's strategy failed because eventually music lovers were able to go online and pay for only the songs they wanted. The online marketplace, epitomized by iTunes's sale of single songs, disintermediated the distribution of CDs through established channels. Cooper argues that this transition from bundled CDs to single song sales resulted in consumers collectively saving somewhere between $5.6 and $9 billion dollars.[15] The music industry's strategy of trying to "lock down competition and slow alternative distribution" failed.[16] Online music, in all its varieties, became a significant substitution for the purchase of physical CDs. *Businessweek* put the matter of disintermediation in the following terms: the music industry "looked up one day to find that Steve Jobs and Apple had taken control of their inventory."[17] The recent history of the music industry may provide insight into the near future of the television industry.

In 2009 the *New York Times* reported that cable television was "the last remaining pillar of the old media business that has not been severely affected by the Internet."[18] The television and movie industries are in the early stages of disintermediation. Unlike the music industry, many players in the video business not only control the content but are also owners of the new distribution system – Internet service providers – and thus "have a direct interest in preventing the disintermediation and have powerful tools to prevent it."[19] Yet this unique position of companies such as Comcast/NBCU – which produce the content, sell cable subscriptions, and sell Internet connections – has not prevented the majority of the video industry's content from ending up online in the hands of pirates. So far both usage-based pricing (making it expensive to download a lot of content) and locking down content (trying to keep it off the Internet) have failed.

Following on the heels of severe disruption within the music industry, we also witnessed Internet-related forces disintermediating the movie rental business when Blockbuster filed for bankruptcy protection in the United States in September 2010 and in Canada in 2011. By 2012 Rogers closed their DVD retail outlets, leaving Canada without a national DVD rental chain. At the peak of the movie rental business in 1989 there were over 70,000 stores in the United States.[20] By 2011 there were only 5,900 left. The storefront rental outlets were replaced by 47,000 DVD rental kiosks such as Redbox. Competition from lower-priced vending machines, online movie streaming, Netflix, iTunes, and piracy brought the 25-year-old movie rental chain Blockbuster to its knees. Its main rival, Hollywood Video, collapsed earlier in the year. Two years later rentals of physical DVDs fell 39 per cent and rentals of DVDs by mail order through companies such as Netflix fell 48 per cent. The bottom is dropping out of the market for rental of movies on physical discs as consumers shift to online options. Spending was clearly shifting: "Revenue from digital streaming was up 545 percent, to $549 million, from about $85 million the year earlier, and total digital revenue rose more than 74 percent, to $1.2 billion from about $699 million."[21] When the online audience decides on a different pattern of viewing and purchasing, the consequences can be swift and severe.

The post-television age has begun at the very time when television has never been more prominent in our lives or more profitable for the industry. The production and distribution of television generates $300 billion in annual revenues.[22] The incumbent players still dominate all aspects of the industry and household television sets still capture over

97 per cent of viewing hours.[23] US domestic spending on filmed entertainment was up 3.1 per cent in 2011 and "consumer-driven revenues
have grown at a 5.8% compounded annual rate since 2000, and the
international revenue for studios for U.S. product has grown at an estimated double-digit pace over the same period."[24] Not all the news is
good. Global advertising revenues fell in 2012 – the first decline since
figures started being compiled.[25] Nonetheless, commercial television is
far from dead.

The Cord-cutting "Myth"

Given the health of the incumbent industry it comes as little surprise
that financial analysts generally see little or no threat from online viewing to established industry players. Consider the appraisal of the cord-
cutting threat provided in 2012 by Bank of Montreal (BMO) Capital
Markets. The financial study argued that "no one watches for free and
for that matter the production of professional content requires revenues
to keep the supply of content coming."[26] It costs money to make television shows so the audience must pay. What they really mean is that
the industry can make far more profit if it makes advertisers pay *and* the
audience pay to watch the shows that carry advertising. Of course, the
daily experience of millions, if not hundreds of millions, of online viewers is that they can and do watch for free. The authors address the issue
of over-the-top viewing and conclude, "The new fear, cord cutting, that
presupposed that content, new and old, would be available at no cost
and with no commercials is a myth."[27] This so-called "myth" contrasts
sharply with the experiences of millions of online viewers who are living the myth every day. The authors appear to have little understanding
of cord-cutting and piracy-supported viewing habits. They wrongly assert that people will not be able to replace cable network subscriptions
with online substitutes because the online viewer will not be able to
find premium content.[28] Again, this flies in the face of a considerable
body of evidence provided by cord cutters' own accounts of their online
viewing experience, which is generally described as "everything I want
to see for free." The financial analysts conclude that "the risk of disintermediation for cable and telcos is relatively low."[29] Yet disintermediation
due to the Internet turns out to be a bit of a nightmare for the music,
newspaper, publishing, and movie rental businesses.

The BMO study also claims that the large file size of television shows
and movies, combined with data caps imposed by Internet service

providers, will severely limit the effects of piracy. The notion that the past of the music industry foretells the future of the television industry is utterly rejected. The belief that "Filmed entertainment content is destined to the same dynamics and similar economic impact as the music business where piracy and portability will facilitate a massive erosion of revenues and profitability from the filmed entertainment industry" is merely a "myth."[30] On the one hand, if this were true one wonders why the television and movie industries are claiming *billions* of dollars in lost revenue from online piracy. Perhaps the MPAA's claims are so big and so bold that they just do not figure within investment advice. On the other hand, one needs only to consider the near future of compression technology to see the faint hope that bandwidth caps and file sizes represent for the television industry's salvation. As Daniel Minoli notes, "there are new compression technologies, such as fractals and wavelets, that if perfected and become cost-effective, will decrease the bandwidth requirement [of online video] by an *order of magnitude or more*."[31]

There is a fallacy in short-term thinking that counts on large file sizes and current bandwidth limitations for forecasting future trends in network traffic and piracy. Michael Powell, president of the National Cable and Telecommunications Association, notes that "the network is getting exponentially faster every year."[32] The day will come when many Internet users will be able to download an entire television season in a few minutes. Cisco Systems predicts that "the average fixed broadband speed is expected to increase nearly fourfold, from 9 Megabits per second in 2011 to 34 Mbps in 2016."[33] By mid-2012 Verizon doubled the speed of its popular Internet service to 50 Mbps and offered download speeds as high as 300 Mbps. At 50 Mbps Verizon customers will be able to download an entire movie in slightly more than two minutes. This move was seen as likely prompting Verizon's rivals to increase the speed of their ISP offerings. Size, speed, and distance are rendered increasingly meaningless with each decade that passes in the lifetime of the Internet.

When we focus on the major incumbent players we find that one of the most distinctive aspects of the cable television industry is a high degree of customer dissatisfaction. Cable companies have the lowest customer satisfaction ratings.[34] If this industry is facing threats of disintermediation it cannot count on consumer loyalty to keep its customers. The unpopular business practices of the television industry have created conditions that compel many customers to seek out disintermediating agents.

The dominant narrative of the television industry insists that online video is a complement to and not a substitute for its existing services. At the 61st annual Cable Show the main subject of presentations and conversations was how to integrate online video into existing operations and business practices. The amount of concern shown over the emerging online audience betrayed the fact that online video was perceived as "a disruptive element in the market place – one that cable operators desperately want to get control of."[35] One observer of the convention, Nathan Ingraham, felt that the incumbent players' main intention was to preserve existing business models and market domination. "Beneath the acknowledgement of the rapid changes underway and cable's need to evolve along with them was a strong defense of providers and networks continuing to do business exactly as they have done for the last four decades or so."[36] The cable industry is unlikely to unbundle its products unless it is forced to do so.

The risk of disintermediation is relatively low for the short term, but things tend to unfold on the Internet at the speed of bytes flying through fibre-optic cables. Even the authors of the BMO financial analysis recognized that "disintermediation is arriving," although they assured investors that the incumbent industry players would successfully manage and control the process.[37] Obviously, I think otherwise. To better understand the risks that the video industry faces, the following will look at how the US television industry currently dominates the flow of television across global markets through its control of time and space. The purpose here is to come to an understanding of how organizational power is exercised within the US television industry and how that type of power stands to be disrupted by the network effects of the Internet. To appreciate the potential for a post-television age we need a picture of how market power is exercised within the dominant television industry. How might that power be disrupted by the peculiar characteristics of the Internet that have caused disintermediation within content and retail sectors and brought twentieth-century business models so much grief?

In *Envisioning Media Power: On Capital and Geographies of Television* (2009) Brett Christophers explored how television exercises market power through control over the flow of television across space and time and through the creation of artificial scarcity.[38] The following will outline Christophers's model of the political economy of television and mine it for insights into how disintermediation could disrupt incumbent industry power.

The US television industry is unique in its reliance on the control of foreign television markets. The majority of national television markets outside the United States are import-dependent on US content and "that dependence has in most cases been increasing."[39] This leads Christophers to argue that "the single most important factor" in the political economy of television is that "global television trade is overwhelmingly dominated by the U.S."[40] The evidence for the global dependency on US television is overwhelming. The US media industry generates "fully 70% of global program trade by volume."[41] The closest competitor, the United Kingdom, generates a mere 10%, with "no other individual country originating more than 4%."[42]

Not only does the United States exercise tremendous global market power but this power has become "increasingly consolidated in the hands of a small number of large [US] firms."[43] Deregulation and rationalization in the US media industry has led to "five major media companies with a stranglehold on the export of US television to international markets. They are NBCUniversal [now Comcast/NBCU], Viacom, Walt Disney, Time Warner, and News Corporation."[44] These five companies also dominate the US domestic broadcast market. The domestic concentration is even greater when one includes program production. After the rules that prevented broadcasters from owning production houses changed in the 1990s, there was "a major shift towards vertical integration of production and distribution."[45] The same companies that once controlled the distribution of television now also control the making of television, "to the degree that nearly all of the most successful and recognized US television shows are now produced by the major broadcast networks' in-house production arms. Thus the percentage of *independent* productions on the networks has fallen from 50% in 1995 to just 18% in 2007."[46] Given that the transnational flow of content is the foundation of economic strength for the US media industry, we must ask what it is that maintains and protects that flow of content across geographies. The answer lies in the control of access and the artificial creation of scarcity through copyright and legal regimes. The US media industry must have effective strategies for preventing leakage of content into uncontrolled foreign (or domestic) competition.

Distributors of cultural products like television and movies must artificially limit access to their products, which would otherwise be available everywhere at once. By controlling when and where video content is shown across various geographies, the industry limits access and thus influences price. A scarce product will command a higher price than one that is readily available simultaneously from multiple sources. Without scarcity "there would be no 'media economy' as we know it."[47] Two things are absolutely paramount to the continued existence of the US media industry in its current form: the maintenance of content scarcity through the licensing of shows within the global television regulatory regime and the control of distribution by the US media oligopoly. Oligopolistic distribution captures domestic and foreign markets and copyright protects the product and ensures that scarcity and price are maintained.

Christophers points to the industry practice of windowing as the central strategy for creating scarcity across global markets. Windowing is the studio process that sees a film or a television show released in the US market first and then gradually appear in cinemas and on television sets in other countries at a later date. The process of gradually releasing content across space and time is complex but the result is well known: the maximization of revenue from each distinct part of international markets. Windowing also involves isolating content on different platforms, such as cinema, television, tablet computers, and smartphones. One platform is used to stimulate demand on another and windowing ensures that a lower-priced market, such as a movie on Amazon for download at a few dollars, does not cannibalize demand for the same movie on a higher priced format, such as a Blu-ray Disc. Thus windowing is a highly developed business practice that "facilitates the *territorialization of scarcity* by virtue of the spatial partitioning of access and copyright … time and space are mediated to engineer local scarcity and maximize local demand."[48] The windowing process ensures that scarcity is maintained in foreign markets and has done so very successfully from the earliest days of the movie and television industry.

This scarcity-creating system has faced numerous threats over the decades from cable television, VHS video, DVD sales, and satellite television distribution, but with each new technology and its threat of disintermediation, Hollywood "has always managed to successfully domesticate them – integrate them into the prevailing market structure, and rework windows to accommodate them *without* changing the basic fabric and logic of the windowing architecture."[49] In response to DVD sales, satellite television, and the Internet the industry adapted its windowing process. Geographical windows have been "converging in the world of television programming" and "many studios are now releasing films internationally on more or less the same date."[50] Due to extraordinary high rates of local online piracy, Disney and Sony Pictures allow Korean audiences to stream movies at home that are currently playing in theatres. Nonetheless, for the most part windowing remains intact as a business practice. A complete collapse in worldwide cinema windows would be catastrophic for the film industry, given that "over 95% of the top 25 films' gross box office receipts are achieved in the first eight weeks in theatres."[51] Windowing ensures that audiences have no choice but to go to the theatres when a movie is initially released while also ensuring that theatres do not have to compete against other, lower-priced distribution platforms such as Netflix.

The current reigning assumption within the media industry is that the Internet will also fall in line with all other previous disintermediating threats and become integrated into the windowing process. Although the seas may be rough, Hollywood will sail past this virtual iceberg. Yet the Internet is not just a new technology that threatens to bring disintermediation in its wake. It is a categorically different order of technology. None of the previous technological threats had the core characteristics of the Internet – a global, distributed network that enabled *billions* of ordinary people to exchange content directly with others at marginal costs. As a distribution system the Internet has thus far defied attempts to impose a territorialization of scarcity. If it is available in one area of the Internet it is freely available in all areas. If it is in the theatres it can also be found online through piracy. The legal availability of television shows and movies on the Internet is subject to industry windowing practices, but the global flow of online piracy renders such windowing practices irrelevant to a significant percentage of the audience.

While there has been very little concrete impact on global piracy in response to the actions of the media industry, the industry itself has been forced to adjust its own practices. Online piracy

> has led rapidly to a trend towards geographical alignment of transmission windows ... The rationale is straightforward: make sure viewers in international markets can watch the programs *on television* as soon as possible after the US airing, otherwise they will get hold of the program illegally and – it is feared – will not watch the television broadcast.[52]

The Australian broadcaster ABC made episodes of the fall 2012 season of *Doctor Who* available online a mere 50 minutes after they appeared in the United Kingdom. In the case of the television show *Lost* the gap was reduced from one year in the 2004 season to four days in 2007. Yet this is a poor example of the industry successfully adapting to the online audience. By 2009 *Lost* was the second most pirated television show on BitTorrent and by 2010 it was number one.[53]

Geo-blocking: Success or Failure?

Christophers asks if the "explicit *territorialization* of the global television economy" can be maintained.[54] He notes that there are early signs that "territory-specific television program release and monetization may in fact be *somewhat* easier to defend and uphold in the online world."[55] These early signs are the use of geo-blocking technologies that, as seen in chapter 3, prevent many Canadians from viewing Hulu. Christophers argues that "geoblocking and comparable technologies do hold out hope for the studios that the Internet's geographical economy will be considerably more controllable than they may have feared."[56] Nonetheless, I remain sceptical. Geo-blocking is easily circumvented and is hardly the stuff to recreate market territorialization within the Internet. Anyone who is going to go to the trouble of cord-cutting is also likely to take the time to learn how to circumvent geo-blocking. In response to a story about geo-blocking in the *Globe and Mail* one reader replied, "even a very novice user can get around it after 10 minutes of research."[57]

In 2007 law professor Dan Svantesson argued that we are "doubtlessly witnessing the Internet undergoing a remarkable change – from the world's first and only 'borderless' communications medium to something that much more resembles our physical world divided by borders of different kinds."[58] Yet five years later the Internet bears only a partial resemblance to a world filled with borders. Even the highest virtual walls, such as those around China and Iran, are circumvented and bypassed. Svantesson based his argument on the growing deployment of geo-blocking technology but, as with all such censoring technologies, an army of hackers is ever present and considers such control strategies nothing more than an interesting challenge easily overcome. Yes, these technologies will affect some, but they have no bearing on online behaviour where there is a combination of willingness and time.

Is geo-blocking truly effective as a technology of territorialization and content control? There appears to be little correlation between geo-blocking and any decline in piracy. For those living outside the United States, circumventing geo-blocking has become synonymous with Hulu and Netflix. Thus far its current role appears to be primarily symbolic – it is used as a form of legal compliance by online media sellers to reassure content providers that some form of territorial protection is in place, but that protection is weak at best. Christophers insists that territorialization will be maintained within the Internet television economy, "even if slightly frayed around the edges."[59] Yet at this point virtual territorialization and windowing are overwhelmed by illegitimate audience practices such as circumvention and online piracy. Legitimate online television services that are geographically restricted do attract millions of paying subscribers but both the global audience and the media industry's content remain beyond the control of the studios. Within any particular geographical market a significant percentage of the industry's legitimate online subscribers and purchasers are also digital pirates.

Legitimate online services work towards the re-territorialization of the Internet television audience while the forces of cord-cutting, circumvention, and piracy work in the opposite direction. To borrow the words of Nick Couldry on media rituals, "there are times when processes of de-territorialization become crucial, even dominant, for example when localised patterns of disorder link up to produce a wider breakdown."[60] Local patterns of piracy link up to global flows of uncontrolled content and the result is the dramatic de-territorialization of media content. Audiences all over the world see television and movies online on their own terms and avoid the restrictions of windowing strategies. There is an ongoing debate among media scholars over the degree to which the Internet renders place irrelevant (and herein I am not claiming that place has no place in conceptualizing online television). David Morley provides a balanced perspective on the issue and is "very sympathetic to the critiques of the more overblown claims of those who announce the 'end of geography.' However, one should not underplay the significance of the transformations of the world's transport and communication systems that have taken place in the last century."[61] And, one might add, in this century.

Assessing the degree and nature of change at this early stage of what is certain to be a long process of upheaval within the media industry requires constant qualification and careful generalization. Television is far from dead but is rapidly mutating into something that, when all the dust has settled, may not look like television at all. On the one hand, Christophers was quite right to argue that by 2009 the studios saw only very marginal erosion of their oligopolistic hold on media power.[62] On the other hand, off the record industry executives quietly worry that studios do not have a firm grasp on anything in cyberspace. The fundamental question here is to what extent will oligopolistic media power, which has traditionally been rooted in the control of time, place, and content, extend into a virtual domain that does not readily comply with established rules for the regulation of time, place, and property rights? To what extent will the normal experience of the twentieth-century television audience be imposed upon the twenty-first-century online audience? That is the $300 billion question.

Prior to the rise of the Internet, the industry's oligopolistic media power was the result of strategies that ensured distribution circuits were monopolized, scarcity was maintained, and territorialization remained intact. The territorialization system was not perfect. There was leakage from VHS recorders, DVD copying, and satellite piracy, and it never held much sway over areas such as China and Russia, but it was far from superfluous. Today, outside of the Internet these strategies continue to function as "economic first principles" and define the "existing spatial architecture of international television distribution" according to Christophers.[63] But others such as Benjamin Craig argue that the Internet "has made the model of territorialising media rights unsustainable."[64]

Craig turns Christophers's argument on its head and claims that territorialization is a "core driver of piracy."[65] Territorialization attempts to enforce geographical restrictions and time zones in a virtual domain that efficiently routes around paywalls and circumvents digital locks. Piracy destroys exclusivity, which is necessary to maintain if territorialization is to be effective: "exclusivity now simply acts as a barrier to supply. Instead of creating the incentive to sign up for the broadcaster's service, consumers can simply obtain the content elsewhere" or directly from the broadcaster via illegitimate means as in the case of circumventing geo-blocking.[66] Imposing territorialization within the Internet introduces higher costs and unnecessary delays that feed the piracy habit while doing little to quell it, thus leading Craig to suggest that the Internet "has made a mockery of the territorial business model."[67]

Ultimately, the problem with territorialization as a business strategy is that it prevents large segments of the online audience from viewing content and compels them to seek out illegitimate means of access. How well can the effort to artificially impose scarcity within the Internet succeed in light of digital plenitude? Media scholars, economists, and even industry executives are suggesting that maintaining artificially created scarcity in the age of the Internet is simply not practical in the long run. News, music, books, even state secrets – pretty well any digital product – exist in a condition of digital plenitude within a global networked media environment. It is not just that scarcity is breaking down online.

It is also breaking down across the television system. Neither of the two principle sources of scarcity – limited broadcast spectrum and "scarcity enforced by technological and legal constraints on illegal reproduction" – remains viable and thus "conventional methods for arbitrating access are approaching their sell-by date."[68] This is hardly a ringing endorsement of the main strategy of the incumbent television industry.

Even within the television industry the forces of competition are eroding practices such as windowing. Consider a recent dispute between Disney, Redbox, and Netflix over preserving the 28-day release-to-DVD sales window that is standard practice: "while Fox and Universal reached agreements with Netflix and Redbox, offering them significant discounts in exchange for accepting the 28-day window, Disney did not follow suit. It wanted more favorable terms than its competitors had received, terms to which Netflix and Redbox would not agree."[69] Instead of accepting Disney's more expensive terms, Redbox and Netflix bought Disney DVDs from other suppliers. Their motive was clear – the new kiosk and online video services wanted to get the movies to their customers faster than Disney was willing to allow. This created a problem for Disney, as their DVD sales fell 16 per cent from the previous quarter. Disney's attempt to preserve the sales window for the more expensive physical DVD format is being eroded by new business models that serve impatient consumers. Disney wishes to preserve scarcity yet other market forces are rapidly eroding such artificially created scarcity.

Does the absence of scarcity, weak control of access, and uncontrolled distribution mean that television has died, as Mark Pesce so boldly stated back in 2004?[70] Here we need to be careful because if the television system is in flames, we may just be staring at a burning phoenix ready to rise again through a new media transformation of its business models and strategies. In the short term there are indications that online viewing is increasing viewership and profits, so we are probably better off contemplating the transformation of an industry rather than the utter destruction of a $300 billion economy. The issue before us is not the impending death of television but the ability of the incumbent industry players to maintain their oligopoly in the face of multiple disintermediating forces.

Christophers leaves us with two cautionary and contradictory statements on the matter. On the one hand, bold and frequent claims that online developments herald an "entirely new television (space) economy" are met with "thin" evidence; "there is certainly nothing *inevitable* about it."[71] Christophers surveys the history of technological innovation – VHS, cable, DVDs – and rightly notes that "the basic economic *and* spatial architectures of television production and distribution have remained strikingly consistent."[72] On the other hand, he also points out that competitive advantage can be "relinquished in the fires of often rapid and profound structural and regulatory change."[73] Yet if we look closely at the first statement about VHS, cable, and DVDs which are presented as a guide to the future of the online television economy, we find apples being compared to oranges.

VHS was a household device isolated from direct connection to VHS machines in other homes. The cable industry was subject to strict regulation and quickly became part of the incumbent industry. Like the early broadcast system, it was a one-to-many distribution system. DVDs were a new media format that were exchanged as physical objects. None of these technologies shared the Internet's features of many-to-many. None led to such unprecedented levels of mass participation in piracy. None enabled masses of amateur and semi-professional videographers to globally distribute their videos at marginal cost. It is not simply a matter that the organizational power of the incumbent television industry prevented these technologies from achieving these things. The technologies in question were, by design, incapable of behaving like the Internet in any meaningful sense. In short, neither VHS, cable, nor DVDs constituted a participatory many-to-many global digital network that connected billions of consumers. Thus past technological innovations within the television system provide poor guidance for predicting how oligopolistic control of access and distribution will fare when faced with a global, decentralized network system that has a history of transforming private digital property into massively shared public property.

Certainly, the threat of disintermediation has not been lost on industry executives. David M. Zaslav, the chief executive of Discovery Communications, says what many have been thinking: "Somebody's going to come over the top" and start selling cable channels via the Internet.[74] Brian Stelter notes that major technology firms such as Apple, Google, Sony, and Intel "have all at least considered such an offering. Those companies could theoretically give consumers new ways to buy bundles of programming, breaking open the cable model – though an incumbent cable or telecommunications company would most likely still need to provide Internet access."[75] At present one of the main things standing in their way is the FCC's definition of a television channel.

The FCC is in the process of rethinking the definition of a channel and considering applying the revised definition to online video distributors such as Netflix, Hulu, and YouTube. The consequences would be widespread: "If it decides that they should [be classified as channels], then more companies could stream TV shows to computers and smartphones, hastening an industrywide shift to the Internet."[76] If the FCC includes these new online distributors in its definition of a channel it would make it easier for them to acquire programming. If the FCC changed the definition of multichannel video programming distributors, then new online distributors would gain the right to redistribute more types of programming. This in turn would reduce the effectiveness of the current strategy of the incumbent television industry, which restricts access to new shows and movies. As Stelter notes, this strategy of limiting access to premium content to starve competition "may explain why the incumbents have opposed any such change."[77] They wish to reduce competition and consumer choice.

In the face of change, the incumbent industry is intent on maintaining the current business model. This is exactly what Zaslav said at the 61st annual national cable television convention: "It's incumbent upon us in the content business to preserve the model so we can reach people and we can invest."[78] The model to which he referred is the one that involves garnering subscriber fees and advertising revenue from bundled channels. Yet this is an industry that suffers from an inflated sense of its own security.

By the fall of 2013 Google was the third-largest company in the United States and had a market capitalization of over $336.82 billion (US), more than the combined market capitalization of Disney, Time Warner Viacom, CBS, and Sony. This gives Google an enormous advantage when it comes to acquisitions and investing in up-front costs such as laying a fibre-optic network. Google is laying fibre in selected American cities as part of a test market for high-speed Internet connections that will be 100 times faster than the national average. The company is also considering building a Google Fiber network in Europe. The final outcomes of these plans are still years in the future. There is the possibility that if cable companies continue to pursue unpopular bandwidth caps that limit the expansion of online television, such strategies will be rendered irrelevant in the face of competition from ultra-high-speed fibre networks. Google is not merely intent on competing with Internet service providers. Google Fiber will also provide access to selected cable channels and Google's growing menu of pay-to-rent movies.

Thus the research group SNL Kagan suggested that pay-TV operators should be "very, very afraid" of Google Fiber because "Google is reinventing the business of pay TV and broadband."[79]

The former FCC commissioner Michael Powell, now head of the National Cable and Telecommunications Association, claimed, "The fact so many Americans stuck with cable through the recession is a testament to our stability and importance," but is this really the case?[80] Unlike Canada, most Americans have only one cable provider per city, leaving consumers with little real choice. In many areas of the United States cable companies enjoy exclusive municipal franchises that prevent competition from offering customers an alternate cable service. As of 2007, only 5 per cent of US households had a choice between two cable television companies.[81] One could easily say that the fact so many Americans stuck with cable through the recession is a testament to the monopolistic character of the television industry. Cable companies make an extra $6 billion per year in profits by avoiding directly competing with each other, and local governments have little interest in changing the situation because they benefit from extra taxes.[82] Once again we encounter collusion between the industry and the state at the consumer's expense.

Content Lockout

Incumbent players within the television industry own the majority of premium content. This allows a handful of firms to intimidate and punish distributors who make deals with online streaming services. We caught a glimpse of the struggle taking place within the television industry over the control of markets when Netflix's chief content officer, Ted Sarandos, publicly complained about cable providers penalizing other television companies that do business with Netflix "in the form of lower carriage fees if they have a Netflix deal."[83] Rumours and outright accusations of incumbent players pressuring cable operators not to sign contracts with online competitors abound.[84] Cable companies and studios may eventually see Netflix as a serious source of competition and raise their licensing fees beyond what Netflix can afford. The incumbent industry's plan might be to get rid of Netflix and use in-house systems to sell content directly to consumers and thus extend their oligopoly into the online market. Both Comcast and Verizon offer streaming services at prices that undercut Netflix. The incumbent industry does not want an outsider providing online access to television content.

Ammori notes that cable operators, multichannel video programming distributors (MVPDs) as they are known in the industry, are aware that the Internet could seriously disrupt the traditional television market and have taken steps to prevent disintermediation. Ammori outlines a number of tactics that the industry is using to achieve content lockout wherein the "incumbents make sure that the most popular programming that consumers would like is not available conveniently online."[85] The intention of content lockout is to "simply starve their competitors of popular shows, movies, and channels" and keep online sources of television content off the family television set.[86] Content lockout follows "the common historical practice of dominant incumbent distributors – from music composers to broadcasters and cable operators – to deprive upstart distributors of the content necessary to compete."[87] Ammori accuses the incumbents of engaging in the violation of network neutrality and overcharging for data in an effort to undermine online television. At the heart of this issue is a television market structure characterized by limited competition, a "stagnant, concentrated market."[88] The FCC has implemented various policies to promote competition within the television industry, but these rules have failed to produce results.

What haunts the television industry is the potential for competitors to put content on television without becoming vertically integrated into the incumbent industry. Ammori describes the common practice of forced vertical integration as a process in which incumbent players "require small programmers to give up much of their companies' equity stock to the MVPDs just to get carried. As one programmer's CEO explained, 'Cable and satellite TV companies want to own you before they put you on television.'"[89] In the past, this practice has ensured that many new programmers were incorporated into the existing ownership structure of the incumbent industry. With the mass deployment of broadband Internet the incumbent industry now faces two major obstacles: new companies can bypass the industry's stranglehold on distribution channels, and new content producers such as Amazon and Google are not about to give up a controlling share of their company to get their content on people's screens.

The primary disintermediation process that is already well under way – the movement of content from the personal computer to the television set, mediated by set-top boxes, smart televisions, Wi-Fi, and related technologies – was described in 2009 as a trend that "terrifies television networks and distributors."[90] There is no stopping this trend.

Audiences have resorted to a combination of legal and illegal services that enable them to get video content on any Internet-enabled screen. This throws into doubt the ability of the incumbent industry to lock down content and control audiences. In the past the incumbent players were able to maintain content lockout and control new programmers because there was no other means of mass distribution. Piracy has demonstrated that an uncontrolled means of distribution exists. Also, as Ammori notes, the economics of Internet-based distribution has reduced the cost of entry into the market for television distributors. One does not need to own satellites, fibre, or coaxial cable networks to become a video content distributor in the Internet age.

The incumbent television industry is also a major supplier of Internet services and often dominates ISP markets in its usual oligopolistic fashion. There is much concern that they could use this market dominance to restrict the flow of competing video streams or impose restrictive cap-and-metered pricing (also known as metered usage, data caps, or bit caps). Jacob Minne suggests that bit caps "are unnecessary to control costs or congestion and primarily serve the anticompetitive purpose of preventing TV subscribers from transitioning to online video services."[91] There is some truth to this and there is also the raw fact that tens of millions of people have nonetheless subscribed to various online video services. Cisco Systems senior analyst Arielle Sumits predicts that data-usage caps and consumption-based pricing will only have a modest impact on the growth rate of Internet traffic.[92] The top 1 per cent of broadband customers generate 20 per cent of Internet traffic. This suggests that data-usage caps may only affect a small percentage of the online audience. We have seen repeated instances of network neutrality violations by companies such as Comcast and Rogers and the imposition of metered Internet usage but neither has thus far stalled the advance of online video.

By mid-2012 the median monthly data usage by Comcast subscribers was 9 gigabytes. Few subscribers were reaching Comcast's 250-gigabyte monthly limit.[93] This is bound to change as the television audience migrates online. By 2014 the average US Internet household used 29 gigabytes of bandwidth per month. Cord cutters now account for 54 per cent of online traffic and consume 212 gigabytes per month (approximately 100 hours of viewable content), over seven times the amount of traffic compared to cable television subscribers.[94] In this environment data caps could operate as a significant deterrent to the adoption of online television.

The arguments over network neutrality and bit caps are complex and reflect different economic doctrines. One side sees government intervention as essential for maintaining fair competition and protecting consumer interests, and the other side believes that "market forces alone are sufficient to ensure that networks advance in the proper direction as no regulator can foresee the future in any case."[95] All sides in the debate tend to be selective in their use of evidence and are guided by deep-seated beliefs.[96]

In the United States the FCC chairman, Tom Wheeler, has proposed new policies governing network neutrality. The forthcoming regulatory framework promises to give Internet service providers the right to put in place a system of tiered broadband rates that would favour their clients, major media corporations, and discriminate against smaller companies. A lead editorial in the *New York Times* described these developments in the following terms: "Mr. Wheeler said on Thursday that he doesn't want the Internet 'divided into "haves" and "have-nots,"' but that's exactly what would happen if the commission creates a regulatory distinction between basic and premium offerings."[97] These new rules may have the potential to stop the evolution of online television dead in its tracks or may prove to be less than the "end of the Internet as we know it," as many fear. It is inevitable that online television will become increasingly expensive under the new rules but this in itself may not be enough to prevent significant disruption to incumbent players in the long term. As Susan Crawford notes, the FCC's decision to allow Internet service providers the right to charge different rates to different online content companies may be the end of Internet neutrality, but "it is not the end of the line for fair and equitable Internet access."[98] The future of the Internet remains unwritten.

In Canada the future of online television may be more secure than in the United States. Under the CRTC Canadian consumers enjoy greater protection of a neutral Internet. While Canadian Internet neutrality rules and their enforcement "are certainly not perfect," Michael Geist argues that the Canadian rules "are better than those found in the U.S. and may provide a competitive advantage for Internet companies seeking a market without paid prioritization" of Internet traffic. According to Geist, "the CRTC policy and the law make it clear that content blocking is unlikely to ever be approved ... paid prioritization – which would result in two-tier speeds based on payment – would face a very tough regulatory road in Canada."[99] Unlike the FCC in the United States, the CRTC in Canada may have more power to regulate Net neutrality and looks like it is willing to assert that power in favour of consumers and innovative Internet companies. This stands in dramatic contrast to the situation in the United States, where the FCC "lacks any legal authority to actually enforce its own net neutrality policies."[100] Yet Geist also calls into question the strength of the Canadian regulatory system when he notes that "the current governing law is ill-suited to address Internet-based video services."[101] Perhaps Canadians may yet find themselves in the same situation as American audiences – hemmed in by a media oligopoly that has captured the government agencies otherwise designed to regulate the television industry with culture and consumers' interests in mind.

While the days of unlimited, unmetered usage of the Internet may be coming to a close, consumer backlash against excessive pricing has thus far had a moderating effect on the market. Lotz suggests that the "freedom of use and open content availability that characterize new technologies in the early years of adoption" tend to be eventually reined in and constrained by dominant firms.[102] Nonetheless, media oligopolies do not always get their own way: "the most likely scenario is a negotiated outcome that will depend greatly on action on the part of informed viewers, consumers, and citizens."[103]

Consumers may become more politically involved with pricing policies if awareness grows about the actual costs of data transmission over the Internet. Michael Geist estimates that cost to be about $0.07 per gigabyte, which suggests that Internet users are being gouged for high-bandwidth service.[104] At present it appears that pricing has had only a moderate impact on the adoption of online video. It is unlikely that content lockout will be achieved through mechanisms such as bit caps and discriminatory practices. In mid-2012 the US Justice Department announced that it was conducting an anti-trust investigation into whether cable companies such as Time Warner Cable and Comcast were unfairly using data caps and other techniques to "quash nascent competition from online video."[105] The business practices of cable companies will be subject to intense public scrutiny as the audience moves online. Regardless of fears over anti-competitive behaviour, "the online television industry appears to be unfolding in a vibrant way."[106]

By 2014 Comcast was seeking the permission of the US government to engage in a $45 billion merger with Time Warner Cable, a move that would transform Comcast "into a powerful gatekeeper, giving it control of 40 percent of the country's Internet service coverage and 19 of the country's top 20 cable markets."[107] Such a merger would give Comcast

considerable bargaining power over carriage (content distribution) negotiations. Comcast is well positioned to defend its interests, with more
than 100 registered lobbyists in Washington whose actions are directed
by a former commissioner of the FCC now in the employ of Comcast.
After such a merger Comcast would have considerable power to exe-
cute content lockout of competitors such as Netflix or simply to increase
their revenue by charging Netflix increased carriage fees. As with the
changing network neutrality situation, no one is really certain what the
consequences of these developments will be for the future of the online
audience.

Ammori argues that content lockout strategies are succeeding in reducing competition. Yet this argument fails to account for the effect that
piracy has upon rendering cord-cutting a viable option for a growing
percentage of the audience and the pressure that cord-cutting is putting on the incumbent players to accommodate the online audience.
Also, content lockout can only work in the long run if two conditions
remain in place: the incumbent industry controls the production of content and also controls access to distribution. Yet the entrance of Google
and other companies investing in new content demonstrates that, in the
long run, the television industry cannot assume it will always be the
dominant creator of quality content.

It does not require rare talent to create much of the trash found on
television. Thus I would not give too much credence to television executives who assure investors that their industry is secure because they
are masters of content creation. It may be that we are on the verge of an
explosion in quality content from a wide variety of sources, including
amateurs and semi-professionals working outside the current production system.

When Ammori claimed that cable operators "have applied considerable pressure on content programmers to keep content offline, and ensure that whatever content is online is unavailable on television
screens," he overlooked the fact that most television and movie content
is already available online and is making its way to an ever-increasing
number of screens.[108] Furthermore, a legion of alternative sources of
quality content has found a home on the Internet, and the Internet itself
is a distribution system that remains beyond the control of the incumbent industry. Lotz described the impact of broadband distribution as
"a radical disruption in television's norm as a medium limited to commercially created content."[109] The bottleneck of distribution and production is bypassed and television's role as the exclusive distributor of

important and quality content is undermined in the Internet age. The same screen that allows me to watch *Game of Thrones* also enables me to watch my students' YouTube videos.

Within the traditional cable and Internet service provider industries, the viability of anti-competitive strategies such as content lockout "ultimately depends on large national market shares" to be effective.[110] On the Internet any market share will pale in comparison to the global volume of digital piracy. The leaky nature of national boundaries in cyberspace suggests that normal economic rules governing scarcity and market share are poor predictors of the future of online television.

Christophers suggests that the "idea that the studios – and everything they bring with them – can be bypassed is ultimately predicated on one great hope, namely the Internet."[111] He argues that if any significant disruption is going to occur a new model must be viable and the old model must be "broken and demonstrably unable to co-exist with the new."[112] Thus far at least, new models such as Netflix and YouTube appear to be viable. The old model appears to be rather wobbly – continually increasing fees, intense consumer dissatisfaction, cable subscribers leaving the old model (through cord-cutting), and nefarious business practices that come with oligopolies. But why must the old model be demonstrably unable to coexist with the new? The music industry suffered a loss of 50 per cent of its revenues because of new Internet-based models and nonetheless is coexisting with innovative alternatives, dominating markets, and continuing to generate profits.[113] While Christophers rightly rejects the "idea of a profitable webcast economy *superseding* a profitable broadcast economy, in anything like the near term," this says little about the long-term risk of disintermediation.[114]

Disintermediation is not necessarily a matter of the utter destruction of an old economic model. There is the possibility that the old model will continue to exist alongside innovative business models, such as virtual cable stations and content producers that are not beholden to the incumbent industry. Indeed, Christophers's model of the political economy of television strongly implies that disintermediation is well under way. Content scarcity, the bedrock of the industry's market power, has been lost to the digital plenitude of the Internet. Territorialization is confounded by the circumvention of geo-blocking. The monopolization of distribution has been undermined by the rise of broadband Internet and mass digital piracy. Each element that has historically assured market power is found wanting in the post-television era. Even the control of production itself, which has been locked up through vertical integration

within the US television oligopoly, is unravelling. All of these phenomena – plenitude, de-territorialization, Internet-based distribution, and
new players in the content production game – are occurring at the edges
of the television system and thus far are only affecting a small percentage of the audience. Yet all the pieces for a new type of television system
are falling into place. In 1999 it would have been true to say that the
music industry was suffering nothing more than marginal erosion.
Ten years later the entire shoreline of the music industry had changed
and the waters continue to rise. If scarcity, windowing, territorialization, and control of production and distribution are indeed the corner-
stones of the television industry's globe-spanning market power, we
need to acknowledge that the Internet is beginning to weaken this
architecture of control.

The threat of disintermediation is not merely a product of the Internet. The television industry is at war with itself. In 2012 Dish Network
began offering a service called Auto Hop that allowed subscribers to
skip commercials while watching shows on DVRs. "As network executives tell it, Dish Network is a friend turned foe, once preserving the
advertising model but now threatening to turn on a doomsday device."[115] Dish did this in an attempt to make television viewing more
attractive in an era when online audiences are learning how to avoid
commercials. Dish was almost immediately sued by Fox, NBCUniversal, and CBS. Dish is the largest satellite television provider in the
United States with 14 million subscribers. Although this is not the first
time that the industry has gone to court over advertising-skipping technology, it is the first time in the Internet age that a network has tried to
make it easier for viewers to avoid commercials.

A more serious threat before the courts in 2012 was the result of a
new online television distributor started by the billionaire Barry Diller,
former CEO of Paramount Pictures and Fox. Diller's latest business
venture is a startup called Aereo, which streams broadcast television
over the Internet. Aereo was immediately sued for copyright infringement by Fox, Univision, PBS, ABC, Disney, CBS, NBCUniversal, Universal Network Television, and Telemundo. By providing broadcast
television online for a nominal fee, Aereo threatened to disintermediate
the entire broadcast system. Although Aereo failed to defend itself in
the courts and is no longer operating, it is indeed curious that a billionaire television executive was willing to create a new business model
that would seriously disrupt the very economic system that made him
a billionaire. There is money to be made in disintermediating the

television system, and some of the very people who helped build the incumbent industry are willing to tear it down and build an alternative system more suited to the post-television generation.

The ecosystem of the television industry is filled with contradictory forces that attempt to reinforce and undermine the existing oligopolies. Other industry sectors provide plenty of examples of the risk of disintermediation as well as the possibility of reintermediation; thus we cannot assume that the Internet is an acid that dissolves all twentieth-century oligopolies. As Lotz also observes, "All too frequently emergent technologies provided multiplicity and diversity in their infancy, only to be subsumed by dominant and controlling commercial interests as they became more established."[116] The fight over the future of television is in essence a fight for control of culture. Any significant disruption of the incumbent television industry will have to find a way around state-corporate collusion that supports market concentration, oligopolies, and the current distribution of cultural power within capitalism. Yet in the end it may be the hubris of the television industry that is its undoing. Consider the lesson of America Online (AOL).

Back in 2003 AOL's chief executive, Jonathan Miller, was facing massive defection by subscribers. He responded by declaring that AOL's new business plan was to build "a big tent so people don't leave AOL to get what they want."[117] When Miller made this bold announcement in 2003 AOL had approximately 25 million subscribers. By 2013 AOL's subscriber base had slid to under 3 million. That was one leaky tent they built. The notion that one company can keep the online audience away from the enormous catalogue of freely available online content is a measure of either an ego fit for a multinational corporation or an indication of an extreme disconnect with the real world of online consumers.

AOL's problem is similar to the issue faced by the cable and television industry – how to keep subscribers within your online properties. Now consider the more recent comments by Neil Smit, president of the American cable giant Comcast: "Let's never give our customers a reason to cord cut. Whether it's an iPad or TV screen or mobile, let's let them view it the way they want to view it."[118] AOL wanted to build a virtual tent so big that people would not want to leave it and Comcast wants to "give customers no reason to go anywhere else."[119] This is all well and good until you realize that a new generation of viewers wants your content and knows how to get it for free. Comcast's basic value proposition to the consumer – a few shows and movies that you want to see bundled with a bunch of garbage that you do not want to see for an average annual subscription fee of around $900 (US) – gives customers plenty of reasons for defecting to less expensive online services. An American household could subscribe to Hulu Plus, Netflix, and Amazon Instant for around $270 a year, and the kids would pirate whatever they cannot find from these services from the Internet.[120] That is over $600 in annual savings in an economy that is at best described as brutal to the American consumer. The truth about television is that it is getting to be a significant part of a household's monthly expenses. The *Wall Street Journal* notes that Americans' cable bills have grown almost 38 per cent from 2000 to 2010.[121] Even Jon Miller, chief digital officer for News Corporation, has publicly recognized that the price gap of $70 or more per month between traditional television subscriptions and new online alternatives such as Netflix is not sustainable.[122] The big tent of big media is beginning to come apart at the seams.

All this is not to say that television is on its deathbed. The US major film studios released 132 films in 2001 and 179 in 2011. Over the same period the critical summer box office revenues have grown from $3.41 to $4.5 billion.[123] Revenue from the top five films in each year went up and down, but the overall trend sees the second half of the decade outperforming the first half.[124] According to the MPAA, international box office revenues are up 35 per cent from five years ago.[125] Although box office sales in the United States and Canada dropped 5 per cent between 2002 and 2011, global box office revenue increased 24 per cent between 2007 and 2011. The fortunes of companies and products in the media industry do rise and fall but according to the *Economist* magazine, things were looking very good in the summer of 2013: "the shares of some firms have reached all-time highs, and over the past five years News Corp, Viacom, Disney, and Time Warner have each delivered more than twice the S&P 500's average return of 6.1%."[126]

Producers are far from trading in their Ferraris for Fords but there are signs that the studios' business model of the past 20 years is rapidly changing. Consider the analysis offered by Peter Chernin, a producer at Fox and a former president of News Corporation. Chernin recently reflected on the situation of many of his former colleagues, which he summarized with the observation, "They're completely broke." Chernin blamed the decline of many of his colleagues' fortunes on the collapse of DVD sales: "The DVD business represented fifty percent of their profits ... The decline of that business means their entire profit could come down between forty and fifty percent for new movies ... the DVD sell-through business is not coming back again. Consumers will buy their movies on Netflix, iTunes, Amazon et al. before they will purchase a DVD."[127] The studios are still reeling from the rapid demise of DVD sales and now they must contend with price competition from streaming services. Netflix is seen as a replacement for more profitable DVD purchases but also adds money to studios' overall revenue.

At present the economic indicators of disruption remain at the margins of the entertainment sector and are often contradictory. In Canada and the United States one of the television industry's biggest problems is its age. It is a mature market faced with an aging population and little room for significant growth. Industry analyst Larry Haverty described the situation in the following terms: "Cable penetration is pretty much at a max in the United States and will probably grow with new household formation but we don't know if that will happen this year or even next."[128] The long-term trend has seen cable companies grow at the expense of broadcast television; "broadcast network viewership levels have suffered steady erosion and fragmentation over the past 25 years ... Each of the four major primetime networks (ABC, CBS, FOX, NBC) has substantially fewer viewers today than five or ten years ago."[129] The broadcast industry has experienced a much longer decline in ratings than is being witnessed in the cable sector: "the live ratings for network programs (that is, the ratings for people who watch shows when they are first broadcast) have declined for 14 straight quarters."[130] This trend continued into 2013, when network ratings and profits continued to fall. Garth Ancier, co-founder of the Fox network, related how former colleagues still in the television business express "tremendous frustration about working in a declining marketplace."[131]

Downward or upward movement in ratings across the cable and broadcast system usually has multiple causes such as time shifting, or watching TV programs at times other than when they are originally aired using DVRs, and the attraction of video gaming. Another reason ratings were down is that people were watching television via online vehicles that are not yet counted by the complex industry ratings system. Nielsen was not yet measuring television consumption on computers, cell phones, or tablets. The audience measurement company began to make modest changes in measuring Internet audiences within households in 2013.[132] Improvements in the ratings system that make better account of online viewing already suggest that online viewers make a substantial contribution to ratings. For example, the Fox network show *New Girl* has 33 per cent of its audience watching the show outside of traditional television.[133]

The main reason for recent changes in ratings may be that more viewers are time shifting and watching on a variety of new platforms such as tablet computers. The audience is no longer bound to watch on the terms set by the broadcast schedule. Jeff Gaspin, former head of entertainment at NBC, looked at the trend in continually lower ratings and concluded, "We are seeing the cumulative effect of nonlinear viewing."[134] The industry is losing control over time – when a show is watched. This is far more than a minor short-term problem for the television and advertising sectors: "many executives say they are concerned that long-term changes in watching habits are taking a significant toll on viewership."[135]

When scholars explored the "looming business battles for the online television markets," they came to the conclusion that the entrance of major cable operators such as Comcast and Time Warner Cable into the Internet television market "should be considered as a means of controlling access and content rather than being a disruptive innovation to the sector." Their strategies include "preserving market power, creating scarcity, and reinventing bottlenecks."[136] When Nicholas Garnham looked at the circulation of power in the cultural industries, he suggested that an industry's power resulted from "artificially limiting access in order to create scarcity" and argued that "cultural distribution, not cultural production" was the "key locus of power and profit."[137] Christophers revisited Garnham's thesis and concluded that strategies that seek to create scarcity are increasingly impractical: "One certainly gets the sense that many in the industry see they are fighting a losing battle; that ultimately it will be impossible to circumscribe and police access (and hence 'create' scarcity where none 'naturally' exists) to the degree that was once possible."[138] Christophers's model of the political economy of the television industry reveals a weakening of the industry's market power. That power stems from the industry's ability to realize scarcity, which Christophers describes as "central to the leading (US) distributors' imperative of retaining and exercising their economic power."[139] This scarcity is maintained because the incumbent industry controls the distribution of media content, but that control is slipping away. After all, there is now a global army of amateur re-broadcasters and file sharers who have created a gift economy of television redistribution. Cultural distribution remains a significant source of power, but the ability to exercise that power is moving out of the boundaries of the industry and relocating to the online audience. Perhaps the erosion of exclusivity over cultural distribution is why Verizon CEO Ivan Seidenberg acknowledged that disintermediation is a near-term threat. "Young people are pretty smart. They're not going to pay for something they don't need to ... Over the top is going to be a pretty big issue for cable. I think cable has some life left in its model ... but it is going to get disintermediated over the next several years."[140]

Unbundling

Few things about the television industry are more controversial than the practice of grouping a bunch of channels together and selling them to cable subscribers as a bundled package. American television viewers only watch 9 per cent of the channels available to them, which amounts to 18 channels out of an average of 189 available.[141] In 2006 the FCC released a report that consumers "would save as much as 13 percent on their cable bills if they could buy only the channels they wanted instead of being forced to pay for hundreds of them."[142] More recently, industry analysts claim that unbundling would strip the US television economy of 50 per cent of its revenues.[143] Both estimates (13 per cent and 50 per cent) are reflections of industry self-interest and have little to do with reality. No one really knows what would happen if the incumbent television industry unbundled its products. Nevertheless, bundling must overcome considerable political and economic resistance if it is to remain a dominant business practice. Consider how cable operators force 100 million American households to pay for ESPN through bundling yet only 25 million households watch the channel.[144] Television economics create 75 million reasons for unbundling. There is a growing risk of unbundling due to a wide variety of threats, such as the possibility of partial unbundling within sports television and rumours of a possible unbundling of HBO's excellent programming. Partial unbundling is already underway as pay-TV providers compete with lower-priced entry-level bundles. As David Carr explained to *New York Times* readers, "if your platform, your programming and your audience are all under attack, the degree of difficulty in selling big packages of entertainment over cable is increasing."[145] There is also growing political support for unbundling coming from lawmakers in the United States and Canada.

In Canada the conservative Harper government announced its intention to require cable providers to unbundle their television packages. Canadian Interior Minister James Moore explained, "We don't think it's right for Canadians to have to pay for bundled television channels that they don't watch. We want to unbundle television channels and allow Canadians to pick and pay for the specific television channels that they want."[146] The television industry will fight this new policy tooth and nail, so it remains to be seen if the government will deliver on its promise. Geist suggests that the CRTC will shortly mandate the unbundling of television packages: "with the government committing to consumer choice for television in the Speech from the Throne, unbundling television is a done deal."[147] If so, it will be a game-changing event for both consumers and the entertainment industry.

The effort to de-bundle subscription television in the United States, spearheaded by Republican Senator John McCain, has gone nowhere. Conventional wisdom, which appears to be driven by industry lobbyists, holds that unbundling will cost consumers dearly, eliminate diversity of content, and end life on the planet as we know it. Perhaps a better way of understanding unbundling is in relationship to the network effects of new media and globalization. Edward Rhodes argues that organizations are losing the ability to control information and markets.[148] The sovereign state, business corporations, and other major institutions are experiencing substantial unravelling in the face of global digital networks and related forces. It would be altogether remarkable if the television industry managed to escape such system-wide forces of change. Bundles are unlikely to disappear completely, yet the industry has little choice but to offer options that match the pick-and-pay flexibility and affordability of online digital content services. As Gregory Gimpel rightly notes, "Industries that do not give customers what they want poise themselves for disruption from outsiders who better satisfy consumer preference."[149]

Summary

When Charlie Ergen, chairman of the largest satellite broadcaster in the United States, admits that "four of his five children have stopped paying for a TV subscription, and the fifth is living at home," it requires a tremendous leap of faith to assume that television is not facing troubled times.[150] Ergen notes that when his daughter and her friends come home and bring out their tablets they surf online "until they find something free that they want to watch."[151] This is not marginal behaviour. This is a highly consequential generational shift in viewing habits.

Disintermediation is occurring in the music, publishing, news, and DVD sectors and is widely expected to occur within the television industry. The incumbent industry players hope to manage the process but executives privately fear that the road ahead will be less than smooth. Some financial analysts insist that the cord-cutting phenomenon is a myth, yet other analysts are citing cord-cutting as a reason for downgrading the valuation of major entertainment companies.

A model of the political economy of the television industry suggests that the industry's power rests in its control of distribution and near-monopoly hold on production. The Internet has forced changes in windowing strategies, but along with territorialization and the artificial creation of scarcity, windowing remains a key to revenue generation. Yet the circumvention of geo-blocking along with global piracy of television and movies is effectively de-territorializing the flow of video for a significant percentage of the online audience. The industry can no longer depend on a limited broadcast spectrum, scarcity, or copyright regimes to protect the foundation of its global market power in the online environment. Past strategies of content lockout were effective, but attempts to limit the availability of online content appear to be unsustainable in the face of emerging business models intent on disintermediation, a growing number and variety of networked consumer technologies, and the digital plenitude these technologies engender.

Although there is much concern about the erosion of network neutrality and the imposition of higher fees through metered Internet use, thus far neither issue has stalled the adoption of online video or prevented tens of millions of individuals from subscribing to online video services. No one can reasonably claim that television has died. Yet there is a growing number of reasons to agree with Lotz when she suggests that the centrality achieved by the incumbent television industry "as controllers of distribution and schedulers of programs" is diminished.[152] Television has contracted a persistent online virus and will never be quite the same again.

8 Post-television Society: Diversity, Citizenship, News, and Global Conflict

The list of indictments brought against television is long: degraded self-esteem, sexism and misogynistic values, poor eating habits, the promotion of violence and racial stereotypes, hyper-consumption, a neoconservative war agenda, anti-Arab sentiment, polarized elections, increased inequality in political involvement, and much more. Of course television has also been a source of progressive values. Herein my purpose is not to revisit the debate between those who see television as a powerful source of capitalist ideologies and those who celebrate the superior interpretive powers of an active audience. Nevertheless, we are on safe ground when we attribute significant influence to dominant media systems. Standing on this ground as a starting point, the following explores social and political aspects of post-television culture: diversity, citizenship, news, and global conflict.

Television is the very engine of capitalist societies; it shapes voter habits and influences public policy, consumer values, and our perception of everyday reality. What is at stake with the rise of a type of television system that is not dominated by the commercial production of programming but one wherein multiple modes of production coexist within reach of the same audiences? One mode in particular is of concern here – the production of video content outside the normal advertising-production-distribution relationship that defines commercial television.

Advertising-supported content played a role in shaping the twentieth century. What happens within social systems when audiences are exposed to video content that is produced from beyond the confines of the commercial production system? This chapter will explore this scenario by taking into serious consideration James Curran's observation that in the past "new media gave rise to new centres of power, which increased tensions within the prevailing structure of authority."[1] The construction of taste, value, and identity within television culture represents the very centre of capitalism's prevailing structure of authority. As such, this structure is under attack from the rise of uncontrolled video production and the migration of audiences to online viewing contexts. The primary centre of authority at risk is the commercial television oligopoly and the corporate and political interests it promotes. The media oligopoly that developed in the twentieth century is at risk of having its economic and cultural power eroded by the diversity that results from a growing number of producers who use a new distribution system to access the audience.

Diversity

Diversity has long been a problem in the television system. Consider the situation in the United States, where it is generally claimed that the free market unleashes the greatest amount of diversity. In *Media Diversity: Economics, Ownership and the FCC* Mara Einstein argued that the FCC "again and again has tried to create diversity in the television marketplace and has failed miserably."[2] The same could be said of many other regulatory regimes across the globe. Deregulation of television is spreading around the world as a policy imperative and as a result content diversity is shrinking. Diversity is usually seen as something that would come from "many types of programming from many different producers providing a breadth of perspective."[3] The source of the lack of diversity is found in how commercial television makes money: "advertising is at the heart of the diversity problem."[4] A commercial television system naturally seeks to produce profitable television, and profitable programming "means programming that serves the interests of advertisers."[5]

Einstein argues that changing owners or producers or creating more channels would not change the nature of the content. Owners are inevitably guided by the vested interests of the television oligopoly. Diversity of producers and expansion of channels within the current television marketplace have failed to produce different content. As long as the same *commercial* system produces television, programming will be designed to suit advertisers. "Given the restrictions of the advertising model, limits are placed on the type of programming that will be produced ... it must not be controversial within the current economic and social frame. If content diversity is the goal, then advertising cannot be the backbone of the television revenue model."[6]

As long as television is under the control of a concentrated handful of media conglomerates, the desire for diversity will remain unfulfilled. This is a system that effectively reduces competition. A lack of competition in turn fosters a lack of diversity. Small television production companies are not economically viable and as a result "independent producers have either been merged into the larger companies or have disappeared."[7] As long as we rely on the existing structure of the television system, neither promoting more producers nor promoting more channels leads to increased diversity. These economic limitations provide insight into the possible effects of a new type of distribution system – the Internet.

Because her 2004 analysis predates the television audience's movement online, Einstein could see only one solution to the problem of diversity: "content diversity cannot be changed without changing the economic structure of the industry."[8] Certainly, we can safely conclude that there are significant changes occurring in the economic structure of the television and film industries. Radical changes in the distribution structure of the industry could expand the number of producers, channels, and diversity of content and audiences, and introduce new economies of television. This appears to be exactly what is happening as a result of the advent of the Internet. Internet-based systems of television production and distribution address a critical need created by commercial media: "there needs to be a space where programming can be created that is untouched by the tentacles of advertising."[9] Advertising certainly exists on the Internet but it does not exercise the same influence over content and audiences as it does in "old" media. Einstein insists that "what is needed is a space within the media marketplace that is insulated from advertising and its accompanying need to produce large, homogenous audiences."[10] The gift economy of amateur videography, early experiments in audience-funded productions, productions co-created by the audience, and other novel video economies suggest that just such a space is being created in cyberspace. Even piracy plays an important role in promoting diversity. File-sharing sites act as a subaltern distribution network and contribute to more cultural diversity "when compared to the mainstream commercial distribution circuit."[11] In China, for example, such sites provide the audience with "a much wider and inclusive cinematic spectatorship than the hegemonic form of theatrical screenings" offered by official sources.[12]

Of course, not everyone agrees that commercial television fails to serve our individual and collective needs. Industry evangelists such as

Evan Shapiro, former president of the Sundance Channel, celebrate commercial television as providing us with "the best, most valuable and most relevant content on earth right now" and extol the virtues of being more engaged with commercial media.[13] Such self-interested claims remind us that the television system is rooted in the ideological territory of capitalism.

In her examination of the changes the television industry is going through in an "emerging post-network era," Amanda Lotz notes that studios, conglomerates, and distributors no longer enjoy the same degree of control over cultural production that they once did in the twentieth century.[14] The incumbent television industry remains important and still holds the centre ground but viewers have gained more control over their television experience. Of course, this new level of control should not be overstated; "commercial interests still control production, and viewers' choice is still limited as there remains much that cannot be found on television."[15] But YouTube and other online venues for distributing video provide an indication of where the audience is headed. The television audience has never had such a vast amount of video material to watch that did not derive from the commercial production system. One could say exactly the opposite of Lotz's observation and be equally correct – commercial interests are losing control of production and viewers' choices are becoming as vast as the entire Internet. The very fact that there remains much that cannot be found on local television is driving the post-television generation to alternative sources to get what can readily be found elsewhere.

As a result of the Internet's role as a new distribution system television is undergoing a radical redesign. Things normally affected by television will also be part of this transformation. As Lotz notes, "how audiences are exercising choice and control require us to revise fundamental ideas about media and culture."[16] All this rests on central aspects of post-television culture: the diversification of content that can be produced for the television audience, the multiplication of video producers, a diminishing degree of control over content and audiences, and new visual economies. Cable television caused a diversification of content, but because this occurred within the established structure of the television industry the net effect was relatively mild. Yet online audiences are watching an unprecedented diversity of video content coming from a vastly expanded number of video producers. As a result of the Internet, video content is being produced via novel entrepreneurial business models and in many cases with little or no regard for economic exchange. Next-generation film-making – video content made specifically for distribution over the Internet and mobile platforms – has created "a new culture of entrepreneurial filmmaking" that is not dependent on the existing film distribution oligopolies.[17]

All this is not to say that the old television system is no longer an influential force. Aymar J. Christian surveyed the fortunes of pioneering independent online video producers and, unsurprisingly, found that "entrepreneurs looking to build portals for independent video face incredible challenges to creative autonomy."[18] Yet this only speaks of those who try to produce content from within a capitalist mode of exchange. The entrepreneurial subjects of Christian's study were trying to create and package content that would attract the support of advertisers. As yet we know little about the possibilities latent in non-market modes of creation, distribution, and exchange that arise as a result of the network effects of the Internet. We must also take into account the inefficiency of the media marketplace. Whereas it is generally assumed that a market approach delivers the widest possible range of goods, within the contemporary media economy we are faced with the negative effects of concentrated markets and their gatekeepers. Susan Christopherson draws our attention to how the concentration of ownership in distribution channels manifests a market failure: "most 'creative' entertainment media cannot easily access their potential consumers."[19] Commercial markets are not the most efficient but they *are* the most powerful.

One example of new visual economies is seen in crowdsourced funding, wherein the audience directly supports a videographer's effort to produce new content. Crowdsourcing is also used as a production process that combines the effort of many individuals to produce written works such as Wikipedia, as well as documentaries and movies. Individually, these new production methods have had little impact on the television industry yet collectively they represent a period of rapid innovation in video production and funding methods. Independent film-makers are "capitalizing on the growing popularity of crowd-sourced financial support for small projects in order to get their films made in the first place."[20] Writing in the *Globe and Mail*, reporter Susan Krashinsky relates how

crowd-funding websites such as Kickstarter and Indiegogo – which invite people to give small amounts of money on the Web toward projects they believe in, like a continuous digital version of a public radio pledge drive, have become a source for many independent filmmakers in search of backing. Seventeen Kickstarter-funded films were at Sundance this year, and 31 went to the South By Southwest film festival.[21]

Sites like Vimeo and DailyMotion enable film-makers to earn money through voluntary donations and pay-to-view and provide further examples of the online business models that are promoting more funding for independent video projects. As Jeff Bercovici suggested to *Forbes* readers, "It's a good time to be an independent filmmaker on the web."[22] Crowdsourcing is not about to compete directly with Hollywood blockbusters that see production costs in the hundreds of millions but it will help introduce new stories to the audience. The type of stories that can be told greatly depends upon the available types of economies and production processes. In the twentieth century producers were subject to the requirements of an oligopolistic visual economy. Crowdsourcing is one example of how the television and movie oligopolies are losing control over production.

It is conventional wisdom among industry workers, scholars, and analysts that only certain types of programs can be profitably produced. Nonetheless, television's recent past has been characterized by a "further diversification in the content produced by the industry and available to viewers."[23] Here Lotz is referring to new types of storytelling and content that appeared on television in the first decade of the twenty-first century. If the post-television age that lies before us is merely destined to diversify content in a similar manner as did *Sex in the City, Survivor,* and *Arrested Development,* then do we really have anything to celebrate or much to look forward to in the next stage of television's evolution? Lotz is certainly correct to suggest that new forms of storytelling await us. Yet how progressive can we expect new stories to be when they are all derived from the same old profit-driven, advertising-supported production system controlled by powerful multinational corporations often working in collusion with governments?

I would argue that new values and progressive change will come from the margins of the emerging post-television system, where the profit motive is diminished. The Internet provides a distribution system wherein the influence of the advertising industry is minimized and often completely eradicated. Online television creates a space for content that defies the imperatives of the corporate media economy. It enhances the ability of content not produced by media corporations to reach the viewing audience. Prior to the integration of the Internet into the television system it was impossible, with rare exception, for amateur videographers, very small production companies, artists, public intellectuals, and professionals working completely outside the media industry to access the television audience. Post-television culture moves alternative content within reach of the online audience.

Indicative of how fast the nature of television is changing, in 2004 P. David Marshall described television as an apparatus that had divided its production capabilities from its reception capabilities.[24] The commercial system produced the shows and the audience watched those shows. Marshall also contrasted television with the personal computer. Yet even while he was writing those words these two systems were converging and coalescing into what is rapidly becoming a highly interconnected production and reception system in which both aspects are available to the audience. We now have a global online sports audience that is illicitly rebroadcasting commercial television from home computers. We have emerging forms of audience-produced video content. This joins a flood of video content made by media professionals, intellectuals, artists, and even armies and insurgents. We have the Internet-based mode of television distribution via P2P, cyberlockers, and other methods of redistribution undertaken by audience members. Televisions are being built with incredible computing power and networking potential. Many flat-panel screens now include a USB port and wireless capabilities which allow a computer, and by extension, the Internet, to be connected. And so it goes – all digital screens are connecting to all other digital screens, and the thing once known as television is flowing between these screens with increasing speed and ease.

Almost everything significant about television derived from its basic distinction between production and reception. The industry produced what the twentieth-century audience watched. The erosion of the divide between producer and audience is one of the definitive characteristics of television in the twenty-first century. I can create a video and upload that to YouTube, other video sites, or my own website, and others can watch that video on their Internet-connected televisions, computers, and mobile digital devices. In the post-television age the audience acquires greatly expanded capabilities of production, distribution, and redistribution. No longer relegated to a relatively passive role, the audience has transformed into a source of competition and disintermediation within the entertainment system.

One might raise numerous objections to this formulation of the twenty-first-century television system on the basis of the marginal nature of amateur and alternative video production and its audiences.

Amateur and alternative content might be marginalized simply by virtue of being buried under the onslaught of a global commercial menu of choices. Apple, Google, or some other corporation might inevitably "own" the interface to television and marginalize content that does not serve its business interests. The audience might have little desire to view content that does not derive from the commercial television system. Digital piracy and illicit redistribution activity may prove to be a transitional phase that will be brought under control as audience behaviour is normalized according to the dictates of state and market forces.

Perhaps these things will come to pass but the Internet community has demonstrated considerable interest in two things: self-representation and viewing alternative sources of content. Arguments to the effect that our ability to self-represent, to produce our own content, or to view alternative sources of content will be diminished fail to account for the online audience's capabilities as a political force. Equally so, it is highly unlikely that the commercial television system will be entirely displaced by alternative sources of content. So what happens to society if the former near-totalizing character of commercial media is breached by flows of videos produced from alternative production systems? The post-television age signifies this new era in which commercial television resides on our screens as only one of many content sources. We have only recently entered the era of online television. Television's possible role in promoting a better tomorrow must be placed in the context of commercial media's historical role as a tool of social control that was often used against our collective interests.

This is not the first time a new television distribution technology arrived accompanied by great promises. In the late 1960s policymakers, industry lobbyists, media activists, and technocrats were singing the praises of cable as a new communication technology that would bring entertainment, news, and information to audiences while serving social, cultural, and educational needs. Cable television promised to create a "wired nation" and harmonize conflict among societies.[25] In the United States the President's Task Force on Communication Policy "enthusiastically suggested that cable television, by allowing minorities and disaffected groups an outlet to express themselves and to communicate with the nation, might reduce their feelings of alienation and thus help solve the 'problem' of the social unrest that was sweeping American society in 1968."[26] In the context of the 1960s counterculture, it was widely thought that cable television could give marginal communities a voice, be a force for social good, and promote democratic social change. Cable would transform the passive audience of network television into active communities that would provide direct feedback and participate in the selection and dissemination of messages and programming directed towards the masses. It was a grand dream that fell apart in the face of oligopolistic market forces and regulatory bodies that were captured by industry interests.

Cable television did bring more channels and more diversity in programming. Thomas Streeter points out that the range of values represented on cable television was "much broader than was ever common on the politically timid big three networks."[27] Yet cable became firmly entrenched in the oligopoly of the television industry, failed to develop two-way forms of communication, and mostly recirculated existing programming. Streeter suggests that minority tastes remain underrepresented and promises of an empowered audience and "abundant, diverse programming for all have not been fully realized."[28] The question naturally arises as to whether the Internet will follow a similar pattern and fall under the control of either the old or a new media oligopoly.

Streeter asks, "Why is desktop video any more 'revolutionary' than super eight cameras, videotape, the original reel-to-reel video portapaks, video cassettes, and numerous other improvements in low-cost visual media of the last forty years?"[29] Here again we run into an apples versus oranges comparison. The video technology of the twentieth century never achieved quite the same low-cost character of contemporary video technology. Processing and distribution costs are now marginal for amateur work. There are billions of video cameras in consumers' hands – a vastly greater number than existed in the twentieth century. In 2011 consumers bought 1 billion mobile phones with cameras and over one-third of the global population owns a digital camera.[30]

Two key technological characteristics render contemporary video exceptional if not revolutionary – digital and networked. The digitization of video technology has rendered it far more malleable, transportable, omnipresent, and inexpensive. The networked character of video technology has enabled amateurs and professionals to distribute their work globally at marginal costs. While it remains to be seen just how progressive all these elements may prove to be, one can hardly deny that significant transformations in video culture are under way as a result of the mass participation in the creation and dissemination of digital, networked video. In short, the current video system, when taken as a whole, bears little resemblance to video, cable, and broadcast television systems of the twentieth century. The simple fact that each month more video content is uploaded to the Internet than has been created by Hollywood in the past 60 years, and that much of that content is produced by amateurs, suggests that we are in a truly extraordinary phase of video culture.

Before we ask what may come of a vast expansion in content available to online television audiences, we need to establish the basic character of content produced by the incumbent television industry. If audiences are already exposed to content that represents a highly diverse set of values, reflects all voices and communities within society, and is ideologically diverse, then the net effect of more content and more producers would be minimal. The degree of change made possible by online television is related to the degree of difference manifested by a new mode of video production and distribution.

Commercial television reflects what Justin Lewis has called "a global drift towards pro-business neoliberalism."[31] Almost everything significant about television arises from the economic imperative that rules over transnational media conglomerates, as former Disney CEO Michael Eisner made clear when he said, "To make money is our only obligation."[32] The primary product of commercial media is audiences packaged and sold to advertisers. The primary effect of television is consumerism – consumer behaviour managed by major corporations. If we reduce this system to merely news and entertainment we overlook its most obvious economic purposes and social consequences – the promotion of commercial interests and the management of mass consumption and public opinion.

This is not a content production and distribution system that acts benignly in consumers' best interests. This is a system that is "anticompetitive by design: it has an in-built ability to influence consumer preferences."[33] This is also a system with substantial political power, as "governments *have* generally chosen to acquiesce to powerful private media interests."[34] The conservative appraisal of commercial media amounts to a shrug of the shoulders because it is believed that public welfare is best served by corporations operating with the minimum of government oversight. Michael Schudson suggests that advertising "may shape our sense of values."[35] Yet if that "may" is the best that can be said about advertising, which funds the bulk of commercial media, then a multi-trillion-dollar scam has been perpetrated by advertisers and the television system against manufacturers of consumer goods.

Commercial television promotes a "pro-corporate consumerist ideology" wherein consumers are encouraged to seek the fulfilment of their desires through consumption even as those very desires are shaped by television.[36] Within the United States no less than 25 per cent of television viewing time is taken up by advertising – propaganda on behalf of the consumer way of life. The needs of advertisers play a central role within the television system. A great bulk of scholarly literature over the past half century confirms Lewis's claims that "advertising degrades television content."[37] The general assumption is that television delivers what audiences want, but this is a system that carefully constructs and directs audience tastes. As Jonathan Gray notes, Hollywood does not dominate the marketplace because of its aesthetic superiority but because it exercises "outright structural control" of markets, regulatory regimes, trade agreements, technologies, and audiences.[38] Programming is not merely a reflection of the popular will. It is the result of a production system that promotes programs that serve advertisers' interests.

Eileen R. Meehan notes that the "first premise in almost any discussion of television is that television gives us the programming we want."[39] Meehan argues that programming has little to do with viewer choice and tastes. Programming is largely directed by the industry's need for inexpensive and innocuous content and advertisers' need for valuable audiences. The structure of the industry effectively insulates "television from its viewership, limits its content, and constricts its technological potential."[40] Once again we encounter the claim that the preference of the television oligopoly "is for the status quo."[41] It is advertisers, not the audience, who are the "primary customers of networks and channels," which in turn renders programming little more than "a vehicle for advertising."[42] This suggests that television creates a need for content not produced by the television industry – content not designed to serve advertisers' purposes and the "version of capitalism that is peculiar to the United States."[43] It also suggests that commercial television creates a need that cannot be fulfilled by Time Warner, News Corporation, Disney, Comcast, Viacom, and other giants of the industry – the need for truly diverse content. While it is generally thought that television gives the audience what it wants, the opposite is closer to the truth. Television restricts audience choice. These realities of commercial television drive increasing numbers of the online audience to alternative sources of content. This migration to alternative content may change television's historical role in the construction of national identities.

National Identity in a Post-television Society

Cracks are beginning to appear in the system that helped form national identities in the nation states of the twentieth century. As the marketplace gains greater power of audience measurement and surveillance as part of its program of manufacturing consumer behaviour, the state risks losing its ability to shape the identity of citizens. The state's regulatory regimes of broadcast content control are at risk of fading into irrelevance with the dawn of a transnational online audience that has the power to watch what it wants to watch, when it wants to watch it.

Joshua Green notes that the "dis-embedding of television programming from nationally bound television systems alters television's relationship with audiences that remain located in them."[44] The attempt to create nationally branded television falls apart in "online environments that privilege television programming over the contexts of its distribution."[45] Audiences long to move beyond the limits of national broadcast systems to get the content they want. Thus the post-television generation is rapidly relocating to a transnational virtual space where the audience is formed "through taste and choice" rather than through geography and regulatory regimes.[46] This has implications for how the identity of individuals as citizens is constructed.

Citizenship was once "the outcome of a chain of production, distribution and consumption that involved relatively few possible variations."[47] A stable and homogeneous visual diet contributed to the creation of the twentieth-century citizen. This suggests that the new modes of audience activity, expanded capabilities of choice, an international menu of visual consumption, and an emasculated regulatory system will see new forms of identity emerge from the viewing habits of the post-television audience. In Canada the right to decide what to watch has been mediated by the CRTC. Bart Beaty and Rebecca Sullivan, associate professors at the Faculty of Communication and Culture, University of Calgary, observed that "the CRTC frequently decides that the public has no right to decide what it would like to watch."[48] Yet how much power do regulatory agencies and media oligopolies have over an audience armed with options such as cord-cutting, piracy, geo-blocking circumvention, and innovative online video services?

In 2006, a lifetime ago in the fast-moving world of online television, Beaty and Sullivan noted that "video files will soon be as hard to control as audio ... [yet] the television industry still battles over the increasingly fallacious idea of simply closing the broadcast system to outside influences."[49] The CRTC is guided by outmoded regulatory concerns as it tries to "keep foreign programming out of Canada," the television oligopoly is resisting any changes to its bundled-content business model, and the Internet is socializing the post-television generation in viewing habits supported by "non-capitalist exchange systems" – piracy.[50] The disconnect between the audience and agents of control has never been greater.

The willingness to control the audience at any cost cannot be overstated. In 2004 the US House of Representatives gave serious consideration to criminalizing the simple act of fast-forwarding through commercials on television and at the beginning of DVDs.[51] Beaty and Sullivan argue that shared interests have fostered state-corporate collusion to control the audience: "the desire for a tightly controlled, homogeneous audience with limited choice serves both a cultural argument for elite nationalist programming and the economic argument for maintaining a captive, manageable audience for maximized profit. The telecommunications infrastructure has been, therefore, developed along strictly homogeneous lines that keep the audience in check."[52] But that is the story of the twentieth century. What remains to be seen is how effective state-corporate collusion will be in maintaining a system of content and audience control in the age of the Internet. The rise of the post-television audience suggests that the right to decide what to watch and, by extension, to form one's own identity is slipping out of the grasp of institutional forces.

Placing the right emphasis on each of the elements of the television system is no easy task when almost everything about television is in a state of unprecedented change. Graeme Turner defends the primacy of the twentieth-century television system and proclaims that "the nation still matters in television studies' account of what television does and what it will do in the future."[53] As Green suggests, "the significance of broadcast television's role for the formation of national identity and citizenship may be lessened, but not yet eradicated."[54] Yes, the nation still matters, but for an increasing number of online viewers it matters less and less. Turner suggests that one of the indications of the continued significance of the nation state for the television audience is "the general preference for local programming over imported programming."[55] While this is a preference that is well established in the industry's statistics and academic analysis, it is safe to say that the study of local preferences frequently fails to account for the vast flow of pirated and legitimate online video content that is rendering national borders and state cultural policies irrelevant. Consider the example of Spanish Internet audiences' preference for foreign series over local Spanish online television programs.[56] This segment of the audience exhibits a general preference for imported programming over local programming – at least in their online behaviour. Likewise, research into Cuban media consumption reveals how movies and television shows originating from the United States and Latin America are exchanged via external hard drives and account for "most of their media consumption."[57]

The defence of local preferences has to account for the illicit flow of video between nations. The online audience uses piracy to redress the lack of locally available television and movies. Until we have a better grasp of the nature and volume of transnational subterranean flows, any claims about the primacy of local programming need to be seen as subject to qualification. The actual viewing habits of the audience are obscured by subterranean practices.

Another example of the disconnect between the subaltern practices of local viewers and claims about state control of viewing habits is found in the example of Chinese audiences. Anthony Y.H. Fung argues that "the cultural terrains colonized by the new and globally connected television always operate under the control of the state."[58] Yet even in the authoritarian context of China the state's control is eroding. China has the largest piracy rates in the world (90 per cent) and almost no legal market exists for American media products such as movie DVDs. China's bootleg market for DVDs grossed $6 billion (US) in 2010.[59] Such an enormous scale of television and movie piracy limits China's control of what audiences are watching. For example, when the Chinese government banned Mel Gibson's film *The Passion of the Christ*, Chinese audiences found easy access to the movie via piracy.

> Although the film was banned in China, both Catholics and Protestants there reportedly viewed illegal copies of it. In Israel the company that held the movie's distribution rights declined to release it but Palestinian Christians, foreign Christian pilgrims, and Muslims in the West Bank nonetheless watched pirated copies of the film. *Passion* bootlegs also circulated in Saudi Arabia, presumably in part because of the controversy over the film in Israel. And unable or unwilling to pay to watch the film in theatres or on legitimate DVDs, Mexicans in both Mexico and the United States purchased cheaper pirated copies instead.[60]

Even in the United States Christian churches resorted to piracy to screen the movie for congregations. Assessments about what the audience is watching, and what role the state is playing, must take into account the habits and capabilities of the online audience.

The New News

In post-television culture the production and distribution of news may no longer be dominated by commercial media conglomerates. There are early.signs that commercial news is beginning to lose its position of primacy among the online audience. Amateur video news, also called citizen-footage, is part of a rising culture of participatory journalism wherein ordinary people create their own videos of events, upload them to sites such as YouTube, and also share them with commercial news organizations.

One day in July 2010 while I was working on this book, a small earthquake struck Ottawa. I grabbed my camera and filmed the water sloshing around in my aquarium and then posted it to YouTube. I spent the rest of the day answering emails from news organizations across the United States and Canada. Television and newspaper organizations wanted permission to include my brief video in their newscasts and on their websites. Millions of people saw the video on television and over 250,000 Internet users watched online. I had a similar experience when there was a small fire in the apartment building directly across from my home office. My video camera twice turned me into an amateur reporter.

When an earthquake struck Japan on 11 March 2011, amateur videos captured the event. In the following week 20 videos, mostly recorded by amateurs, were viewed 96 million times.[61] The Pew Research Center's Project for Excellence in Journalism analysed such citizen-footage and concluded that "news is becoming a major part of what Americans watch on YouTube."[62] Nevertheless, YouTube's amateur news videos are "probably still outpaced by the audience for news on conventional television worldwide."[63] Commercial news organizations produced 51 per cent of the most popular news videos on YouTube, amateurs accounted for 39 per cent, and activists produced 5 per cent.[64]

The Pew study noted another use of YouTube by amateurs, one to which my students often draw my attention: the posting of videos from Fox News with the purposes of highlighting and criticizing "controversial comments made by the channel's pundits or guests."[65] This use of YouTube to produce commentary on biased commercial news highlights the erosion of commercial media's cultural authority under the conditions of post-television culture. If commercial news is not perceived to be fair and balanced, the online audience will produce a counter-discourse. Amateur videographers are becoming an agenda-setting force which represents a challenge to traditional news sources. Amateurs are imitating the style of news commentary seen on television in the *Colbert Report* and *The Daily Show*. The American video blogger Philip Franchina, known on YouTube as Philip DeFranco, attracted 2 million subscribers on YouTube with his sarcastic commentary on celebrities and current events.

While some might argue that amateur news sources fail to live up to the standards of traditional journalistic sources, the gross failure of commercial sources such as Fox News to provide fair and balanced reporting suggests that, in many cases, numerous commercial news sources have long abdicated any claim to journalistic integrity. Video content provided by corporations to news agencies is eroding the integrity of television news. It is curious that citizen-produced video news is generally seen as lacking journalistic integrity when the measure of such integrity is news organizations that use a "substantial amount of commercial content," which often is little more than corporate public relations and thinly veiled advertising.[66] We need to assess the significance of amateur news production beyond metrics defined by industry standards.

Where the production of video news by citizens is taking us is hard to say at this moment. News organizations are attempting to co-opt citizen production of news but it is unlikely that such an effort will dull its ideological challenge. Entrepreneurs and established news organizations are trying to figure out how to profit from or, in the jargon of business, "monetize" free amateur labour, but such efforts may be irrelevant to the growth, viability, and import of citizen-produced news. Contrary to the reigning assumptions of capitalism, not everything must enter into the purview of the marketplace to be sustainable and consequential.

Amateur-produced video news is one more example of how digital plenitude within a media system confounds the logic of scarcity. In the pre-Internet media context the issue of audience power was framed in terms of the audience's "incapacity" to question or challenge the news selection process, an incapacity which leads to withdrawal: "In a mediascape characterized by scarcity, that is, finite numbers of news outlets which often share similar routines, primary sources and journalistic cultures, audience 'power' may be reduced to little more than blunt veto, that is, the option to disengage from news media as, indeed, increasing numbers of especially younger audiences have been doing."[67] Artificial scarcity affected the production of news and influenced the audience's possible responses to a relatively homogeneous system of news production.

Luke Goode argues that the empowered and productive online audience "does not signal the end of agenda-setting by professional or elite media organizations. Such institutions still break and frame a large proportion of the news stories circulating through the online sphere and this is unlikely to change in the near future. But those institutions must now vie for attention in competition with a diverse range of alternative news sources, from hyperlocal sites to unofficial and untamed celebrity gossip sites." Goode makes the important point that, once online, commercial news loses its privileged status: "Stories, once online, confront various possible fates: they may be more easily buried in this vast new attention economy if they do not capture the imagination quickly and strongly enough; or they may be amplified, sustained and potentially morphed as they are re-circulated, reworked, and reframed by online networks." This privileged status is further eroded when the news audience is armed with a video camera and an Internet connection. "Citizen journalism allows members of the public to engage in agenda-setting not merely by producing original content (though this is certainly a significant development) but also by rendering the agenda-setting processes of established professional media outlets radically provisional, malleable and susceptible to critical intervention."[68] Again and again we encounter the assertion that the online audience gains greater powers of production, distribution, and discourse.

Online news is one of the more potent examples of the erosion of scarcity in the networked media economy. Amateurs who aspire to be serious news commentators, along with those who mimic a critical, comedic style and ordinary people who capture an event on camera, demonstrate our collective "movement away from an oligopolistic-based scarcity associated with broadcasting toward a more differentiated abundance or saturation associated with a proliferation of new and old television services, technologies and providers."[69] But this is a change that will face resistance. Much is at stake when news has such a weighty impact on defining the public's impression of the nature of a situation. In both democratic and authoritarian states there exists a long historical record of the repression of the radical press. Lee Slater suggests that "state repression is more common when media projects threaten to move out of the margins and are connected to social or political movements that threaten the authority of the state or functioning of the economy. Where the domination of a medium's technological form and content by the state or corporations has not been possible, tensions do arise between alternative and mainstream uses in which legal repression becomes necessary."[70] Slater documents a long list of legal actions against online independent news organizations. The Internet does not completely protect independent news media from state coercion. Indeed, a sign of the growing influence of amateur-produced news may be the increasing coercion of alternative sources of news by corporate and state actors. Nevertheless, alternative models of online news delivery provide ample evidence that the Internet continues to deliver a counter-discourse. This is particularly true in the domain of local online news.

Local online news may find a natural fit with the Internet's ability to reach niche audiences. There are approximately 4,600 active local online news sites in the United States alone.[71] News corporations have not found great success in developing hyper-local online news services, yet this says nothing of the potential for non-market and alternative models of local news production. Whereas some see a failure of the commercial hyper-local news model, others argue that "hyperlocal journalism is thriving."[72] Local news does not fade away or lose relevance in a post-television culture.

Independent online news resembles the role of public service broadcasting (PSB) in its attempt to provide reporting and analysis beyond the influence of market forces. In nations where PSB is isolated from the influence of advertisers and the state, researchers found that public broadcasting leads to increased knowledge of current affairs.[73] This positive effect is greatest when public broadcasters were largely disconnected from market pressure and state intervention. Unfortunately, across most nations PSB faces large cuts in funding and pressure to integrate into the market system. Fortunately, as states renege on their responsibility to provide information systems that promote democratic accountability, the Internet appears well placed to revive the role of local news and an independent and critical press.

Global Conflict

The television system of the twentieth century was controlled by authoritarian and paternalistic states and by major corporations. In all cases the result was the same – audiences had limited access to a limited selection of content. Each system of control limited different types of content for different reasons. Over time the globalization of the market-place along with the deployment of cable and satellite expanded the variety of content available to audiences in statist and market-based television systems, but both nations and markets continue to exercise considerable influence over what the audience can and cannot see.

Television and movies have always been subject to varying degrees of censorship and controlled distribution. This history of control has tremendous implications for a post-television culture characterized by uncontrolled audiences and content. Content is not merely a neutral product of a communication system. Content carries meanings. Meanings shape behaviour and behaviour must be managed within capitalism. Thus for any type of contemporary social order, statist, capitalist, or otherwise, the flow of uncontrolled video content across the globe represents a potential loss of control over mass behaviour. The following explores the darker implications of video content flowing across borders and evading the local regulatory regime. When populations are exposed to video content that contradicts their local belief system, the result is often conflict and violence.

In September 2012 violence once again spread across the Arab world because of content on the Internet. A movie trailer for a D-list movie, *Innocence of Muslims*, that ridicules the Prophet Muhammad was posted to YouTube and led to riots in Libya and Egypt. The producer of the film, Nakoula Basseley Nakoula, is a Coptic Christian living in Southern California who was on probation after his conviction for financial crimes. According to Khaled Elgindy, the video was made by "a handful of Christian extremists" and eventually found its way over the Internet to Muslim extremists in Egypt.[74] Prior to the video coming to the attention of people in Libya it existed in obscurity until a version was dubbed in Arabic. YouTube refused to remove the video after determining that, according to its own guidelines, the video was not hate speech. YouTube released the following statement:

> We work hard to create a community everyone can enjoy and which also enables people to express different opinions. This can be a challenge because what's OK in one country can be offensive elsewhere.
>
> This video – which is widely available on the Web – is clearly within our guidelines and so will stay on YouTube. However, given the very difficult situation in Libya and Egypt we have temporarily restricted access in both countries.[75]

On its own the YouTube video did not create the tensions between various religious groups. In Egypt Muslims and Coptic Christians have been bickering violently for centuries. Various parties participated in creating the video clip and then used it to inflame conflict: "the video was given prominence in Egypt when a clip from it was screened on the Al-Nas television channel by the conservative Muslim host Sheikh Khaled Abdalla."[76] Sarah Carr, an Egyptian British journalist, described the sheikh as "part of a school of particularly shrill religious demagogues who turn every possible event into an attack on Islam."[77] By 14 September the protests spread because they reflected "pent-up resentment of Western powers in general … The anger stretched from North Africa to South Asia and Indonesia and in some cases was surprisingly destructive."[78] In the words of Issandr El Amrani, "The resulting cascade of outrage is now predictable: Islamophobes in the West will say 'we told you they're fanatics' and the crowd-riling demagogues here will say 'we told you they disrespect us.'"[79]

According to the *New York Times*, "Millions of people across the Muslim world, though, viewed the video as one of the most inflammatory pieces of content to circulate on the Internet. From Afghanistan to Libya, the authorities have been scrambling to contain an outpouring of popular outrage over the video and calling on the United States to take measures against its producers."[80] Google temporarily blocked access to the video in Egypt, Libya, India, Malaysia, Saudi Arabia, and Indonesia but did not remove the video. Even a request from the White House failed to convince Google to remove the video. Even if Google did remove the video it would still be available on numerous other websites.

Blocking access was widely seen as an ineffectual method of preventing people in Egypt or elsewhere from viewing the video. The fact of the matter is that once a video is popular or controversial, no company or country can remove it from the Web or completely prevent Internet users from seeing it. Within a few days of the initial riots in Egypt and Libya, violent protests had spread to nearly 20 countries, from North Africa to Indonesia. Meanwhile views of the trailer for *Innocence of Muslims* grew from 122,000 to over 7 million within three days. A version of the trailer given Arabic subtitles garnered over 3 million views in three days, with Egypt providing the most viewers. Within a week total views for all the various versions of the trailer had grown from a few thousand to over 25 million.

Numerous nations frequently request that Google remove content. Often Google complies with such requests but not always. When a

Canadian made a video that depicted himself urinating on his passport and flushing it down the toilet, Google refused the Canadian government's request to remove the video. Likewise, corporations make frequent requests for videos to be taken down that go far beyond copyright concerns and Google may or may not remove the video in question. In every case where a video is removed, if the audience demands to see it online it will be found somewhere else. Often, censorship is ineffectual on the Internet. As a result, every country has had to deal with a flood of uncontrolled content across its borders to a degree that did not happen in the twentieth century.

Such incidents as just described demonstrate how uncontrolled content can lead one culture to react violently to another culture's values. The notion of rights and freedoms differs greatly between the West and the East, with the West emphasizing the primacy of an individual's rights while Egyptians, for example, "put a greater emphasis on the rights of communities, families and religious groups."[81] Cultural groups were kept in relative isolation from each other under the content regime of twentieth-century television. This isolation is breaking down under the global flow of Internet content. As a result, conflict over values expressed by secular and fundamentalist belief systems is growing. The movement of uncontrolled content across national borders is taking place within a historical context of empires, client states, and repression. For example, there was also no small amount of resentment among the Egyptian population over the 30 years of American support for the brutal Mubarak dictatorship. In a context rife with historical grievances and cultural differences an otherwise obscure and meritless video can become consequential. A video that would otherwise most likely have been seen by very few became President Obama's "most serious foreign policy crisis of the election season."[82]

Predictably, *Globe and Mail* columnist Margaret Wente heaped scorn on the "many liberal intellectuals – and now, unbelievably, the U.S. administration" who acknowledged the role that the West has played in the Middle East and dare suggest that "it's partly our fault when Western insults to Islam lead to riots in the streets." Given the US and British support of various tyrants in the Middle East, Wente's attempt to lay the source of the blame for the violence entirely on Muslim intolerance is simplistic.[83] The expansion of the global audience's representational powers must be placed in a context of systemic social injustice, the violence of empires, the role of the market as a censor, and grievous economic inequality if we are to fully appreciate the implications of unconstrained video production and distribution.

Summary

Television is the super-peer of consumer culture. It informs voters, shapes consumer habits, moulds identity, and generates support for the interests of tyrants, empires, and major corporations. Television supports the prevailing structures of authority through an anti-democratic system of manufactured tastes, preferences, and value creation. In short, it serves the interests of the few under the guise of apparently giving the many what they want. Television is rightly seen as an agent of social control and consumer management because it has been owned and operated by powerful interests that restricted access to the audience and limited the variety of available content. The rise of broadband Internet has created a new type of distribution vehicle for video content that allows content to flow across borders and beyond the confines of markets and local governments.

Because the societies of the twentieth century were significantly influenced by the content disseminated by corporations and statist broadcast systems, any dramatic change in the structure of content dissemination will present a challenge to the prevailing structures of authority. The rise of the online television audience represents one more aspect of the struggle to control the means of production and communication. Audiences, along with a wide variety of semi-professional and professional film-makers, are using the Internet to produce and globally distribute video outside the direct control of media corporations and regulatory regimes. Also, audiences are redistributing pirated video content and further eroding the influence of the dominant television system. Low-cost video production and distribution are leading to greater diversity of producers and content.

Increased diversity of content represents a threat to the television oligopoly because commercial television is limited in what type of content it can produce. Commercial television's content must be profitable, attractive to advertisers, and, above all else, non-threatening to the interests of major corporations and the state. The rise of uncontrolled audiences, producers, and content subverts the role of television and movie industries as forms of social control that were established in the twentieth century. This subversion is manifested in areas such as the containment of audience choice, the management of national identity, the production of news, and the isolation of cultural regions.

Many of the effects of a post-television system of content creation and distribution remain unknown. Nonetheless, we are witnessing the rapid expansion of content available to audiences and a transformation in the status of the audience from consumers to producers of video. The uncontrolled flow of online video across national borders erodes the influence of regulatory regimes and threatens to undermine the state's management of national identity. The amateur production of news challenges the corporate sector's ability to manage public opinion through the agenda-setting character and definitional power of commercial news. In a borderless online world, video content acts as if it is everywhere at once. Censorship efforts by states and by corporations have little effect on the availability of controversial content, and as a result intercultural conflict is being aggravated by online content produced outside of the confines of the incumbent television system. The loss of centralized control within capitalism's content system appears to have the same effect as the loss of centralized control in the breakup of authoritarian states – a rise of conflict between belief systems.

Conclusion: Post-television Culture

With each passing year in Canada and the United States cable prices are rising faster than the rate of inflation. Piracy is out of control and a younger generation is being socialized in the expectation that entertainment should be free. Meanwhile the audience is learning to flex political muscle and prevent any draconian closure of online freedoms. These phenomena represent an extraordinary matrix of forces. Yet the post-television age has not begun with a complete rupture of our collective viewing habits. Commercial television is an addiction that will not be quickly tossed aside like a dirty needle that pricked our collective consciousness. It remains a powerful drug. We should celebrate the possibility that the online audience is demonetizing content, eroding brands, and disrupting the television system. It is a representational system that deserves significant disruption.

Regardless of all the disruptive potential of the Internet age, we are confronted with what we do not know. We do not know how many people will cut the cord, cancel their cable subscriptions, and move to an entirely online television experience or simply "shave the cable" – reduce their cable bill and supplement their viewing with online sources. We do not have a clear picture of how many will use piracy as their primary means of accessing television and movies. We do not know how many young people will grow up with the expectation that television and movies should be free (and act on that expectation). We do not have a clear picture of the full effect of multiple viewing platforms and mobile screens, and we do not know if online television audiences are more or less social than the audiences of the twentieth century. These are just a few of the uncertainties that obscure the future of a post-television age.

When I look at how my own viewing habits have changed I find that my television experience is more often than not advertising-free. I rarely watch a television show at its scheduled time. I am watching far more international fare than is available from my television provider. I watch more video content that did not derive from the television industry – from both amateur and professional sources. With increasing frequency I sit down in front of a computer screen to watch shows and movies instead of plopping down in front of the old tube. I still share many of Archie Bunker's television habits but have complemented them with a variety of digital devices and viewing habits that are distinctly twenty-first century.

The signs of an emerging post-television culture are everywhere and growing. When the fourth season of *Breaking Bad* was made available to Netflix subscribers, 50,000 viewers watched the entire season in 24 hours. Canadians are watching online video on more laptops, tablet computers, and smartphones than on television sets.[1] While we are watching video on a greater variety of screens we are also watching an increasing amount of Web video on our televisions. One survey reports that 45 per cent of consumers use television as "their primary Web video screen, up from 33 percent last year."[2] Television is migrating online and the Web is migrating to television sets. Meanwhile, the audience is exploring online television services and even opting out of cable altogether. Thirty-four per cent of millennials in the United States watch mostly online video or no broadcast television.[3] The television industry generally denies that cord-cutting is an issue, yet online discussions provide ample evidence that the audience is seeking ways to move its television viewing to less expensive and more varied online sources. The Internet is enabling the audience to replace traditional television and movie providers with inexpensive and free (if not often illegal) alternatives. Meanwhile, commercial television is responding with innovative ways of telling stories that attempt to bind the audience more securely to the corporate screen.[4] From extraordinary examples of binge viewing to incremental changes in online audience habits, we stand witness to the impact of the Internet on Archie Bunker's children.

It is fairly common to see claims that industry standards and regulatory regimes will determine the structure of online television. In 2004 Christopher T. Marsden described the future of Internet video as being defined by standards bodies, regulatory regimes, and market forces.[5] Governments and corporations do affect the online audience and will play a role in shaping the future of the television system. Equally so, it must also be recognized that the Internet enables the audience to circumvent regulations, subvert markets, and route around technological barriers. This renders the audience a potent force for shaping the emerging online television system. The forces of political power, capital, and regulation will continue to mitigate the potential of consumer choice and subterranean audience practices, but the Internet has redrawn the battle lines and states and markets are struggling to catch up.[6]

Online video acts as a complement to television. Broadcasters upload short clips, promotional segments, news items, and background material that foster deeper engagement with commercial media. Entire newscasts, full movies, complete television series, and the almost complete reproduction of television's flow of content have found their way online. Online audiences also watch a growing body of high-quality video content that does not derive from the television oligopoly. Forces of integration are met with the counter-force of disruptive audience behaviour. Elizabeth Evans suggests that an online audience practice such as downloading television from the Internet "ultimately offers a greater disruption to the temporal structure of broadcasting than earlier recording technologies, in turn offering greater autonomy over their engagement with it."[7] The online audience is more disruptive and autonomous than the offline audience of the twentieth century. As a result, the commercial sector is losing control over the flow of programs and movies and is at risk of losing its position as the primary arbiter of audience tastes and choices. The entertainment industry tends to assume that audiences will keep watching because commercial television produces the best content, but this ingenuous argument overlooks how television, as an oligopolistic marketplace, shapes audience tastes and limits choice.

In the emerging post-television age commercial television is not going to disappear but old oligopolies may well be replaced by new media oligopolies, perhaps dominated by Google and Apple or other types of innovative firms yet to be invented. An established marketplace that relies on a controlled distribution system is confronted with the appearance of a new distribution system that affords competitive advantages. Thus Lotz has observed that the broadcast sector fears that Google, Yahoo!, and AOL could take over the role played by incumbent broadcasters such as CBS, NBC, and ABC.[8] The television system of the twentieth century risks being compared to the railway system when it was confronted with the rise of mass air travel.

In *Television Truths* one of the pioneers of cultural studies, John Hartley, surveys the field of television studies and identifies the "pervasive, persuasive, and powerful" TV truths that structure our lives.[9] In light of the audience's enhanced capabilities as producers of content Hartley calls for a "new paradigm for understanding television" and sees television as intimately connected to the future of knowledge production.[10] Hartley explores the usual set of issues: the audience as active makers of meaning, an enhanced public sphere, globalization, Americanization, identity, citizenship, choice, aesthetics, liveness, authenticity, historical memory, and pedagogy.

In keeping with the general perspective of cultural studies, Hartley tends to privilege the audience's position in the determination of meanings. He sees the source of meaning as having shifted from the church of the Middle Ages to the private life of the modern citizen.[11] Yet perhaps the source of meaning finds its centre not in the private life of modern citizens but in the public life of the postmodern consumer. It is odd to see the individual privileged as the source of meaning when the contemporary individual is so firmly entrenched within the context of globalized institutions of meaning-production, which are pervasive and extremely well financed. John Fiske's argument that popular pleasures contain elements of resistance is unassailable.[12] Yet this critically important insight needs to be balanced with a constant return to the simple fact that however audiences may read films, programs, and commercials, these resistive audiences still end up in the shopping mall. Consumption is the preferred meaning of television. Very-large-scale mass societies of informational-industrial capitalism are based upon equally large-scale modes of behaviour management. The primary task of television is the reproduction of the consumer. It executes this task with amazing efficiency by replacing meaning-making functions once performed by the family, the education system, and the church.[13] This industrialization of meaning-making presents a significant challenge to individual capabilities of independent thought and action. As David Morley, a founding member of the cultural studies field, has noted, "The power of viewers to reinterpret meanings is hardly equivalent to the discursive power of centralized media institutions to construct the texts which the viewer then interprets, and to imagine otherwise is simply foolish."[14] Many scholars recognize the constraining character of commercial media. Thus Jonathan Gray and Amanda Lotz remind us that the cultural studies and political economy approaches to television are not as far apart as many accounts often portray them to be.[15]

In the twentieth century the relationship between institutionalized systems of representation and commercial promotion was pervasive. Even when we look at the earliest years of government-funded and highly regulated broadcasters such as the BBC it is clear that television in all its forms served to consolidate the relationship between culture and commerce.[16] Across the globe, corporations spent $163 billion (US) in 2012 on television advertising with the intention of reinforcing the relationship between watching and consuming. This suggests that the primary meaning of the television system is found in the imperative to consume according to the dictates of the corporate production system and the primary response of the audience is found in their actions as consumers. This in turn implies that meaning-making capabilities possessed by the audience pale in comparison to the ability of commercial media to shape values and desires that drive mass patterns of consumption. The active audience is most active as consumers and not as resisters to marketplace messages. Television has been called a $150 to $300 billion marketplace, but a full economic account of television must follow the flow of content to the flow of consumer dollars. Television sits atop a global consumer economy that sees consumers spend well over $20 trillion annually. Not every one of those dollars falls under the influence of television but such an economic system is critically dependent upon commercial television's promotional force.

The high-technology industry associated with the Internet and modern communication systems is itself the product of considerable propaganda on behalf of consumption. Samsung alone spends over $4 billion (US) annually on global advertising. The consumer devices that deliver Internet connectivity, mobility, communication, recording, and other digital capabilities are composed of toxic materials and implicated in social injustice and environmental degradation at the levels of mining, manufacturing, and disposal. For example, over 140 million cell phones end up in landfills in America every year, along with over 80 per cent of obsolete consumer electronics. Silicon Valley is "home to some of the most toxic industries in the nation ... a site of extreme social inequality."[17] As an industrial system the Internet replicates the worst of capitalism and does its best to implicate us in capitalism. Google plans to feature users' names, photographs, and online posts as tools for promoting products. Facebook, Twitter, and cell phone companies are developing more ways to deliver users to advertisers. We have never seen such sophistication in the commercial collection of personal data. This is bound to have an effect on the corporate sector's ability to promote its own interests and influence consumer behaviour.

As much as cultural studies and proponents of the active audience have contributed to our understanding, any reassessment of audience power must account for the connection between commercial media and consumption. As Newman and Levine have cogently argued, television scholarship has proven to be a "key site for the legitimation of television."[18] This legitimation takes place through bias in the scholarly assessment of what constitutes quality television, an overestimation of the interpretive powers and resistive stance of the active audience, and academic research centres that receive financial support from major media conglomerates. Any new paradigm of television studies needs greater connection to the centre of the television system – consumption. Jason Mittell reminds us, "consumer capitalism is a primary component of American ideology that is conveyed in nearly every television program."[19] When we look at children's relationship to television many parents will attest to a direct link between watching and wanting. As we age this link does not weaken so much as gain cultural sophistication and psychological subtlety. Television should be seen as a promotional system entrenched within a production system wrapped within the enigma of global consumer culture. We are not going to be able to kick the habits of hyper-consumption and ecological destruction within advanced capitalism without wrestling with the pusher. If there is to be a new paradigm for understanding television it must provide a better account of television's role as the voice of capitalism in the age of global military-industrial-media empires. If it is to be the case, as J.P. Kelly suggests, that online television engenders a heightened level of engagement with commercial television, then we must be doubly wary of calls for collaboration with this visual mode of manufacturing consent.[20] To update Raymond Williams's notion of television's flow, we need to follow the flow of money within the television system.

The changes television is going through have redefined its identity and function. Television in the twentieth century was defined by the state and market's firm control of where and when programs could be viewed. This twentieth-century conception of television no longer fits the subject in question. Consider P. David Marshall's suggestion that in some cases, "online video collapses the distinction between video produced by television and video produced from some other source."[21] Under such conditions, what happens to our notion of television as a particular type of experience arising from a specific production system?

The standard definition of television starts at the production side and privileges professional, marketplace-based economies of scale. In 2004 Michael L. Katz defined television as the asymmetrical flow of content that derives from programming created by professionals for relatively large audiences. This programming "comes in discrete units of between

15 minutes and several hours."[22] Yet this definition unduly privileges twentieth-century television and fails to account for how new technologies and mediums are changing the viewing experience. As Hartley argued, "television is not simply a resource supplied commercially to markets."[23] When Hartley wrote these words in 1999 in *Uses of Television* few people imagined that the uses of television would include the audience making their own television content. Books about the uses of television written in the twentieth century serve as a benchmark for measuring how the audience's capacities have expanded and how modes of television production and distribution have evolved.

With increasing frequency, commercial television is making use of content that derives from the audience, as in news and weather programming. The online context of the audience is changing the power relations that defined twentieth-century television. We see this in Uricchio's observation that "we are witnessing nothing less than the emergence of a new production system generated within communities of interest, not states and corporations."[24] When a television set is transformed into just another screen connected to the Internet, the viewing experience is no longer defined by or restricted to any one particular system of content production. The experience of being the audience is expanded to encompass all forms of video content from all sources. Because television was initially controlled by either corporations or states the temptation is to continue to restrict the definition of television to content systems that are owned and operated by governments and media conglomerates. It is easy to forget that almost exactly a century ago in 1920, television was "not dominated by giant corporate conglomerates" but was defined by the inventors and amateurs that tinkered with the technology.[25] The role of piracy, amateurs, and online tinkering with production and distribution models that is found at the centre of post-television culture serves to remind us that the "commercial, one-way model of 'television' is not inherent to the medium itself but has been constructed by specific regulatory policies and economic practices."[26] Television's own history suggests that a better approach to defining the medium would be to conceptualize television as not limited to a particular production system or mode of watching. Television's lack of specificity results from the changing nature of production, distribution, economics, and the emerging role of the audience as producers and distributors of video. As it becomes an omnipresent, multi-platform, multipurpose media experience, television loses any essential character and becomes the media environment itself.

Such a radical change in the nature of a distribution system, from the twentieth-century broadcast mode of distribution to the contemporary era of the Internet, has scholars and industry experts anticipating a wide variety of changes to the television system. New producers, new stories, new roles for the audience, shifting power relationships in the political economy of television, greater diversity and choice, the erosion of video content's status as private property, and many other forces are at work. Formerly unprofitable modes of storytelling and programming are becoming viable, and unconventional programming no longer needs to conform to dominant business models or controlled distribution systems. These changes carry consequences because television is the DNA of capitalism. Toby Miller summarized a century of critical intellectual output on the matter when he observed that "consciousness has been customized to the requirements of economical media production."[27] Commercial media, with television triumphant at the centre, provided much of the coding for mass belief and action. It appears that we are tampering with our media DNA. Television may not have been the primary cause of many aspects of the twentieth century but it was certainly guilty by association. This is a system designed to "compete with our experience and influence our interpretation of it."[28] Television played a significant role in a significant number of lives. If twentieth-century television was indeed a vast wasteland, as Newton Minnow so famously overstated in 1962, it was far from impotent. The second half of the last century testifies to the consequential nature of television's structure. When we look to the future of online television we face the uncertainty of unintended consequences.

Walter Cummins and George Gordon have suggested that in the twentieth century many of television's consequences were "unintended, unstated, and even unknown to those involved in its programming. Indeed, the history of television's influence is more a history of unanticipated side effects than it is of predictable outcomes."[29] We can anticipate that erosion of control over content will have widespread economic, social, and political effects, particularly when the content in question is video, moving pictures, the very stuff we love to watch. Yet it is difficult and somewhat foolish to predict the precise outcome of a post-television generation that gets most of its viewing fare from online sources. Online television could strengthen the market position of the cable TV industry: "it is very possible that cable's overall market position will be even stronger in five to ten years."[30] Perhaps little more will change than television power shifting from an old oligopoly to a new one. There is also the risk that the online television ecosystem will become as hyper-concentrated as other sectors of the digital economy. Whatever direction the online audience takes, modest adjustments in the television industry seem unlikely, given the differences that exist between broadcast-based and Internet-based communication systems. The possibility for extreme changes is increased when we consider the difference between the context of the twentieth and the twenty-first century.

Television came of age at the dawn of the era of mass consumption. In many ways it was the midwife of consumer culture. It sold something everyone wanted, the American Dream, a comfortable middle-class lifestyle, easy credit and lots to spend it on. When television came of age in the early 1960s and entered the majority of our homes, we were barely aware of the consequences of unfettered consumption. Half a century later there is a greater level of awareness among audiences regarding the ecological and social impact of production and consumption because the effects of the consumer lifestyle are much more obvious. Mass involvement in video making, the rise of amateur reporters and budding documentarians, the simple ability to point a camera and upload the scene, almost instantly, to a global audience – all this new media activity will play a role in the struggle to define exactly what our local and global situation is and what should be done about it. Context will condition content. This is not to say that the audience will have a uniform response to whatever crisis faces them. How they respond will depend on local cultures and contexts. Republican white males in Texas make choices with their cameras and television remote controls in a very different manner than do Muslims in the Middle East.

Unidirectional commercial and state television has transformed into a multidirectional networked public sphere, an arena in which local, regional, and global conflicts are played out by ordinary people armed with cameras and Internet access. Participatory networked television is a tool and a weapon, with the audience playing the role of content producer and distributor. In *Legitimating Television* Michael Z. Newman and Elana Levine see access to Web-based content as a "further distancing of TV use from the pre-convergence era's broadcasting status quo."[31] Under these conditions online television contributes to conflict as cultures collide in cyberspace and content is distributed outside the control of regulatory regimes. In this context Archie Bunker and his family do more than just struggle over evolving social norms in the comfort and privacy of their shared domestic space. They point the camera at themselves and each other, they transmit their cultural wars into cyberspace, and we the people formerly known as the audience are likewise drawn into the struggle.

The post-television era is movement towards high-definition reality. Cathode ray tube television of the twentieth century was a grainy experience of small screens that delivered low-quality images, mediocre sound, and commercialized reality. Now flat-panel televisions deliver ultra-high-definition images that shift the cultural status of television towards the cinematic. The *New York Times* described the difference in terms of "looking through a window rather than looking at a picture."[32] These new screens of post-television culture are high definition not merely in the technical and optical sense. They move the audience beyond the confines of a commercially defined realm of moving images and representation. Post-television culture delivers more capacity to participate in creating social realities. Perhaps it is unwise to speak of new media as delivering a more authentic experience of reality, but certainly different forms of realism are mediated through new modes of video production arising out of the Internet.

The status of television has always been caught up in issues of class-based distinctions of taste and value. It remains to be seen how the integration of outsider content into the viewing experience will change the cultural status of TV. Newman and Levine note that "discourses of legitimation" emanating from the industry and from academia describe viewers as empowered by new technologies such as DVDs, which give greater control over time and supplant the networks' role as programmer.[33] These discourses also speak of the new television era as liberating the audience from crass commercialism and advertising "in so far as they interrupt the authentic content of television."[34] Yet there is no such thing as a commercial-free viewing experience within commercial television when the show itself is an advertisement for a lifestyle and products play the role of secondary characters. When the industry speaks of freedom, empowerment, and the agency of the audience it engages in a form of doublespeak that masks the marketplace's intention to own eyeballs, invade privacy, gather personal data, and manage consumption patterns.

Newman and Levine describe television as being "no longer impoverished by comparison to movies."[35] There is another aspect of television's poverty that must be taken into account – the poverty of advertising-driven content. Post-television culture is not marked by the demise of commercial television, at least not as long as we live within capitalism's social order. Changes that merely affect the delivery of commercial media would at best be cosmetic and convenient. We will know we are in post-television culture when the online audience is engaged with audience-produced content that relentlessly challenges the dominant economic and political assumptions of the day. Henry Jenkins, the renowned interpreter of fan culture, is mistaken to enthusiastically embrace the kind of collaboration that sees the audience becoming more involved in the creation and dissemination of commercial television. Newman and Levine argue that "he sees one ultimate purpose of his scholarship as helping media industries to better make and sell their wares."[36] Perhaps the day is coming when a significant amount of our viewing time is taken up by experiences no longer impoverished by their association with capitalism. Post-television culture gains consequential force when we the people formerly known as the audience are the producers, distributors, and storytellers of our own versions of reality.

One of the greatest contradictions of post-television culture is in the realm of economics and advertising. The digital nature of online viewing enables better surveillance of audience habits and delivers more targeted advertising. Social aspects of online viewing also "generate richer information about audiences for precision-targeted and perhaps more valued type of advertising."[37] Combine the data gathered from digital viewing with the knowledge of consumer habits gained through digital spending and the result is managerial capitalism on steroids. At the same time the ecology of online viewing enables the audience to escape from advertising, if they so desire (and of course many do). In light of these contradictory forces we cannot position the future of the post-television audience as an inevitable emancipation from the constraints of media corporations and the firms they serve.

Hartley asserts that television studies, as an "only recently established and still contested field," must account for the productive capabilities of the audience. These new productive capabilities are nothing less than "the most important innovation in television … the *democratization of productivity*."[38] Along with an increase in productive capabilities the audience is also experiencing expanded powers of distribution, circumvention, and choice. Many of the activities formerly reserved for the owners and operators of commercial television are now shared in some form or another by the audience. Certainly, not all of the audience has equal access to these new capabilities and not all who do have access will make use of them. Yet it may only take a small percentage of billions of Internet-connected audience members to make a big difference. For example, a mere 5 per cent or so of citizens are engaged as activists in the political arena. Where would we be without that active minority? Furthermore, the online audience is becoming more, not less, active with each passing year. Between 2009 and 2013 the percentage of American adult Internet users who uploaded videos doubled and now stands at a remarkable 31 per cent. Among 18- to 29-year-old Internet users this productive activity rises to an incredible 41 per cent.[39] The act of being a video creator and distributor may soon be mainstream audience behaviour.

Productive audiences act as a counter-force to trends of digital enclosure that Mark Andrejevic fears will strip networked individuals of their autonomy. According to Andrejevic, the productive activity of Internet users "promises little more than the reproduction of the social relations it purports to overcome."[40] Here the analytical tools of Marxist analysis are applied to the subject with all the subtlety of a massive hammer and sickle. There is far more promise in our online productive activity than the mere reproduction of capitalism's social relations, even when our productions flow through commercial sites such as YouTube. Google received over 100 million requests to take down piracy-related links in 2013 yet piracy remains rampant. This suggests control mechanisms are both enhanced and degraded in the highly decentralized context of the Internet. History clearly demonstrates that subversion can take place in spite of the repressive structures that surround the individual. Uncontrolled flows of online content stand as a reminder that for all their power and capabilities, market and state mechanisms of digital enclosure have yet to eliminate counter-discourses and the transformation of fee into free. The Internet is not a virtual iron cage.

Andrejevic's dismissal of the value of mundane acts of production by ordinary people contrasts sharply with Sean Cubitt's valuation of the productive activity of twentieth-century artists who "have been profoundly at odds with the dominant presuppositions of capital and its workings."[41] Too often the Left positions intellectuals and artists as resisters of capitalism and ordinary people as reproducers of capitalism. Nonetheless, Cubitt looks to electronic media as the source of a new type of productivity that holds forth "the possibility of change so profound that nothing will ever be the same again."[42] As Cubitt and many others note, capitalism has made many enemies. Now those enemies of capitalism have the ability to participate in the production of televisual content and do so beyond the institutional, market, and technological controls of the twentieth century. This is a source of hope that there lies something within our grasp beyond a society moulded to the demands of capital. This hope is usually dampened within the critical literature by the oft-repeated observation that new mass media are "quickly dominated by centralized and centralizing corporations."[43] Thus in *The Master Switch* Tim Wu draws a picture of twentieth-century media as a circle that endlessly repeats the cycle of innovation, enhanced individual communication capabilities, consolidation by the state and corporations, and demise of individual communicative capabilities. In other words, there is never anything really very new in new media systems.[44] This argument is tantamount to proposing that the forces of capital represent an end of history. The market has already decided the fate of online television. This theory merely serves to reproduce television's own ideology of control. Nothing less than the future itself is controlled by the market and its handmaid, media.

Uricchio reminds us that television's ideology of control was developed in the context of an industrial economy which promoted "increasing constraints on expression with the appearance of each new technology."[45] Behind the artificial scarcity, limited programming availability, and regulatory regimes of twentieth-century television was the imperative to maintain "strict message control" on behalf of dominant economic and political interests.[46] Yet in spite of these forces of constraint, as the twentieth century waned viewers gained greater control over the medium through VCRs, DVDs, DVRs, and the Internet itself. As a result, television operates as "a medium in a near constant state of transition" and constraining forces continue to be confounded by the countermoves of the audience.[47] More is afoot here than a straightforward reproduction of the social relations of capitalism. Consider James Carey's observation that "structures of consciousness parallel structures of communication."[48] It is this fundamental relationship that leads Manuel Castells to suggest that the productive activity of the online audience may be "rewiring our minds."[49] The transformation the television system is undergoing is part of a process that sees new content changing the character of our collective symbolic environment. The online environment provides greater autonomy for the individual as a communicating subject and this in turn increases "the chances for the introduction of messages challenging dominant values and interests ... Reprogramming networks of meaning substantially affects the exercise of power throughout all of the networks."[50] In contrast to fears that the Internet will merely reproduce dominant systems of power, the type of communicative autonomy expressed through amateur videography, guerrilla rebroadcasting, and digital piracy "is directly related to the development of social and political autonomy."[51]

I have argued that previously fringe aspects of television viewing – piracy, cord-cutting, the failure to adopt pay-TV at all (cord nevers), alternative modes of video production and distribution – are growing increasingly consequential. The degree to which any of these activities will become mainstream remains to be seen. It is far too early to start writing eulogies for commercial television. We do not yet know if on-line modes of television consumption are displacing or merely comple-menting our extensive diet of commercial media.[52] I have suggested that, in spite of industry voices to the contrary, there remains the pos-sibility that the television industry could follow a path similar to that of the music industry and see the loss of control over its content within the Internet. The adoption of online television has lagged behind the adop-tion of digital music, so time will need to pass before we can draw more certain conclusions about the fate of digital media in networked en-vironments. Nevertheless, when you add up all the forces at work it appears that an oligopolistic media system is facing the possibility of disintermediation, losing control over audiences and content, and is unable to adapt quickly because of legacy technology, contractual com-mitments, and executives invested in maintaining the status quo. Yet such a broad concept as loss of control needs careful qualification. Regulatory regimes still have legal weight, the industry has many tech-nologies and tactics at its disposal for keeping audience members in the fold, and not everyone is a digital pirate reaching for the scissors, ready to cut the cord. After all, online television has only recently emerged within the context of a much older media economy that absolutely dominates the audience's leisure time and saturates our collective im-agination. And yet the vast majority of the time when people hand me their laptop, smartphone, or tablet computer to look at a video, it is not commercial television being shared. Other media experiences are musc-ling their way into our entertainment time. Television is everywhere – but so much more than just the television of Time Warner and Rupert Murdoch. The audience is displacing the role of commercial gatekeep-ers in the media system.

The question that *Post-TV* seeks to answer is this: can there be any-thing more to television than what is offered to us by the current varia-tions of commercial and state-run media? In *Watching TV Is Not Required* Bernard McGrane and John Gunderson suggest that "from the point of view of critical sociology, we could say that as a social institution, tele-vision serves the purpose of conditioning us to find it more and more difficult to be interested in anything *other* than television."[53] The forces addressed herein imply that online television is the very thing that could break the conditioning of commercial media. The conditioning McGrane and Gunderson speak of flows from the logic of television: "Keep watching, buy something, and come back tomorrow."[54] The irony of the television industry's rush to adapt to the online environment is that it may be laying the foundation for a type of viewing experience that, to some degree, undermines what television wants – compliant consumers and passive citizens.

Post-television Culture

Cultural systems are shaped by their communication technologies, and the uses of communication technologies are shaped by their cultural context. When new modes of communication appear we often witness changes in the way meanings are created and distributed, which in turn affects patterns of behaviour. We are currently in the midst of a global shift away from a highly centralized era of television that has tremendous implications for the way meanings are produced and disseminated. Lotz notes that twentieth-century television "circulated ideas in a way that asserted and reinforced existing power structures and dominant ways of thinking." This is the central message delivered by the critical study of television – power is exercised through television. Television's cultural role shifts when it is no longer the source of a broad and heterogeneous audience. Lotz argues that "it has become increasingly unlikely that television functions as a space for the negotiation of contested beliefs among diverse groups simply because audiences are now more narrow and specialized."[55] Here we see the fear that television is gathering more power unto itself as it isolates groups and suppresses civic debate. Yet, once again, exactly the opposite may be occurring as a result of the structure of online television.

YouTube's rich field of comments and oppositional videos suggests that this new television space is rife with contested beliefs. An otherwise obscure trailer for a meritless movie can become the basis for increased dialogue *and* conflict between groups. As television moves beyond the control of corporate entertainment networks and state regulation, as it evolves from a one-way offline flow to a multidirectional online flow of content, and as audiences increasingly play the role of producers and distributors, television begins to mirror the general character of the Internet itself – an unconstrained flow of counter-discourses, a clash of contested beliefs, and a veritable renaissance of diversity. Such a structure of television flow is unlikely to reduce the communicative capabilities of the audience.

In so far as we could speak of a television culture in the twentieth century, the forces mapped herein suggest that there is something after television, that the television system is changing to such a degree that what it is becoming will be as different as the iPhone is to the rotary phone. When Joke Hermes observes in *After the Break* that "any amateur who wishes to make television can do so," he reveals one of the key features of the "break" between the old and new television systems.[56] Such a statement would be nonsensical in the previous century. The democratization of production and distribution and the Internet-ization of commercial television invite us to consider what defines post-television culture as a distinct historical moment. Obviously, it is not the death of visual culture or the end of moving pictures. Post-television culture inscribes a new mode of producing and distributing "moving pictures" that disrupts the twentieth century's hermetically sealed system of representation but also may be the beginning of a global culture deeply engaged with screens far beyond our current situation.

In 1995 Peter d'Agostino and David Tafler described the arrival of a post-television culture as a direct challenge to mainstream television's ability to "structure overall consciousness." They proposed that "in a post-television environment, television first turns to video."[57] This certainly seems to be the case as the audience moves online. Video is seen by many critical theorists as not merely a different technology than television but as something that produces reality differently than television. Video "revolutionizes television" by giving communities the ability to maintain their values, define their own reality, and confront television's pretension to represent the whole community.[58] Beyond these familiar claims, the outlines of post-television culture remain skeletal, a frame waiting to be fleshed out. Twenty years later the non-stop series of transformations brought on by the Internet allow us to offer a more meaty description of post-television culture.

Post-television culture denotes a collection of technology-enabled forces, none of which are entirely new but which together collectively constitute a break from the structure of twentieth-century television. Forces such as mobility, ubiquitous presence of both screens and video recording devices, and an expansion in modes of production and distribution arguably have undermined the corporate/state control of visual representation. Contradictions abound in this cultural system just as they do in capitalism itself. Piracy operates as an anti-economy, an alternative mode of distribution, a politicizing agent, and a stimulus to purchasing. To this the corporate-state alliance responds with mass criminalization of otherwise benign audience behaviours. The digital environment enables circumvention but also ensures expanded surveillance capabilities. The audience gains new powers of speech even as commercial media threatens to overwhelm the visual environment and drown out independent thought. Forces latent in the twentieth century as varied and oppositional as surveillance and counter-discourse increase in magnitude even as the risks and dangers facing the human race threaten to overwhelm the foundation of our existence. Post-television culture fundamentally alters how meanings are produced, what meanings can be produced, and who gets to participate in their production and distribution. It represents an unprecedented level of participation in the creation and global distribution of the raw materials used for building social orders – words, stories, images, videos. Post-television culture is changing the quantity, accessibility, and nature of the very building blocks of cultural systems – widely available meanings.

The Last Word on Internet Piracy?

It should be kept in mind that in this book I have not argued that the online audience is in total control of its television experience. Christine Quail notes that the "popular myth of user control over all media, all content" lends itself to the false argument that the online audience is "in total control of their viewing experience."[59] In actuality, neither freedom nor control is complete in online or offline contexts. Whereas Quail argues that the American and Canadian television industries' control of access, international distribution deals, and government regulation "largely structure the global online television context," I have clearly taken issue with the notion that government and industry *largely* structure online television viewing.[60] Time will need to pass before the trajectory of the online audience is undeniable. Nonetheless, cord cutters, cord nevers, pirates, and other emerging forms of online audience behaviour demonstrate that structuring forces of the twentieth century are being eroded. Evasion of regulations, transgression of laws, and circumvention of technologies are definitive characteristics of the online television audience. Thus claims such as those made by Elissa Nelson to the effect that "consumers make choices within a system controlled by conglomerate structures" require careful qualification in light of the online audience's considerable capabilities when it comes to evading structures of control and making their own viewing choices outside of technological and regulatory constraints.[61] Theirs is not a highly structured or firmly controlled viewing experience.

The public pronouncements of industry and government consistently insist that the end of piracy is just around the corner (although privately they will often tell a very different story). The general trend has been towards the mass criminalization of everyday behaviour and increasingly draconian penalties for downloading something that is otherwise of marginal worth. Yet it is unlikely that such policy changes will stem the tide. As a headline in the *New York Times* proclaimed in the summer of 2012, "Internet Pirates Will Always Win." In this news story Nick Bilton suggests, "It is only going to get worse."[62] Piracy rates will continue to vex the entertainment industry and governments will continue to write laws that deliver punishments that far exceed the damage done.

There is a terrible irony to the state of copyright law. Under pressure from the entertainment industry, governments have changed laws, increased penalties, decreased consumer rights, and eroded the principles of fair dealing and fair use. All this has resulted from the dissemination of overblown statistics and propaganda from the media industry. In other words, the policymaking process has been captured by major corporations that lied to government officials, distorted facts, eroded public rights, and advanced private interests at the expense of common culture. If we were serious about crime we would demand that the media industry make reparations for influencing public officials, warping legislation, and criminalizing mass behaviour. Some of the richest corporations in the world have manipulated public policy to unjustly advance private gain. A terrible crime has been committed against all of us. These economic and political inequities provide fertile ground for a disruptive post-television culture to take root among the global online audience.

Notes

Introduction

1 Cisco, "Cisco Visual Networking Index: Forecast and Methodology, 2011–2016." Also see Sandvine, "Global Internet Phenomena Spotlight: Netflix Rising." In 2011 the media measurement firm Sandvine reported that 40 per cent of North American broadband traffic was taken up with delivering video.

2 Lotz, *The Television Will Be Revolutionized*, 2.

3 Holt and Sanson, "Introduction," 1.

4 D'Agostino and Tafler, "Introduction," xv.

5 Gray, *Television Entertainment*, 9.

6 Ibid., 8.

7 Gripsrud, "Broadcast Television," 211.

8 Lotz, *The Television Will Be Revolutionized*, 146.

9 Fixmer and Sherman, "TV Networks Fueled by Netflix Effect."

10 "For the 2008–2009 TV season, the amount of television watched reached an all-time high as Americans spent four hours and 49 minutes a day on average in front of the TV, up four minutes from last year and up 20% from 10 years ago. The average household watched eight hours and 21 minutes a day on average, also at an all-time high." Nielsen, "Average TV Viewing for 2008–09 TV Season at All-Time High."

11 Here I have appropriated Richard Chalfen's description of domestic analogue home movie practices of the mid-twentieth century as the "simplest situation." When compared to the current highly fragmented, disbursed, and interactive modes of production and viewing, the relatively homogeneous, domesticated, and controlled television audiences of the analogue broadcast era can be said to represent the simplest situation in

the history of the television audience. Chalfen, "Home Movies as Cultural Documents," 130.

12 McLuhan and Fiore, *The Medium Is the Massage*, 61.

13 D'Agostino and Tafler, "Introduction," xiii.

14 Ibid., xvi–xvii.

15 Moore, "What Does 'Watching TV' Mean in the Post-TV Age?"

16 Born, "Inside Television," 424.

17 De Valck and Teurlings, "After the Break," 8.

18 Ibid., 11.

19 Ibid., 8.

20 Chmielewski, "Netflix Executive Upends Hollywood."

21 Tay and Turner, "Not the Apocalypse," 33.

22 Hart, "Video on the Internet," 136.

23 Bignell and Fickers, "Introduction," 48.

24 Ibid., 34.

25 Baloo, comment on Michael Geist's blog post, "Is the CRTC Ready to Hit the Reset Button on Television Regulation in Canada?"

26 Nielsen, "January 2011: Online Video Usage Up 45%." In January 2011 the time spent viewing video on computers and laptops from home and work increased by 45 per cent from a year earlier, but the number of unique online viewers only increased by 3 per cent during the same period. According to one report, "total digital video views rose 30% year over year for the first quarter of 2013." See Whitney, "Streaming Users Double Up."

27 Newman, "Free TV," 3.

28 Geist, "Canadian Broadcasters and BDUs."

29 Ibid. Geist argues, "The Internet based streams effectively reduce the value of a cable or satellite television subscription since much of what is now offered through those services is, by Bell's own definition, of no market value."

30 Baysinger, "Sports Summit."

31 Lotz, *The Television Will Be Revolutionized*, 7.

32 Crawford, *Captive Audience*, 11.

33 Tay and Turner, "Not the Apocalypse," 32.

34 Vicha, Facebook status update, 14 June 2011.

35 Hartley, "Invisible Fictions," 122.

36 Oliveira, "Online Video Surging in Canada."

37 Ladurantaye, "For This Man, the Show Must Go On."

38 Cheng, "Cutting the Cable Cord Gets Easier."

39 Hauser, *Vernacular Voices*, 109.

40 Block, "Cable Convenes in D.C. under a Cloud of Uncertainty."

41 Born, "Inside Television," 421.

42 Lawton, "More Households Cut the Cord on Cable."
43 Schechner, "TV Networks See Key Audience Erode."
44 Berr, "Television as We Know It Is Fading."
45 Gatmaitan, "Network TV: An Industry in Decline"; College News, "Television News in Rapid Decline."
46 Burgess, "Online Movie Streaming Will Overtake DVD Sales This Year in U.S." In 2012 online movie streaming made up 94 per cent of all movie purchases.
47 Cervantes, "Poll: Are Blu-ray and DVD Movies Now Obsolete?"
48 D'Agostino and Tafler, "Introduction," xvii.
49 Gray, *Television Entertainment*, 11.

1. From the Remote Control to Out of Control: Music Piracy and the Future of Television

1 While some argue that markets are less concentrated and consumers have more choice, the opposite is the case. Choice occurs across a set of media products offered by a decreasing number of firms. Winseck, "The State of Media Ownership and Media Markets."
2 Jenkins, "The Cultural Logic of Media Convergence," 33.
3 McChesney, *The Problem of the Media*, 177. Indicative of market concentration, the American cable giant Comcast faced an $875 million antitrust lawsuit in 2012. The lawsuit contends that Comcast "entered into agreements with its competitors to allocate the nation's regional cable markets amongst themselves" and "used its monopoly power to raise cable prices to artificially high, supra-competitive levels." Milford and Bathon, "Comcast Heads to Trial in Case Alleging Monopolization." McChesney notes that cable rates in the United States have increased at three times the inflation rate (*The Problem of the Media*, 179).
4 Ibid., 178–9.
5 Winseck, "Big Media in the Hot Seat at CRTC Hearings." Winseck dismissed Church as little more than a "hired-gun" for Bell Canada.
6 Ibid.
7 Ibid.
8 Uricchio, "Television's Next Generation," 170.
9 Ibid.
10 Ibid.
11 Seiter et al., *Remote Control*, 2.
12 Denick, *Media and Global Civil Society*, 54.
13 Kellner, *Television and the Crisis of Democracy*, 95.

14 Linder, *Public Access Television*, xxv.
15 Downing, *Radical Media: Rebellious Communication and Social Movements*, 3.
16 Boyle, "From Portapak to Camcorder," 68.
17 Ibid., 69.
18 Downing, *Radical Media: The Political Experience of Alternative Communication*, 7, 352.
19 Uricchio, "Television's Next Generation," 178.
20 Ibid., 178, 177.
21 Negroponte, *Being Digital*, 153.
22 Associated Press, "Netflix Future Tied to Using Internet Video Streaming Insights to Improve Recommendations."
23 Black et al., "More than 'Just Shopping,'" 37.
24 Thomas, "When Digital Was New," 64.
25 Wolff, "It's War! Hollywood Strikes Back."
26 Ibid.
27 Thomas, "When Digital Was New," 67.
28 Ibid.
29 Seltzer, "The Broadcast Flag," 214.
30 "The Betamax Case."
31 Ibid.
32 Varona, "Changing Channels and Bridging Divides," 115.
33 Ibid.
34 Gruenwal, "As Hollywood Watches, SOPA Champion Berman Fights for His Seat."
35 Masnick, "Some Data on How Much the Big Media Firms Are Donating to SOPA/PIPA Sponsors."
36 Wyatt, "F.C.C. Commissioner Leaving to Join Comcast."
37 Thomas, "When Digital Was New," 71.
38 Ibid., 72.
39 Zittrain, *The Future of the Internet and How to Stop It*.
40 Bennett and Brown, "Introduction," 6.
41 Smith, "DVD Technologies and the Art of Control," 130.
42 Ibid., 147.
43 Rosen, "The People Formerly Known as the Audience."
44 Murdoch, "Speech by Rupert Murdoch to the American Society of Newspaper Editors."
45 Elliott, "Adding to the Annual Spectacle."
46 Rosen, "The People Formerly Known as the Audience."
47 *Economist*, "Among the Audience."
48 Edgecliffe-Johnson, "Media Wants to Break Free."

49 Covert, "A Decade of iTunes Singles Killed the Music Industry."
50 Ibid.
51 Porter, "The Perpetual War." The International Federation of the Phonographic Industry (IFPI) claims that approximately 95 per cent of music downloads (in 2010) were illegal. The IFPI is hardly an unbiased source for data, but this number may be closest to the truth. See Morrissey, "O.K., Downloaders, Let's Try This Song Again."
52 Sweney, "Global Recorded Music Sales Fall Almost $1.5bn amid Increased Piracy."
53 Wikström, "A Typology of Music Distribution Models," 17.
54 Recording Industry Association of America, "For Students Doing Reports."
55 Manjoo, "Sour Notes."
56 Economist, "Counting the Change."
57 Ibid.
58 Barnett, "Spotify 'Helps Curb Music Piracy.'" See also Giletti, "Why Pay if It's Free?"
59 Atkinson, "Pandora Effect."
60 Also noteworthy, "94 percent of digital sales now come from streaming music services, while 6 percent come from downloads." Ingham, "Swedish Music Market Grows 12% in H1 2013."
61 Wikström, "A Typology of Music Distribution Models," 9.
62 Steirer, "The Personal Media Collection in an Era of Connected Viewing," 92.
63 Barlow, The DVD Revolution, 27.
64 Rifkin, "The Age of Access," 43.
65 Sabbagh, "Hollywood in Turmoil as DVD Sales Drop and Downloads Steal the Show."
66 Goodkind, "Netflix Introduces New Pricing Plan." Indicative of a highly active audience, this article generated over 2,220 comments from cord cutters, Netflix users, digital pirates, and other members of the post-television generation.
67 Bilton, "Disruptions."
68 Ibid.
69 Ibid.
70 Manjoo, "Sour Notes."
71 Ibid.
72 Etherington, "iTunes Match and iCloud."
73 Kahn, "Music Industry Failing to Promote Legal Alternatives to Piracy."
74 Miller, "How to End Content Piracy Right Now."

75 Harris, "'Game of Thrones' Piracy Arguments Proven Wrong by History."

76 Oberholzer-Gee and Strumpf, "The Effect of File Sharing on Record Sales." The authors conclude that "file sharing has had only a limited effect on record sales" (2).

77 Peitz and Waelbroeck, "Why the Music Industry May Gain from Free Downloading – The Role of Sampling," and Hu et al., "Does Sampling Influence Customers in Online Retailing of Digital Music?"

78 Aguiar and Martens, "Digital Music Consumption on the Internet," 15.

79 "Court Orders Bell to Pay Quebecor $1M in Piracy Lawsuit." Videotron has asked the court for an additional $173 million from Bell for lost revenue due to the piracy allowed by Bell.

80 Chenoweth, "Murdoch Cops Blast over Pay TV Pirates."

81 Doyle, "How the Murdoch Scandal Turned Paranoia into Reality."

82 Strangelove, *The Empire of Mind*, 87.

83 Pfanner, "Copyright Cheats Face the Music in France."

84 Geuss, "French Anti-P2P Law Cuts Back Pirating, but Music Sales Still Decline."

85 Lescure, "Contribution aux politiques culturelles à l'ère numérique."

86 Giblin, "Evaluating Graduated Response," 60.

87 *Economist*, "Singing a Different Tune."

88 enigmax, "Young File-sharers Respond to Tough Laws by Buying a VPN." Also see enigmax, "File-sharing Prospers Despite Tougher Laws."

89 Mulligan, "What Happened to the RIAA's Missing 3.5 Million?"

90 Andy, "Piracy Collapses as Legal Alternatives Do Their Job."

91 Pakinkis, "Piracy Rising in UK, According to Ofcom Report."

92 Lunden, "U.S. Music Sales Down as Streaming Up 24% to 51B Tracks in 6 Months."

93 Shinai, "As Streaming Replaces Downloading, Music Revenue Stagnates."

94 Anderson, "Only 9% (and Falling) of US Internet Users Are P2P Pirates."

95 Ibid.

96 Pakinkis, "Piracy Rising in UK."

97 Waterman, Ji, and Rochet, "Enforcement and Control of Piracy, Copying, and Sharing in the Movie Industry," 284.

98 NetNames, "Netnames Piracy Analysis," 3.

99 Rostami, "Free Is Hard to Beat," 7.

100 Associated Press, "RIAA Stops Piracy Lawsuit Strategy."

101 Bangerman, "RIAA Anti-P2P Campaign a Real Money Pit, According to Testimony."

102 Giletti, "Why Pay if It's Free?" 30.

103 Koh, Murthi, and Raghunathan, "Shift in Demand for Music," 18.
104 Stop Music Piracy, "Music Piracy & Organized Crime."
105 Karaganis et al., "Does Crime Pay?" 2.
106 Sweney, "Government Wants to Cut Illegal Filesharing by 80% by 2011."
107 Geist, "Copyright Lobby Demands Rollback of Recent Canadian Reforms in Secretive Trade Deal." According to Geist, "lobby groups are hoping to use secretive trade negotiations to forge legislative change. Later this week, the International Intellectual Property Alliance, an umbrella organization that represents movie, music, and software associations, will urge the U.S. government to pressure Canada to enact further reforms as part of the Trans Pacific Partnership trade negotiations."
108 Cubbison, "A Dark Day on the Internet Leads to a Sea Change in Copyright Policy," 25.
109 Engleman, "Web Piracy Bills 'Dead' in U.S. from Lobbying, Dodd Says."
110 Lee, "Paramount Exec Faces Skeptical Crowds on Post-SOPA Outreach Tour."
111 Goel, Miesing, and Chandra, "The Impact of Illegal Peer-to-peer File Sharing on the Media Industry." The authors conclude, "Our tests show a significant increase in stock prices on average that is consistent with the proposition that sophisticated investors believe that the industry's current strategy of protecting its revenues through tighter laws and stronger enforcement is associated with an expectation of higher future cash flows" (27).
112 Yang, "All for Love," 527.
113 Tryon and Dawson, "Streaming U," 226.
114 Goldacre, "Illegal Downloads and Dodgy Figures."
115 For example, see Cammaerts and Meng, "Creative Destruction and Copyright Protection."
116 Smith and Telang, "Assessing the Academic Literature Regarding the Impact of Media Piracy on Sales," 1.
117 United States Government Accountability Office, "Intellectual Property."
118 Karaganis, "Introduction," iii; "Rethinking Piracy," 1, 9, 8.
119 Ibid., 40–1. Another study looking at US media companies finds "combined revenues for 10 major media in the United States have steadily declined as a proportion of overall economic activity or gross domestic product (GDP) from 1999 to at least 2009" but also notes "the exception of television and video games, whose revenues have so far kept pace with GDP." This study concludes that "we may be entering an era of a declining size of media industries in terms of conventional measures, but not necessarily a falling supply of media products themselves." See Waterman and Ji, "Online Versus Offline in the U.S.," 285.

120 Cammaerts, Mansell, and Meng, "Copyright & Creation," 7.
121 Karaganis, "Rethinking Piracy," 41.
122 Ibid., 42.
123 Kal Raustiala and Chris Sprigman examined the economic costs of online piracy and also concluded, "So what's the real number? At this point, we simply don't know" ("Piracy Really Hurt the U.S. Economy?").

2. Television and Movie Piracy: Simple, Fast, and Free

1 "Would You Pay for a Legal Alternative to Film Piracy?"
 2 Online comments on "Would You Pay for a Legal Alternative to Film Piracy?"
 3 Oldernwiser, comment on "Would You Pay for a Legal Alternative to Film Piracy?"
 4 Economist, "Ahoy There!"
 5 Bodó and Lakatos, "Theatrical Distribution and P2P Movie Piracy," 443.
 6 Danaher and Smith, "Gone in 60 Seconds," 1.
 7 Peukert, Claussen, and Kretschmer, "Piracy and Movie Revenues," 2. George Ford of the policy think tank Phoenix Center claims that Peukert, Claussen, and Kretschmer's study suffers from a "poorly designed statistical model." Who are we to believe, a peer-reviewed academic study or the pronouncements of a policy think tank? See Cooke, "New Paper Disputes Claim that MegaUpload Helped Mid-sized Movies."
 8 Bainbridge, "Austar Boss Fears Piracy Explosion under NBN."
 9 Loebbecke and Fischer, "Pay TV Piracy and Its Effect on Pay TV Provision," 18.
10 Siri and Reimontas, Digital & Physical Piracy in GB, 5.
11 Venturini, Marshall, and Di Alberto, "Accenture Video-over-Internet Consumer Survey 2012," 9.
12 De Kosnik, "Piracy Is the Future of Television," 2.
13 Ibid., 12.
14 Bruns, "The User-led Disruption," 2.
15 Brown, "How Hollywood Uses Megaupload."
16 Rosen, "How Hollywood Can Capitalize on Piracy."
17 Brown, "How Hollywood Uses Megaupload."
18 Castells and Cardoso, "Piracy Cultures," 826.
19 De Kosnik, "The Collector Is a Pirate," 529.
20 Ibid.
21 Castells and Cardoso, "Piracy Cultures," 826.
22 Ibid., 827.

23 Tryon, *On-Demand Culture*, 41.
24 Lisanti, "TV Cord-cutting on the Rise."
25 Wilkerson, "Cord-cutting Thwarted for Now by Big Media: Nomura."
26 De Kosnik, "Piracy Is the Future of Television," 16.
27 Mann, "Google's Brin Slams Hollywood Piracy Stance."
28 Pakinkis, "Piracy Rising in UK."
29 DtecNet, "Television Piracy," 3.
30 Gibbons, "Cable Show 2012."
31 Gillespie, *Wired Shut*, 244.
32 Keane, *Media and Democracy*, 162.
33 Karaganis, "Rethinking Piracy," 4.
34 Ibid., 8.
35 "Top 10 Most Pirated TV-Shows of 2011." Outside the United States the demand for pirated US shows remains strong. In 2011 *Dexter* had the most pirated single television episode at 3,620,000 downloads, up from 2,780,000 in 2009. Yet the most pirated television episode in 2009, *Heroes*, had 6,580,000 downloads.
36 Szalai, "CW Online Push Causes Ratings, Cord Cutting Concerns (Report)."
37 Wallenstein, "CW Shortens Web Streaming Delay to Battle Piracy."
38 Bookman, "CW's Streaming Audience May Be Up by 60 Percent."
39 Karaganis, *"Media Piracy in Emerging Economies,"* 46.
40 Ibid., 47.
41 Stelter, "Fox Show Will Start Worldwide."
42 Ibid.
43 Wallenstein, "'Touch' Latest Show to Bow Day-and-Date Worldwide."
44 Ibid.
45 Irvine, "Youth Shaping Future of Online TV, Movies, Music."
46 Turner, "Global Online TV and Video Revenues Predicted to Nudge $22 Billion by 2016." "The U.S. will remain the dominant territory for online TV and video revenues, with 54 percent of the global market in 2010 – but this will drop to around 36 percent of the total global market in 2016" (ibid.).
47 Stross, "Yes, Norma Desmond, the Pictures Are Getting Small Again."
48 *Economist*, "Online Video in China."
49 *Economist*, "The Chinese Stream."
50 Kokas, "American Media and China's Blended Public Sphere," 149.
51 O'Halloran, "Online Video Markets to Surge over Next Five Years."
52 Cisco, "Cisco Visual Networking Index: Forecast and Methodology, 2010–2015."

53 Greenberg, "The Year's Most Pirated Videos."
54 treetops, comment on Burgess, "Online Movie Streaming Will Overtake DVD Sales This Year in U.S."
55 Learmonth, "Fox's 'Prison Break' Free on Hulu, but 1 Million Prefer BitTorrent."
56 Pesce, "Piracy Is Good?" 8.
57 Ibid., 2.
58 Jenkins, "When Piracy Becomes Promotion."
59 Condry, "Cultures of Music Piracy," 345.
60 Seetoo, "Can Peer-to-peer Internet Broadcast Technology Give Fans Another Chance?" 386.
61 Bruns, "The User-led Disruption," 3.
62 Masur and Katz, "ISP Licensing," 286.
63 Stelter and Stone, "Digital Pirates Winning the Battle with Studios."
64 Wang et al., "Steal This Movie," 15.
65 Brioux, "Point, Click – and Get Geo-blocked."
66 Newman, "Free TV," 5.
67 MelissaB, comment on Brioux, "Point, Click – and Get Geo-blocked."
68 Seles, "It's (Not) the End of TV as We Know It," 26.
69 Ibid., 7.
70 jk2011, comment on Pamela McClintock, "MPAA Chief Christopher Dodd Says SOPA Debate Isn't Over, Defends Hosting Harvey Weinstein Even as He Attacked Over 'Bully,'" *Hollywood Reporter*, 5 April 2012.
71 Anonymous Coward, comment on Leigh Beadon, "Just How Much Do Shows Like Game of Thrones Owe to Piracy?" *Techdirt*, 9 April 2012.
72 Karaganis, *"Rethinking Piracy,"* 10.
73 BBC News, "Online Film Piracy 'Set to Rise.'"
74 Bai and Waldfogel, "Movie Piracy and Sales Displacement in Two Samples of Chinese Consumers," 9.
75 Noonan, "A Slight Change of Heart among Movie Thieves."
76 Andy, "Piracy Collapses as Legal Alternatives Do Their Job."
77 Waterman, Ji, and Rochet, "Enforcement and Control of Piracy, Copying, and Sharing in the Movie Industry," 256, 280.
78 "Faster, Better, Cheaper," 28.
79 Khrennikov, "Netflix Clones in Russia Get a Head Start with Piracy Law."
80 Some empirical studies that show piracy hurting video rentals, purchases, and movie-going are Bounie, Waelbroeck, and Brourreau, "Piracy and the Demand for Films"; Rob and Waldfogel, "Piracy on the Silver Screen"; and De Vany and Walls, "Estimating the Effects of Movie Piracy on Box-office Revenues." Also see Bialik, "Putting a Price Tag on Film Piracy."
81 Smith and Telang, "Competing with Free."

82 Rob and Waldfogel, "Piracy on the Silver Screen," 382.
83 Bagnasco, "Why Do Pirates Demand Movies?" 63.
84 Danaher and Waldfogel, "Reel Piracy," 11.
85 McBride and Fowler, "Studios See Big Rise in Estimates of Losses to Movie Piracy." Such a claim is hard to reconcile with a 2009 academic study that concluded, "File-sharing, on average, does not reduce the sales of movie DVDs in the short-term" (Martikainen, "Does File Sharing Reduce DVD Sales?" 31).
86 Karaganis, *Media Piracy in Emerging Economies*, 45.
87 Cammaerts, Mansell, and Meng, "Copyright & Creation," 8.
88 Ernesto, "Top 10 Most Pirated Movies of 2009," "*Avatar* Crowned the Most Pirated Movie of 2010," "Top 10 Most Pirated Movies of 2011," "*Project X* Most Pirated Movie of 2012," and "'The Hobbit' Most Pirated Film of 2013."
89 Mann, "Rising Box Office Receipts Threatened by Online Piracy." Global box office receipts increased 3 per cent from 2010 and totalled $32.6 billion (US) in 2011.
90 Karaganis, "Rethinking Piracy," 10.
91 Danaher and Waldfogel, "Reel Piracy," 3.
92 Ibid., 21.
93 Mann, "Rising Box Office Receipts Threatened by Online Piracy."
94 Waterman, Ji, and Rochet, "Enforcement and Control of Piracy, Copying, and Sharing in the Movie Industry," 261.
95 Yamato, "Universal Chief Ron Meyer Addresses VOD Fiasco, Admits Cowboys & Aliens, Land of the Lost, Wolfman Kinda Stunk."
96 Karaganis, "Rethinking Piracy," 45.
97 "Faster, Better, Cheaper."
98 Karaganis, "Rethinking Piracy," 46.
99 Mattelart, "Audiovisual Piracy, Informal Economy, and Cultural Globalization," 747.
100 Baumgärtel, "The United States of Piracy," 7.
101 Yar, "The Global 'Epidemic' of Movie 'Piracy': Crime-wave or Social Construction?" 691.
102 Ibid., 690.
103 Comment by Renegade Knight on Greg Sandoval, "Post-SOPA Surprise: Common Ground for Tech, Big Media," cNet, 5 April 2010.
104 Cox, "But Who Are the Real Pirates?"
105 Senior, "How Do You Police the Entire Internet?"
106 Holson, "Studios Moving to Block Piracy of Films Online."
107 Cohen, "Scant Gains in War on Piracy."
108 Baumgärtel, "The United States of Piracy," 394.

109 static416, reply to Michael Geist, "Hurt Locker P2P Lawsuit Comes to Canada," DSLReports.com, 26 January 2007.
110 MattHunX, reply to "Why PIRACY IS a POSITIVE Thing," RationalSkepticism.org, 22 January 2012.
111 Baumgärtel, "The United States of Piracy," 6.
112 Steinmetz and Tunnell, "Under the Pixelated Jolly Roger," 53.
113 Lindgren and Linde, "The Subpolitics of Online Piracy," 10.
114 Mylonas, "Piracy Culture in Greece," 727.
115 Li, "From D-Buffs to the D-Generation," 559. See also Kiriya, "The Culture of Subversion and Russian Media Landscape."
116 Rose, "Lights, Camera, Revolution."
117 Li, "From D-Buffs to the D-Generation," 560.
118 Mylonas, "Accumulation, Control and Contingency."
119 Andersson, "The Quiet Agglomeration of Data," 599.
120 Vonderau, "Beyond Piracy," 114.
121 Fredriksson, "Piracy, Globalisation and the Colonisation of the Commons," 8.
122 Caraway, "Survey of File-sharing Culture," 581.
123 Dent, "Piracy, Circulatory Legitimacy, and Neoliberal Subjectivity in Brazil," 44.
124 Mylonas, "Accumulation, Control and Contingency," par. 2.1.
125 Ibid.
126 Ibid., par. 2.4.
127 Haggart, "Lessons from Canada's Decade of Copyright Reform."
128 Green, "When Stealing Isn't Stealing."
129 Ibid.
130 Newman, "Free TV."
131 Ibid., 2.
132 Ibid.
133 Ibid.
134 Ibid., 4.
135 Newman and Levine, *Legitimating Television*, 133.
136 Ibid., 171.
137 Pomerantz, "Hollywood Faces Grave Threat from Popcorn Time."

3. Sports Television Piracy: They Stream. They Score!

1 NBC, "London Olympics on NBC Is Most-watched Television Event in U.S. History."
2 Truong, "Olympics Fans Use the Web to Sneak around Tape Delay."

3 Chozick, "NBC Unpacks Trove of Data from Olympics."
4 Hutchins and Rowe, *Sport beyond Television*, 10.
5 Frankel, "Why Aren't More People Cutting the Cord?"
6 Ibid.
7 Ibid.
8 Peters, "MLB Blackout Only Hurts the Fans, Network."
9 Ibid.
10 Dickey, "Joey Votto's New Contract Is like a Mortgage-backed Security."
11 Sakthivel, "4G Peer-to-peer Technology – Is It Covered by Copyright?" 310.
12 Green, "Why Do They Call It TV When It's Not on the Box?" 101.
13 anguis, comment on Burgess, "Online Movie Streaming Will Overtake DVD Sales This Year in U.S."
14 David and Millward, "Football's Coming Home?" 359.
15 Mann, "20m Pirate World Cup Viewers."
16 Taylor, "Premier League Shuts Down 30,000 Illegal Streams."
17 Birmingham and David, "Live-streaming," 70.
18 NetResult, *Background Report on Digital Piracy of Sporting Events*, 4.
19 Hutchins, "Robbing the World's Largest Jewelry Store," 10. Also see Smith, "Interview."
20 Brett Hutchins suggests that this claim is an instance of the industry inflating piracy statistics. Hutchins, "Robbing the World's Largest Jewelry Store," 4.
21 Hutchins and Rowe, "From Broadcast Scarcity to Digital Plenitude," 356.
22 Dickey, "Joey Votto's New Contract Is Like a Mortgage-backed Security."
23 Birmingham and David, "Live-streaming."
24 PricewaterhouseCoopers, "Discovering Behaviors and Attitudes Related to Pirating Content."
25 Blain, "Sports over IP," 22.
26 Larson, Bender, and Laker, "The Aging Sport Fan," 791.
27 "The national television package of the National Football League was worth $900 million per year in 1990–93. Starting in 2006, the NFL received $3.1 billion per year from CBS, FOX, NBC and ESPN. Adjusting for inflation, this means the real growth of television revenue for the NFL approximately doubled from 1990 to 2006. Major League Baseball and the National Basketball Association also experienced similar growth during this period of time." Seetoo, "Can Peer-to-peer Internet Broadcast Technology Give Fans Another Chance?" 377.
28 Hutchins and Rowe, "From Broadcast Scarcity to Digital Plenitude," 354.
29 Ibid., 355.
30 Ibid., 357, 358.

31 Ibid., 360.
32 Crawford, *Consuming Sport*.
33 Hutchins and Rowe, "From Broadcast Scarcity to Digital Plenitude," 365.
34 Ibid., 366, 367.
35 Solomon, "Friend or Foe?" 253.
36 Hutchins, "Robbing the World's Largest Jewelry Store," 1.
37 Ibid., 6.
38 Ibid.
39 This is revealed in an online comment in a conversation about how to access free streaming sports: "The people involved in streaming with myp2p are just regular people who engage in highly illegal activity and have absolutely nothing to gain, other than providing many happy people with coverage of sports they wouldn't otherwise see." Comment by hiteleven on the post, "I'm interested in streaming sports from around the world in Canada; what are my options?" MetaFilter.com, 24 May 2010.
40 Bruns, "The User-led Disruption," 2.
41 Ibid., 3.
42 Mudhar, "Sports Moving Online, But Warily."
43 Hutchins, "Robbing the World's Largest Jewelry Store," 7.
44 Carter, "WWE's Business Model Is an Endangered Species."
45 Stelter, "2.1 Million Streamed the Super Bowl, NBC Says."
46 Greenfield, "NBC Claims Super Bowl Streaming Victory, But Viewers Cry 'Fail.'"
47 Neagle, "Insatiable Demand for Streaming Video Puts Pressure on Providers."
48 Slater, "Who's Streaming March Madness?"
49 Ogg, "With 3M Downloads, MLB App Hits It Out of the Park."
50 Mudhar, "Sports Moving Online, But Warily."
51 Troianovski, "Video Speed Trap Lurks in New iPad."
52 Ibid.
53 Middleton, "TURNER and CBS to Charge for March Madness Streaming."
54 Dreier, "Why Your March Madness Will Now Cost You."
55 Ibid.
56 Ozer, "NBA League Pass."
57 Shirky, "The Year of the Newspaper Paywall."
58 Scott, "The Fall of Rome," 8.
59 Johnson, "Everything New Is Old Again," 116.
60 Harper, "Global Sports Media Consumption Report."
61 Ibid., 11.
62 Ibid., 17.

63 Ibid., 18.
64 Ibid., 25.
65 Ibid., 30.
66 Ibid., 44.
67 David and Millward, "Football's Coming Home?"
68 Castells, *The Informational City*.
69 David and Millward, "Football's Coming Home?" 363.
70 Ibid.
71 Ibid., 364.
72 Ibid., 365.
73 Boyle and Haynes, *Power Play*, 220.
74 Boyle and Haynes, *Football in the New Media Age*, 37.
75 Ibid., 59.
76 Ibid., 156.
77 Hutchins and Rowe, *Sport beyond Television*, 4.
78 Ibid., 34–5.
79 Ibid., 41.
80 Ibid., 70.
81 Kirton and David, "The Challenge of Unauthorized Streaming to the English Premier League and Television Broadcasters," 91.
82 Hutchins and Rowe, "Reconfiguring Media Sport for the Online World," 711.
83 Hutchins and Rowe, *Sport beyond Television*, 71.
84 Ibid., 181.
85 Meân, "Sport, Identities, and Consumption," 178.
86 McNutt, "The #NBCFail Olympics," 126.
87 Blain, "Sports over IP," 129.
88 Hiestand, "NBC Marquee TV Sports Events to Be Streamed Digitally."
89 Sandomir, Miller, and Eder, "To Protect Its Empire, ESPN Stays on Offense."
90 Witkowski, Hutchins, and Carter, "E-sports on the Rise?"
91 In 2011, a total of 567,000 simultaneous viewers watched the final match of the Value Corporation's Dota 2 tournament, *The International 2*, streamed live via the Internet.
92 Gaudiosi, "Twitch Rides Video Game Streaming to Global Success."
93 Wingfield, "With Twitch Acquisition Talks, Validation of Games as a Spectator Sport."
94 Weiss and Schiele, "Virtual Worlds in Competitive Contexts," 1.
95 Scholz, "New Broadcasting Ways in IPTV," 17. Also see Taylor, *Raising the Stakes*, 215.

96 Goel and Stelter, "Social Networks in a Battle for the Second Screen."
97 David and Millward, "Football's Coming Home?" 365.

4. Television's Scariest Generation: Cord Cutters and Cord Nevers

1 This audience behaviour is so new that when I began writing *Post-TV* I could find no scholarly articles specifically devoted to the subject.
2 Turner, "My Media Consumption Habits with the iPad."
3 O'Neill, "iPad Owners, Potential Owners More Likely to Cut Cord, Downgrade Pay-TV Buy."
4 Turner, "My Media Consumption Habits with the iPad."
5 Banerjee, Alleman, and Rappoport, "Analysis of Video-viewing Behavior in the Era of Convergent and Connected Devices," 2.
6 Ibid., 33.
7 Ibid., 31.
8 Nielsen, "Busting the Cord-cutting Myth."
9 Gelles, "Comcast-NBCU Merger Pays Dividends."
10 Szalai, "Analysts: Fourth-quarter Pay TV Sub Momentum Allays Some Cord Cutting Fears." Another report notes, "Almost five percent of the almost 60 million cable service customers ended the relationship with their provider sometime between 2010 and 2011. Across New Jersey, cable customers are dropping like flies. In the same time span, Comcast lost 2.5 percent of its customers in the area, and Cablevision lost another 1.6 percent. These numbers are, however, still less than the national average for dropped service, based on the findings of market research conducted by the Board of Public Utilities" (techmichelle, "Cable Viewers Bail in Favor of Programming on Demand").
11 Lieberman, "Big Media Q4 Corporate Earnings Roundup."
12 Bednarski, "Iger Sees Little Cord-cutting, Says Netflix Is Good, Not Dominant."
13 Ibid.
14 Miller, "Ari Emanuel Takes on Silicon Valley and Internet Piracy."
15 Hall, "Fox COO."
16 Szalai, "Time Warner Cable CFO."
17 Lieberman, "Moguls Are 'In Denial' about Poverty, Time, Warner Cable CEO Says."
18 Frankel, "Nielsen: 1.5M U.S. Households Cut the Cord in 2011."
19 Fraser, "Comcast and the Cord-cutting Trend." Fraser reported that an estimated 4.7 per cent of television subscribers (4.7 million American

households) will have cut the cord by the end of 2013, a percentage that closely aligned with Nielsen's own data.

20 Luckerson, "The Fight for Streaming TV."

21 Wallenstein, "Top Wall Street Analyst." Later in 2013 Moffett described the situation in the following terms: "the numbers aren't huge, but they are statistically significant" (Edwards, "Analyst Sounds Warning on Death of TV").

22 Canadian Press, "Cord Cutting."

23 Oliveira, "Canadian TV 'Cord Cutters' Reach 8 Per Cent of Population."

24 Canadian Press, "Measuring the Canadian 'Cord-cutting' Population." The Canadian Press reports on comScore's finding that "About one in four respondents aged 18 to 24 said they were a cord cutter, as did about one in five of those aged 25 to 34. About 15 per cent of those over 35 said they had cut the cord ... Among 18- to 24-year-olds, the number of cord cutters has grown by 60 per cent (to about 25 per cent) since 2010, according to comScore. And the growth rate is 270 per cent for those aged 25 to 34 (to about 19 per cent)" (ibid.).

25 Beach, "Canadians Cut the Cord in Q1."

26 Vlessing, "Netflix Canada Has Local Carriers Losing the Cord-cutting War."

27 Boon Dog Professional Services, "'Cord Cutting' in Canada Increases."

28 Freeman, "Cord-cutting Canadians Not a Threat to Cable Business."

29 Bradshaw, "More Canadians Cutting the Cord?"

30 The second quarter of 2012 alone saw "the overall industry shed more than 400,000 subscribers" in the United States (ibid.).

31 Ramachandran, "Evidence Grows on TV Cord-cutting."

32 Shapiro, "TV: An Intervention." Also noteworthy, in 2012 it was observed that "38 percent of all homes that cut the cord, did so in the past 12 months" (ibid.).

33 Lee, "TV Subscriptions Fall for First Time as Viewers Cut the Cord."

34 Shapiro, "TV: An Intervention."

35 Leichtman Research Group, "Multi-channel Video Industry Has First-ever Annual Net Subscriber Loss." Comparing first-quarter (Q1) subscriber net gains from 2011 to 2013 also reveals a dramatic decline: 470,000, Q1 2011; 445,000, Q1 2012; 195,000, Q1 2013.

36 SNL Kagan, "U.S. Multichannel Video Subscribers Drop for Second Straight Quarter."

37 Pomerantz, "12 Million Households Expected to Cut the Cord by 2015." The market analysis company Motley Fool also made an argument for

continued growth in cord-cutting and suggested that any peak in cord-cutting is still years away. Bylund, "Why Cord-cutting Won't Slow Down in 2012."

38 Baumgartner, "Cord Cutting No Longer an 'Urban Myth.'" Moffett reported 2013 Q2 declines of 360,000, a small decline of only 0.3 per cent, but one that follows on the heels of a net loss of 911,000 subscribers in 2012 and 258,000 in 2011.

39 King, "How 'Cord Never' Generation Poses Sales Drag for Pay TV."

40 Ibid.

41 Fetto, "Rise in Cord-cutting Creates Opportunities for Marketers."

42 Clancy, "Despite the Hype, Millennials Aren't Cutting the Cord, That Much."

43 Bode, "Time Warner CEO Still Thinks Most Cord Cutters Live with Mom."

44 Shapiro, "TV: An Intervention."

45 Wise, "More Media Consumers Are Cutting the Cable Cord."

46 Lieberman, "Moguls Are 'In Denial' About Poverty, Time Warner Cable CEO Says."

47 Ibid.

48 Leamy, "FCC: High Cable Prices Consumers' Biggest Problem."

49 Tharp, "Cable Bills to Pass $200 a Month by 2020: Industry Forecast."

50 Lieberman, "Moguls Are 'In Denial' About Poverty, Time Warner Cable CEO Says."

51 Joe, comment on Lieberman, "Moguls Are 'In Denial' About Poverty, Time Warner Cable CEO Says."

52 Crupi, "Cable Commands 70 Percent of Prime-time GRPs." Crupi notes, "According to GfK Media, some 6.9 million U.S. households bailed on subscription TV in 2011, bringing the number of homes served exclusively by over-the-air TV to around 20.7 million – 18 percent of the 114.1 million TV households universe."

53 Steward, "Over the Air TV Catches Second Wind, Aided by the Web."

54 Dix and Jenks, "Viewers Tuning Out Basic, Premium TV." The authors note an increase in advertising avoidance and year-over-year increases in premium-pay TV cancellations "across all major age demographics."

55 Perren, "Business as Usual," 74.

56 Matin, "Digital Rights Management (DRM) in Online Music Stores." Matin concludes, "Digital Rights Management (DRM) does not prevent piracy or provide the music industry with any benefit" (292).

57 Greenberg, "Confront the Causes of Cord-cutting Now."

58 Greenberg, "HBO's 'Game of Thrones' on Track to Be Crowned Most Pirated Show of 2012."

59 AAP, "Downloads Don't Matter."
60 Reimold, "A Cord-cutter's Life."
61 Ibid.
62 Ibid.
63 Ibid.
64 Ibid.
65 Jamie Allyant, comment on Reimold, "A Cord-cutter's Life."
66 Donohue, "Cisco: Set-top Data Could Boost 'TV Everywhere.'"
67 Flint, "Analyst Warns of Bleak Outlook for Cable Industry."
68 jimmy6p, comment on Canadian Press, "Cord Cutting."
69 Lisanti, "TV Cord-cutting on the Rise."
70 Lotz, *The Television Will Be Revolutionized*, 18.
71 Fixmer, "New TV Season, and Fewer Viewers."
72 mrpainless2003, comment on Yahoo! Answers, "Why do people post priated [*sic*] tv shows on the internet?"
73 Frieden, "The Opportunities and Threats from Next Generation Television," 20.
74 Gershon, "TV's Scariest Generation."
75 Fixmer, "New TV Season, and Fewer Viewers."
76 Barnes, "Web Deals Cheer Hollywood, Despite Drop in Moviegoers."
77 Greenfield, "How Many Cord Nevers Are There?"
78 Nelson, "Young Americans Won't Pay for TV." Pay-TV here refers to traditional television services known as cable, satellite, or telco TV.
79 Ibid.
80 Ibid.
81 Callahan, "You Watch Television?"
82 Ibid.
83 Zimmett, "Get Ready for TV 2.0."
84 Krashinsky, "TV's Digital Switch Boosts Appeal of Cord-cutting."
85 urgman, comment on Krashinsky, "TV's Digital Switch Boosts Appeal of Cord-cutting."
86 Mark William Kennedy, comment on Krashinsky, "TV's Digital Switch Boosts Appeal of Cord-cutting."
87 Crawford, "The Discriminatory Incentives to Bundle in the Cable Television Industry," 42.
88 Crawford and Cullen, in "Bundling, Product Choice, and Efficiency," conclude that consumers may indeed benefit from à la carte sales of cable networks.
89 Farrell, "Survey Says: 92% of Consumers Want a la Carte."
90 Ibid.

91 Ultracat, comment on Krashinsky, "TV's Digital Switch Boosts Appeal of Cord-cutting."

92 JimmyK, comment on Krashinsky, "TV's Digital Switch Boosts Appeal of Cord-cutting."

93 not_from_here, comment on Krashinsky, "TV's Digital Switch Boosts Appeal of Cord-cutting."

94 peekaboo, comment on Krashinsky, "TV's Digital Switch Boosts Appeal of Cord-cutting."

95 gfin, comment on Krashinsky, "TV's Digital Switch Boosts Appeal of Cord-cutting."

96 slapdash dapoint, comment on Krashinsky, "TV's Digital Switch Boosts Appeal of Cord-cutting."

97 Kennedy, comment on Krashinsky, "TV's Digital Switch Boosts Appeal of Cord-cutting."

98 Ezinky, comment on samzenpus, "Millions of Subscribers Leaving Cable TV for Streaming Services," Slashdot, 5 April 2012.

99 MDillenbeck, comment on samzenpus, "Millions of Subscribers Leaving Cable TV for Streaming Services."

100 TheRaven64, comment on samzenpus, "Millions of Subscribers Leaving Cable TV for Streaming Services."

101 StormWeaver, comment on samzenpus, "Millions of Subscribers Leaving Cable TV for Streaming Services."

102 pecosdave, comment on samzenpus, "Millions of Subscribers Leaving Cable TV for Streaming Services."

103 Craig Ott, comment on Ramachandran, "Dish Chief: TV Needs to Change."

104 Kelty Logan notes that "while OTV advertising may be held to a higher creative standard than traditional TV advertising, there is no indication that entertainment value contributes to an improved attitude toward advertising in the OTV environment" ("And Now a Word from Our Sponsor").

105 Ibid.

106 Moskovciak, "When Cord-cutting Is Better than Cable."

107 allison1211, comment on Moskovciak, "When Cord-cutting Is Better Than Cable."

108 Townsend, "Cord Cutting (Cable TV)."

109 Anonymous Coward, comment on samzenpus, "Millions of Subscribers Leaving Cable TV for Streaming Services."

110 brokeninside, comment on samzenpus, "Millions of Subscribers Leaving Cable TV for Streaming Services."

111 Chetty et al., "'You're Capped!'" 1.
112 Seppo, "Cutting-the-cord, Bandwidth Usage and Data Caps in Practice."
113 Gonzalez, "Cable TV Cost Is High but Streaming TV Could Cost More."
114 Townsend, "Cord Cutting (Cable TV)."
115 paulinwaterloo, comment on Canadian Press, "Cord Cutting."
116 Macoute, comment on Canadian Press, "Cord Cutting."
117 lefty, comment on Canadian Press, "Cord Cutting."
118 Cinemaven, comment on Canadian Press, "Cord Cutting."
119 Pott, "Pirates Not to Blame for Big Media's Sales Plunge."
120 Szalai, "Hulu Plus Subscription Service Crosses 2 Million User Mark."
121 Nice, "Five Reasons You Should Give Up TV Bills – Plus Five Reasons You Shouldn't."
122 Wolff, "It's War."
123 John Weber, comment on Fruhlinger, "Tuning Up Web TV."
124 John Damron, comment on Fruhlinger, "Tuning Up Web TV."
125 Fruhlinger, "Tuning Up Web TV."
126 Lotz, *The Television Will Be Revolutionized*, 244.
127 Rowell, "When Did Watching TV Become Such a Hassle?"
128 Griggs, "My Cable Cutting Experience."
129 Ibid.
130 Umiastowski, "Picture Isn't Pretty for Cable TV Stocks."
131 Ramayah et al., "Testing a Causal Model of Internet Piracy Behavior among University Students," 208.
132 "Facebook App by FreeCast.com Fuels Cord Cutting Growth."
133 Bowery and Rimmer, "Rip, Mix, Burn."
134 Tay and Turner, "What Is Television?" 76.
135 Bruns, "Reconfiguring Television for a Networked, Produsage Context," 86.
136 Ibid., 92.
137 Mann, "US Cable Launches Connected Awareness Campaign."
138 Yao, "Cable Companies See Customers Cutting Back."

5. Disruption: Viewing Habits of the Post-television Generation

1 There are indications that as with the remote control and VHS, the DVR is not as disruptive as first thought. David Poltract, president of CBS research division, reports, "In a DVR survey conducted by CBS, persons in non-DVR households watched 5.1 hours of TV a day, while DVR households watched 5.7 hours: a 12% increase for DVR households ... When polled, 70% of people say they used a DVR to fast-forward through commercials; electronic data puts the figure at 50%. People tend to skip ads selectively;

they tend to stop early to avoid fast-forwarding through the show, and they stop for ads they like. Finally, 21% of people who fast-forward through ads still remember what they are promoting, which is more than people who don't try to skip them" (Rauch, "TV's New Economics").

2 Hess, "Nielsen and Google AdWords Study Younger TV Viewers."
3 Ha, Leconte, and Savidge, "From TV to the Internet to Mobile Phones," 281.
4 Poeter, "NPD: Rising Tide for Streaming Media Players."
5 Cisco, "Cisco Visual Networking Index: Forecast and Methodology, 2011–2016." Online video doubled in volume in 2011 and was projected to increase sixfold by 2016.
6 Oliveira, "One in Four Canadians Watch More Online Video than TV."
7 Ha, Leconte, and Savidge, "From TV to the Internet to Mobile Phones," 296.
8 Accenture, "Video-over-Internet Consumer Survey 2013," 2.
9 Goggin, "Sport and the Rise of Mobile Media," 20.
10 Stanton, "51% of Total US Population Watches Streaming Video Weekly."
11 Horváth, Csordás, and Nyirö, "Rewritten by Machine and New Technology," 526.
12 Ibid., 548.
13 Accenture, "Video-over-Internet Consumer Survey 2013," 6.
14 Venturini, Marshall, and Di Alberto, "Accenture Video-over-Internet Consumer Survey 2012," 6.
15 Dennen, "State of the Internet."
16 Gannes, "YouTube Changes Everything," 151. Industry studies tend to overlook the issues of "free" and commercial avoidance when explaining online audience behaviour.
17 Cha and Chan-Olmsted, "Substitutability between Online Video Platforms and Television," 261.
18 Ibid., 262.
19 Bondad-Brown, Rice, and Pearce, "Influences on TV Viewing and Online User-shared Video Use."
20 Cha and Chan-Olmsted, "Relative Advantages of Online Video Platforms and Television According to Content, Technology, and Cost-related Attributes."
21 Bondad-Brown, Rice, and Pearce, "Influences on TV Viewing and Online User-shared Video Use," 488.
22 Tryon, On-Demand Culture, 74.
23 Ibid., 75.
24 See-To, Papagiannidis, and Cho, "User Experience on Mobile Video Appreciation," 1484.

25 Phalen and Ducey, "Audience Behavior in the Multi-Screen 'Video-verse,'" 148.
26 Solsman, "Netflix Is Giving People Their Net Fix, Nielsen Says."
27 Brzoznowski, "Survey: 7 in 10 U.S. TV Watchers Are Binge Viewers."
28 Ha, Leconte, and Savidge, "From TV to the Internet to Mobile Phones," 294.
29 Cui, Chipehase, and Jung, "Personal TV," 203.
30 Sun et al., "A Cross-cultural Study of User Experience of Video on Demand on Mobile Devices," 468.
31 TiVo, "Netflix Not Cannibalizing Traditional TV Viewing."
32 Banerjee, Alleman, and Rappoport, "Analysis of Video-viewing Behavior in the Era of Convergent and Connected Devices," 4.
33 Powers and Comstock, "The Rumors of Television's Demise Have Been Greatly Exaggerated," 6.
34 Berman and Kesterson-Townes, *Beyond Digital*, 6.
35 Gibs, "The New Screen for Video," 27. Likewise, another 2010 study of Hungarian university students concluded, "It seems that television consumption has hardly decreased" (Horváth, Csordás, and Nyirö, "Rewritten by Machine and New Technology," 547).
36 Yu, "Mobile TV has Station Owners Intrigued, Flummoxed."
37 Ballvé, "Mobile Video."
38 Berman and Kesterson-Townes, *Beyond Digital*, 1.
39 "Over 50 percent of global mainstream consumers have adopted a wide range of digital consumption behaviors: from checking news and watching video online, to accessing mobile services, participating in social networking and visiting user-generated content sites." Ibid., 3.
40 Moore, "71% of Online Adults Now Use Video-sharing Sites." Accenture found online video viewing to be at 92 per cent in a 2012 survey covering the United States, Argentina, Brazil, the United Kingdom, Germany, Italy, Spain, and France, up 77 per cent from a year earlier (Venturini, Marshall, and Di Alberto, "Accenture Video-over-Internet Consumer Survey 2012," 4).
41 Oliveira, "One in Four Canadians Watch More Online Video than TV."
42 Canadian Press, "More Canadians Watching TV Online, Opting for Wireless over Landlines."
43 Ha, Leconte, and Savidge, "From TV to the Internet to Mobile Phones," 287.
44 Ibid., 295.
45 Ibid., 290–1.
46 Spangler, "Why 'TV Everywhere' Still Isn't Everywhere."
47 "In China, the UK and the U.S., over half of early adopters and mainstream consumers consume online video such as Hulu and Netflix on their

PCs and video on demand on their home TVs." Berman and Kesterson-Townes, *Beyond Digital*, 4.

48 Moshe, "Media Time Squeezing," 68.

49 McAdams, "Yet Another 3-screen Study." "The amount of time participants spent watching content on TV accounted for 90.2 percent of their aggregate multiscreen consumption. PCs accounted for 9.3 percent, while mobile was 0.5 percent." Also from the same study, "simultaneous usage of TV and video sites was more limited than simultaneous usage of broadcast and cable TV with social, search and email sites. Around 90 percent of the test participants accessed email, search or social media sites while watching TV, while 65 percent of TV viewers simultaneously accessed network online video sites."

50 Venturini, Marshall, and Di Alberto, "Accenture Video-over-Internet Consumer Survey 2012," 6.

51 Ibid.

52 Digitalsmiths, "New Study Spotlights 'Cord-cheating.'"

53 Spangler, "Netflix, Hulu Dominate Mobile TV Viewing."

54 Wakefield, "Tweeting with the Telly On."

55 Harper, "Global Sports Media Consumption Report," 5.

56 Lee and Andrejevic, "Second-screen Theory," 43.

57 Dawson, "Little Players, Big Shows," 245.

58 Ibid.

59 Berman and Kesterson-Townes, *Beyond Digital*, 4. In the United States 90 percent of mainstream consumers split their attention between the television and second and third screens. Google, "The New Multi-screen World."

60 Nielsen, "Double Vision." "In the U.S., 88 percent of tablet owners and 86 percent of smartphone owners said they used their device while watching TV at least once during a 30-day period. For 45 percent of tablet-tapping Americans, using their device while watching TV was a daily event, with 26 percent noting simultaneous TV and tablet use several times a day. U.S. smartphone owners showed similar dual usage of TV with their phones, with 41 percent saying they use their phone at least once a day while tuned in. Device owners in the U.K. also logged heavy usage for tablets (80%) and smartphones (78%) while watching TV. British daily usage of smartphones or tablets while watching TV rivaled that of the U.S. Nearly a quarter (24%) of those surveyed claiming to use their device several times a day while watching TV."

61 Interactive Advertising Bureau, "The Multi-screen Marketer."

62 McAdams, "HDTV Remains Most Popular Video Viewing Platform, CEA Says."

63 Ibid.
64 Interactive Advertising Bureau, "The Multi-screen Marketer," 13.
65 Smith and Boyles, "The Rise of the 'Connected Viewer,'" 5.
66 Interactive Advertising Bureau, "The Multi-screen Marketer," 23.
67 McAdams, "Yet Another 3-screen Study."
68 De Meulenaere, Van den Broeck, and Lievens, 319.
69 Goggin, *Cell Phone Culture*, 185.
70 Holmes, Josephson, and Carney, "Visual Attention to Television Programs with a Second-screen Application."
71 Roettgers, "ABC Executive."
72 Steinberg, "Behind Fox News' Primetime Shuffle, an Effort to Thwart Digital Distraction."
73 Friedman, "TV Viewers Use Twitter During Ads."
74 Smith and Boyles, "The Rise of the 'Connected Viewer,'" 2.
75 Malik, "LTE, Smartphones & Video Are Adding Up to a Mobile Data Boom."
76 Cisco, "Cisco Visual Networking Index: Forecast and Methodology, 2011–2016."
77 Kovach, "Time Spent Watching Video on Mobile Devices Has Doubled in the Last Year."
78 Whitney, "Mobile Video Viewing Could Lead to Cord-cutting."
79 Ibid. Also see Business Insider, "The Mobile Industry: In-Depth," and Nielsen, "Cross-platform Report: How We Watch from Screen to Screen." In the United States the mobile video audience increased 77 per cent between 2010 and 2012.
80 Chozick and Wingfield, "In Search of Apps for Television," and Sanger, "Streaming TV on Mobile Phones Will Rocket to 240 Million by 2014." According to Ericsson, there will soon be 3 billion smartphone subscriptions. Also noteworthy, soon 85 per cent of the world's population will have high-speed (3G) access to the Internet through mobile phones and 50 per cent will have 4th-generation high-speed connections. "Traffic and Market Report on the Pulse of the Networked World."
81 Oliveira, "One in Four Canadians Watch More Online Video than TV."
82 Danova, "Mobile Usage."
83 Farman, *Mobile Interface Theory*, 9.
84 O'Neill, "iPad Owners, Potential Owners More Likely to Cut Cord, Downgrade Pay-TV Buy." A survey by the Diffusion Group (TDG) found that 33.9 per cent of iPad owners "are to varying degrees likely to cancel their PayTV service in the next six months. The survey found that among people considering buying an iPad, 13.5 percent are prone to cord-cutting.

Both numbers significantly outstrip the number of cord cutters among average adult broadband users, which is less than 10 percent. TDG said nearly 13 percent of iPad owners are highly likely to drop pay-TV services, twice the rate of iPad Intenders (6.4 percent) and three times the rate among average adult broadband users (4.3 percent)." The 2010 results probably overstate the iPad effect on cord-cutting but the possibility remains that certain types of mobile viewing devices will foster the impulse to cut the cord.

85 Cui, Chipehase, and Jung, "Personal TV," 204.
86 Katz, "Conclusion," 310.
87 Rushton, "YouTube Chief."
88 The Arbitron/CIMM study found that out-of-home video consumption "accounted for 13 percent of the total time spent with TV and online video sites" (SNL Kagan, "SNL Kagan Finds Over-the-Top and TV Everywhere Swallowing up Mobile Video").
89 Lee, Yoo, and Kwak, "Consumers' Preferences for the Attributes of Post-PC." In 2012 an estimated 368 million PCs, 106 million tablet computers, 654 million smartphones, 100 million Internet-enabled televisions, and 25 million video game consoles were sold.
90 Danova, "Mobile Usage."
91 O'Neill, "Connected-TV Shipments Globally to Nearly Triple by 2016." Nielsen reports that 49 per cent "Never" watch online television with others and that 35 per cent "Rarely" do so.
92 Thompson, "The Post-PC World Is Real and It's Here." The IBM study arrives at slightly different numbers: "By 2015 consumers will purchase an estimated 780.8 million Internet-enabled mobile devices but only 479.1 million personal computers (PCs)" (Berman and Kesterson-Townes, *Beyond Digital*, 5).
93 Baig and Snider, "Mobile Devices Star in Prime Time at Home."
94 Ibid.
95 Ha, Leconte, and Savidge, "From TV to the Internet to Mobile Phones," 295.
96 "All over the world, except for Japan and South Korea, mobile broadcast services based on the DVB-H technology have struggled to develop a sustainable ecosystem and to build a substantial subscriber base." Evens and Prario, "Mobile Television in Italy," 66.
97 Evens et al., "Access to Premium Content on Mobile Television Platforms," 37.
98 Foremski, "The Media Industry's 2nd Apocalypse."
99 Goggin, "The Eccentric Career of Mobile Television," 119.

100 Goggin, *Global Mobile Media*, 82.
101 Goggin, "Sport and the Rise of Mobile Media," 26.
102 Ibid., 32–3.
103 Ibid., 33.
104 Manovich, *Software Takes Command*, 227.
105 Goggin, *Global Mobile Media*, 97.
106 Ibid.
107 Castells et al., *Mobile Communication and Society*, 246.
108 Ling and Donner, *Mobile Communication*, 139, 140.
109 Goggin, "Changing Media with Mobiles," 199.
110 Ibid.
111 Goel and Stelter, "Social Networks in a Battle for the Second Screen."
112 Ibid.
113 Interactive Advertising Bureau, "The Multi-screen Marketer," 17.
114 Pase, "Inbound and Outbound," 9.
115 Marques, "TV without a Remote."
116 Gibs, "Do We Watch the Web the Same Way We Watch TV?"
117 On social isolation and new media see Turkle, *Alone Together*.
118 Farman, *Mobile Interface Theory*, 134.
119 Wohn and Na, "Tweeting about TV."
120 Gray, *Television Entertainment*, 93.
121 Tryon, *On-Demand Culture*, 127.
122 Fuchs, "Information and Communication Technologies and Society," 84.
123 Baig and Snider, "Mobile Devices Star in Prime Time at Home."
124 Ibid.
125 Nielsen, "The Follow-Back."
126 Napoli, "Program Value in the Evolving Television Audience Marketplace," 10.
127 Sharma and Vranica, "Tweets Provide New Way to Gauge TV Audiences."
128 Harrington, Highfield, and Bruns, "More than a Backchannel," 4.
129 Lee, "Tweeting about Twerking Seen as Lifeline for TV Industry."
130 Bennett, "Transformations through Twitter," 522–3.
131 Griffin, "Surveillance of Audience Labor Using New Media."
132 Hill, Nalavade, and Benton, "Social TV."
133 Hart and Taylor, "Social Media Use While Watching Prime-time TV," 37.
134 Yarow, "Twitter Is Still Very Small."
135 Van Dijck, "The Internet in Flux," 236.
136 Van Dijck, *The Culture of Connectivity*, 157.
137 Ryssdal, "The Future of Television."

138 Puopolo et al., "The Future of Television," 3.
139 Ibid., 4.
140 Ibid.
141 Ibid., 5.

6. Innovation: New Sources of Competition for Online Audiences

1 Daswani, "More than Half of U.S. Broadband Homes Use Netflix."
2 Gara, "Amazon Takes a Shot, but Netflix Is Still King of the Stream." An
   early 2013 study by Piper Jaffray found that of the top 50 movies available
   for streaming over the past three years Netflix had 14 percent, Hulu
   offered 0 percent, and Amazon had only 11 percent available. Of the top
   75 television shows available over the past four years Netflix had 33 percent, Hulu had 44 percent, and Amazon offered only 7 percent.
3 Evens, "Platform Leadership in Online Broadcasting Markets," 478.
4 Christian, "The Web as Television Reimagined?" 340.
5 Dawson, "Defining Mobile Television," 255.
6 Keilbach and Stauff, "When Old Media Never Stopped Being New," 80.
7 Ibid., 89.
8 Cubitt, *Videography*, xv.
9 Ibid., 10.
10 Ibid., 134.
11 Ibid.
12 Ibid., 202.
13 Ibid., 91.
14 Edwards, "Intel Confident of Obtaining Programs for Web TV Service."
15 De Valck and Teurlings, "After the Break," 15.
16 Tossell, "Digital Killed the Video Store, What Will Replace It?"
17 Ibid.
18 Ibid.
19 Ladurantaye, "For This Man, the Show Must Go On."
20 Ibid.
21 Oliveira, "Netflix Subscribers Now Nearly a Third of English Canada."
   Also see Silcoff, "CRTC Paints Picture of Canada's Netflix Boom." Silcoff
   notes that "10 per cent of Canadian adults subscribed to the online
   on-demand movie and TV show service as of last fall [2010], up from 6 per
   cent the previous spring." By fall 2012 the percentage of Canadian Netflix
   viewers had jumped to 17 per cent. See Vlessing, "U.S. Network TV Still
   King in Canada, but Netflix Popularity Growing."

22 faustushood, comment on Tossell, "Digital Killed the Video Store, What Will Replace It?"

23 Kafka, "Netflix Still Eats a Third of the Web Every Night." Also see Adhikari et al., "Unreeling Netflix." This paper is the first systematic academic study to look into the architecture of Netflix video streaming.

24 Bond, "Netflix Might Be Most-watched 'Cable Network' in the U.S. Today."

25 eMarketer, "TV Watchers Want Original Content, No Matter the Platform."

26 Whitney, "Streaming Users Double Up, Tablet Views Grow Six Times."

27 Hall, "More Streamers Adding Hulu or Amazon to Netflix." Between 2010 and 2011, revenue for VOD services such as iTunes grew 75 per cent to $273 million while revenue for SVOD services such as Netflix grew by 10,000 per cent to $454 million.

28 Ibid. In 2012 Hulu was less than 10 per cent of the size of Netflix.

29 Cryan, "Netflix Surpasses Apple to Take Lead in U.S. Online Movie Business in 2011." Netflix's share of the online movie market grew from 0.5 per cent in 2011 to 44 per cent in 2012. This growth appears to have come at the expense of Apple's iTunes market share, which was 60.8 per cent in 2010 but only 32.3 per cent in 2011.

30 Nielsen, "What Netflix and Hulu Users Are Watching … and How."

31 O'Halloran, "Cord-cutting Creeps Up as 49% of US Homes Take Connected TV."

32 Szalai, "Time Warner CEO." Also see Szalai, "Viacom CEO Defends Nickelodeon's Netflix Deal Again." Viacom, the owner of Nickelodeon, defended their content deal with Netflix and described Netflix viewing as not "completely cannibalistic." Szalai reports that "time spent on Nickelodeon content on Netflix is about 2 percent of the time spent on the Nickelodeon TV channel."

33 Frankel, "We've Got Hard Data." Among streamers of Nickelodeon's flagship channel, usage "dropped 6 percent from the year-over-year average; viewing also declined a whopping 11 percent for Nick Toons and Teen Nick. For non-streamers, ratings actually grew 2 percent for Nickelodeon, 5 percent for Nick Toons and 26 percent for Teen Nick (a huge 37 percent differential). Among streamers, ratings increased 11 percent for Disney's boy-targeted XD channel, but they grew far more – 27 percent – among households that don't stream. The dynamic was the same for the Time Warner Inc.–owned Cartoon Network, which saw viewership increase by 9 percent among the streaming group but 12 percent among non-streamers."

34 Friedman, "Cable Ratings Impacted by Streaming Rivals." Anthony DiClemente, a media analyst at Barclays Capital, suggested that "most of the ratings weakness is concentrated in syndicated and rerun programming, a genre that now has more direct competition from online platforms like Netflix, iTunes, and Amazon."

35 Tossell, "Digital Killed the Video Store, What Will Replace It?" Tossell notes, "Those without the service watch roughly 16 hours of regular and Internet TV each week, while those with Netflix watch about 21 hours per week, including TV, Internet TV and more than five hours of Netflix programming combined." Also see Szalai, "Analyst: Online Streaming Now Hurting Some TV Networks' Ratings."

36 Stone and Stelter, "Some Online Shows Could Go Subscription-Only."

37 Ray, "NFLX 'Whacking' Kids Shows, Threatens Disney, Viacom, Says Bernstein."

38 Frankel, "Dish's Ergen: Streaming on Netflix 'Devalues' Mad Men."

39 Ibid.

40 Crupi, "DISH Network Threatens to Drop AMC."

41 Wallenstein, "Netflix Exec Defends Impact on TV Biz." Wallenstein reports that "Sarandos also cited the output deals Netflix has with TV networks the CW and AMC as crucial to the financial health of those operations. 'What's important to note is that you look at programming at CW, Netflix license fees makes that content profitable,' he said. 'Without it, it was struggling along. Same would be true of AMC shows as well.'"

42 Carr, "TV Foresees Its Future."

43 Chmielewski, "Netflix Executive Upends Hollywood."

44 Tryon, "Make Any Room Your TV," 288.

45 Ibid., 298.

46 Adegoke, "Netflix: The New Arch-Frenemy."

47 Boorstin, "Disney CEO Bob Iger Talks Earnings, 'Avengers,' and International Growth."

48 Knee, "Why Content Isn't King."

49 Reardon, "Netflix Is Cable's 'Frenemy.'"

50 Barr, "Television's Newcomers," 3.

51 Clancy, "A Fifth of US Netflix Users Have Cut the Cord."

52 Jakab, "Netflix's Uphill Battle for Subscriber Growth."

53 "Editorial: In Broadband Race, USA Is Not No. 1." Also, Trevor Barr describes the overall availability of "good broadband" in the United States as "actually very patchy" (Barr, "Television's Newcomers," 8).

54 Snider and Yu, "Cheap Broadband, PCs Aimed at Low-income Families."

55 Barr, "Television's Newcomers," 8.

56 Spangler, "Amazon Streams More Video than Hulu or Apple."
57 Waldfogel, "Cinematic Explosion," 8.
58 Ibid., 31. Waldfogel notes the explosion in independent movie production: "Independent movies – those produced outside the major Hollywood studios – make up large and growing shares of what succeeds in the market: between 2000 and 2012 the independent share of theatrical box office revenue rose from 20 to 40 percent, while the independent share of top DVD rental rose from 20 to 50 percent. The independent share of titles in the iTunes top 100 has exceeded 50 percent since 2009, and the independent share of the top 50 titles by release vintage at Vudu, roughly 10 percent from 1980 to 2005, reached 40 percent in 2010" (ibid., 6).
59 comScore, "The 2010 U.S. Digital Year in Review."
60 Perez, "Hulu Announces Adding 1 Million Paid Subscribers in Q1 2013."
61 Nielsen, "What Netflix and Hulu Users Are Watching … and How."
62 Nielsen, "Detailing the Digital Revolution."
63 Couts, "ComScore: YouTube Still Crushing the Competition, but Hulu Wins on Ads."
64 kanic121, comment on Moskovciak, "When Cord-cutting Is Better than Cable."
65 Damratoski et al., "An Investigation into Alternative Television Viewership Habits of College Students," 75.
66 Gutman, "Evan Shapiro on Why TV Isn't Dead and How Marketers Need to See It."
67 Stelter, "A DVR Ad-eraser Causes Tremors at TV Upfronts."
68 Ibid. Perhaps this is why James L. McQuivey, vice president and analyst for Forrester Research, concluded, "The fact that Dish would be willing to anger some of its most important content partners just goes to show how desperate these times we live in really are."
69 Chozick and Stelter, "An Online TV Site Grows Up."
70 Chozick and Stelter, "Hulu Faces a Nebulous Future as It Seeks a New Owner."
71 Spangler, "Hulu's Advertising Chief Is Latest Exec to Exit."
72 "Apple iTunes Dominates Internet Video Market." By the end of 2012 iTunes achieved a 67 per cent market share of electronic sell-through (EST) for television shows and 65 per cent EST market share for feature-length movies.
73 Falcone, "Which Streaming Media Device Is Right for You?"
74 Akkad, "BlackBerry 10's Open Secret."
75 Krosse, comment on Nathaniel Wice, "Streaming with Apple TV," *Barron's*, 26 May 2012. Similarly, the *CNET* review notes that Apple TV is "a much

less useful box if you don't have other Apple devices or don't buy your content from iTunes. Roku's competing boxes offer more streaming services, including Amazon Instant, Hulu Plus, HBO Go, and Pandora. The Roku LT is also available at half the price" ("Apple TV Review").

76 Santo, "The Biggest Impact from an Apple TV Could Be Unbundled Channels."
77 Kosner, "It's the Content, Stupid!"
78 Van Dijck, *The Culture of Connectivity*, 122.
79 In *The Culture of Connectivity* Van Dijck makes an extended case for Google's strategy of interoperability and convincingly argues that this business strategy has more to do with gaining market power than with empowering consumers.
80 Pogue, "Chromecast, Simply and Cheaply, Flings Web Video to TVs."
81 Brustein, "Google Reels in Its Latest Internet-TV Device."
82 Ibid.
83 Stewart and Ramachandran, "Google Seeks TV Content for Streaming Service."
84 Van Dijck, *The Culture of Connectivity*, 121.
85 Guynn, "Google TV Undergoes a Trial by Partisans."
86 Cubitt, *Videography*, xvi.
87 Atkinson, "YouTube Considering Introducing Subscription-based Streaming Service."
88 Thompson, "YouTube May Be Worth $20 Billion by 2020."
89 Baig and Snider, "Mobile Devices Star in Prime Time at Home."
90 Carr, "A Glimpse of Murdoch Unbound."
91 Van Dijck, *The Culture of Connectivity*, 112, 119.
92 Ibid., 128.
93 Wasko and Erickson, "The Political Economy of YouTube," 383.
94 Seabrook, "Streaming Dreams."
95 Ibid.
96 On the similarities between YouTube and television, see Vermeer, "What's on the Tube Today?"
97 Uricchio, "The Future of a Medium Once Known as Television," 27.
98 Ibid., 31.
99 Ibid., 34.
100 Ibid.
101 Marques, "TV without a Remote."
102 Uricchio, "The Future of a Medium Once Known as Television," 32.
103 Uricchio, "Television's Next Generation," 180.
104 Van Dijck, *The Culture of Connectivity*, 121.

105 Ibid., 122.
106 Van Dijck, "YouTube beyond Technology and Cultural Form," 153.
107 Ibid., 156.
108 Uricchio, "The Future of a Medium Once Known as Television," 32.
109 Van Dijck, "YouTube beyond Technology and Cultural Form," 156.
110 Ibid.
111 Ibid., 157.
112 Williams, *Television: Technology and Cultural Form*, 20–1.
113 See chapter 2, "The Home and Family on YouTube," in Strangelove, *Watching YouTube*.
114 Van Dijck, "YouTube beyond Technology and Cultural Form," 157.
115 Uricchio, "The Future of a Medium Once Known as Television," 37.
116 Cubitt, *Videography*, 102.
117 Daidj, "Corporate Strategies, Business Ecosystems and Convergence," 1104.
118 Merrin, "Still Fighting 'the Beast,'" 108.
119 Ibid., 113.
120 Moglen, "Freedom in the Cloud."
121 Ibid.
122 McCann, "Hulu Said to Disclose Users' Viewing Habits."
123 Spigel, "Smart Homes," 243.
124 Ibid., 240.
125 Ibid., 243.
126 Ibid., 244.
127 Ibid.
128 Ibid.
129 Donohue, "SeaChange, Tellabs to Target Ads on iPad Based on Web Viewing Habits."
130 Green, "Why Do They Call It TV When It's Not on the Box?" 101.
131 Levy, "No More Hulu for You."
132 Spangler, "Is 'TV Everywhere' Liberating or Coercive?"

7. Disintermediation: The Political Economy of Television

1 Martin and Medina, *The Future of TV*, 1.
2 Spangler, "Cord-cutting Alert." Content consumption via TV Everywhere surged 246 per cent between 2013 and 2014 but the service lacks the variety of content that can be found via piracy and remains restrictive.
3 Wood, "TV Apps Are Soaring in Popularity."
4 Ammori, "TV Competition Nowhere," 40.

5 Bachman, "Will Hulu Join Netflix in Rush for Cable-TV Partners?"
6 Taneja and Young, "Television Industry's Adoption of the Internet," 219, 239.
7 Winseck, "Bell-Astral Deal Should Be Stopped in Its Tracks."
8 Ibid.
9 Tichur and Ladurantaye, "As Headwinds Gather, Rogers Seeks Its Next Windfall."
10 Ibid.
11 Cooper, "Structured Viral Communications," 18.
12 Ibid., 25.
13 Ibid., 28.
14 Ibid., 29.
15 Ibid., 31.
16 Ibid., 41.
17 Grover, Lowery, and Edwards, "Revenge of the Cable Guys."
18 Arango, "Cable TV's Big Worry."
19 Cooper, "Structured Viral Communications," 45.
20 Pilieci, "Rogers Abandons Video-rental Business."
21 Cieply, "Report Shows Quarterly Decline in Video Rental Revenue."
22 Di Piazza, "The Television and Movie Industry Explained," 1.
23 "Faster, Better, Cheaper," 26.
24 Ibid., 3.
25 Ibid.
26 Logsdon, Hoskin, and Anderson, *Perspectives on the Filmed Entertainment Industries 2012*, 38.
27 Ibid., 164.
28 Ibid., 38.
29 Ibid., 39.
30 Ibid.
31 Minoli, *Linear and Nonlinear Video and TV Applications*, 32.
32 Donohue, "What's Comcast Cooking for the Cable Show?"
33 Spangler, "Net Video to Keep Eating More Bandwidth."
34 "May 2012 and Historical ACSI Scores."
35 Bookman, "Cable's Move to Absorb the Online Video Threat."
36 Ibid.
37 Tichur and Ladurantaye, "As Headwinds Gather, Rogers Seeks Its Next Windfall," 4.
38 Christophers, *Envisioning Media Power*.
39 Ibid., 132.
40 Ibid.

41 Ibid.
42 Ibid.
43 Ibid.
44 Ibid., 133.
45 Ibid.
46 Ibid.
47 Ibid., 137.
48 Ibid., 142.
49 Ibid., 143.
50 Ibid., 145. The BMO report refutes the notion that windowing in the film business is going away anytime soon: "the most frequently used term to describe the distribution window for years has been 'collapsing,' which in our opinion is nowhere near accurate and disregards the exclusivity window for theatrical runs and practical reality of distribution for most home video releases" (Logsdon, Hoskin, and Anderson, *Perspectives on the Filmed Entertainment Industries 2012*, 132).
51 Ibid.
52 Christophers, *Envisioning Media Power*, 157.
53 "Top 10 Most Pirated TV-shows of 2010."
54 Christophers, *Envisioning Media Power*, 158.
55 Ibid.
56 Ibid., 158–9.
57 Innocent Bystander, comment on Ted Kritsonis, "Media-hungry Canadians Seek Access to Geoblocked Hulu, Spotify," *Globe and Mail*, 20 October 2009.
58 Svantesson, "'Imagine There's No Countries …,'" 1.
59 Christophers, *Envisioning Media Power*, 159.
60 Couldry, *Media Rituals*, 15.
61 Morley, *Home Territories*, 194.
62 Christophers, *Envisioning Media Power*, 159.
63 Ibid.
64 Craig, "Media sans Frontiers," 17.
65 Ibid., 16.
66 Ibid., 26.
67 Ibid., 33.
68 Christophers, *Envisioning Media Power*, 192.
69 Fritz, "Disney Feuds with Redbox and Netflix over 'John Carter' DVD."
70 Pesce, "Piracy Is Good?"
71 Christophers, *Envisioning Media Power*, 428.
72 Ibid.
73 Ibid., 427.

74　Stelter, "If Video Sites Could Act like Cable Companies."

75　Ibid.

76　Ibid.

77　Ibid.

78　Block, "Cable Show 2012."

79　Yao, "Why Pay TV Operators Should Fear Google Fiber."

80　Ibid.

81　Hazlett, "Cable TV Franchises as Barriers to Video Competition," 81. Hazlett notes that "cable franchise remains in place across more than 30,000 local jurisdictions." These local franchises effectively exclude competition and maintain high prices and poor service. Also, "cable operators have won awards from their national trade association for successfully lobbying for 'level playing field' laws, state statutes explicitly designed to limit competition by raising cable franchise barriers" (8).

82　Ibid., 6.

83　Bond, "Netflix CCO Ted Sarandos Reveals His Strategy for Expansion."

84　Stelter, "Gatekeepers of Cable TV Try to Stop Intel." Also see Fixmer and Sherman, "Time Warner Cable Content Incentives Thwart New Web TV."

85　Ammori, "Copyright's Latest Communications Policy," 379.

86　Ibid.

87　Ibid., 380.

88　Ammori, "TV Competition Nowhere," 6.

89　Ammori, "Copyright's Latest Communications Policy," 385. Ammori notes that this practice continues in spite of its illegality. Any programmers who file a carriage complaint against a distributor are collectively blackballed by distributors and thus shut out from the television system.

90　Stone and Stelter, "Some Online Shows Could Go Subscription-Only."

91　Minne, "Data Caps."

92　Spangler, "Net Video to Keep Eating More Bandwidth."

93　Spangler, "Comcast to Shift from Broadband Caps to Usage-based Pricing."

94　Neel, "Cord Cutters Dominate Broadband Usage."

95　Atkinson, "Economic Doctrines and Network Policy," 425.

96　Ibid., 415.

97　Editorial Board, "Searching for Fairness on the Internet."

98　Crawford, "The Wire Next Time."

99　Geist, "Different Regulations, Different Regulators."

100　Holt, "Regulating Connected Viewing," 23.

101　Geist, "CRTC vs. Netflix."

102　Lotz, *The Television Will Be Revolutionized*, 145.

103 Ibid., 146.
104 Geist, "Canada's Usage Based Billing Controversy," 40.
105 Catan and Schatz, "U.S. Probes Cable for Limits on Net Video."
106 Waterman, Sherman, and Ji, "The Economics of Online Television," 33.
107 Mahler, "As Netflix Resists, Most Firms Just Try to Befriend Comcast."
108 Ammori, "Copyright's Latest Communications Policy," 408.
109 Lotz, *The Television Will Be Revolutionized*, 148.
110 Waterman, Sherman, and Ji, "The Economics of Online Television," 3.
111 Christophers, *Envisioning Media Power*, 316.
112 Ibid., 317.
113 According to the Recording Industry Association of America, US revenues declined 50 per cent from 2000 to 2011. Reuters, "Analysis – Key to Universal-EMI Decision."
114 Christophers, *Envisioning Media Power*, 317.
115 Stelter, "A DVR Ad-eraser Causes Tremors at TV Upfronts."
116 Lotz, *The Television Will Be Revolutionized*, 151.
117 Hansell, "Beyond War News."
118 Reardon, "Cable Fights to Stay Relevant in Online World."
119 Szalai, "Comcast Cable Chief Talks Sub Trends, Streampix."
120 Flacy, "Comcast Continues Losing Cable Subscribers to Cord-cutting."
121 Cheng, "Cutting the Cable Cord Gets Easier."
122 Richmond, "New Research Shows Netflix Is a Catalyst for Cord-cutting and Cord-shaving."
123 Logsdon, Hoskin, and Anderson, *Perspectives on the Filmed Entertainment Industries 2012*, 128–9.
124 Ibid., 131. In a paper presented at the 2011 Telecommunications Policy Research Conference, David Waterman and Sung Wook Ji draw a similar picture and note that although "combined revenues for 10 major media in the U.S. have steadily declined as a proportion of overall economic activity (GDP) from 1999 to at least 2009," the exception is "television and video games, which have continued to expand or at least keep pace with overall economic activity in the U.S." ("Online vs. Offline in the U.S.," 2, 21).
125 MPAA, "Theatrical Market Statistics, 2011."
126 *Economist*, "Breaking Up Is Not So Very Hard to Do."
127 Obst, "Hollywood Is Completely Broken."
128 Adegoke, "Media's Cable Engine Splutters, Writedowns Loom."
129 Logsdon, Hoskin, and Anderson, *Perspectives on the Filmed Entertainment Industries 2012*, 149. Also noteworthy here, "Given that many of the cable networks are owned by primetime broadcast players, the ultimate

economics have not gone away for ABC, NBC, and FOX" (ibid., 150). The BMO analysis substantially discounts the impact of the Internet on the television industry: "The latter options [Internet and video gaming] are often overweighed, in our opinion, as local TV viewership minutes continue to climb" (ibid.).

130 Carter, "Prime-time Ratings Bring Speculation of a Shift in Habits." Another report from April 2013 noted that "total primetime commercial ratings fell 8 percent across the board, marking the sixth straight quarter of total TV declines – and the steepest drop since the third quarter of 2009" (Stelter, "As TV Ratings and Profits Fall, Networks Face a Cliffhanger").

131 Stelter, "As TV Ratings and Profits Fall, Networks Face a Cliffhanger."

132 James, "Nielsen to Include Internet Viewers in Its Definition of TV Homes." For an overview of the changing nature of audience measurement, see Buzzard, *Tracking the Audience*.

133 Strachan, "Viewers Watching More Traditional TV, Exec Insists."

134 James, "Nielsen to Include Internet Viewers in Its Definition of TV Homes."

135 Ibid.

136 Donders and Evens, "Cable Wars and Business Battles in Broadcasting Markets," 9.

137 Garnham, "Concepts of Culture," 30–1.

138 Christophers, "Television's Power Relations in the Transition to Digital," 253.

139 Christophers, *Envisioning Media Power*, 18.

140 Kafka, "Hey Cable Guys!"

141 Spangler, "Cord-cutting Alert."

142 Belson, "F.C.C. Sees Cable Savings in à la Carte."

143 Martin and Medina, *The Future of TV*, 1.

144 Sandomir, Miller, and Eder, "To Protect Its Empire, ESPN Stays on Offense."

145 Carr, "New Challenges Chip Away at Cable's Pillar of Profit."

146 Brustein, "Cable TV Companies Forced to Unbundle in Canada."

147 Geist, "Is the CRTC Ready to Hit the Reset Button on Television Regulation in Canada?"

148 Rhodes, "Challenges of Globalization, Flattening and Unbundling," 17.

149 Gimpel, "Five Pressing Issues Shaping the Future of TV & Video," 11.

150 Ramachandran, "Dish Chief."

151 Ibid.

152 Lotz, *The Television Will Be Revolutionized*, 254.

8. Post-television Society: Diversity, Citizenship, News, and Global Conflict

1 Curran, *Media and Power*, 55.
2 Einstein, *Media Diversity*, 210.
3 Ibid.
4 Ibid., 212.
5 Ibid.
6 Ibid.
7 Ibid., 218.
8 Ibid., 220.
9 Ibid., 221.
10 Ibid., 226.
11 Cardoso et al., "P2P in the Networked Future of European Cinema," 819.
12 Li, "From D-Buffs to the D-Generation," 559. Angela Xiao Wu argues that diversity within China requires media markets structured by institutional forces, yet her research did not extend beyond 2005 and thus says little about the current flow of online pirated filmed entertainment. See Wu, "Broadening the Scope of Cultural Preferences," 515.
13 Gutman, "Evan Shapiro on Why TV Isn't Dead and How Marketers Need to See It."
14 Lotz, *The Television Will Be Revolutionized*, 254.
15 Ibid.
16 Ibid., 247.
17 Ryan and Hearn, "Next Generation 'Filmmaking,'" 133. See also Cunningham, Silver, and McDonnell, "Rates of Change."
18 Christian, "Beyond Big Video," 84.
19 Christopherson, "Hollywood in Decline?" 150.
20 Krashinsky, "Fake Enemies Stoke Indie Film Buzz."
21 Ibid.
22 Bercovici, "Vimeo, DailyMotion Court Filmmakers in YouTube's Shadow."
23 Ibid.
24 Marshall, *New Media Cultures*, 93.
25 Smith, "The Wired Nation," 602.
26 Streeter, "Blue Skies and Strange Bedfellows," 234.
27 Ibid., 236.
28 Ibid., 237.
29 Ibid., 239.
30 Anderssen, "Photo-overload."
31 Lewis, "The Myth of Commercialism," 337.
32 Sun and Picker, *Mickey Mouse Monopoly*.

33 Lewis, "The Myth of Commercialism," 342.
34 Ibid., 341.
35 Schudson, *Advertising*, 210.
36 Lewis, "The Myth of Commercialism," 343.
37 Ibid., 346.
38 Gray, *Television Entertainment*, 98.
39 Meehan, *Why TV Is Not Our Fault*, 50.
40 Ibid., 51.
41 Ibid., 4.
42 Ibid., 5.
43 Ibid., 4.
44 Green, "Why Do They Call It TV When It's Not on the Box?" 102.
45 Ibid.
46 Ibid., 103.
47 Turner, "Television and Cultural Studies," 376.
48 Beaty and Sullivan, *Canadian Television Today*, 103.
49 Ibid., 127. A similar study of the German television industry "character-ized by strong (national) regulation and common national IP and distribu-tion rights" such as is found in Canada concluded that convergence with international television flows and the growth of non-linear viewing are general trends affecting the German audience. Loebbecke, "Broadcaster-driven Video-on-Demand (VoD) Platforms in the Era of Disrupting and Converging Media Value Chains," 1.
50 Ibid., 130.
51 Ibid., 115.
52 Ibid., 113.
53 Turner, "Television and the Nation," 63.
54 Green, "Why Do They Call It TV When It's Not on the Box?" 103.
55 Turner, "Television and the Nation," 62.
56 Sanz, "Statistical, Ecosystems and Competitiveness Analysis of the Media and Content Industries," 41.
57 Pertierra, "If They Show Prison Break in the United States on a Wednes-day, by Thursday It Is Here," 399.
58 Fung, "Globalizing Televised Culture," 184.
59 Levin and Horn, "DVD Pirates Running Rampant in China."
60 Curtis, "Preface," vii.
61 Journalism Project Staff, "YouTube and News," 2.
62 Ibid.
63 Ibid., 5.
64 Ibid., 15.

65 Ibid., 16.
66 Wood et al., "Tonight's Top Story," 807.
67 Goode, "Social News, Citizen Journalism and Democracy," 1292.
68 Ibid., 1293.
69 Moran and Malbon, *Understanding the Global TV Format*, 10.
70 Slater, "Democracy and Online News."
71 Schaffer, "Innovations in the Delivery of Online Local News," 544.
72 Paulussen and D'heer, "Using Citizens for Community Journalism," 588.
73 Soroka et al., "Auntie Knows Best?"
74 Mackey et al., "Updates on Protests over Anti-Islam Film."
75 Sutter, "YouTube Restricts Video Access over Libyan Violence."
76 Mackey et al., "Updates on Protests over Anti-Islam Film."
77 Ibid.
78 Gladstone, "Anti-American Protests Flare Beyond the Mideast."
79 El Amrani, "The Politics of Outrage Is Still an Irresistible Temptation."
80 Miller, "As Violence Spreads in Arab World, Google Blocks Access to Inflammatory Video."
81 Kirkpatrick, Cooper, and Landler, "Egypt, Hearing from Obama, Moves to Heal Rift from Protests."
82 Baker and Landler, "U.S. Is Preparing for a Long Siege of Arab Unrest."
83 Wente, "It's Too Easy to Lay All the Blame on a Crude Video."

Conclusion: Post-television Culture

1 Silcoff, "CRTC Paints Picture of Canada's Netflix Boom."
2 Kafka, "Tipping Point?"
3 Beaujon, "Third of Millennials Watch Mostly Online Video or No Broadcast TV."
4 Ross, *Beyond the Box*. Also see Gillan, *Television and New Media*.
5 Marsden, "The Challenges of Standardization," 137.
6 For a survey of policy approaches to television at the dawn of online TV, see Ward, *Television and Public Policy*.
7 Evans, *Transmedia Television*, 154.
8 Lotz, *The Television Will Be Revolutionized*, 133.
9 Hartley, *Television Truths*, 1.
10 Ibid., 11.
11 Ibid., 22.
12 Fiske, *Television Culture*.
13 Kinder, *Playing with Power in Movies, Television, and Video Games*, 37.
14 Morley, "Theoretical Orthodoxies," 125.

15 Gray and Lotz, *Television Studies*, 104.
16 Turnock, *Television and Consumer Culture*.
17 Pellow, Parks, and Park, *The Silicon Valley of Dreams*, xi.
18 Newman and Levine, *Legitimating Television*, 152.
19 Mittell, *Television and American Culture*, 272.
20 Kelly, "Beyond the Broadcast Text," 135.
21 Marshall, "Screens," 42.
22 Katz, "Industry Structure and Competition Absent Distribution Bottlenecks," 32.
23 Hartley, *Uses of Television*, 23.
24 Uricchio, "The Recurrent, the Recombinatory and the Ephemeral," 32.
25 Ouellette, "Will the Revolution Be Televised?" 167.
26 Ibid.
27 Miller, *Television Studies*, 112.
28 Press, "Women Watching Television," 55.
29 Cummins and Gordon, *Programming Our Lives*, x.
30 Wirth and Rizzuto, "Future Prospects for Cable Telecommunications in an Over-the-top World," 41. Also see Bar and Taplin, "Cable's Digital Future."
31 Newman and Levine, *Legitimating Television*, 109.
32 Brinkley, "HDTV."
33 Newman and Levine, *Legitimating Television*, 134.
34 Ibid.
35 Ibid., 128.
36 Ibid., 168.
37 Marshall, "Screens," 46.
38 Hartley, "Less Popular but More Democratic," 30.
39 Purcell, "Online Video 2013," 2. Only 18 per cent of adult Internet users post videos they have created themselves, but this type of activity is also bound to increase with the ongoing deployment of smartphones.
40 Andrejevic, "Surveillance in the Digital Enclosure," 315.
41 Cubitt, "Lost Generations," 18.
42 Ibid.
43 Miller, *Television Studies*, 180.
44 Wu, *The Master Switch*.
45 Uricchio, "Constructing Television," 68.
46 Ibid., 73.
47 Ibid., 77.
48 Carey, *Communication as Culture*, 161.
49 Castells, *Communication Power*, 413.
50 Ibid.

51 Ibid., 414.
52 Gunter, *Television versus the Internet*, 105.
53 McGrane and Gunderson, *Watching TV Is Not Required*, 80.
54 Ibid.
55 Lotz, *The Television Will Be Revolutionized*, 33.
56 Hermes, "Caught," 35.
57 D'Agostino and Tafler, "Introduction," xv.
58 Ibid., xvi–xvii.
59 Quail, "Television Goes Online," 4.
60 Ibid., 11.
61 Nelson, "Windows into the Digital World," 73.
62 Bilton, "Internet Pirates Will Always Win."

Bibliography

AAP. "Downloads Don't Matter." *Sydney Morning Herald*, 26 February 2013.

Accenture. "Video-over-Internet Consumer Survey 2013." Accenture.com. pp. 1–16.

Adegoke, Yinke. "Media's Cable Engine Splutters, Writedowns Loom." Reuters, 25 April 2012.

– "Netflix: The New Arch-Frenemy." Reuters, 4 May 2012.

Adhikari, Vijay Kumar, Yang Guo, Fang Hao, Matteo Varvello, Volker Hilt, Moritz Steiner, and Zhi-Li Zhang. "Unreeling Netflix: Understanding and Improving Multi-CDN Movie Delivery." *Proceedings of the IEEE International Conference on Computer Communications*, University der Bundeswehr München, Munich, Germany, 30 July–12 August 2012.

Aguiar, Luis, and Bertin Martens. "Digital Music Consumption on the Internet: Evidence from Clickstream Data." Institute for Prospective Technological Studies Digital Economy working paper. Seville, Spain: European Commission Joint Research Centre, 2013.

Akkad, Omar El. "BlackBerry 10's Open Secret: It's Aimed at the Walled Garden." *Globe and Mail*, 11 May 2012.

Ammori, Marvin. "Copyright's Latest Communications Policy: Content-Lock-Out and Compulsory Licensing for Internet Content." *Commlaw Conspectus* 18 (2010): 375–420.

– "TV Competition Nowhere: How the Cable Industry Is Colluding to Kill Online TV." Free Press, January 2010, 1–40.

Anderson, Nate. "Only 9% (and Falling) of US Internet Users Are P2P Pirates." *ars technica*, 23 March 2011.

Anderssen, Erin. "Photo-overload: Everyone's Taking Pics, But Is Anyone Really Looking?" *Globe and Mail*, 23 June 2012.

Andersson, Jonas. "The Quiet Agglomeration of Data: How Piracy Is Made Mundane." *International Journal of Communication* 6 (2012): 585–605.

Andrejevic, Mark. "Surveillance in the Digital Enclosure." *The Communication Review* 10 (2007): 295–317.

Andy. "Piracy Collapses as Legal Alternatives Do Their Job." *TorrentFreak*, 16 July 2013.

Appadurai, Arjun. *Modernity at Large*. Minneapolis: University of Minnesota Press, 1996.

"Apple iTunes Dominates Internet Video Market." NDP Group, 23 April 2013.

"Apple TV Review." *CNET*, 16 March 2012.

Arango, Tim. "Cable TV's Big Worry." *New York Times*, 23 June 2009.

Associated Press. "Netflix Future Tied to Using Internet Video Streaming Insights to Improve Recommendations." 9 April 2012.

– "RIAA Stops Piracy Lawsuit Strategy." 21 December 2008.

Atkinson, Claire. "Pandora Effect: Digital Music Sales Tumble." *New York Post*, 11 October 2013.

– "TV in a Bad 'Spot': Fragmented Audience Is Threatening Ad Sales." *New York Post*, 30 April 2013.

– "YouTube Considering Introducing Subscription-based Streaming Service." *New York Post*, 11 May 2012.

Atkinson, Robert. "Economic Doctrines and Network Policy." *Telecommunications Policy* 35 (June 2011): 413–25.

Bachman, Justin. "Will Hulu Join Netflix in Rush for Cable-TV Partners?" *Businessweek*, 18 October 2013.

Bagnasco, Anna Maria. "Why Do Pirates Demand Movies? Empirical Evidence from Italy." Paper presented at the International Conference on Applied Economics, Universidad de Alicante, Alicante, 16–19 June 2010.

Bai, Jie, and Joel Waldfogel. "Movie Piracy and Sales Displacement in Two Samples of Chinese Consumers." Unpublished paper. 17 September 2009, pp. 1–23.

Baig, Edward C., and Mike Snider. "Mobile Devices Star in Prime Time at Home." *USA Today*, 1 June 2012.

Bainbridge, Amy. "Austar Boss Fears Piracy Explosion under NBN." *Australian Broadcasting Corporation*, 15 March 2012.

Baker, Peter, and Mark Landler. "U.S. Is Preparing for a Long Siege of Arab Unrest." *New York Times*, 15 September 2012.

Ballvé, Marcelo. "Mobile Video: Mobile's Big Monetization Opportunity as Audiences Boom." *Business Insider*, 9 April 2013.

– "Why This TV Season Will Confirm Mobile's Unstoppable Rise as a Complementary 'Second Screen.'" *Business Insider*, 20 September 2013.

Banerjee, Aniruddha, James Alleman, and Paul Rappoport. "Analysis of Video-viewing Behavior in the Era of Convergent and Connected Devices." Paper presented to the 19th ITS Biennial Conference, Bangkok, Thailand, 18–21 November 2012.

Bangerman, Eric. "RIAA Anti-P2P Campaign a Real Money Pit, According to Testimony." *ars technica*, 3 October 2007.

Bar, François, and Jonathan Taplin. "Cable's Digital Future." In Sarah Banet-Weiser, Cynthia Chris, and Anthony Freitas, eds., *Cable Visions: Television beyond Broadcasting*, 66–84. New York: New York University Press, 2007.

Barlow, Andrew. *The DVD Revolution: Movies, Culture, and Technology*. Westport, CT: Praeger, 2004.

Barnes, Brooks. "Web Deals Cheer Hollywood, Despite Drop in Moviegoers." *New York Times*, 24 February 2012.

Barnett, Emma. "Spotify 'Helps Curb Music Piracy.'" *The Telegraph*, 6 November 2009.

Barr, Trevor. "Television's Newcomers: Netflix, Apple, Google, and Facebook." *Telecommunications Journal of Australia* 61 (2011): 1–10.

Baumgärtel, Tilman. "The United States of Piracy." Keynote speech presented at the Asia Cultural Forum, University of the Philippines, Manila, 2006.

Baumgartner, Jeff. "Cord Cutting No Longer an 'Urban Myth.'" *Multichannel News*, 6 August 2013.

Baysinger, Tim. "Sports Summit: Lazarus – TV Everywhere Protects Pay TV Ecosystem." *Multichannel News*, 19 June 2013.

BBC News. "Online Film Piracy 'Set to Rise.'" 9 July 2004.

Beach, Jamie. "Canadians Cut the Cord in Q1." *IP&TV News*, 3 July 2013.

Beaty, Bart, and Rebecca Sullivan. *Canadian Television Today*. Calgary: University of Calgary Press, 2006.

Beaujon, Andrew. "Third of Millennials Watch Mostly Online Video or No Broadcast TV." *Poynter Mediawire*, 10 October 2013.

Bednarski, P.J. "Iger Sees Little Cord-cutting, Says Netflix Is Good, Not Dominant." *MediaPost*, 24 September 2013.

Belson, Ken. "F.C.C. Sees Cable Savings in à la Carte." *New York Times*, 10 February 2012.

Bennett, James, and Tom Brown. "Introduction: Past the Boundaries of 'New' and 'Old' Media." In James Bennett and Tom Brown, eds., *Film and Television After DVD*, 1–18. London: Routledge, 2008.

Bennett, Lucy. "Transformations through Twitter: The England Riots, Television Viewership and Negotiations of Power through Media Coverage." *Participations: Journal of Audience & Reception Studies* 9 (November 2012): 511–25.

Bercovici, Jeff. "Vimeo, DailyMotion Court Filmmakers in YouTube's Shadow." *Forbes*, 19 September 2012.

Berman, Saul, and Lynn Kesterson-Townes. *Beyond Digital: Connecting Media and Entertainment to the Future.* Somers, NY: IBM Global Business Services, 2012.

Berr, Jonathan. "Television as We Know It Is Fading." *MSN Money*, 14 May 2013.

Bialik, Carl. "Putting a Price Tag on Film Piracy." *Wall Street Journal*, 5 April 2013.

Bignell, Jonathan, and Andreas Fickers. "Introduction: Comparative European Perspectives on Television History." In Jonathan Bignell and Andreas Fickers, eds., *A European Television History*, 1–54. Malden, MA: Blackwell, 2008.

Bilton, Nick. "Disruptions: For HBO, Still Beholden to a Cable Company." *New York Times*, 10 June 2012.

– "Internet Pirates Will Always Win." *New York Times*, 4 August 2012.

Birmingham, Jack, and Matthew David. "Live-streaming: Will Football Fans Continue to Be More Law Abiding than Music Fans?" *Sport in Society* 14 (2011): 69–80.

Black, Jason, Kieran Downes, Frank Field, and Aleksandra Mozdzanowska. "More than 'Just Shopping': Personalization, Privacy, and (Ab)use of Data." Paper presented to the Science, Society and Sustainability Conference, Athens, Greece, 26 May 2006.

Blain, Emmanuel. "Sports over IP: Dynamics and Perspectives." Master of Science in Technology and Policy Dissertation, MIT, June 2010.

Block, Alex Ben. "Cable Convenes in D.C. under a Cloud of Uncertainty." *Hollywood Reporter*, 10 June 2013.

– "Cable Show 2012: 'We Don't Know What the Customer Wants,' Says Discovery's David Zaslav." *Hollywood Reporter*, 21 May 2012.

Bode, Karl. "Time Warner CEO Still Thinks Most Cord Cutters Live with Mom." *Broadband DSLReports*, 30 May 2014.

Bodó, Balázs, and Zoltán Lakatos. "Theatrical Distribution and P2P Movie Piracy." *International Journal of Communication* 6 (2013): 413–45.

Bond, Paul. "Netflix CCO Ted Sarandos Reveals His Strategy for Expansion." *Hollywood Reporter*, 30 May 2012.

– "Netflix Might Be Most-watched 'Cable Network' in the U.S. Today." *Hollywood Reporter*, 4 April 2013.

Bondad-Brown, Beverly A., Ronald E. Rice, and Katy E. Pearce. "Influences on TV Viewing and Online User-shared Video Use: Demographics, Generations, Contextual Age, Media Use, Motivations, and Audience Activity." *Journal of Broadcasting and Electronic Media* 56 (2012): 471–93.

Bookman, Samantha. "Cable's Move to Absorb the Online Video Threat." *FierceOnlineVideo*, 30 May 2012.

– "CW's Streaming Audience May Be Up by 60 Percent." *FierceOnlineVideo*, 15 May 2014.

Boon Dog Professional Services. "'Cord Cutting' in Canada Increases." *Broadcaster*, 13 August 2013.

Boorstin, Julia. "Disney CEO Bob Iger Talks Earnings, 'Avengers,' and International Growth." CNBC, 8 May 2012.

Born, Georgina. "Inside Television: Television Studies and the Sociology of Culture." *Screen* 41 (Winter 2000): 404–24.

Bounie, David, Patrick Waelbroeck, and Marc Bourreau. "Piracy and the Demand for Films: Analysis of Piracy Behavior in French Universities." *Review of Economic Research on Copyright Issues* 3 (2006): 15–27.

Bowery, Kathy, and Matthew Rimmer. "Rip, Mix, Burn: The Politics of Peer to Peer and Copyright." *First Monday* 7 (July 2005).

Boyle, Deirdre. "From Portapak to Camcorder: A Brief History of Guerrilla Television." *Journal of Film and Video* 44 (1992): 67–79.

Boyle, Raymond, and Richard Haynes. *Football in the New Media Age*. London: Routledge, 2004.

– *Power Play: Sport, the Media and Popular Culture*. Edinburgh: Edinburgh University Press, 2009.

Bradshaw, James. "More Canadians Cutting the Cord?" *Globe and Mail*, 15 May 2014.

Briel, Robert. "After Cord-cutting There Is Cord-cheating." *Broadband TV News*, 5 September 2013.

Brinkley, Joel. "HDTV: High Definition, High in Price." *New York Times*, 20 August 1998.

Brioux, Bill. "Point, Click – and Get Geo-blocked." *Toronto Star*, 31 January 2009.

Broder, John M. "Climate Change Seen as Threat to U.S. Security." *New York Times*, 8 August 2012.

Brown, Jesse. "How Hollywood Uses Megaupload." *Maclean's*, 30 March 2012.

Bruns, Axel. "Reconfiguring Television for a Networked, Produsage Context." *Media International Australia* 126 (February 2008): 82–94.

– "The User-led Disruption: Self-(Re)broadcasting at *Justin.tv* and Elsewhere." Paper presented at EuroTV'09, Leuven, Belgium, 2009.

Brustein, Joshua. "Cable TV Companies Forced to Unbundle in Canada." *Businessweek*, 14 October 2013.

– "Google Reels in Its Latest Internet-TV Device." *Businessweek*, 26 August 2013.

Brzoznowski, Kristin. "Survey: 7 in 10 U.S. TV Watchers Are Binge Viewers." *WorldScreen*, 30 April 2014.

Burgess, Rick. "Online Movie Streaming Will Overtake DVD Sales This Year in U.S." *TechSpot*, 23 March 2012.

Business Insider. "The Mobile Industry: In-Depth." BI Intelligence, 10 October 2012.

Buzzard, Karen. *Tracking the Audience: The Ratings Industry from Analog to Digital*. London: Routledge, 2012.

Bylund, Anders. "Why Cord-cutting Won't Slow Down in 2012." *The Motley Fool*, 10 April 2012.

Callahan, Michael. "You Watch Television? How Very Lowbrow of You." *The Philly Post*, 7 March 2012.

Cammaerts, Bart, Robin Mansell, and Bingchun Meng. "Copyright & Creation: A Case for Promoting Inclusive Online Sharing." London: LSE Media Policy Project, September 2013.

Cammaerts, Bart, and Bingchun Meng. "Creative Destruction and Copyright Protection: Regulatory Responses to File-sharing." London: LSE Media Policy Project, March 2011.

Canadian Press. "Cord Cutting: 200,000 Canadian Households Could Cancel Cable in 2012." *Huffington Post*, 30 December 2011.

– "Measuring the Canadian 'Cord-cutting' Population." *Ottawa Business Journal*, 11 July 2013.

– "More Canadians Watching TV Online, Opting for Wireless over Landlines." *Globe and Mail*, 26 September 2013.

– "Rogers Reports 15 Per Cent Increase in First-quarter Profits, Revenue Up." *Toronto Star*, 22 April 2013.

Caraway, Brett Robert. "Survey of File-sharing Culture." *International Journal of Communication* 6 (2012): 564–84.

Cardoso, Gustavo, Miguel Caetano, Rita Espanha, Pedro Jacobetty, and Tiago Lima Quintanilha. "P2P in the Networked Future of European Cinema." *International Journal of Communication* 6 (2012): 795–821.

Carey, James. *Communication as Culture: Essays on Media and Society*. London: Routledge, 1989.

Carr, David. "A Glimpse of Murdoch Unbound." *New York Times*, 29 January 2012.

– "New Challenges Chip Away at Cable's Pillar of Profit." *New York Times*, 27 April 2014.

– "TV Foresees Its Future. Netflix Is There." *New York Times*, 21 July 2013.

Carter, Bill. "Prime-time Ratings Bring Speculation of a Shift in Habits." *New York Times*, 22 April 2012.

Carter, Michael. "WWE's Business Model Is an Endangered Species." *The Motley Fool*, 24 April 2012.

Castells, Manuel. *Communication Power*. Oxford: Oxford University Press, 2009.
– *The Informational City: Economic Restructuring and Urban Development*.
  Oxford: Blackwell, 1989.
Castells, Manuel, and Gustavo Cardoso. "Piracy Cultures." *International
  Journal of Communication* 6 (2012): 826–33.
Castells, Manuel, Mireia Fernández-Ardèvol, Jack Linchuan Qiu, and Araba
  Sey. *Mobile Communication and Society: A Global Perspective*. Cambridge, MA:
  MIT Press, 2009.
Catan, Thomas, and Amy Schatz. "U.S. Probes Cable for Limits on Net Video."
  Wall Street Journal, 13 June 2012.
Cervantes, Edgar. "Poll: Are Blu-ray and DVD Movies Now Obsolete?" *Phan-
  droid*, 25 March 2012.
Cha, Jiyoung, and Sylvia M. Chan-Olmsted. "Relative Advantages of Online
  Video Platforms and Television According to Content, Technology, and
  Cost-related Attributes." *First-Monday* 17 (October 2012).
– "Substitutability between Online Video Platforms and Television." *Jour-
  nalism & Mass Communication Quarterly* 89 (June 2012): 261–78.
Chalfen, Richard. "Home Movies as Cultural Documents." In Sari Thomas,
  ed., *Film Culture: Explorations of Cinema in Its Social Context*, 126–38. London:
  Scarecrow Press, 1982.
Cheng, Roger. "Cutting the Cable Cord Gets Easier." *Wall Street Journal*,
  13 October 2010.
Chenoweth, Neil. "Murdoch Cops Blast over Pay TV Pirates." *Financial
  Review*, 27 March 2012.
Chetty, Marshini, Richard Banks, A.J. Bernheim Brush, Jonathan Donner, and
  Rebecca E. Grinter. "'You're Capped!' Understanding the Effects of Band-
  width Caps on Broadband Use in the Home." Paper presented at the ACM
  SIGCHI Conference on Human Factors in Computing Systems, Austin,
  Texas, 5–10 May 2012.
Chmielewski, Dawn C. "Netflix Executive Upends Hollywood." *Los Angeles
  Times*, 25 August 2013.
Chozick, Amy. "NBC Unpacks Trove of Data from Olympics." *New York Times*,
  25 September 2012.
Chozick, Amy, and Brian Stelter. "Hulu Faces a Nebulous Future as It Seeks
  a New Owner." *New York Times*, 23 June 2013.
– "In Search of Apps for Television." *New York Times*, 27 April 2012.
– "An Online TV Site Grows Up." *New York Times*, 16 April 2012.
Christian, Aymar Jean. "Beyond Big Video: The Instability of Independent
  Networks in a New Media Market." *Continuum: Journal of Media & Cultural
  Studies* 26 (2012): 73–87.

- "The Web as Television Reimagined? Online Networks and the Pursuit of Legacy Media." *Journal of Communication Inquiry* 36 (October 2012): 340–56.
Christophers, Brett. *Envisioning Media Power: On Capital and Geographies of Television*. Lanham, MD: Lexington Books, 2009.
- "Television's Power Relations in the Transition to Digital." *Television and New Media* 9 (May 2008): 239–57.
Christopherson, Susan. "Hollywood in Decline? US Film and Television Producers beyond the Era of Fiscal Crisis." *Cambridge Journal of Regions, Economy and Society* 6 (2013): 141–57.
Cieply, Michael. "Report Shows Quarterly Decline in Video Rental Revenue; Digital Streaming Increases." *New York Times*, 29 April 2012.
Cisco. "Cisco Visual Networking Index: Forecast and Methodology, 2010–2015." Cisco White Paper, 1 June 2011.
- "Cisco Visual Networking Index: Forecast and Methodology, 2011–2016." Cisco White Paper, 30 May 2012.
Clancy, Michelle. "Despite the Hype, Millennials Aren't Cutting the Cord, That Much." *RapidTVNews*, 1 May 2014.
- "A Fifth of US Netflix Users Have Cut the Cord." *RapidTVNews*, 19 July 2013.
Cohen, David S. "Scant Gains in War on Piracy." *Variety*, 15 April 2012.
comScore. "The 2010 U.S. Digital Year in Review." 7 February 2011.
Condry, Ian. "Cultures of Music Piracy: An Ethnographic Comparison of the US and Japan." *International Journal of Cultural Studies* 7 (2004): 343–63.
Cooke, Chris. "New Paper Disputes Claim that MegaUpload Helped Mid-sized Movies." Complete Music Update, 18 September 2013.
Cooper, Mark. "Structured Viral Communications: The Political Economy and Social Organization of Digital Disintermediation." *Journal on Telecommunication and High Technology Law* 9 (2011): 15–46.
Couldry, Nick. *Media Rituals: A Critical Approach*. London: Routledge, 2003.
"Court Orders Bell to Pay Quebecor $1M in Piracy Lawsuit." *Toronto Sun*, press release, QMI Agency, 25 July 2012.
Couts, Andrew. "ComScore: YouTube Still Crushing the Competition, but Hulu Wins on Ads." *Digital Trends*, 17 June 2011.
Covert, Adrian. "A Decade of iTunes Singles Killed the Music Industry." *CNNMoney*, 25 April 2013.
Cox, Alex. "But Who Are the Real Pirates?" *The Guardian*, 27 May 2002.
Craig, Benjamin. "Media sans Frontiers: How the Territorialisation of Rights Drives Consumer Piracy." Filmmaking.net, 6 September 2007.
Crawford, Garry. *Consuming Sport: Fans, Sport and Culture*. London: Routledge, 2004.

Crawford, Gregory S. "The Discriminatory Incentives to Bundle in the Cable Television Industry." *Quantitative Marketing and Economics* 6 (2008): 41–78.

Crawford, Gregory S., and Joseph Cullen. "Bundling, Product Choice, and Efficiency: Should Cable Television Networks Be Offered à la Carte?" *Information Economics and Policy* 19 (October 2007): 379–404.

Crawford, Susan. *Captive Audience: The Telecom Industry and Monopoly Power in the New Gilded Age.* New Haven, CT: Yale University Press, 2003.

– "The Wire Next Time." *New York Times,* 27 April 2014.

Crupi, Anthony. "Cable Commands 70 Percent of Prime-time GRPs." *Ad Age,* 21 June 2012.

– "DISH Network Threatens to Drop AMC." *Adweek,* 4 May 2012.

Cryan, Dan. "Netflix Surpasses Apple to Take Lead in U.S. Online Movie Business in 2011." Press release, HIS Technology, 1 June 2012.

Cubbison, Laurie. "A Dark Day on the Internet Leads to a Sea Change in Copyright Policy." In Clancy Ratliff, ed., *The CCCC-IP Annual: Top Intellectual Property Developments of 2011,* 25–8. The Intellectual Property Caucus of the Conference on College Composition and Communication, March 2012.

Cubitt, Sean. "Lost Generations." In Peter D'Agostino and David Tafler, eds., *Transmission: Toward a Post-Television Culture,* 1–19. London: Sage, 1994.

– *Videography: Video Media as Art and Culture.* New York: St Martin's Press, 1993.

Cui, Yanqing, Jan Chipehase, and Younghee Jung. "Personal TV: A Qualitative Study of Mobile TV Users." In Pablo Cesar, Konstantinos Chorianopoulos, and Jens F. Jensen, eds., *Interactive TV: A Shared Experience,* 196–204. Berlin: Springer, 2007.

Cummins, Walter, and George Gordon. *Programming Our Lives: Television and American Identity.* London: Praeger, 2006.

Cunningham, Stuart, Jon Silver, and John McDonnell. "Rates of Change: Online Distribution as Disruptive Technology in the Film Industry." *Media International Australia* 136 (August 2010): 119–32.

Curran, James. *Media and Power.* London: Routledge, 2002.

Curtis, Marez. "Preface." *American Quarterly* 59 (September 2007): vii–ix.

D'Agostino, Peter, and David Tafler. "Introduction." In Peter D'Agostino and David Tafler, eds., *Transmission: Toward a Post-Television Culture,* xiii–xxxi. London: Sage, 1994.

– eds. *Transmission: Toward a Post-Television Culture.* London: Sage, 1994.

Daidj, Nabyla. "Corporate Strategies, Business Ecosystems and Convergence." Paper presented at the International Conference on Technology and Business Management, American University in the Emirates, Dubai, 18–20 March 2013.

Damratoski, Katie J., April R. Field, Katie N. Mizell, and Michael C. Budden. "An Investigation into Alternative Television Viewership Habits of College Students." *Journal of Applied Business Research* 27 (January/February 2011): 69–76.

Danaher, Brett, and Michael D. Smith. "Gone in 60 Seconds: The Impact of the Megaupload Shutdown on Movie Sales." Social Science Research Network, 6 March 2013.

Danaher, Brett, and Joel Waldfogel. "Reel Piracy: The Effect of Online Film Piracy on International Box Office Sales." Social Science Research Network working paper, 16 January 2012.

Danova, Tony. "Mobile Usage: How Today's Audiences Consume Media on Phones and Tablets and What It Means for Mobile." *Business Insider*, 21 August 2013.

Daswani, Mansha. "More Than Half of U.S. Broadband Homes Use Netflix." *WorldScreen*, 2 May 2014.

David, Matthew, and Peter Millward. "Football's Coming Home? Digital Reterritorialization, Contradictions in the Transnational Coverage of Sport and the Sociology of Alternative Football Broadcasts." *The British Journal of Sociology* 63 (2012): 349–69.

Dawson, Max. "Defining Mobile Television: The Social Construction and Deconstruction of New and Old Media." *Popular Communication* 10 (2012): 253–68.

– "Little Players, Big Shows: Format, Narration, and Style on Television's New Smaller Screen." *Convergence: The International Journal of Research into New Media Technologies* 13 (2007): 231–50.

Dejean, Sylvain. "What Can We Learn from Empirical Studies about Piracy?" CESifo Economic Studies, M@rsouin working paper, August 2008.

De Kosnik, Abigail. "The Collector Is a Pirate." *International Journal of Communication* 6 (2012): 529–41.

– "Piracy Is the Future of Television." Convergence Culture Consortium, MIT, 17 March 2010.

De Meulenaere, Jonas, Wendy Van den Broeck, and Bram Lievens. "From Era of Plenty to Era of Overflow: What Shall I Watch?" *Journal of Communication Inquiry* 36 (July 2012): 305–21.

Denick, Lina. *Media and Global Civil Society*. New York: Palgrave Macmillan, 2012.

Dennen, Steve. "State of the Internet: Video, Mobile and Social." comScore, 1 February 2011.

Dent, Alexander S. "Piracy, Circulatory Legitimacy, and Neoliberal Subjectivity in Brazil." *Cultural Anthropology* 27 (2012): 28–49.

De Valck, Marijke, and Jan Teurlings. "After the Break: Television Theory Today." In Marijke de Valck and Jan Teurlings, eds., *After the Break: Television Theory Today*, 7–17. Amsterdam: Amsterdam University Press, 2013.

De Vany, Arthur, and W. David Walls. "Estimating the Effects of Movie Piracy on Box-office Revenues." *Review of Industrial Organization* 30 (2006): 291–301.

Dickey, Jack. "Joey Votto's New Contract Is Like a Mortgage-backed Security." Deadspin, 4 April 2012.

Digitalsmiths. "New Study Spotlights 'Cord-cheating.'" Press release, Research Triangle Park, NC, 3 September 2013.

Di Piazza, Guy. "The Television and Movie Industry Explained: Where Does All the Money Go?" Strategy Analytics, June 2007.

Dix, James, and Alicia Jenks. "Viewers Tuning Out Basic, Premium TV." *Barron's*, 15 May 2012.

Donders, Karen, and Tom Evens. "Cable Wars and Business Battles in Broadcasting Markets: Implications for Internet Television." Paper presented at EUROCPR 2011, Ghent, Belgium, 27–9 March 2011.

Donohue, Steve. "Cisco: Set-top Data Could Boost 'TV Everywhere.'" *Light Reading*, 19 November 2009.

– "SeaChange, Tellabs to Target Ads on iPad Based on Web Viewing Habits." *FierceCable*, 16 May 2012.

– "What's Comcast Cooking for the Cable Show?" *FierceCable*, 17 May 2012.

Downing, John D.H. *Radical Media: Rebellious Communication and Social Movements*. Thousand Oaks, CA: Sage, 2001.

– *Radical Media: The Political Experience of Alternative Communication*. Cambridge, MA: South End Press, 1984.

Doyle, John. "How the Murdoch Scandal Turned Paranoia into Reality." *Globe and Mail*, 28 March 2012.

Dreier, Fred. "Why Your March Madness Will Now Cost You." *Forbes*, 15 March 2012.

DtecNet. "Television Piracy: It's the New Fall Season." DtecNet.com, November 2009.

Economist. "Ahoy There!" 29 April 2010.

– "Among the Audience." 20 April 2006.

– "Breaking Up Is Not So Very Hard to Do." 22 June 2013.

– "The Chinese Stream." 9 November 2013.

– "Counting the Change." 17 August 2013.

– "Online Video in China: Watch This Space." 17 March 2012.

– "Singing a Different Tune." 12 November 2009.

Edgecliffe-Johnson, Andrew. "Media Wants to Break Free." *Financial Times*, 17 May 2009.

"Editorial: In Broadband Race, USA Is Not No. 1." *USA Today*, 6 December 2011.

Editorial Board. "Searching for Fairness on the Internet." *New York Times*, 15 May 2014.

Edwards, Cliff. "Intel Confident of Obtaining Programs for Web TV Service." *Bloomberg*, 25 June 2013.

Edwards, Jim. "Analyst Sounds Warning on Death of TV." *Business Insider*, 8 August 2013.

Einstein, Mara. *Media Diversity: Economics, Ownership and the FCC*. Mahwah, NJ: Lawrence Erlbaum, 2004.

El Amrani, Issandr. "The Politics of Outrage Is Still an Irresistible Temptation." *The National*, 13 September 2012.

Elliott, Stuart. "Adding to the Annual Spectacle, NBC and the N.F.L. Take the Super Bowl to Cyberspace." *New York Times*, 18 December 1995.

eMarketer. "TV Watchers Want Original Content, No Matter the Platform." eMarketer.com, 1 October 2013.

Engleman, Eric. "Web Piracy Bills 'Dead' in U.S. from Lobbying, Dodd Says." *Bloomberg*, 12 April 2012.

enigmax. "File-sharing Prospers Despite Tougher Laws." *TorrentFreak*, 22 May 2012.

– "Young File-sharers Respond to Tough Laws by Buying a VPN." *TorrentFreak*, 1 May 2012.

Envisional. "An Estimate of Infringing Use of the Internet." Cambridge, London. January 2011.

Ernesto. "*Avatar* Crowned the Most Pirated Movie of 2010." *TorrentFreak*, 20 December 2010.

– "'The Hobbit' Most Pirated Film of 2013." *TorrentFreak*, 31 December 2013.

– "*Project X* Most Pirated Movie of 2012." *TorrentFreak*, 27 December 2012.

– "Top 10 Most Pirated Movies of 2009." *TorrentFreak*, 20 December 2009.

– "Top 10 Most Pirated Movies of 2011." *TorrentFreak*, 24 December 2011.

Etherington, Darrell. "iTunes Match and iCloud: Pirate Reward or Anti-theft Measures?" *The Apple Blog*, 9 June 2011.

Evans, Elizabeth. *Transmedia Television: Audiences, New Media, and Daily Life*. London: Routledge, 2011.

Evens, Tom. "Platform Leadership in Online Broadcasting Markets." In Mike Friedrichsen and Wolfgang Mühl-Benninghaus, eds., *Handbook of Social Media Management*, 477–91. Berlin: Springer, 2013.

Evens, Tom, Katrien Lefever, Peggy Valcke, Dimitri Schuurman, and Lieven De Marez. "Access to Premium Content on Mobile Television Platforms: The Case of Mobile Sports." *Telematics and Informatics* 28 (2011): 32–9.

Evens, Tom, and Benedetta Prario. "Mobile Television in Italy: The Key to Success, the Cause of Failure." *International Journal of Digital Television* 3 (2012): 53–68.

"Facebook App by FreeCast.com Fuels Cord Cutting Growth." Freecast.com press release. Orlando, FL, 30 April 2012.

Falcone, John P. "Which Streaming Media Device Is Right for You?" *CNET*, 26 March 2012.

Farman, Jason. *Mobile Interface Theory: Embodied Space and Locative Media.* London: Routledge, 2012.

Farrell, Mike. "Survey Says: 92% of Consumers Want a la Carte." *Multichannel News*, 18 April 2012.

"Faster, Better, Cheaper: Making Money in a Digital World." Ipsos MediaCT, November 2009.

Fetto, John. "Rise in Cord-cutting Creates Opportunities for Marketers." *OnlineVideoInsider*, 5 May 2014.

Fiske, John. *Television Culture*. New York: Methuen & Co., 1987.

Fixmer, Andy. "New TV Season, and Fewer Viewers." *Bloomberg Businessweek*, 15 September 2011.

Fixmer, Andy, and Alex Sherman. "Time Warner Cable Content Incentives Thwart New Web TV." *Bloomberg*, 12 June 2013.

– "TV Networks Fueled by Netflix Effect Introduce Most New Shows Since 2004." *Bloomberg*, 20 May 2011.

Flacy, Mike. "Comcast Continues Losing Cable Subscribers to Cord-cutting." *Digital Trends*, 3 November 2011.

Flint, Joe. "Analyst Warns of Bleak Outlook for Cable Industry." *Los Angeles Times*, 28 November 2011.

Foremski, Tom. "The Media Industry's 2nd Apocalypse: The Rapid Rise of Mobile." ZDNet, 8 June 2014.

Frankel, Daniel. "DISH's Ergen: Streaming on Netflix 'Devalues' Mad Men." *paidContent*, 7 May 2012.

– "Nielsen: 1.5M U.S. Households Cut the Cord in 2011." *paidContent*, 4 May 2012.

– "We've Got Hard Data: Netflix Really Is Killing Nickelodeon." *paidContent*, 26 April 2012.

– "Why Aren't More People Cutting the Cord? Regional Sports Networks." *paidContent*, 9 March 2012.

Fraser, Chad. "Comcast and the Cord-cutting Trend." InvestingDaily.com, 2 May 2013.

Fredriksson, Martin. "Piracy, Globalisation and the Colonisation of the Commons." *Global Media Journal* 6 (2012): 1–8.

Freeman, Sunny. "Cord-cutting Canadians Not a Threat to Cable Business." *Huffington Post*, 31 October 2013.

Frieden, Rob. "The Opportunities and Threats from Next Generation Television." Working paper, Penn State University, November 2011.

Friedman, Wayne. "Cable Ratings Impacted by Streaming Rivals." *MediaDaily-News*, 5 June 2012.

– "TV Viewers Use Twitter During Ads." *MediaDailyNews*, 20 September 2013.

Fritz, Ben. "Disney Feuds with Redbox and Netflix over 'John Carter' DVD." *Los Angeles Times*, 8 June 2012.

Fruhlinger, Joshua. "Tuning Up Web TV." *Wall Street Journal*, 16 March 2012.

Fuchs, Christian. "Information and Communication Technologies and Society: A Contribution to the Critique of the Political Economy of the Internet." *European Journal of Communication* 24 (2009): 69–87.

Fung, Anthony Y.H. "Globalizing Televised Culture: The Case of China." In Graeme Turner and Jinna Tay, eds., *Television Studies After TV: Understanding Television in the Post-Broadcast Era*, 178–88. London: Routledge, 2009.

Gannes, Liz. "YouTube Changes Everything: The Online Video Revolution." In Darcy Gerbarg, ed., *Television Goes Digital*, 147–55. New York: Springer, 2009.

Gara, Tom. "Amazon Takes a Shot, But Netflix Is Still King of the Stream." *Wall Street Journal*, 24 June 2013.

Garnham, Nicholas. "Concepts of Culture: Public Policy and the Cultural Industries." *Cultural Studies* 1 (1986): 23–37.

Gatmaitan, James. "Network TV: An Industry in Decline." *The Alligator*, 14 May 2013.

Gaudiosi, John. "Twitch Rides Video Game Streaming to Global Success." *CNN Money*, 4 October 2013.

Geist, Michael. "Canada's Usage Based Billing Controversy: How to Address the Wholesale and Retail Issues." Working paper, 2011.

– "Canadian Broadcasters and BDUs: Can They Compete with 'Free'?" michaelgeist.ca, 24 May 2011.

– "Copyright Lobby Demands Rollback of Recent Canadian Reforms in Secretive Trade Deal." michaelgeist.ca, 24 September 2012.

– "CRTC vs. Netflix: Has Canada's Broadcast Regulator Started a Fight It Can't Win?" michaelgeist.ca, 29 September 2014.

– "Different Regulations, Different Regulators: Behind Canada's Net Neutrality Advantage." michaelgeist.ca, 28 April 2014.

– "Is the CRTC Ready to Hit the Reset Button on Television Regulation in Canada?" michaelgeist.ca, 28 April 2014.

Gelles, David. "Comcast-NBCU Merger Pays Dividends." *Financial Times*, 15 February 2011.

Gershon, Bernard. "TV's Scariest Generation." *Ad Age*, 2 December 2011.

Geuss, Megan. "French Anti-P2P Law Cuts Back Pirating, but Music Sales Still Decline." *ars technica*, 1 April 2012.

Gibbons, Kent. "Cable Show 2012: Multicultural Viewers Have Appeal – And Choices." *Multichannel News*, 22 May 2012.

Giblin, Rebecca. "Evaluating Graduated Response." Pre-publication copy. Social Sciences Research Network, 6 September 2013, pp. 1–61.

Gibs, Jon. "Do We Watch the Web the Same Way We Watch TV? Not Really." *Nielsenwire*, 4 February 2012.

– "The New Screen for Video." In Darcy Gerbarg, ed., *Television Goes Digital*, 11–28. New York: Springer, 2009.

Giletti, Theodore. "Why Pay if It's Free? Streaming, Downloading, and Digital Music Consumption in the 'iTunes Era.'" Master of science dissertation, Department of Media and Communications, London School of Economics and Political Science, August 2011.

Gillan, Jennifer. *Television and New Media: Must Click TV*. London: Routledge, 2011.

Gillespie, Tarleton. *Wired Shut: Copyright and the Shape of Digital Culture*. Cambridge, MA: MIT Press, 2007.

Gimpel, Gregory. "Five Pressing Issues Shaping the Future of TV & Video." MIT Center for Digital Business, May 2012, pp. 1–16.

Gladstone, Rick. "Anti-American Protests Flare beyond the Mideast." *New York Times*, 14 September 2012.

Goel, Sanjay, Paul Miesing, and Uday Chandra. "The Impact of Illegal Peer-to-peer File Sharing on the Media Industry." *California Management Review* 52 (Spring 2010): 6–33.

Goel, Vindu, and Brian Stelter. "Social Networks in a Battle for the Second Screen." *New York Times*, 2 October 2013.

Goggin, Gerard. *Cell Phone Culture: Mobile Technology in Everyday Life*. London: Routledge, 2006.

– "Changing Media with Mobiles." In John Hartley, Jean Burgess, and Axel Bruns, eds., *A Companion to New Media Dynamics*, 193–208. West Sussex, UK: Wiley-Blackwell, 2013.

– "The Eccentric Career of Mobile Television." *International Journal of Digital Television* 3 (June 2012): 119–40.

– *Global Mobile Media*. London: Routledge, 2010.

– "Sport and the Rise of Mobile Media." In Brett Hutchins and David Rowe, eds., *Digital Media Sport: Technology and Power in the Network Society*, 19–36. London: Routledge, 2013.

Goldacre, Ben. "Illegal Downloads and Dodgy Figures." *The Guardian*, 5 June 2009.

Gonzalez, Barb. "Cable TV Cost Is High but Streaming TV Could Cost More." *Tech Goes Strong*, 23 March 2012.

Goode, Luke. "Social News, Citizen Journalism and Democracy." *New Media & Society* 11 (November 2009): 1287–305.

Goodkind, Nicole. "Netflix Introduces New Pricing Plan." *Yahoo! Finance*, 25 April 2013.

Google. "The New Multi-screen World: Understanding Cross-platform Consumer Behavior." Google.com, August 2012.

Gray, Jonathan. *Television Entertainment*. London: Routledge, 2008.

Gray, Jonathan, and Amanda D. Lotz. *Television Studies*. Cambridge, UK: Polity, 2012.

Green, Joshua. "Why Do They Call It TV When It's Not on the Box? 'New' Television Services and Old Television Functions." *Media International Australia, Incorporating Culture & Policy* 126 (February 2008): 95–105.

Green, Stuart P. "When Stealing Isn't Stealing." *New York Times*, 26 March 2012.

Greenberg, Andy. "HBO's 'Game of Thrones' on Track to Be Crowned Most Pirated Show of 2012." *Forbes*, 9 May 2012.

– "The Year's Most Pirated Videos." *Forbes*, 8 May 2009.

Greenberg, Mark. "Confront the Causes of Cord-cutting Now." *Variety*, 10 May 2013.

Greenfield, Rebecca. "How Many Cord Nevers Are There? An Office Survey." *Atlantic Wire*, 29 August 2012.

– "NBC Claims Super Bowl Streaming Victory, But Viewers Cry 'Fail.'" *Atlantic Wire*, 7 February 2012.

Griffin, Brian L. "Surveillance of Audience Labor Using New Media: Three Innovations of Television Broadcast Networks." iConference 2013 Proceedings, Fort Worth, TX, 12–15 February 2013, pp. 885–90.

Griggs, Raymond. "My Cable Cutting Experience." *JR's 2 Cents*, 22 March 2012.

Gripsrud, Jostein. "Broadcast Television: The Chances of Its Survival in a Digital Age." In Lynn Spigel and Jan Olsson, eds., *Television After TV: Essays on a Medium in Transmission*, 210–23. Durham, NC: Duke University Press, 2004.

Grover, Ronald, Tom Lowery, and Cliff Edwards. "Revenge of the Cable Guys." *Bloomberg Businessweek*, 11 March 2011.

Gruenwal, Juliana. "As Hollywood Watches, SOPA Champion Berman Fights for His Seat." *National Journal*, 7 April 2012.

Gunter, Barrie. *Television versus the Internet: Will TV Prosper or Perish as the World Moves Online?* Oxford: Chandos, 2010.

Guynn, Jessica. "Google TV Undergoes a Trial by Partisans." *Los Angeles Times*, 18 August 2010.

Gutman, Brandon. "Evan Shapiro on Why TV Isn't Dead and How Marketers Need to See It." *Forbes*, 9 May 2012.

Ha, Louis, Dominik Leconte, and Jennifer Savidge. "From TV to the Internet to Mobile Phones: A National Study of U.S. College Students' Multiplatform Video Use and Satisfaction." In Francis L.F. Lee, Louis Leung, Jack L. Qiu, and Donna S.C. Chu, eds., *Frontiers in New Media Research*, 278–98. London: Routledge, 2013.

Haggart, Blayne. "Lessons from Canada's Decade of Copyright Reform." Blayne Haggart's Orangespace, 12 April 2012.

Hall, Gina. "Fox COO: 'People Will Give up Food and a Roof over Their Head before They Give up TV.'" *L.A. Biz*, 9 August 2013.

– "More Streamers Adding Hulu or Amazon to Netflix." *L.A. Biz*, 5 June 2013.

Hansell, Saul. "Beyond War News, AOL's Broadband Plan May Face a Struggle." *New York Times*, 24 March 2003.

Harper, Chris. "Global Sports Media Consumption Report." London: TV Sports Market, 2013, pp. 1–62.

Harrington, Stephen, Tim Highfield, and Axel Bruns. "More than a Backchannel: Twitter and Television." *Participations: Journal of Audience & Reception Studies* 10 (May 2013): 1–5.

Harris, Andrew. "'Game of Thrones' Piracy Arguments Proven Wrong by History." *Australian Financial Review*, 20 May 2014.

Hart, Jeffrey A. "Video on the Internet: The Content Question." In Darcy Gerbarg, ed., *Television Goes Digital*, 131–45. New York: Springer, 2009.

Hart, William, and Erica Taylor. "Social Media Use While Watching Primetime TV." In *Proceedings of the Second Annual Social Media Technology Conference & Workshop*, Bowie State University, 27–28 September 2012, pp. 31–8.

Hartley, John. "Invisible Fictions: Television Audiences, Paedocracy, Pleasure." *Textual Practice* 1 (1987): 121–38.

– "Less Popular but More Democratic: Corrie, Clarkson and the Dancing Cru." In Graeme Turner and Jinna Tay, eds., *Television Studies After TV: Understanding Television in the Post-Broadcast Era*, 20–30. London: Routledge, 2009.

– *Television Truths*. Oxford: Blackwell, 2008.

– *Uses of Television*. London: Routledge, 1999.

Hauser, Gerard A. *Vernacular Voices: The Rhetoric of Publics and Public Spaces*. Columbia: University of South Carolina Press, 1999.

Hazlett, Thomas W. "Cable TV Franchises as Barriers to Video Competition." *Virginia Journal of Law and Technology* 12 (Winter 2007): 1–82.

Hiestand, Michael. "NBC Marquee TV Sports Events to Be Streamed Digitally." *USAToday*, 11 April 2013.

Hill, Shawndra, Aman Nalavade, and Adrian Benton. "Social TV: Real-time Social Media Response to TV Advertising." Paper presented at KDD 2012, the 18th ACM SIGKDD Conference on Knowledge Discovery and Data Mining, 12 August 2012, Beijing, China, pp. 1–9.

Hermes, Joke. "Caught." In Marijke de Valck and Jan Teurlings, eds., *After the Break: Television Theory Today*, 35–49. Amsterdam: Amsterdam University Press, 2013.

Hess, Shawn. "Nielsen and Google AdWords Study Younger TV Viewers." *WebProNews*, 17 May 2012.

Holmes, Michael E., Sheree Josephson, and Ryan E. Carney. "Visual Attention to Television Programs with a Second-screen Application." Proceedings of the Symposium on Eye Tracking Research and Applications, Santa Barbara, CA, 28–30 March 2012, 397–400.

Holson, Laura M. "Studios Moving to Block Piracy of Films Online." *New York Times*, 25 September 2003.

Holt, Jennifer. "Regulating Connected Viewing: Media Pipelines and Cloud Policy." In Jennifer Holt and Kevin Sanson, eds., *Connected Viewing: Selling, Streaming, & Sharing Media in the Digital Era*, 19–39. London: Routledge, 2014.

Holt, Jennifer, and Kevin Sanson. "Introduction: Mapping Connections." In Jennifer Holt and Kevin Sanson, eds., *Connected Viewing: Selling, Streaming, & Sharing Media in the Digital Era*, 1–15. London: Routledge, 2014.

Horváth, Dóra, Tamás Csordás, and Nóra Nyirö. "Rewritten by Machine and New Technology: Did the Internet Kill the Video Star?" *Participations: Journal of Audience & Reception Studies* 9 (November 2012): 526–57.

Hu, Nan, Ling Lui, Indranil Bose, and Jialie Shen. "Does Sampling Influence Customers in Online Retailing of Digital Music?" *Information Systems and e-Business Management* 8 (November 2010): 357–77.

Hurst, Nathan. "Apple, Amazon Dominating Tablet, E-reader Market, RJI Survey Shows." University of Missouri News Bureau, 4 June 2012.

Hutchins, Brett. "Robbing the World's Largest Jewelry Store: Digital Sports Piracy, Industry Hyperbole, and Barriers to an Alternative Online Business Model." In Alison Henderson, ed., *Refereed Proceedings of the Australian and New Zealand Communication Association Conference: Communication on the Edge*, Hamilton, New Zealand, 6–8 July 2011.

Hutchins, Brett, and David Rowe. "From Broadcast Scarcity to Digital Plenitude: The Changing Dynamics of the Media Sport Content Economy." *Television and New Media* 10 (April 2009): 354–70.

– "Reconfiguring Media Sport for the Online World: An Inquiry into 'Sports News and Digital Media.'" *International Journal of Communication* 4 (2010): 696–718.

– *Sport beyond Television: The Internet, Digital Media and the Rise of Networked Media Sport*. London: Routledge, 2012.

Ingham, Tim. "Swedish Music Market Grows 12% in H1 2013." *MusicWeek*, 21 July 2013.

Interactive Advertising Bureau. "The Multi-screen Marketer." New York: Econsultancy, May 2012.

Irvine, Martha. "Youth Shaping Future of Online TV, Movies, Music." Associated Press, 18 February 2012.

Jakab, Spencer. "Netflix's Uphill Battle for Subscriber Growth." *Wall Street Journal*, 22 April 2012.

James, Meg. "Nielsen to Include Internet Viewers in Its Definition of TV Homes." *Los Angeles Times*, 7 May 2013.

Jenkins, Henry. "The Cultural Logic of Media Convergence." *International Journal of Cultural Studies* 7 (2004): 33–43.

– "When Piracy Becomes Promotion." *Reason*, December 2006.

Johnson, Victoria E. "Everything New Is Old Again: Sport Television, Innovation, and Tradition for a Multi-platform Era." In Amanda D. Lotz, ed., *Beyond Prime Time: Television Programming in the Post-Network Era*, 114–37. London: Routledge, 2009.

Journalism Project Staff. "YouTube and News: A New Kind of Visual Journalism." Pew Research Center, Washington, DC, 16 July 2012.

Kafka, Peter. "Hey Cable Guys! Cord Cutting Is Real, and It's a Problem, Says Verizon CEO." *All Things Digital*, 23 September 2010.

– "Netflix Still Eats a Third of the Web Every Night." *All Things Digital*, 14 May 2013.

– "Tipping Point? We're Watching More Web Video on TVs Than on PCs." *All Things Digital*, 27 September 2012.

Kahn, Urmee. "Music Industry Failing to Promote Legal Alternatives to Piracy." *The Guardian*, 8 March 2010.

Karaganis, Joe. "Introduction." In Joe Karaganis, ed., *Media Piracy in Emerging Economies*, i–vi. Social Sciences Research Council, 2011.

– "Rethinking Piracy." In Joe Karaganis, ed., *Media Piracy in Emerging Economies*, 1–73. Social Sciences Research Council, 2011.

Karaganis, Joe, Pedro Mizukami, Lawrence Liang, John Cross, and Olga Sezneva. "Does Crime Pay? MPEE's Findings on Piracy, Organized Crime, and Terrorism." Social Sciences Research Council, 2011.

Katz, James E. "Conclusion." In James E. Katz, ed., *Mobile Communication Dimensions of Social Policy*, 303–10. London: Transaction Publishers, 2011.

Katz, Michael L. "Industry Structure and Competition Absent Distribution Bottlenecks." In Eli Noam, Jo Groebel, and Darcy Gerbarg, eds., *Internet Television*, 31–59. Mahwah, NJ: Lawrence Erlbaum, 2004.

Keane, John. *Media and Democracy*. Cambridge, UK: Polity Press, 1991.

Keilbach, Judith, and Markus Stauff. "When Old Media Never Stopped Being New: Television's History as an Ongoing Experiment." In Marijke de Valck and Jan Teurlings, eds., *After the Break: Television Theory Today*, 79–98. Amsterdam: Amsterdam University Press, 2013.

Kellner, Douglas. *Television and the Crisis of Democracy*. Boulder, CO: Westview, 1990.

Kelly, J.P. "Beyond the Broadcast Text: New Economies and Temporalities of Online TV." In Paul Grainge, ed., *Ephemeral Media: Transitory Screen Culture from Television to YouTube*, 122–37. New York: Palgrave Macmillan, 2011.

Khrennikov, Ilya. "Netflix Clones in Russia Get a Head Start with Piracy Law." *Businessweek*, 31 July 2013.

Kinder, Marsha. *Playing with Power in Movies, Television, and Video Games: From Muppet Babies to Teenage Mutant Ninja Turtles*. Berkeley: University of California Press, 1991.

King, Ian. "How 'Cord Never' Generation Poses Sales Drag for Pay TV." *Bloomberg*, 18 September 2013.

Kiriya, Ilya. "The Culture of Subversion and Russian Media Landscape." *International Journal of Communication* 6 (2012): 446–66.

Kirkpatrick, David D., Helene Cooper, and Mark Landler. "Egypt, Hearing from Obama, Moves to Heal Rift from Protests." *New York Times*, 13 September 2012.

Kirton, Andrew, and Matthew David. "The Challenge of Unauthorized Streaming to the English Premier League and Television Broadcasters." In Brett Hutchins and David Rowe, eds., *Digital Media Sport: Technology and Power in the Network Society*, 81–96. London: Routledge, 2013.

Knee, Jonathan A. "Why Content Isn't King." *Atlantic*, July/August 2011.

Koh, Byungwan, B.P.S. Murthi, and Srinivasan Raghunathan. "Shift in Demand for Music: Causal Effect of Online Music Piracy and Digital Music on Album Sales." Working paper, School of Management, University of Texas, November 2010.

Kokas, Aynne. "American Media and China's Blended Public Sphere." In Jennifer Holt and Kevin Sanson, eds., *Connected Viewing: Selling, Streaming, & Sharing Media in the Digital Era*, 144–57. London: Routledge, 2014.

Kosner, Anthony Wing. "It's the Content, Stupid! Maybe the FCC, Not Tim Cook, Will Decide If Apple's iTV Is Viable." *Forbes*, 30 May 2012.

Kovach, Steve. "Time Spent Watching Video on Mobile Devices Has Doubled in the Last Year." *Business Insider*, 19 June 2013.

Krashinsky, Susan. "Fake Enemies Stoke Indie Film Buzz." *Globe and Mail*, 17 August 2012.

- "TV's Digital Switch Boosts Appeal of Cord-cutting." *Globe and Mail,* 23 August 2011.

Ladurantaye, Steve. "For This Man, the Show Must Go On." *Globe and Mail,* 29 June 2013.

Larson, Brian V., A. Douglas Bender, and Dennis R. Laker. "The Aging Sport Fan: A Model for Marketing Spectator Sports to Baby Boomers." In Rodney A. Oglesby and Marjorie G. Adams, eds., *Business Research Yearbook: Global Business Perspectives,* 787–92. Beltsville, MD: International Academy of Business Disciplines, 2008.

Lawton, Christopher. "More Households Cut the Cord on Cable." *Wall Street Journal,* 28 May 2009.

Leamy, Elisabeth. "FCC: High Cable Prices Consumers' Biggest Problem." *ABC News,* 21 April 2012.

Learmonth, Michael. "Fox's 'Prison Break' Free on Hulu, but 1 Million Prefer BitTorrent." *Business Insider,* 3 September 2008.

Lee, Edmund. "TV Subscriptions Fall for First Time as Viewers Cut the Cord." *Bloomberg,* 19 May 2014.

- "Tweeting about Twerking Seen as Lifeline for TV Industry." *Bloomberg,* 7 October 2013.

Lee, Hye Jin, and Marc Andrejevic. "Second-screen Theory: From the Democratic Surround to the Digital Enclosure." In Jennifer Holt and Kevin Sanson, eds., *Connected Viewing: Selling, Streaming, & Sharing Media in the Digital Era,* 40–61. London: Routledge, 2014.

Lee, Joo-Suk, Seung-Hoon Yoo, and Seung-Jun Kwak. "Consumers' Preferences for the Attributes of Post-PC: Results of a Contingent Ranking Study." *Applied Economics* 38 (2006): 327–34.

Lee, Timothy B. "Paramount Exec Faces Skeptical Crowds on Post-SOPA Outreach Tour." *ars technica,* 12 April 2012.

Leichtman Research Group. "Multi-channel Video Industry Has First-ever Annual Net Subscriber Loss." Press release, Durham, NH, 20 May 2013.

Lescure, Pierre. "Contribution aux politiques culturelles à l'ère numérique." Minister of Culture and Communication, France, May 2013.

Levin, Dan, and John Horn. "DVD Pirates Running Rampant in China." *Los Angeles Times,* 22 March 2011.

Levy, Josh. "No More Hulu for You." *Save the Internet,* 1 May 2012.

Lewis, Justin. "The Myth of Commercialism: Why a Market Approach to Broadcasting Does Not Work." In Jeffery Klaehn, ed., *The Political Economy of Media and Power,* 337–56. New York: Peter Lang, 2010.

Li, Jinying. "From D-Buffs to the D-Generation: Piracy, Cinema, and an Alternative Public Sphere in Urban China." *International Journal of Communication* 6 (2012): 542–63.

Lieberman, David. "Big Media Q4 Corporate Earnings Roundup: Can Moguls Stop Worrying about Cord-cutting as the Economy Improves?" *Deadline*, 20 February 2012.

– "Moguls Are 'In Denial' about Poverty, Time Warner Cable CEO Says." *Deadline*, 1 March 2012.

Linder, Laura R. *Public Access Television: America's Electronic Soapbox*. Westport, CT: Praeger, 1999.

Lindgren, Simon, and Jessica Linde. "The Subpolitics of Online Piracy: A Swedish Case Study." Paper presented at the XVII ISA World Congress of Sociology, Gothenburg, Sweden, 16 July 2010.

Ling, Rich, and Jonathan Donner. *Mobile Communication*. Malden, MA: Polity Press, 2009.

Lisanti, Joseph. "TV Cord-cutting on the Rise." *Variety*, 18 February 2012.

Loebbecke, Claudia. "Broadcaster-driven Video-on-Demand (VoD) Platforms in the Era of Disrupting and Converging Media Value Chains." Social Science Research Network working paper, 31 March 2012.

Loebbecke, Claudia, and Matthias Fischer. "Pay TV Piracy and Its Effect on Pay TV Provision." *Journal of Media Business Studies* 2 (2005): 17–34.

Logan, Kelty. "And Now a Word from Our Sponsor: Do Consumers Perceive Advertising on Traditional Television and Online Streaming Video Differently." *Journal of Marketing Communication* 18 (February 2012): n.p.

Logsdon, Jeffrey, Jeffrey B. Hoskin, and Kara Anderson. *Perspectives on the Filmed Entertainment Industries 2012*. Toronto: BMO Capital Markets, April 2012.

Lotz, Amanda D. *The Television Will Be Revolutionized*. New York: New York University Press, 2007.

Luckerson, Victor. "The Fight for Streaming TV." *Time*, 16 May 2013.

Lunden, Ingrid. "U.S. Music Sales Down as Streaming Up 24% to 51B Tracks in 6 Months." *TechCrunch*, 19 July 2013.

Mackey, Robert, David Goodman, Jennifer Preston, and Christine Hauser. "Updates on Protests over Anti-Islam Film." *New York Times*, 14 September 2012.

Mahler, Jonathan. "As Netflix Resists, Most Firms Just Try to Befriend Comcast." *New York Times*, 1 May 2014.

Majek, Dee. "Webtelevision, Webseries and Webcasting: Case Studies in the Organization and Distribution of Television-style Content Produced Online." Master's thesis, Stockholm University, 2012.

Malik, Om. "LTE, Smartphones & Video Are Adding Up to a Mobile Data Boom." *Gigacom*, 3 June 2013.

Manjoo, Farhad. "Sour Notes." *Salon*, 30 July 2002.

Mann, Colin. "20m Pirate World Cup Viewers." *Advanced Television*, 25 July 2014.

– "Google's Brin Slams Hollywood Piracy Stance." *Advanced Television*, 16 April 2012.

– "Rising Box Office Receipts Threatened by Online Piracy." *Advanced Television*, 2 April 2012.

– "US Cable Launches Connected Awareness Campaign." *Advanced Television*, 7 May 2012.

Manovich, Lev. *Software Takes Command*. London: Bloomsbury Academic, 2013.

Marques, Caroline. "TV without a Remote: A Teen's Take on Streaming." *Ypulse*, 19 April 2012.

Marsden, Christopher T. "The Challenges of Standardization: Toward a Next Generation Internet." In Eli Noam, Jo Groebel, and Darcy Gerbarg, eds., *Internet Television*, 113–41. Mahwah, NJ: Lawrence Erlbaum, 2004.

Marshall, P. David. *New Media Cultures*. London: Arnold, 2004.

– "Screens: Television's Dispersed 'Broadcast.'" In Graeme Turner and Jinna Tay, eds., *Television Studies After TV: Understanding Television in the Post-Broadcast Era*, 41–50. London: Routledge, 2009.

Masnick, Mike. "Some Data on How Much the Big Media Firms Are Donating to SOPA/PIPA Sponsors." *TechDirt*, 5 December 2011.

Martikainen, Emmi. "Does File Sharing Reduce DVD Sales?" Social Science Research Network working paper, 18 January 2011.

Martin, Laura, and Dan Medina. *The Future of TV*. New York: Needham Insights, 2013.

Masur, Steven, and Cynthia Katz. "ISP Licensing: A Carrot to the Stick of Three-strikes Laws." *SMU Science and Technology Law Review* 13 (Summer 2010): 283–99.

Matin, Ali. "Digital Rights Management (DRM) in Online Music Stores: DRM-encumbered Music Downloads' Inevitable Demise as a Result of the Negative Effects of Heavy-handed Copyright Law." *Loyola of Los Angeles Entertainment Law Review* 28 (January 2008): 265–94.

Mattelart, Tristan. "Audiovisual Piracy, Informal Economy, and Cultural Globalization." *International Journal of Communication* 6 (2012): 735–50.

"May 2012 and Historical ACSI Scores." American Consumer Satisfaction Index, 15 May 2012.

McAdams, Deborah D. "HDTV Remains Most Popular Video Viewing Platform, CEA Says." *TVTechnology*, 14 May 2012.

– "Yet Another 3-screen Study: Alternative Platforms Are Additive." *TVTechnology*, 11 June 2012.

McBride, Sarah, and Geoffrey A. Fowler. "Studios See Big Rise in Estimates of Losses to Movie Piracy." *Wall Street Journal*, 3 May 2006.

McCann, Nick. "Hulu Said to Disclose Users' Viewing Habits." Court House News Service, 11 May 1012.

McChesney, Robert W. *The Problem of the Media: U.S. Communication Politics in the 21st Century*. New York: Monthly Review Press, 2004.

McGrane, Bernard, and John Gunderson. *Watching TV Is Not Required: Thinking about Media and Thinking about Thinking*. London: Routledge, 2010.

McLuhan, Marshall, and Quentin Fiore. *The Medium Is the Massage: An Inventory of Effects*. New York: Bantam, 1967.

McNutt, Myles. "The #NBCFail Olympics: Access, Liveness and the Public Interest." *Journal of Popular Television* 1 (2013): 121–8.

Meân, Lindsey J. "Sport, Identities, and Consumption: The Construction of Sport at ESPN.com." In Andrew C. Billings, ed., *Sports Media: Transformation, Integration, Consumption*, 162–80. London: Routledge, 2011.

Meehan, Eileen R. *Why TV Is Not Our Fault: Television Programming, Viewers, and Who's Really in Control*. Lanham, MD: Rowman & Littlefield, 2005.

Mellis, Michael J. "Internet Piracy of Live Sports Telecasts." *Marquette Sports Law Review* 18 (Spring 2008): 259–84.

Merrin, William. "Still Fighting 'the Beast': *Guerrilla Television* and the Limits of YouTube." *Cultural Politics* 8 (2012): 97–119.

Middleton, Chad. "TURNER and CBS to Charge for March Madness Streaming." 600 ESPN El Paso, 16 February 2012.

Milford, Phil, and Michael Bathon. "Comcast Heads to Trial in Case Alleging Monopolization." *Bloomberg*, 13 April 2012.

Miller, Claire Cain. "As Violence Spreads in Arab World, Google Blocks Access to Inflammatory Video." *New York Times*, 13 September 2012.

Miller, Michael J. "Ari Emanuel Takes on Silicon Valley and Internet Piracy." *PC Magazine*, 31 May 2012.

Miller, Ron. "How to End Content Piracy Right Now." FierceContentManagement, 6 May 2013.

Miller, Toby. *Television Studies: The Basics*. London: Routledge, 2010.

Minne, Jacob. "Data Caps: How ISPs Are Stunting the Growth of Online Video Distributors and What Regulators Can Do about It." Social Science Research Network, 1 May 2012.

Minoli, Daniel. *Linear and Nonlinear Video and TV Applications: Using IPv6 and IPv6 Multicast*. Hoboken, NJ: John Wiley & Sons, 2012.

Mittell, Jason. *Television and American Culture.* Oxford: Oxford University Press, 2010.

Moglen, Eben. "Freedom in the Cloud: Software Freedom, Privacy, and Security for Web 2.0 and Cloud Computing." Software Freedom Law Center, 5 February 2010.

Moore, Frazier. "What Does 'Watching TV' Mean in the Post-TV Age?" *Associated Press*, 19 June 2008.

Moore, Kathleen. "71% of Online Adults Now Use Video-sharing Sites." Pew Research Center's Internet and American Life Project, 26 July 2011.

Moran, Albert, and Justin Malbon. *Understanding the Global TV Format.* Bristol: Intellect, 2006.

Morley, David. *Home Territories: Media, Mobility and Identity.* London: Routledge, 2000.

– "Theoretical Orthodoxies: Textualism, Constructivism and the New Ethnography in Cultural Studies." In Marjorie Ferguson and Peter Golding, eds., *Cultural Studies in Question*, 121–37. London: Sage, 1997.

Morrissey, Janet. "O.K., Downloaders, Let's Try This Song Again." *New York Times*, 3 September 2011.

Moshe, Mira. "Media Time Squeezing: The Privatization of the Media Time Sphere." *Television and New Media* 13 (January 2012): 68–88.

Moskovciak, Matthew. "When Cord-cutting Is Better than Cable." *CNET*, 2 May 2012.

MPAA. "Theatrical Market Statistics, 2011." January 2011.

Mudhar, Raju. "Sports Moving Online, But Warily." *Toronto Star*, 19 March 2012.

Mulligan, Mark. "What Happened to the RIAA's Missing 3.5 Million?" *Music Industry Blog*, 16 April 2012.

Murdoch, Rupert. "Speech by Rupert Murdoch to the American Society of Newspaper Editors." News Corporation, 13 April 2005.

Mylonas, Yiannis. "Accumulation, Control and Contingency: A Critical Review of Intellectual Property Rights' 'Piracy.'" *First Monday* 16 (2011).

– "Piracy Culture in Greece: Local Realities and Civic Potentials." *International Journal of Communication* 6 (2012): 710–34.

Napoli, Philip M. "Program Value in the Evolving Television Audience Marketplace." Washington, DC: Time Warner Cable, 2012, pp. 1–32.

NBC. "London Olympics on NBC Is Most-watched Television Event in U.S. History." NBC Sports Group Press Box, 13 August 2012.

Neagle, Colin. "Insatiable Demand for Streaming Video Puts Pressure on Providers." *PCWorld*, 15 March 2012.

Neel, K.C. "Cord Cutters Dominate Broadband Usage." *FierceCable*, 16 May 2014.

Negroponte, Nicholas. *Being Digital*. New York: Alfred A. Knopf, 1995.

Nelson, Elissa. "Windows into the Digital World: Distributor Strategies and Consumer Choice in an Era of Connected Viewing." In Jennifer Holt and Kevin Sanson, eds., *Connected Viewing: Selling, Streaming, & Sharing Media in the Digital Era*, 62–78. London: Routledge, 2014.

Nelson, Rebecca. "Young Americans Won't Pay for TV. Will They Ever?" *Time*, 9 May 2013.

NetNames. "Netnames Piracy Analysis: Sizing the Piracy Universe." NetNames.com, September 2013.

NetResult. *Background Report on Digital Piracy of Sporting Events*. London: Envision and NetResult, 2008.

Newman, Michael Z. "Free TV: File-sharing and the Value of Television." *Television and New Media* (October 2011): 1–9.

Newman, Michael Z., and Elana Levine. *Legitimating Television: Media Convergence and Cultural Status*. London: Routledge, 2011.

Nice, Dianne. "Five Reasons You Should Give Up TV Bills – Plus Five Reasons You Shouldn't." *Globe and Mail*, 30 November 2011.

Nielsen. "Average TV Viewing for 2008–09 TV Season at All-time High." Nielsen.com, 10 November 2009.

– "Busting the Cord-cutting Myth: Video in the Interactive Age." Nielsen.com, 16 June 2010.

– "Cross-platform Report: How We Watch from Screen to Screen." Nielsen.com, 3 May 2012.

– "Detailing the Digital Revolution: Social, Streaming and More." Nielsen.com, 24 February 2012.

– "Double Vision – Global Trends in Tablet and Smartphone Use While Watching TV." Nielsen.com, 5 April 2012.

– "January 2011: Online Video Usage Up 45%." Nielsen.com, 11 February 2011.

– "The Follow-Back: Understanding the Two-way Causal Influence Between Twitter Activity and TV Viewership." Nielsen.com, 6 August 2013.

– "What Netflix and Hulu Users Are Watching ... and How." Nielsen.com, 27 July 2011.

Noonan, Amy. "A Slight Change of Heart among Movie Thieves." *The Telegraph (Australia)*, 4 June 2012.

Oberholzer-Gee, Felix, and Koleman Strumpf. "The Effect of File Sharing on Record Sales: An Empirical Analysis." *Journal of Political Economy* 115 (February 2007): 1–42.

Obst, Lynda. "Hollywood Is Completely Broken." *Salon*, 15 June 2013.

Ogg, Erica. "With 3M Downloads, MLB App Hits It Out of the Park." *Gigacom*, 12 April 2012.

O'Halloran, Joseph. "Cord-cutting Creeps Up as 49% of US Homes Take Connected TV." *RapidTVNews*, 9 June 2014.

– "Online Video Markets to Surge over Next Five Years." *RapidTVNews*, 9 November 2011.

Oliveira, Michael. "Canadian TV 'Cord Cutters' Reach 8 Per Cent of Population." *Globe and Mail*, 3 April 2013.

– "Netflix Subscribers Now Nearly a Third of English Canada." Canadian Press, 2 April 2014.

– "One in Four Canadians Watch More Online Video than TV: Survey." *Globe and Mail*, 2 May 2012.

– "Online Video Surging in Canada." *Globe and Mail*, 28 April 2011.

O'Neill, Jim. "Connected-TV Shipments Globally to Nearly Triple by 2016." *FierceOnlineVideo*, 2 May 2012.

– "iPad Owners, Potential Owners More Likely to Cut Cord, Downgrade Pay-TV Buy." *FierceOnlineVideo*, 12 November 2010.

Ouellette, Laurie. "Will the Revolution Be Televised?" In Peter D'Agostino and David Tafler, eds., *Transmission: Toward a Post-Television Culture*, 165–87. London: Sage, 1994.

Ozer, Jan. "NBA League Pass: The Future of Online Sports Video." *Streaming Media*, 22 March 2012.

Pakinkis, Tom. "Piracy Rising in UK, According to Ofcom Report." *MusicWeek*, 30 May 2013.

Pase, André Fagundes. "Inbound and Outbound: When Applications Invade TV and Change Our Rooms." Presented at the Unstable Platforms: The Promise and Peril of Transition Conference, 13–15 May 2011, MIT, Cambridge, MA.

Paulussen, Steve, and Evelien D'heer. "Using Citizens for Community Journalism." *Journalism Practice* 7 (2013): 588–603.

Peitz, Martin, and Patrick Waelbroeck. "Why the Music Industry May Gain from Free Downloading – The Role of Sampling." International University in Germany working paper no. 41, October 2005.

Pellow, David Naguib, Lisa Sun-Hee Parks, and Lisa Park. *The Silicon Valley of Dreams: Environmental Injustice, Immigrant Workers, and the High-tech Global Economy*. New York: New York University Press, 2002.

Perez, Sarah. "Hulu Announces Adding 1 Million Paid Subscribers in Q1 2013." *TechCrunch*, 30 April 2013.

Perren, Alisa. "Business as Usual: Conglomerate-sized Challenges for Film and Television in the Digital Era." *Journal of Popular Film and Television* 38 (2010): 72–8.

Pertierra, Anna Cristina. "If They Show Prison Break in the United States on a Wednesday, by Thursday It Is Here: Mobile Media in Twenty-first-century Cuba." *Television and New Media* 13 (August 2012): 399–414.

Pesce, Mark. "Piracy Is Good? New Models for the Distribution of Television Programming." Unpublished paper, Australian Film, Television and Radio School, Sydney, Australia, 2005.

Peters, Colleen. "MLB Blackout Only Hurts the Fans, Network." *The Telescope*, 21 April 2012.

Peukert, Christian, Jörg Claussen, and Tobias Kretschmer. "Piracy and Movie Revenues: Evidence from Megaupload: A Tale of the Long Tail?" Social Sciences Research Network, 20 August 2013.

Pfanner, Eric. "Copyright Cheats Face the Music in France." *New York Times*, 19 February 2012.

Phalen, Patricia F., and Richard V. Ducey. "Audience Behavior in the Multi-screen 'Video-verse.'" *International Journal on Media Management* 14 (2012): 141–56.

Pilieci, Vito. "Rogers Abandons Video-rental Business." *Vancouver Sun*, 17 April 2012.

Poeter, Damon. "NPD: Rising Tide for Streaming Media Players." *PC Magazine*, 1 May 2013.

Pogue, David. "Chromecast, Simply and Cheaply, Flings Web Video to TVs." *New York Times*, 31 July 2013.

Pomerantz, Dorothy. "12 Million Households Expected to Cut the Cord by 2015." *Forbes*, 20 July 2011.

– "Hollywood Faces Grave Threat from Popcorn Time." *Forbes*, 24 March 2014.

Porter, Eduardo. "The Perpetual War: Pirates and Creators." *New York Times*, 4 February 2012.

Pott, Trevor. "Pirates Not to Blame for Big Media's Sales Plunge." *The Register*, 16 April 2012.

Powers, Jack, and George Comstock. "The Rumors of Television's Demise Have Been Greatly Exaggerated: What the Data Say about the Future of Television Content in a Child's Digital World." *Mass Communication and Journalism* 2 (2012): 1–8.

Press, Andrea L. "Women Watching Television: Issues of Class, Gender, and Mass Reception." In Peter D'Agostino and David Tafler, eds., *Transmission: Toward a Post-Television Culture*, 53–89. London: Sage, 1994.

PricewaterhouseCoopers. "Discovering Behaviors and Attitudes Related to Pirating Content." Washington, DC, 2011.

Puopolo, Scott, Carlos Cordero, William Gerhardt, Kate Griffin, Leszek Izdebski, and David Parsons. "The Future of Television: Sweeping Change at Breakneck Speed." San Jose, CA: Cisco Internet Business Solutions Group, 2011.

Purcell, Kristen. "Online Video 2013." Pew Research Center's Internet & American Life Project, Washington, DC, 10 October 2013.

Quail, Christine. "Television Goes Online: Myths and Realities in the Contemporary Context." *Global Media Journal* 12 (Spring 2012): 1–15.

Ramachandran, Shalini. "Dish Chief: TV Needs to Change." *Wall Street Journal*, 7 June 2012.

– "Evidence Grows on TV Cord-cutting." *Wall Street Journal*, 7 August 2012.

Ramayah, T., Noor Hazlina Ahmad, Lau Geuk Chin, and May-Chiun Lo. "Testing a Causal Model of Internet Piracy Behavior among University Students." *European Journal of Scientific Research* 29 (2009): 206–14.

Rauch, Peter, ed. "TV's New Economics." MIT Communications Forum, 8 March 2006.

Raustiala, Kal, and Chris Sprigman. "Piracy Really Hurt the U.S. Economy?" Freakanomics.com, 1 January 2012.

Ray, Tiernan. "NFLX 'Whacking' Kids Shows, Threatens Disney, Viacom, Says Bernstein." *Barron's*, 26 April 2012.

Reardon, Marguerite. "Cable Fights to Stay Relevant in Online World." *CNET News*, 14 June 2011.

– "Netflix Is Cable's 'Frenemy.'" *CNET News*, 23 May 2012.

Recording Industry Association of America. "For Students Doing Reports." riaa.com, n.d.

Reimold, Dan. "A Cord-cutter's Life: 10 Lessons Learned." *PBS Mediashift*, 27 February 2012.

Reuters. "Analysis – Key to Universal-EMI Decision: Has Music Business Lost Control?" 16 May 2012.

Rhodes, Edward. "Challenges of Globalization, Flattening and Unbundling." *South Asian Journal of Business and Management* 2 (June 2013): 17–23.

Richmond, Will. "New Research Shows Netflix Is a Catalyst for Cord-cutting and Cord-shaving." *VideoNuze*, 14 June 2011.

Rifkin, Jeremy. "The Age of Access: The New Politics of Culture vs. Commerce." Unpublished paper, n.d., pp. 43–8.

Rob, Rafael, and Joel Waldfogel. "Piracy on the Silver Screen." *Journal of Industrial Economics* 55 (September 2007): 379–95.

Roettgers, Janko. "ABC Executive: Second Screen Can Be a Distraction." Gigacom, 11 September 2013.

Rose, Steve. "Lights, Camera, Revolution: The Birth of Libyan Cinema after Gaddafi's Fall." *The Guardian*, 1 October 2012.

Rosen, Jake. "How Hollywood Can Capitalize on Piracy." *MIT Technology Review*, 17 October 2013.

Rosen, Jay. "The People Formerly Known as the Audience." *Pressthink*, 27 June 2006.

Ross, Sharon Marie. *Beyond the Box: Television and the Internet*. Oxford: Blackwell, 2008.

Rostami, Flora. "Free Is Hard to Beat: A Closer Look at the Digital Music Download Dilemma." *UCLA Journal of Law & Technology* 15 (Spring 2011): 1–34.

Rostow, Eugene V. *President's Task Force on Communications Policy, Final Report*. Washington, DC: US Government Printing Office, 1968.

Rowell, Rainbow. "When Did Watching TV Become Such a Hassle?" *Omaha World-Herald*, 27 May 2012.

Rushton, Katherine. "YouTube Chief: Mobile Will Soon Eclipse TV." *London Telegraph*, 11 October 2012.

Ryan, Mark David, and Gregory N. Hearn. "Next Generation 'Filmmaking': New Markets, New Methods and New Business Practices." *Media International Australia* 136 (August 2010): 133–45.

Ryssdal, Kai. "The Future of Television: Content Still Matters." *Marketplace*, 11 January 2012.

Sabbagh, Dan. "Hollywood in Turmoil as DVD Sales Drop and Downloads Steal the Show." *The Guardian*, 3 May 2011.

Sakthivel, M. "4G Peer-to-peer Technology – Is It Covered by Copyright?" *Journal of Intellectual Property Rights* 16 (July 2011): 309–12.

Sandomir, Richard, James Andrew Miller, and Steve Eder. "To Protect Its Empire, ESPN Stays on Offense." *New York Times*, 26 August 2013.

Sandvine. "Global Internet Phenomena Spotlight: Netflix Rising." 17 May 2011.

Sanger, Steve. "Streaming TV on Mobile Phones Will Rocket to 240 Million by 2014." *WorldTVPC*, 9 May 2012.

Santo, Michael. "The Biggest Impact from an Apple TV Could Be Unbundled Channels." Examiner.com, 3 June 2012.

Sanz, Esteve. "Statistical, Ecosystems and Competitiveness Analysis of the Media and Content Industries: European Television in the New Media Landscape." Joint Research Centre of the European Commission, Luxembourg, 2012.

Schaffer, Jan. "Innovations in the Delivery of Online Local News." *I/S: A Journal of Law and Policy for the Information Society* 8 (2013): 543–63.

Schechner, Sam. "TV Networks See Key Audience Erode." *Wall Street Journal*, 27 May 2011.

Scholz, Tobias M. "New Broadcasting Ways in IPTV: The Case of the Starcraft Broadcasting System." Paper presented at the World Media Economics & Management Conference, 23–27 May 2012, Thessaloniki, Greece.

Schudson, Michael. *Advertising: The Uneasy Persuasion*. New York: Basic Books, 1986.

Scott, Mark. "The Fall of Rome: Media after Empire." A.N. Smith Memorial Lecture in Journalism, University of Melbourne, 14 October 2009.

Seabrook, John. "Streaming Dreams." *The New Yorker*, 16 January 2012.

See-To, Eric W.K., Savvas Papagiannidis, and Vincent Cho. "User Experience on Mobile Video Appreciation: How to Engross Users and to Enhance Their Enjoyment in Watching Mobile Video Clips." *Technology Forecasting and Social Change* 79 (October 2012): 1484–94.

Seetoo, Chia-heng. "Can Peer-to-peer Internet Broadcast Technology Give Fans Another Chance?" *University of Illinois Journal of Law, Technology & Policy* 2 (2007): 369–94.

Seiter, Ellen, Hans Borchers, Gabriele Kreutzner, and Eva-Maria Warth, eds. *Remote Control: Television, Audiences, and Cultural Power*. London: Routledge, 1989.

Seles, Sheila. "It's (Not) the End of TV as We Know It." Convergence Culture Consortium, MIT, 17 March 2010.

Seltzer, Wendy. "The Broadcast Flag: It's Not Just TV." *Federal Communications Law Journal* 57.2 (2005): 209–14.

Senior, Antonia. "How Do You Police the Entire Internet?" *The Guardian*, 1 April 2012.

Seppo. "Cutting-the-cord, Bandwidth Usage and Data Caps in Practice." *Thoughts by Pilvi*, 24 February 2012.

Shapiro, Evan. "TV: An Intervention." *Huffington Post*, 5 June 2012.

Sharma, Amol, and Suzanne Vranica. "Tweets Provide New Way to Gauge TV Audiences." *Wall Street Journal*, 6 October 2013.

Shinai, John. "As Streaming Replaces Downloading, Music Revenue Stagnates." *USA Today*, 22 May 2014.

Shirky, Clay. "The Year of the Newspaper Paywall." Reuters, 6 January 2012.

Silcoff, Sean. "CRTC Paints Picture of Canada's Netflix Boom." *Globe and Mail*, 4 September 2012.

Siri, Jean-Philippe, and Rimantas Reimontas. *Digital & Physical Piracy in GB*. London: Ipsos, 2007.

Slater, Chuck. "Who's Streaming March Madness? You'd Be Surprised." *Fast Company*, 16 March 2012.

Slater, Lee. "Democracy and Online News: Indymedia and the Limits of Participatory Media." *Scan Journal* 3 (June 2006): n.p.

Smith, Aaron, and Jan Lauren Boyles. "The Rise of the 'Connected Viewer.'" Pew Research Center's Internet & American Life Project, Washington, DC, 17 July 2012.

Smith, Jo T. "DVD Technologies and the Art of Control." In James Bennett and Tom Brown, eds., *Film and Television After DVD*, 129–48. London: Routledge, 2008.

Smith, Michael D., and Rahul Telang. "Assessing the Academic Literature Regarding the Impact of Media Piracy on Sales." Social Sciences Research Network, 19 August 2012, pp. 1–22.

– "Competing with Free: The Impact of Movie Broadcasts on DVD Sales and Internet Piracy." *MIS Quarterly* 33 (June 2008): 321–38.

Smith, Patrick. "Interview: NetResult CEO Christopher Stokes on Tackling Football TV Pirates." PaidContent, 22 September 2009.

Smith, Ralph Lee. "The Wired Nation." *Nation*, 18 May 1972, 582–602.

Snider, Mike. "Analysis Details Digital Lives in the USA." *USA Today*, 24 February 2012.

Snider, Mike, and Roger Yu. "Cheap Broadband, PCs Aimed at Low-income Families." *USA Today*, 9 December 2011.

SNL Kagan. "SNL Kagan Finds Over-the-top and TV Everywhere Swallowing up Mobile Video." SNL Kagan press release, 24 May 2012.

– "U.S. Multichannel Video Subscribers Drop for Second Straight Quarter." 17 November 2010.

Solomon, Bari. "Friend or Foe? The Impact of Technology on Professional Sports." *CommLaw Conspectus: Journal of Communications Law and Policy* 20 (January 2012): 253–83.

Solsman, Joan. "Netflix Is Giving People Their Net Fix, Nielsen Says." *CNET*, 18 September 2013.

Soroka, Stuart, Blake Andrew, Toril Aalberg, Shanto Iyengar, James Curran, Sharon Coen, Kaori Hayashi, Paul Jones, Gianpetro Mazzoleni, June Woong Rhee, David Rowe, and Rod Tiffen. "Auntie Knows Best? Public Broadcasters and Current Affairs Knowledge." *British Journal of Political Science* 43 (2013): 719–39.

Spangler, Todd. "Amazon Streams More Video Than Hulu or Apple, But It's Still Miles Behind Netflix." *Variety*, 8 April 2014.

– "Comcast to Shift from Broadband Caps to Usage-based Pricing." *Multichannel News*, 17 May 2012.

– "Cord-cutting Alert." *Multichannel News*, 6 May 2014.

– "Hulu's Advertising Chief Is Latest Exec to Exit." *Variety*, 1 October 2013.

- "Is 'TV Everywhere' Liberating or Coercive?" *Multichannel News*, 2 May 2012.
- "Netflix, Hulu Dominate Mobile TV Viewing." *Variety*, 3 June 2013.
- "Net Video to Keep Eating More Bandwidth." *Multichannel News*, 30 May 2012.
- "Why 'TV Everywhere' Still Isn't Everywhere." *Multichannel News*, 30 April 2012.

Spigel, Lynn. "Smart Homes: Digital Lifestyles Practiced and Imagined." In Jostein Gripsrud, ed., *Relocating Television: Television in the Digital Context*, 238–56. London: Routledge, 2010.

Stanton, David. "51% of Total US Population Watches Streaming Video Weekly." Gfk.com, 10 September 2013.Steinberg, Brian. "Behind Fox News' Primetime Shuffle, an Effort to Thwart Digital Distraction." *Variety*, 7 October 2013.

Steinmetz, Keven F., and Kenneth D. Tunnell. "Under the Pixelated Jolly Roger: A Study of Online Pirates." *Deviant Behavior* 34 (2013): 53–67.

Steirer, Gregory. "The Personal Media Collection in an Era of Connected Viewing." In Jennifer Holt and Kevin Sanson, eds., *Connected Viewing: Selling, Streaming, & Sharing Media in the Digital Era*, 78–95. London: Routledge, 2014.

Stelter, Brian. "2.1 Million Streamed the Super Bowl, NBC Says." *New York Times*, 7 February 2012.
- "As TV Ratings and Profits Fall, Networks Face a Cliffhanger." *New York Times*, 12 May 2013.
- "A DVR Ad-eraser Causes Tremors at TV Upfronts." *New York Times*, 16 May 2012.
- "Fox Show Will Start Worldwide." *New York Times*, 21 March 2012.
- "Gatekeepers of Cable TV Try to Stop Intel." *New York Times*, 12 June 2013.
- "If Video Sites Could Act Like Cable Companies." *New York Times*, 22 May 2012.

Stelter, Brian, and Brad Stone. "Digital Pirates Winning the Battle with Studios." *New York Times*, 5 February 2009.

Steward, Christopher S. "Over the Air TV Catches Second Wind, Aided by the Web." *Wall Street Journal*, 21 February 2012.

Stewart, Christopher S., and Shalini Ramachandran. "Google Seeks TV Content for Streaming Service." *Globe and Mail*, 17 July 2013.

Stone, Brad, and Brian Stelter. "Some Online Shows Could Go Subscription-Only." *New York Times*, 29 March 2009.

Stop Music Piracy. "Music Piracy & Organized Crime." stoppiracy.org.za, n.d.

Strachan, Alex. "Viewers Watching More Traditional TV, Exec Insists." *Ottawa Citizen*, 24 August 2013.

Strangelove, Michael. *The Empire of Mind: Digital Piracy and the Anti-Capitalist Movement*. Toronto: University of Toronto Press, 2005.

– *Watching YouTube: Extraordinary Videos by Ordinary People*. Toronto: University of Toronto Press, 2010.

Streeter, Thomas. "Blue Skies and Strange Bedfellows: The Discourse of Cable Television." In Lynn Spigel and Michael Curtin, eds., *The Revolution Wasn't Televised: Sixties Television and Social Conflict*, 221–42. London: Routledge, 1997.

Stross, Randall. "Yes, Norma Desmond, The Pictures Are Getting Small Again." *New York Times*, 7 July 2012.

Sun, Chyng, and Miguel Picker. *Mickey Mouse Monopoly: Disney, Childhood, and Corporate Power*. Video, 52 min. Media Education Foundation, 2001.

Sun, Na, Dominik Frey, Robert Jin, Hui Huang, Zhe Chen, and Pei-Luen Patrick Rau. "A Cross-cultural Study of User Experience of Video on Demand on Mobile Devices." *Lecture Notes in Computer Science* 8024 (2013): 468–74.

Sutter, John D. "YouTube Restricts Video Access over Libyan Violence." CNN, 13 September 2012.

Svantesson, Dan. "'Imagine There's No Countries …' – Geo-identification, the Law and the Not So Borderless Internet." *Journal of Internet Law* 10 (March 2007): 1–21.

Sweney, Mark. "Global Recorded Music Sales Fall Almost $1.5bn amid Increased Piracy." *The Guardian*, 28 March 2011.

– "Government Wants to Cut Illegal Filesharing by 80% by 2011." *The Guardian*, 25 July 2008.

Szalai, George. "Analyst: Online Streaming Now Hurting Some TV Networks' Ratings." *Hollywood Reporter*, 4 June 2012.

– "Analysts: Fourth-quarter Pay TV Sub Momentum Allays Some Cord Cutting Fears." *Hollywood Reporter*, 24 February 2012.

– "Comcast Cable Chief Talks Sub Trends, Streampix." *Hollywood Reporter*, 29 February 2012.

– "CW Online Push Causes Ratings, Cord Cutting Concerns (Report)." *Hollywood Reporter*, 20 April 2012.

– "Hulu Plus Subscription Service Crosses 2 Million User Mark." *Hollywood Reporter*, 17 April 2012.

– "Time Warner Cable CFO: Pay TV Bill Costs Consumers Only 30 Cents per TV Hour." *Hollywood Reporter*, 28 February 2012.

– "Time Warner CEO: Netflix Deal Affecting Nickelodeon Ratings." *Hollywood Reporter*, 2 April 2012.

– "Viacom CEO Defends Nickelodeon's Netflix Deal Again." *Hollywood Reporter*, 3 April 2012.

Taneja, Harsh, and Heather Young. "Television Industry's Adoption of the Internet: Diffusion of an Inefficient Innovation." In Alan B. Albarran, ed., *Media Management and Economic Research in a Transmedia Environment*, 219–41. London: Routledge, 2013.

Tay, Jinna, and Graeme Turner. "Not the Apocalypse: Television Futures in the Digital Age." *International Journal of Digital Television* 1 (2010): 31–50.

– "What Is Television? Comparing Media Systems in the Post-broadcast Era." *Media International Australia* 126 (February 2009): 71–81.

Taylor, Jim. "Premier League Shuts Down 30,000 Illegal Streams." BBC Radio 1 Newsbeat, 16 August 2012.

Taylor, T.L. *Raising the Stakes: E-sports and the Professionalization of Computer Gaming*. Cambridge, MA: MIT Press, 2012.

techmichelle. "Cable Viewers Bail in Favor of Programming on Demand." *DTVUSA Forum*, 4 June 2012.

"Television News in Rapid Decline." *CollegeNews*, 14 April 2013.

Tharp, Paul. "Cable Bills to Pass $200 a Month by 2020: Industry Forecast." *New York Post*, 10 April 2012.

"The Betamax Case." Electronic Frontier Foundation, n.d.

Thomas, Julian. "When Digital Was New: The Advanced Television Technologies of the 1970s and the Control of Content." In James Bennett and Niki Strange, eds., *Television and Digital Media*, 52–75. Durham, NC: Duke University Press, 2011.

Thompson, Cadie. "YouTube May Be Worth $20 Billion by 2020." *CNBC*, 16 May 2013.

Thompson, Hugh. "The Post-PC World Is Real and It's Here." *Globe and Mail*, 5 April 2012.

Tichur, Rita, and Steve Ladurantaye. "As Headwinds Gather, Rogers Seeks Its Next Windfall." *Globe and Mail*, 28 April 2012.

TiVo. "Netflix Not Cannibalizing Traditional TV Viewing." Press release, San Jose, CA, 29 July 2013.

"Top 10 Most Pirated TV-shows of 2010." *TorrentFreak*, 31 December 2010.

Tossell, Ivor. "Digital Killed the Video Store, What Will Replace It?" *Globe and Mail*, 25 April 2012.

Townsend, Keith. "Cord Cutting (Cable TV)." *Virtualized Geek*, 10 April 2012.

"Traffic and Market Report on the Pulse of the Networked World." Ericsson, Stockholm, Sweden, June 2012.

Troianovski, Anton. "Video Speed Trap Lurks in New iPad." *Wall Street Journal*, 22 March 2012.

Truong, Alice. "Olympics Fans Use the Web to Sneak around Tape Delay." Yahoo! News, 3 August 2012.

Tryon, Chuck. "'Make Any Room Your TV': Digital Delivery and Media Mobility." *Screen* 53 (Autumn 2012): 287–300.

– *On-Demand Culture: Digital Delivery and the Future of Movies*. New Brunswick, NJ: Rutgers University Press, 2013.

Tryon, Chuck, and Max Dawson. "Streaming U: College Students and Connected Viewing." In Jennifer Holt and Kevin Sanson, eds., *Connected Viewing: Selling, Streaming, & Sharing Media in the Digital Era*, 217–33. London: Routledge, 2014.

Turkle, Sherry. *Alone Together: Why We Expect More from Technology and Less from Each Other*. New York: Basic Books, 2011.

Turner, Elliot. "My Media Consumption Habits with the iPad." *Compounding My Interests*, compoundingmyinterests.com, 9 April 2012.

Turner, Graeme. "Television and Cultural Studies: Unfinished Business." *International Journal of Cultural Studies* 4 (2001): 371–84.

– "Television and the Nation: Does This Matter Anymore?" In Graeme Turner and Jinna Tay, eds., *Television Studies after TV: Understanding Television in the Post-Broadcast Era*, 54–64. London: Routledge, 2009.

Turner, Mimi. "Global Online TV and Video Revenues Predicted to Nudge $22 Billion by 2016." *Hollywood Reporter*, 10 December 2012.

Turnock, Rob. *Television and Consumer Culture: Britain and the Transformation of Modernity*. London: I.B. Tauris, 2007.

Umiastowski, Chris. "Picture Isn't Pretty for Cable TV Stocks." *Globe and Mail*, 28 August 2013.

United States Government Accountability Office. "Intellectual Property: Observations of Efforts to Quantify the Economic Effects of Counterfeit and Pirated Goods." April 2010.

Uricchio, William. "Constructing Television: Thirty Years that Froze an Otherwise Dynamic Medium." In Marijke de Valck and Jan Teurlings, eds., *After the Break: Television Theory Today*, 65–78. Amsterdam: Amsterdam University Press, 2013.

– "The Future of a Medium Once Known as Television." In Pelle Snickars and Patrick Vonderau, eds., *The YouTube Reader*, 24–39. Sweden: National Library of Sweden, 2009.

– "The Recurrent, the Recombinatory and the Ephemeral." In Paul Grainge, ed., *Ephemeral Media: Transitory Screen Culture from Television to YouTube*, 24–36. New York: Palgrave Macmillan, 2011.

– "Television's Next Generation: Technology/Interface Culture/Flow." In Lynn Spigel and Jan Olsson, eds., *Television After TV: Essays on a Medium in Transmission*, 163–82. Durham, NC: Duke University Press, 2004.

Van Dijck, José. *The Culture of Connectivity: A Critical History of Social Media*. Oxford: Oxford University Press, 2013.

– "The Internet in Flux: Twitter and the Interpretative Flexibility of Microblogging." In Francis L.F. Lee, Louis Leung, Jack L. Qiu, and Donna S.C. Chu, eds., *Frontiers in New Media Research*, 223–40. London: Routledge, 2013.

– "YouTube beyond Technology and Cultural Form." In Marijke de Valck and Jan Teurlings, eds., *After the Break: Television Theory Today*, 147–59. Amsterdam: Amsterdam University Press, 2013.

Varona, Anthony E. "Changing Channels and Bridging Divides: The Failure and Redemption of American Broadcast Television Regulation." *Minnesota Journal of Law, Science & Technology* 6 (2005): 3–116.

Venturini, Francesco, Charles Marshall, and Egidio Di Alberto. "Accenture Video-over-Internet Consumer Survey 2012." Accenture, 12 April 2012.

Vermeer, Frank. "What's on the Tube Today? On the Ontology of Television and YouTube." Master's thesis, Universiteit Utrecht, 2011.

Vlessing, Etan. "Netflix Canada Has Local Carriers Losing the Cord-cutting War." *Hollywood Reporter*, 7 June 2013.

– "U.S. Network TV Still King in Canada, but Netflix Popularity Growing." *Hollywood Reporter*, 27 September 2013.

Vonderau, Patrick. "Beyond Piracy: Understanding Digital Markets." In Jennifer Holt and Kevin Sanson, eds., *Connected Viewing: Selling, Streaming, & Sharing Media in the Digital Era*, 99–123. London: Routledge, 2014.

Wakefield, Jane. "Tweeting with the Telly On." *BBC News*, 22 March 2011.

Waldfogel, Joel. "Cinematic Explosion: Movies, Gatekeepers, and Product Delivery in the Digital Age." Unpublished paper, Carlson School of Management, University of Minnesota. September 2013.

Wallenstein, Andrew. "CW Shortens Web Streaming Delay to Battle Piracy." *Variety*, 13 March 2012.

– "Netflix Exec Defends Impact on TV Biz." *Variety*, 30 May 2012.

– "Top Wall Street Analyst: Pay TV 'Cord-cutting Is Real.'" *Variety*, 3 June 2013.

– "'Touch' Latest Show to Bow Day-and-Date Worldwide." *Variety*, 22 March 2012.

Wang, Ryuou, Yan Shoshitaishvili, Christopher Kruegel, and Giovanni Vigna. "Steal This Movie: Automatically Bypassing DRM Protection in Streaming Media Services." Proceedings of the 22nd USENIX Conference on Security, USENIX Association, Berkeley, CA, 2013, 687–702.

Ward, David, ed. *Television and Public Policy: Change and Continuity in an Era of Global Liberalization*. New York: Lawrence Erlbaum, 2008.

Wasko, Janet, and Mary Erickson. "The Political Economy of YouTube." In
    Pelle Snickars and Patrick Vonderau, eds., *The YouTube Reader*, 372–86.
    Stockholm: National Library of Sweden, 2009.
Waterman, David, and Sung Wook Ji. "Online Versus Offline in the U.S.: Are
    the Media Shrinking?" *The Information Society* 28 (2012): 285–303.
– "Online vs. Offline in the U.S.: Are the Media Shrinking?" Paper presented
    at the Telecommunications Policy Research Conference, George Mason
    University School of Law, Arlington, VA, 23–25 September 2011.
Waterman, David, Sung Wook Ji, and Laura R. Rochet. "Enforcement and
    Control of Piracy, Copying, and Sharing in the Movie Industry." *Review of
    Industrial Organization* 30 (2007): 255–89.
Waterman, David, Ryland Sherman, and Sung Wook Ji. "The Economics of
    Online Television: Revenue Models, Aggregation, and '*TV Everywhere.*'"
    Paper presented at the Digital Media and New Media Platforms: Policy and
    Marketing Strategies Conference, National Chengchi University, Taipei,
    Taiwan, 29 March 2012.
Weiss, Thomas, and Sabrina Schiele. "Virtual Worlds in Competitive Contexts:
    Analyzing eSports Consumer Needs." *Electronic Markets: The International
    Journal on Networked Business* 19 (April 2013): 1–10.
Wente, Margaret. "It's Too Easy to Lay All the Blame on a Crude Video." *Globe
    and Mail*, 18 September 2012.
Whitney, Daisy. "Mobile Video Viewing Could Lead to Cord-cutting." *Online
    VideoInsider*, 25 April 2014.
– "Streaming Users Double Up, Tablet Views Grow Six Times." *Online Video-
    Insider*, 30 May 2013.
– "Who Needs a DVR?" Solutions Research Group, 6 January 2009.
Wikström, Patrik. "A Typology of Music Distribution Models." *International
    Journal of Music Business Research* 1 (April 2012): 7–20.
Wilkerson, David B. "Cord-cutting Thwarted for Now by Big Media:
    Nomura." *Market Pulse*, 21 September 2011.
Williams, Raymond. *Television: Technology and Cultural Form*. 2nd edn. London:
    Routledge, 1990.
Wingfield, Nick. "With Twitch Acquisition Talks, Validation of Games as a
    Spectator Sport." *New York Times*, 19 May 2014.
Winseck, Dwayne. "Bell-Astral Deal Should Be Stopped in Its Tracks." *Globe
    and Mail*, 16 March 2012.
– "Big Media in the Hot Seat at CTRC Hearings." *Globe and Mail*, 20 June 2011.
– "The State of Media Ownership and Media Markets: Competition or
    Concentration and Why Should We Care?" *Sociological Compass* 2 (January
    2008): 34–47.

Wirth, Michael O., and Ron Rizzuto. "Future Prospects for Cable Telecommunications in an Over-the-top World." In Alan B. Albarran, ed., *Media Management and Economic Research in a Transmedia Environment*, 18–45. London: Routledge, 2013.

Wise, Lindsay. "More Media Consumers Are Cutting the Cable Cord." *Miami Herald*, 16 September 2013.

Witkowski, Emma, Brett Hutchins, and Marcus Carter. "E-sports on the Rise? Critical Considerations on the Growth and Erosion of Organized Digital Gaming Competitions." In *Proceedings of the 9th Australasian Conference on Interactive Entertainment: Matters of Life and Death*, ACM, New York, NY, 2013, article 43, 2 pp.

Wohn, D. Yvette, and Eun-Kyung Na. "Tweeting about TV: Sharing Television Viewing Experiences Via Social Media Message Streams." *First Monday* 16 (March 2011).

Wolff, Michael. "It's War! Hollywood Strikes Back." *GQ Magazine*, 5 April 2012.

Wood, Michelle L., Michelle R. Nelson, Jaeho Cho, and Ronald A. Yaros. "Tonight's Top Story: Commercial Content in Television News." *Journalism and Mass Communication Quarterly* 81 (December 2004): 807–22.

Wood, Molly. "TV Apps Are Soaring in Popularity." *New York Times*, 4 June 2014.

"Would You Pay for a Legal Alternative to Film Piracy?" *New Zealand Herald*, 8 April 2012.

Wu, Angela Xiao. "Broadening the Scope of Cultural Preferences: Movie Talk and Chinese Pirate Film Consumption from the Mid-1980s to 2005." *International Journal of Communication* 6 (2012): 501–29.

Wu, Tim. *The Master Switch: The Rise and Fall of Information Empires*. New York: Alfred A. Knopf, 2011.

Wyatt, Edward. "F.C.C. Commissioner Leaving to Join Comcast." *New York Times*, 11 May 2011.

Yamato, Jen. "Universal Chief Ron Meyer Addresses VOD Fiasco, Admits Cowboys & Aliens, Land of the Lost, Wolfman Kinda Stunk." *Movieline*, 3 November 2011.

Yang, Ling. "All for Love: The Corn Fandom, Prosumers, and the Chinese Way of Creating a Superstar." *International Journal of Cultural Studies* 12 (September 2009): 527–43.

Yao, Deborah. "Cable Companies See Customers Cutting Back: 'The Beginning of Cord Cutting.'" *Huffington Post*, 8 February 2009.

– "Why Pay TV Operators Should Fear Google Fiber." SNL Kagan, 7 August 2012.

Yar, Majid. "The Global 'Epidemic' of Movie 'Piracy': Crime-wave or Social Construction?" *Media, Culture & Society* 27 (2005): 677–96.

Yarow, Jay. "Twitter Is Still Very Small." *Business Insider*, 27 September 2013.

Yu, Roger. "Mobile TV Has Station Owners Intrigued, Flummoxed." *USA Today*, 10 April 2013.

Zimmett, Eric. "Get Ready for TV 2.0." *StateCollege.com*, 15 April 2012.

Zittrain, Jonathan. *The Future of the Internet and How to Stop It*. New Haven, CT: Yale University Press, 2008.

Index

Tim Blackmore, *War X: Human Extensions in Battlespace*

Michael Dartnell, *Insurgency Online: Web Activism and Global Conflict*

Janine Marchessault and Susan Lord, eds., *Fluid Screens, Expanded Cinema*

Barbara Crow, Michael Longford, and Kim Sawchuk, eds., *The Wireless Spectrum: The Politics, Practices, and Poetics of Mobile Media*

Michael Strangelove, *Watching YouTube: Extraordinary Videos by Ordinary People*

Arthur Kroker and Marilouise Kroker, eds., *Critical Digital Studies: A Reader, second edition*

Michael Strangelove, *Post-TV: Piracy, Cord-Cutting, and the Future of Television*